ALBION ASCENDANT

ENGLISH HISTORY, 1660–1815

WILFRID PREST

OXFORD UNIVERSITY PRESS

1998

Oxford University Press, Great Clarendon Street, Oxford OX2 6DP

Oxford New York
Athens Auckland Bangkok Bogota Bombay
Buenos Aires Calcutta Cape Town Dar es Salaam Delhi
Florence Hong Kong Istanbul Karachi
Kuala Lumpur Madras Madrid Melbourne
Mexico City Nairobi Paris Singapore
Taipei Tokyo Toronto Warsaw
and associated companies in
Berlin Ibadan

Oxford is a trade mark of Oxford University Press

Published in the United States
by Oxford University Press Inc., New York

© *Wilfrid Prest 1998*

British Library Cataloguing in Publication Data
Data available

Library of Congress Cataloging in Publication Data
Data applied for

ISBN 0–19–820417–5
ISBN 0–19–820418–3 pbk

Typeset by Alliance Phototypesetters, Pondicherry
Printed in Great Britain
on acid-free paper by
Biddles Ltd., Guildford and
King's Lynn

THE SHORT OXFORD HISTORY OF THE MODERN WORLD

General Editor: J. M. ROBERTS

THE CRISIS OF PARLIAMENTS: ENGLISH HISTORY, 1509–1660
Conrad Russell

EMPIRE, WELFARE STATE, EUROPE: ENGLISH HISTORY, 1906–1992
Fourth Edition
T. O. Lloyd

BARRICADES AND BORDERS: EUROPE, 1800–1914
Second Edition
Robert Gildea

THE OLD EUROPEAN ORDER, 1660–1800
Second Edition
William Doyle

ENDURANCE AND ENDEAVOUR: RUSSIAN HISTORY, 1812–1992
Fourth Edition
J. N. Westwood

THE BRITISH EMPIRE, 1558–1995
Second Edition
T. O. Lloyd

MODERN INDIA: THE ORIGINS OF AN ASIAN DEMOCRACY
Second Edition
Judith M. Brown

THE LIMITS OF LIBERTY: AMERICAN HISTORY, 1607–1992
Second Edition
Maldwyn A. Jones

REBELLIONS AND REVOLUTIONS: CHINA FROM THE 1800S TO THE 1980S
Jack Gray

BRITISH HISTORY, 1815–1906
Norman McCord

THE EUROPEAN DYNASTIC STATES, 1494–1660
Richard Bonney

England, the better part of the best Island in the whole world, anciently with Scotland called Britain, and sometimes Albion. . . .

Edward Chamberlayne, *Anglia Notitia: or the Present State of England* (1669)

PREFACE

This book spans just over one and a half centuries—about two full lifetimes by modern Western standards, although nearly twice that for people born in England between 1660 and 1815. It opens with the collapse of the first, perhaps last, English republic, and ends with a famous victory over Napoleonic France at the battle of Waterloo. The time frame within which any historical narrative or interpretation is presented inevitably influences its contents and direction. Thus beginning in 1660 serves to emphasize both the manifold legacies of the mid-seventeenth century English Revolution, and the firm rejection of its more radical aspects, even before the demise of the republican regime. Earlier or later points of departure would be compatible with other (to my mind less compelling) views of the significance of the 1640s and 50s. As for 1815 rather than 1783, 1789, or 1832, the conclusion of the last of many wars fought over the centuries between England and France plainly marked a major turning point, no less in domestic matters than foreign policy, something which could not be said so confidently of other possible closing dates.

These 155 years also derive a certain coherence from encompassing the transformation of a small and comparatively insignificant offshore island into a colonial, economic, and military superpower, the most formidable the world had yet seen. How and why that remarkable—and as it may now seem, curiously evanescent—transition occurred, with what effects, for whose benefit, and at whose expense, is a major theme of this outline history. Yet not everything interesting and important about the lives of the five generations which extended over that period can be or is here related to the nation's emerging geo-political role and status.

That story itself is as much a part of European, and indeed global history, as of the history of England alone, or that of the British Isles. Historians have good reason to be more conscious than once they were that British and English history are by no means the same thing. Indeed, a major theme of recent scholarship has been the process of constructing a British identity after the political Union of England and Scotland in 1707. But while attempting to take some account of Scottish, Irish, and Welsh developments and structures at various points along the way, the main focus of this book is upon England (or England and Wales together). At the same time I have sought to confine the term 'Britain' to the political unit created by the Act of Union, rather than using 'England' to include Scotland, let alone Ireland.

In accordance with the General Editor's preface to earlier volumes in this series, I have not hesitated to emphasize 'society and its structure at the expense of traditional political narrative'. But while the following pages are by no means exclusively devoted to high politics, they do include an account of constitutional and political change, which is intended to stand in its own right as well as to provide a context for the exploration of cultural, economic, and social themes. In general I have sought to pay attention to ordinary people as well as the elite, and where possible to identify the distinctive nature of women's experiences, although without confining or marginalizing these in separate chapters or sections.

After serving my historical apprenticeship on a slightly earlier period, I have found myself increasingly drawn to the later seventeenth and eighteenth centuries, in the hope of better understanding 'what came of it at last'. Perhaps I am not alone in this, for the last ten or fifteen years have seen an astounding surge of published research on every aspect of English history from the later seventeenth to the early nineteenth centuries. No one book by a single author could possibly digest and make full use of this enormous torrent of scholarship. My aim here is merely to provide a reasonably balanced overview of what I take to be the main themes of English history between the Restoration and the end of the French wars, especially for readers who have little or no previous acquaintance with the subject. Those wishing to pursue particular aspects in more detail or depth will find suggestions for further reading in the footnotes and at the end of the volume.

I have sometimes found it difficult to identify the source of particular ideas or information; while I have tried to acknowledge my intellectual debts, I should be glad to know of any inadvertent omissions.

W. R. P.

ACKNOWLEDGEMENTS

While no one else should be held responsible for the outcome, my task has been greatly eased by some generous advisers and critics. In particular I thank those who have read or heard some or all of the text: John Beattie, Christine Churches, Pene Corfield, Martin Fitzpatrick, Mark Goldie, Jo Innes, Dave Lemmings, Iain McCalman, Christine MacLeod, Anthony Page, Jonathan Pincus, John Roberts, Barry Smith, David Spring, Ellis Wasson, my own undergraduate students, an anonymous collective of graduate students, and an anonymous publisher's reader. Many other friends and colleagues have helped with particular issues and problems; it would be invidious to mention names for fear of omissions, but they know who they are, and I hope they will accept this general expression of thanks. The support of Tony Morris of OUP and my departmental colleagues (especially Robert Dare, Roger Hainsworth, and Frank McGregor) has been indispensable. The forbearance of Sabina (once again) and the dedicatees is the least of their virtues.

Margaret Hoskings, Marie Robinson, and Susan Woodburn eased my access to the rich resources of the University of Adelaide's Barr Smith Library; I also thank staff at the State Library of South Australia, Flinders University, the Australian National Library, the Australian National University, the British Library, the Henry E. Huntington Library, the University of London's Institute of Historical Research, and the University of Otago. This book could not have been written without a visiting fellowship at the Humanities Research Centre of the Australian National University in 1994–5, followed by financial support towards a year's teaching relief from the Australian Research Council, and Professor Mary O'Kane, then Deputy Vice-Chancellor (Research), now Vice-Chancellor of the University of Adelaide.

W. R. P.

CONTENTS

List of Figures, Maps, and Table   xv
List of Abbreviations   xvi

PART I: RESTORATION ENGLAND, 1660–1688   I

1. ENGLAND AND THE ENGLISH   3
   Time, Land, People   3
   Getting and Spending   7
   Hierarchies   12
   Government   16
   Church and Dissent   20
   Culture and Ideas   23
   England, Britain, Europe, and the Wider World   28

2. SETTLEMENT DEFERRED   34
   Restoration, Accommodation, Demobilization   34
   Cavaliers, Conspirators, Dissenters   36
   Charles II and the Crisis of 1666–1667   38
   Unstable Alliances, 1668–1677   41
   Popish Plot, Reaction, and Proscription   44
   James II, 1685–1688: A Threat to Church and State?   49
   William of Orange and the Protestant Wind   52

PART II: POST-REVOLUTIONARY ENGLAND, 1689–1715   57

3. GLORIOUS REVOLUTION?   59
   Revolutionary Practice and Principles   59
   Crown and Parliament   62
   Law, Liberty, and Toleration: How Much and for Whom?   65
   Historians and the Revolution   66

4. THE RAGE OF PARTY   69
   Political Assumptions, Ideologies, Structures   69
   War and Peace, 1689–1701   72
   Queen Anne and a Church Militant, 1702–1710   75
   Jacobitism and the Protestant Succession, 1710–1715   78

5. WAR AND THE STATE   81
   Revolution, Diplomacy, and War   81
   The Sinews of War   82

The State's Servants   86
Great Britain as World Power   89

6. TRADE AND THE TOWNS   93
   Commercial Revolution   93
   Middling Orders   96
   Urbanity: London and the Provinces   99
   Economic Concepts and Calculations   103

PART III: GREAT BRITAIN: LIBERTY AND
PROPERTY, 1707–1745   107

7. THE STATE OF THE UNION   109
   Defoe's England   109
   Wales   111
   Scotland   113
   Ireland   116

8. FROM PARTY STRIFE TO ONE-PARTY RULE   120
   The Elector of Hanover, King George I   120
   The Venetian Oligarchy Inaugurated   122
   Parliamentary Management   125
   Opposition, War and Walpole's Fall   127
   Crown and Parliament: Who Ruled Britain?   131

9. RELIGIOUS BELIEF AND PRACTICE   134
   Church and Chapel   134
   Latitudinarianism and Freethinking   138
   'Serving the Designs of Enthusiasm'   140
   Confessional State or Secularizing Society?   143

10. PRODUCTION AND CONSUMPTION   147
    The Landed Interest: Depression and Improvement   147
    Manufactures and Manufacturing   150
    Consumers and Consumerism   152
    Government and the Economy   156

PART IV: EMPIRES WON AND LOST, 1746–1788   159

11. PEOPLE   161
    Population Growth   161
    The Common People   162
    'The Upper Part of Mankind'   168
    Childhood   172

Education and Literacy 174
Love and Marriage 179
Minorities 184

12. POLITICS, POPULARITY, AND PATRIOTISM 187
The Old Corps: Pelham and Newcastle 187
William Pitt and War with France 189
A New Reign, a New Politics? 192
'Wilkes and Liberty!' 195

13. RULING INSTITUTIONS 199
Blackstone and the Rule of Law 199
Crime and Punishment 202
The Established Church, Dissent, and Disability 205

14. BURDENS AND FRUITS OF EMPIRE 211
Attitudes to Empire 211
George III, Lord North, and the American Revolution 212
The Strains of War 214
Ireland: Patriots and Volunteers 216
Pitt and Recovery 218
India and the East 220
The Pacific 222

15. SENSE AND SENSIBILITY 224
The British Enlightenment 224
Science and Medicine 227
Good Works 230
Humanity and Nature 233

PART V: ECONOMIC EXPANSION AND
DIVERSIFICATION, 1750–1815 237

16. INDUSTRIALIZING ENGLAND 239
Historiography 239
Feeding the People 241
Infrastructure: Canals and Turnpikes 244
Power 246
Industry and Invention 248
Trade 251
Banking and Finance 255
Law, Policy, and the State 257
Organization of Work and Workers 260
Labour and Capital 263

Standards of Living	267
Regional and National Dimensions	270
Revolution or Evolution?	273
PART VI: REFORM, REVOLUTION, REACTION, 1789–1815	277
17. RADICALS, REFORMERS AND THE FRENCH REVOLUTION, 1789–1793	279
Radical and Reformist Traditions	279
'Bliss was it in that dawn to be alive'	282
Burke and Paine	284
Jacobins and Loyalists	286
18. THE LAST FRENCH WARS, 1793–1815	292
Mobilization and Repression	292
Dearth and Famine, Discontent and Mutiny	294
Ireland: Rebellion and Union	297
A Peace to be Glad of	299
Worldwide War	301
Victory and Misery	304
19. RETROSPECT AND CONCLUSION	308
Change and Continuity, 1660–1815	308
The Peculiarities of the English	313
APPENDICES	319
I. Monarchs and First Ministers, 1660–1815	319
II. Main British Colonies and Overseas Possessions, 1660–1815	321
Chronology	323
Further Reading	330
Index	345

FIGURES

1. Real wages trends, 1650–1780   9

   Source: E. H. Phelps-Brown and S. Hopkins, 'Seven centuries of the prices
   of consumables, compared with builders' wage rates', *Economica* (1956),
   and *The Agrarian History of England and Wales v. 1640–1750*,
   ed. J. Thirsk (1985), ii. 879.

2. Genealogy of the Houses of Stuart and Hanover   46

3. Patents and inventions, 1700–99   249

   Source: C. MacLeod, *Inventing the Industrial Revolution* (1988), 146–50.

4. Foreign trade, 1700–99   252

   Source: *EHB*, 188

MAPS

1. British Isles: regions and topography   xvii

2. Counties of England   xviii

3. England, Wales, and Scotland: places mentioned in text   xix

4. London, *c*.1714   xx

   Source: C. Wilson, *England's Apprenticeship 1603–1760* (1965). Reprinted
   with permission from Addison Wesley Longman Ltd.

TABLE

1. Average annual tertiary education admissions, selected decades   176

ABBREVIATIONS

DNB	*Dictionary of National Biography*
EHB	*Economic History of Britain since 1700, i. 1700–1860*, ed. R. Floud and D. McCloskey, 2nd edn. (1994)
EcHR	*Economic History Review*, 2nd series
EHD, 1660–1714	*English Historical Documents, viii. 1660–1714*, ed. A. Browning (1966)
EHD, 1714–1783	*English Historical Documents, ix. 1714–1783*, ed. D. B. Horn and M. Ransome (1969)
EHD, 1783–1832	*English Historical Documents, xi. 1783–1832*, ed. A. Aspinall and E. A. Smith (1959)
EHR	*English Historical Review*
HJ	*Historical Journal*
HMC	Historical Manuscripts Commission
P&P	*Past and Present*

CURRENCY

The main unit of English currency during the period covered by this book was the pound (£), made up of 20 shillings (a guinea was 21 shillings). Twelve pennies (pence) made one shilling.

MAP 1. British Isles: regions and topography

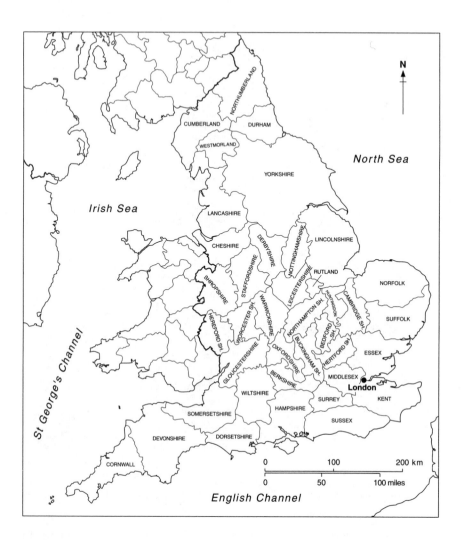

MAP 2. Counties of England

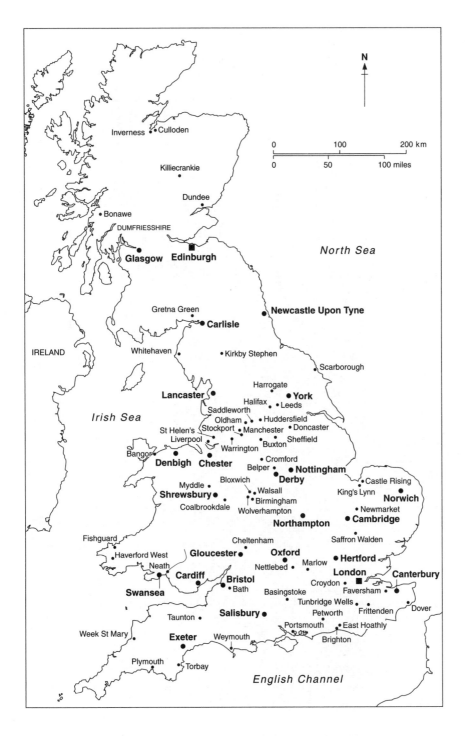

Map 3. England, Wales, and Scotland: places mentioned in text

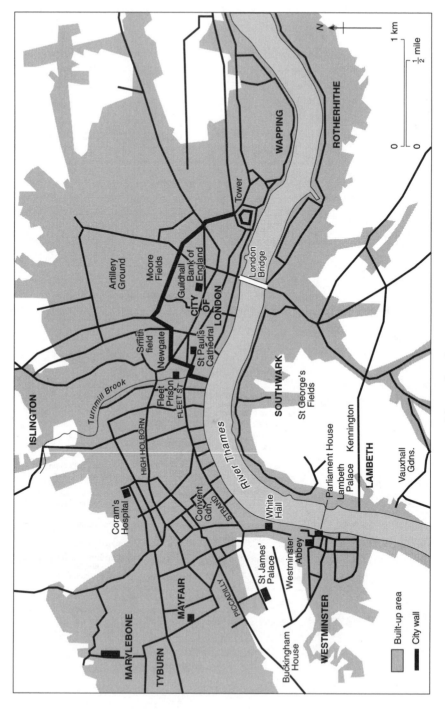

MAP 4. London, c.1714

PART I

Restoration England 1660–1688

1

ENGLAND AND THE ENGLISH

Time, Land, People

Precise and uniform measurement of time, to which we today attach such importance, was neither feasible nor necessary in early modern England. Clocks, found mainly in churches and other public buildings, rarely possessed minute hands until the late seventeenth century, while portable watches were expensive and inaccurate curiosities. Most people relied upon church bells or sundials for the hour of day or night, and no standard clock time was kept throughout the country. The fact that the south-western port of Plymouth ran a quarter-hour later then London hardly mattered much when communications were slow, and the pace of human activities was still governed largely by movements of the heavenly bodies and the passage of the seasons.

While quantitatively accurate timekeeping was of little concern, the quality of time over the course of each year was also far from uniform. The agricultural cycle of ploughing, sowing, and harvesting provided a basic rhythm for most rural communities. Cities and towns also had their municipal cycle, of market-days, court-days, feasts, and civic elections. The traditional ecclesiastical calendar of the Church of England, with its red-letter days and festivals marking events in the life of Christ, shaped another communal set of meanings, not least when the traditional celebration of Christmas Day with plum pudding and mince pies was revived at Charles II's restoration. The enthusiasm or solemnity with which the populace kept national commemorative festivals, such as the monarch's accession day, and November the Fifth or 30 January (anniversaries respectively of the discovery of Guy Fawkes's unsuccessful attempt to blow up Parliament early in James I's reign, and of Charles I's execution) provide a useful index of public opinion in the later seventeenth and early eighteenth centuries.

Calendrical arrangements also had ideological connotations. Thanks to a combination of unreflective conservatism, political inertia, and Protestant hostility to a measure devised by a Counter-Reformation pope, the Gregorian calendar was not adopted until 1752 (see below, p. 188). Before this—by no means uncontested—change brought the British Isles into line with most of Continental Europe, England's dates, based on the older Julian calendar, ran nearly a fortnight behind those kept by most of her diplomatic and trading partners. Moreover, the official English civil year began on 25 March, although in popular usage New Year's Day was 1 January (as it was in Scotland since the beginning of the seventeenth century). Dates between 1 January and 24 March were often given in both Old and New Styles (according to which the final dissolution of the Long Parliament, for example, occurred on 16 March 1659/60). Apart from inconveniencing contemporary diplomats, merchants, travellers, and letter writers, these odd arrangements still occasionally cause trouble to historians.

The geographical boundaries of modern England have barely changed since the later seventeenth century. England still ends more or less where the Welsh mountains begin to the west, and the land narrows and rises at the Cheviot hills to the north (although the Anglo-Scots border was not properly mapped until the 1740s). The mere fact that England covers a larger expanse of ground than Ireland, Scotland, or Wales helps explain her economic and political predominance within the British Isles. Yet by Continental standards England was and is a political unit of only middling size; some ten times larger than the Netherlands, but with less than half the landed area of peninsular Italy and about a third that of Louis XIV's France. When travellers, information, and orders moved no faster than a horse could gallop, such relative compactness, and hence ease and speed of internal communications, had far greater significance than it does today. For example, it explains (in part at least) why an effective centralized government and legal system were established much earlier in England than elsewhere in Europe. This in turn helps account for the distinctive course of English constitutional development, both before and during the period covered by this book.

Yet in assessing the impact of geography on history, mere surface area may be less important than climate and topography. According to the eulogistic account of Edward Chamberlayne (1616–1703) first published in 1669, his country was particularly well favoured in both these latter respects.[1] Besides an exceptionally mild climate (thanks to the surrounding seas, which moderated extremes of temperature), it was 'blessed with very wholesome soil', 'watered abundantly with springs and streams' and having 'few barren mountains or craggy rocks'. Perhaps only an Englishman could sing the praises of English weather, especially during an era of climatic recession now known as the little Ice Age, when average summer temperatures throughout northern Europe fell by around 1 degree centigrade. Yet Chamberlayne's patriotic boosterism was not wholly unfounded. In fact a significantly higher proportion of England's total land area was readily available for cultivation than in Ireland, Scotland or Wales, where the prominence of lake, marsh, moor, and mountain made for a generally less productive if more picturesque terrain.

Otherwise the sheer variety of the English landscape, moulded over the centuries by the interplay of weather and human activity, is still its most striking

---

[1] Modelled originally on a handbook to France published in 1661, some thirty-eight successively updated editions of Chamberlayne's *Anglia Notitia: or, The Present State of England* appeared between 1669 and 1755.

characteristic. Some forty distinct types of farming region, each characterized by a different combination of soils, rainfall, and agricultural regime, have been identified in early modern England. All such local variations were underpinned by the fundamental division between highland and lowland zones. Eastern and southern England are characteristically low-lying, flat or gently undulating, with soils generally rich and often heavy, equally well suited to a wide variety of grain crops and to pasturing stock. At the beginning of our period most of the relatively densely settled population encouraged by these conditions lived in rural villages, usually numbering at least several hundred souls, each usually with its parish church and manor house, outward symbols of spiritual and worldly authority. Moving north and west, across an imaginary line running from near Scarborough on the Yorkshire coast down to the port of Weymouth in Dorset, the countryside becomes noticeably more rugged, hilly or mountainous, wetter and bleaker, with thinnish, poorer soils, generally better suited for grazing animals than growing crops. In the seventeenth and early eighteenth centuries this highland zone supported a relatively sparser and more scattered population, living in small hamlets and isolated farmsteads rather than substantial villages or towns. These people frequently supplemented whatever their labours on the land might yield with income generated from various forms of 'by-employment' (part-time work), typically domestic spinning, weaving or some form of piece-rate metalworking.

According to Chamberlayne, England 'in shape triangular, contains by computation about 30 millions of acres'. The heavily indented, irregular coastline made such calculations extremely tricky. Even the eminent astronomer Edmund Halley (1656–1742), who in 1690 ingeniously attempted to work out the surface area of England by weighing pieces of a paper map and a circle of known area cut from the same map (the same technique modern botanists use to calculate the surface area of a leaf), could not get within a million acres of the right answer (37.3m., or 13m. hectares). The motivation behind such enquiries was to determine the total area of potential farming land, and hence the maximum population which might be supported once all remaining forest, fenland, heath, and other 'wilderness' was brought under cultivation. Around the same time Gregory King (1648–1712), a pioneering social scientist, surmised that about one-quarter of the country was still 'heaths, moors, mountains and barren land' while a further eighth consisted of 'woods ... forests, parks and commons'.[2] King's estimates were almost certainly exaggerated, but the amount of woodland and open space not devoted to agriculture was perhaps twice what remains today. Another notable difference between the landscape then and now was the persistence, especially in the Midlands and East Anglia, of very large open fields and common pastures. This communal pattern of land use, dating back to medieval times, was shortly destined to be replaced by the patchwork of smaller fields, enclosed with hedgerow or stone walls, which had

---

[2] J. P. Cooper and J. Thirsk (eds.), *Seventeenth-Century Economic Documents* (1972), 779.

already spread over much of the north and west of the country, and today seems to embody the traditional essence of rural England.

But demography, not topography, constituted the largest single material difference between England then and now. Today there are about ten times more people living in England than were there at the time of Charles II's restoration. Although the first national census was not conducted until 1801, the administrative, financial and military benefits of establishing how many people lived within the realm were coming to be increasingly recognized from the mid-seventeenth century. Chamberlayne's *Anglia Notitia* actually provides one of the earliest contemporary estimates. Asserting that each parish in the realm (9,725, he believed) contained, on average, eighty families, and allowing seven persons per family, he reached a grand total of 5,446,000 men, women, and children. Although this calculation was based on assumption and guesswork rather than empirical research, the outcome is surprisingly close to the best modern estimate of 5.03m. That figure was computed by the backwards projection of nineteenth-century census data, adjusted according to pre-1801 aggregate birth and death rates derived from a national sample of 404 parishes, with the aid of sophisticated mathematical techniques which few historians feel equipped to comprehend, let alone criticize.[3]

Yet if we may assume the validity of those procedures, the middle years of the seventeenth century evidently saw a significant slowing in the population growth which had been a marked feature of the previous 150 years. Demographic change is never easily explained, but the main causal factor underlying this retreat was probably a declining birth rate (rather than rising mortality). Births diminished because a smaller proportion of the population chose to marry at all, while there was also a perceptible increase in the average age of those who did. Since illegitimacy rates were very low, and contraceptive techniques limited both in efficacy and acceptability, the main variables affecting the number of live births were the proportion of women in the population who married, and the age at which they did so. In early modern England, as today, newly-weds usually wanted to establish a separate household in which to start their life together, rather than continue living with either set of parents. Both husband and wife would normally contribute to achieving the financial independence which this goal required. But it was obviously more easily won when times were relatively good than in hard economic conditions, like the prolonged depression which set in during the second decade of the seventeenth century and was worsened by the disruptions of civil war in the 1640s.

Demographic growth did not merely falter after the mid-seventeenth century, but actually went into reverse. The national population total may have fallen below 5m. in the 1670s and again in the 1690s, as the effects of a lower birth rate were exacerbated by substantial emigrant flows to English colonies in

[3] More numerate readers may, however, consult appendices 11–15 of E. A. Wrigley and R. S. Schofield, *The Population History of England, 1541–1871: a Reconstruction* (1989).

North America and the West Indies, together with severe outbreaks of epidemic disease (mainly bubonic plague, smallpox, and typhus). Population growth resumed again in the early eighteenth century, but at a slower rate than before 1650. So the demographic peak of some 5.3m. reached in the late 1650s was not surpassed for another seventy years.

The demographic experience of early modern England—a cycle of growth, stagnation and growth—reflects a basic pattern identified towards the end of our period by the clergyman Thomas Robert Malthus (1766–1834). Malthus argued that animal (including human) populations always tend to press hard upon the resources available to feed and otherwise support them. Their continued increase is therefore only restrained by the 'positive checks' of famine, epidemic, war, and other disasters, or—preferably—by less traumatic 'preventative' or 'moral' factors. Given the prevailing absence of artificial family limitation (other than prolonged breast-feeding in order to inhibit conception), Malthus and his contemporaries assumed that these amounted to people consciously deciding to postpone marriage, thereby effectively limiting the numbers of children born, in order to protect their living standards. As noted above both mechanisms helped bring about the post-1650 demographic slow down. However, the 'moral check' of delayed and forgone marriage seems to have been the more important of the two. The result, apparent over two generations, from the 1660s to the 1720s, was a slight but crucial easing of population-induced pressures on the basic necessities of life.

Getting and Spending

A growing tendency to distinguish economic issues from their moral, political, or social context was apparent during the sixteenth and seventeenth centuries. The notion of an autonomous economic sphere pervades the writings of the merchant Thomas Mun (1571–1641), whose important pamphlet proclaiming *England's Treasure by Forraign Trade* first appeared in print in 1664, having been written during a commercial crisis forty years before. Mun insisted on the futility of the Crown's attempts to accumulate money in the form of gold and silver bullion, whether by exchange controls or other state-imposed regulatory devices; only if England exported each year more than she imported, thus generating a favourable 'balance of trade', would national wealth be increased. This was anything but an impartial thesis. Mun was writing on behalf of the East India Company, which needed to ship large quantities of silver out of the country in order to purchase cloves, pepper and other spices, and textiles in Asia for profitable resale in England and elsewhere. But what made his case something more than commercial special pleading was the depiction of England's commercial and financial transactions as a self-contained system, controlled in the last analysis by impersonal market forces, not government policies, let alone moral or religious precept.

Mun's mechanistic analysis was perfectly attuned to the intellectual and social temper of the later seventeenth century. The notion that both the world of nature and human society could be thought of as huge machines, designed by God, who had laid down their operating principles but did not interfere with their day-to-day running, became very fashionable from the 1660s onwards. Within this paradigm mathematics was seen as the tool which could both unlock the secrets of the universe and assist governments 'to preserve the subject in peace and plenty'. These last words are attributed to Sir William Petty (1623–87), who described his own demographic and statistical researches as 'political arithmetic'—that is, computations dedicated to the service of the *polis*, or state. Petty, like his friend the demographer John Graunt (1620–74), and their follower Gregory King (mentioned above, p. 5) tried to give administrators and politicians precise numerical data about the human and natural resources of the kingdom, although it must be said that their figures were usually based as much upon inspired guesswork and a priori deduction as solid, systematic information.[4]

For despite the enormous advantage of first-hand acquaintance with their own society, the early political arithmeticians laboured under all the disadvantages facing pioneers in a new field of intellectual enquiry, including very limited resources for collecting and collating data. Modern historians have sought to overcome these deficiencies by compiling systematic retrospective statistics for this proto-statistical age, although sheer lack of evidence makes it impossible to replicate the comprehensive economic series available in most modern industrialized societies. Nevertheless, sufficient data on prices and wage rates have been gathered to calculate something like a consumer price index, as well as indicators of the earning capacity of agricultural labourers and skilled building craftsmen (carpenters, stonemasons, etc.) working in southern England. As Figure 1 shows, a crucial point on which these modern index series are in broad agreement is that by the beginning of our period prices were no longer generally rising and real wages falling, as they had done for most of the preceding century. On the contrary, the statistical evidence suggests that from the 1650s or early 1660s the overall trend of price movements was generally stagnant or downwards, especially for grains and other foodstuffs, while money wages remained stable and even rose slightly towards the end of the century.

Sceptics may well wonder how much faith can be placed in such figures. Like all statistics, they inevitably abstract from and blur the infinite variety of individual human experience. The sources from which they derive do not represent the country as a whole, being heavily biased to the more populous and prosperous south. Hourly or weekly wage rates can be at best a rough and ready guide to income levels among wage-earners, since the amount of work available

---

[4] J. Graunt and W. Petty, *Natural and Political Observations on the London Bills of Mortality* (1662), 67–8; for the authorship of this work, see C. H. Hull (ed.), *The Economic Writings of Sir William Petty* (1899), vol. i.

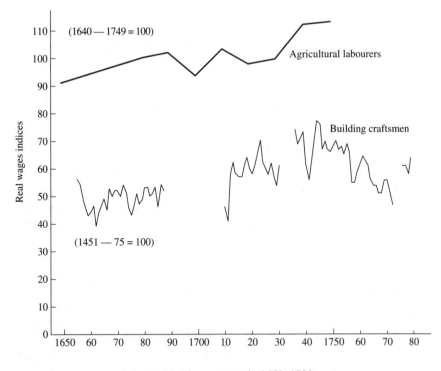

FIG. 1. Real wages trends, 1650–1780

and the hours actually worked were both subject to seasonal and regional fluctuation. The proportion of the population wholly or mainly dependent on wages rather than subsistence farming or some other form of family maintenance was certainly increasing, but we cannot now determine its actual size, nor calculate national rates of unemployment and underemployment. Wages were often paid in kind as well as cash, and supplemented by home-grown or gathered produce. Last, but hardly least, female wage rates are totally ignored for the purposes of these calculations, although together with the earnings of children they undoubtedly made a crucial contribution to many, perhaps most, family budgets. Yet even after all these qualifications, the reality of the post-1650 stabilization and decline in price inflation still seems clear enough, although the impact of this trend upon the living standards of the bulk of the population may be slightly more problematical.

The levelling-off of prices evident from the mid-seventeenth century obviously made things harder for producers and those with goods to sell, while benefiting consumers who bought on the open market. Because the economy was still overwhelmingly agrarian, in terms of both output and employment, the rural sector was the most heavily affected. As grain and wool prices edged downwards, landowners sought to maintain income by increasing agricultural productivity. Advanced techniques for improving the soil with fertilizers, nitrogen-fixing clovers, and other pasture grasses were borrowed from the Netherlands, together with new field crops (potatoes and other vegetables, turnips for winter cattle feed, woad and similar dye plants for cloth-making). Large-scale enclosure of open fields, wastes, and commons, land drainage and reclamation, selling timber or mining coal and other minerals tended to be expedients open mainly to substantial landholders; smaller proprietors turned to dairy-farming, or raising pigs and other livestock, but might also engage in drainage and enclosure schemes. Needless to say, agricultural improvement and innovation were by no means immediately or universally adopted. Yet towards the century's end the productivity of arable land was perhaps twice what it had been two hundred years before. Indeed England had become a net exporter of grain, rather than relying on imports from the Continent in order to stave off dearth and famine.

Early modern England is frequently characterized as 'pre-industrial'. Yet by 1660 industry and trade already played a major role, both economic and social. This was not merely a matter of village craftsmen supplying isolated communities with a limited range of articles and services, like the blacksmiths, carpenters, cutlers, millers, spinners, tailors, and weavers who lived and worked in the remote Cornish village of Week St Mary during the second half of the seventeenth century. Regional industrial clusters included textiles in East Anglia, the south-west counties (notably Gloucester, Wiltshire, Somerset, Dorset, and Devon), and the West Riding of Yorkshire, iron-making on the Sussex and Kentish Weald, and the fabrication of metal wares in the West Midlands.

As these examples suggest, manufacturing industry before the steam age was not confined to cities and towns. On the contrary, dependence upon animal or water power, plus desire to avoid the irksome regulatory oversight of urban craft guilds, had long encouraged industries to migrate to the countryside. Upland pastoral regions, where labour could often be more readily recruited than in mixed farming (grain and grazing) areas, tended to be particularly favoured. The interpenetration of agriculture and industry was a function of location, labour market (dual, seasonal, and part-time employment being very common, for women and children as well as men) and, last but not least, raw materials. The production of woollen cloth had long been England's predominant manufacturing activity; as Chamberlayne wrote in 1669, 'not onely all sorts from the highest to lowest are clothed therewith; but so much hath been heretofore transported beyond the seas'.

Woollen textiles remained England's major export commodity until late in the eighteenth century. The industry was fickle, its booms and busts dictated mainly by conditions in foreign markets, which now stretched from Muscovy to North Africa and across the Atlantic to the New World. Such a geographically extensive trade had developed only recently, as the traditional export line of heavy, warm, and durable broadcloths was supplemented by the 'new draperies', a range of cheaper, lighter, and more brightly coloured worsted or mixed fabrics. But in the second half of the seventeenth century increased competition from foreign manufacturers, particularly the Dutch and French, together with growing demand from domestic consumers enjoying a little more surplus cash in their pockets, meant that export sales of cloth were generally less buoyant than those on the home market.

Although we cannot put exact figures on domestic trade and consumption trends, both experienced vigorous growth after 1660. The continued expansion of London and the kingdom's other 'great trading towns' such as Bristol, Norwich, and Exeter (which a contemporary described as the nation's 'strength and glory') necessarily increased the proportion of the total population dependent for their basic existence upon foodstuffs grown by others.[5] Because towns were growing faster than the population as a whole (towns of 2,500 inhabitants or more held nearly a fifth of the national population by the end of the seventeenth century), the seductive appeal of urban fashions in dress and other consumer goods also influenced an ever wider audience. Burgeoning small industries supplied buoyant domestic demand for ribbons, buttons, glass, paper, pins, knitted stockings, straw hats, crockery, cutlery, and much besides. Meanwhile sugar and tobacco imported from the 'plantations' (colonies) of the West Indies and North America not only sweetened English puddings and filled English pipes, but were re-exported in considerable quantities to eager European customers.

Official attitudes towards foreign trade before the civil wars had been somewhat ambivalent. While customs duties paid by merchants provided a valuable source of Crown revenues, neither merchants nor their business were regarded with special enthusiasm or favour at Court. Foreign policy tended to be determined largely by dynastic and religious imperatives, rather than commercial considerations. A major shift in values after 1660 was signalled by the retention and strengthening of the protectionist Navigation Acts, which the restored monarchy took over from its republican predecessors, with the aim of cutting out or at least minimizing foreign competition (especially the Dutch) in trade with Europe and British plantations across the seas. An eyewitness report exemplifies the importance now attached to fostering English maritime commerce as a source of both profit and power. Standing by the fireside before dinner on 15 December 1661, King Charles II asked a courtier 'whether all navigation [foreign trade] were not good and profitable to the commonwealth?'; receiving an equivocal response to this (evidently rhetorical) question, the King riposted, 'You may as well make me believe this fire does not burn.'[6]

[5] J. Eachard, *Grounds and Occasions of the Contempt of the Clergy and Religion* (1670), 147.
[6] *The Diary of Henry Townshend, 1640–1663*, ed. J. W. Bund (1920), i. 83.

Hierarchies

On 1 May 1660 Parliament formally declared that 'according to the ancient and fundamental Laws of this Kingdom, the government is, and ought to be, by King, Lords and Commons'. The return of the Stuart dynasty promised a comprehensive renewal of order, an end to social confusion as well as political instability. As the republic gradually collapsed inwards upon itself in the autumn and winter of 1659, there had been reason to fear a resurgence of radical sectarian attempts to turn the whole world upside down. On the eve of the royalist triumph, the ambitious young diarist Samuel Pepys (1633–1703) recorded his conviction that any other outcome would mean 'the gentry and citizens throughout England, and [the] clergy must fall'.[7]

While all known societies seem to be hierarchical, the nature and extent of inequality between their members varies enormously. In early modern times social distinctions were generally far more complex, overt, and pervasive than they are in modern Western societies. And whereas today the rhetoric of democracy asserts the innate equality of all human beings, the conventional wisdom of three centuries ago was explicitly anti-egalitarian. According to this dominant discourse, human differences in material, physical, political, and social terms were entirely natural and hence unproblematical, part of the divinely ordained regime which embraced all Creation. Propagated, not always consciously, in families, schools, and churches, this notion of a 'Great Chain of Being' was reflected in the structure of most social institutions and powerfully reinforced by everyday experience. Thus nutritional differences and consequent variations in average height permitted most members of the aristocracy and gentry to look down, quite literally, upon their social—and physical—inferiors.

Yet this highly stratified world-view never commanded total acceptance. Some links in the great chain had begun to fray even before 1640, under the corrosive influence of evangelical Protestant fervour and humanist individualism. The subsequent trauma of civil war stimulated the expression of widespread if hitherto largely inarticulate popular grievances and resentments. During the 1640s and 1650s Levellers, Diggers, Fifth Monarchists, Quakers, and other non-elite activists rejected the existing social order and its anti-egalitarian ideology in pressing for greater economic, political, religious, and social rights. The emergence of these 'fanatics' seriously alarmed the propertied classes, and was a major reason why they eventually supported the monarchy's return (see below, Ch. 2).

Informal speech and usage recognized a basic social dichotomy between the 'aristocracy', 'gentry', 'gentlemen', or 'better sort' on the one hand, and the 'common people', 'commonalty', 'peasantry', or 'vulgar' on the other. But

---

[7] Entry for 18 Apr. 1660: a paperbound abridgement of the superb modern edition is now available as *The Shorter Pepys*, ed. R. Latham (1987).

more ambitious contemporary descriptions of early modern England struggled to characterize the complexities of a society aptly described by one modern historian as 'highly differentiated but … far from uniform, rigid or unchanging in its patterns of inequality'.[8] Most authorities depicted a vertical ladder of degrees, estates or ranks, ranging downwards from the select body of titular peers (sometimes designated as the upper nobility), defined by their legal titles and membership of the House of Lords, through the gentry (or lesser nobility—baronets, knights, esquires, gentlemen) to the plebeian majority of yeomen, husbandmen, cottagers, labourers, and paupers. There was a roughly parallel if less elaborate hierarchy of female ranks and titles, for while men and women both derived status initially from their fathers, married women generally took their husband's rank.

All such schemes evoked an earlier, simpler, idealized social world. They could not easily accommodate the professions (clergy, lawyers, physicians, army and navy officers, and government functionaries, plus a mixed bag of apothecaries, architects, men of letters, and teachers), nor the burgeoning urban elites (import–export merchants, wholesalers, some large-scale manufacturers, and other businessmen). While these groups both cut across and stood apart from the major divisions of traditional agricultural–military society, their growing numbers, influence, and wealth could hardly be ignored altogether. Hence an alternative social-structural map developed during the seventeenth century, with the insertion of an intermediate 'middling sort' between the familiar upper/lower, noble/ignoble, aristocratic/popular division. The result was a three-tiered pyramid, anticipating the more modern social world, conceptualized in terms of essentially economic class divisions, which undoubtedly had emerged by the late eighteenth century. At the beginning of our period, however, both ways of thinking seem to have coexisted. Thus in the 1690s Gregory King distinguished a vertical hierarchy of twenty-six different 'ranks' or 'degrees' among the population at large in his 'Scheme of the income and expense of the several families of England', whom on another occasion he simply divided into the 'better', 'middle', and 'poorest sort'.[9]

Part of the reason why contemporary models of the later Stuart social order were far from straightforward or consistent must be that what they sought to represent lacked clear and stable definition. An individual's social standing did not necessarily remain fixed for life, but fluctuated according to a matrix of distinct if related criteria, including family origins, education, occupation, bearing and dress, property-holding, and income. Age, birth order, marital status, and gender were also of considerable importance. Theoretically at least, in both domestic and public transactions, husbands took precedence over wives, sons preceded daughters, and the first-born son came before his younger

[8] K. Wrightson, 'The social order of early modern England: three approaches', in L. Bonfield *et al.* (eds.), *The World we Have Gained* (1986), 177–202.

[9] Cooper and Thirsk, *Seventeenth-Century Economic Documents*, 780–1, 795.

siblings. Parish registers of baptisms, marriages, and burials might categorize people in as many as six different ways: according to their gender (male or female), their degree or rank (husbandman, yeoman, gentleman), their occupation (labourer, carpenter, servant), their marital status (bachelor, spinster, widow), their birth-order (first-born, only, younger son or daughter) and, with the increasing use of the cryptic designation 'pauper', their wealth—or lack of it.

Just to complicate matters further, multiple designations and occupations were by no means uncommon. At the upper end of the social spectrum, a man who held a baronetcy or knighthood would be referred to by name and title, even if he were no country gentleman living off his estates, but a rich London merchant or financier, like the nouveau riche Sir John Banks (1629–99).[10] Lawyers and other professional practitioners were, however, likely to be identified by an occupational label (such as 'attorney', 'barrister', or 'counsellor-at-law'), and sometimes also by the title of an office they held, as well as by their customary 'addition' of 'gent.' or 'esquire'. These complexities help explain how a person could be assigned to different social categories in documents of approximately the same date. For example, thirteen of the 264 yeomen from the hundred of Kineton, Warwickshire, listed as subscribing to an allegedly 'Free and Voluntary Gift' of emergency cash for Charles II in 1661 appear in other contemporary sources as 'gentleman', and four of the 119 gentlemen as 'esquire'.[11]

Such anomalies may sometimes reflect the mobility of individuals, as well as a general inflation of status and discounting of titles. This process was much condemned, as by a royalist exile at Charles II's court in The Hague who complained in 1653 that the usage 'esquire' was 'now so increased, as he is a very poor and inconsiderable person that writes himself less'.[12] Since the criteria for determining social status were neither clear nor unambiguous, the perceptions of those actually making the classification assumed prime importance. The medieval College of Arms still claimed sole right to determine the correct placement of individuals within the social order, conducting county visitations which publicly 'disclaimed' men who used heraldic coats of arms or the style of 'gentleman' without proper warrant. Yet long before the last official commission to conduct such an enquiry was issued in 1686, contemporary usage had extended the title 'gent.' well beyond those whose names, pedigrees, and armorial crests appeared in the herald's books. Conversely, some so listed, after paying a substantial fee for the privilege of a more or less fictitious pedigree constructed by the College, might still be scornfully dismissed by their neigh-

---

[10] D. C. Coleman, *Sir John Banks: Baronet and Businessman* (1963).

[11] P. Styles, 'Social structure of Kineton Hundred in the reign of Charles II', *Birmingham Archaeological Society Transactions*, 78 (1962), 98–9.

[12] Edward Walker, 'Observations upon the Inconveniences that have attended the frequent Promotions to Titles', in Bodleian Library Ms. Rawlinson D 392, fo. 287.

bours as a mere 'gentleman of paper and wax'. In any case, the heralds were primarily concerned with a select minority (numbering perhaps 10 per cent of the total population) who claimed the dignity of gentle status, among whom birth or family counted far more than was the case further down the social hierarchy. Yet even within this relatively exclusive company, the monarch's prerogative of creating knights and peers significantly diluted the hereditary principle, quite apart from the various other informal avenues to gentle status, including education, occupation, and wealth.

Social classifications and distinctions were no less subtle and various among the vast non-gentle majority whom heralds and genealogists largely ignored. The crafts and trades had complex internal hierarchies; apprenticeship and marriage data show goldsmiths, grocers, and glovers consistently outranking butchers, bakers, and candlestick makers. Skilled workers, even cottage craftsmen, seem always to have been more highly regarded than mere manual labourers, although many of the latter might also find indoors employment in the metal or textile crafts during the winter. On the land, yeomen and husbandmen varied enormously in wealth and social status, rubbing shoulders with the lower or parochial gentry at one end of the spectrum, but sharing the hard lot of the landless agricultural day-labourer at the other. Regional differences add to the difficulty of generalization; the yeomen of Kent, for example, were famously well-to-do, especially by comparison with their nominal counterparts from the Midlands counties.

To emphasize the complexity and fluidity of social distinctions in early modern England is not at all to deny their reality or significance. The very fuzziness of status rankings may have tended to encourage a preoccupation with precedence and other outward signs of social status, such as the wearing of swords by gentlemen—and the code of honour which governed their use in the arcane but often fatal ritual of the duel. The tiny English titular peerage, comprising no more than 150 males in Charles II's reign, enjoyed notably fewer formal privileges than their aristocratic counterparts in Continental Europe. Yet the exclusive legal rights which peers did possess, including immunity from corporal punishment or arrest for debt, and the right to trial by a jury of fellow nobles, were not only valuable in themselves, but also powerful symbolic markers of social difference.

Even so, European visitors frequently remarked upon a relative lack of distance between the English upper aristocracy, the gentry, and the middling mercantile and professional sort. In 1668 a touring Italian count noted with mixed surprise and disapproval that knights apprenticed their sons to 'masters of the lowest trades, such as tailors, shoemakers, innkeepers ... Thus we see men of the noblest blood mixing with the lowest class without being distinguished by their clothes or anything else.'[13] Such blurring of social distinctions was a

---

[13] *Lorenzo Magalotti at the Court of Charles II*, ed. and tr. W. E. K. Middleton (1980), 114.

necessary consequence of primogeniture, the legal rule of inheritance which reserved estate and title to the first-born son, leaving his younger brothers and
sisters to make their own way in the world. But upward social mobility also produced similar results, according to the conservative Chamberlayne, who complained that the excessive 'wealth, insolence and pride' of the lower orders
prevented 'that humble respect and awful reverence which in other kingdoms is
usually given to nobility, gentry and clergy'. Fortunately for those who shared
his outlook, the demographic and economic factors which had made the preceding century an era of almost unprecedented social change gave way after
1660 to more stable conditions, appropriate to a renewed 'emphasis on elite
solidarity, social hierarchy and control'.[14]

Government

Seventeenth-century English governments, whether monarchical or republican, were fortunate to inherit a very long tradition of political integration and
effective centralized rule. Despite well-developed localist sentiment and county
loyalties, early modern England was a unitary state. No ethnic or territorial
enclaves existed where the central government's writ did not run, although
communication difficulties could diminish the effectiveness of its reach at a
long remove from London. Potentially more serious difficulties arose from the
fact that whoever governed England and Wales also ruled the kingdoms of
Scotland and Ireland, together with the Channel Isles, the Isle of Man, and a
mixed bag of colonial settlements and trading posts in Africa, Asia, and the
Americas.

   On the whole the authority of government within England's borders was not
exercised autocratically, but constrained by certain conventional and theoretical limits. Pre-eminent among these was an accepted obligation to rule—or
at least appear to rule— according to law. This implied the competence of the
lawcourts to review and possibly invalidate executive actions infringing subjects' legal rights, for example by arbitrary imprisonment or expropriation of
their property. Law here meant the common law, so-called because current
throughout the land, a national code distinct from the civil or Roman law
which prevailed in Scotland and most of Continental Europe. Common law
was a mixture of unwritten custom (or prescription) long accepted as binding
by the courts, and positive enactments (or parliamentary statutes). The executive arm of government, whether republican or monarchical, could not make
such law by itself; fears that the early Stuart kings did not accept this principle
underlay much of the political opposition they encountered. All measures
which imposed penalties for non-compliance, or infringed the property rights
of individuals in order to raise taxation for government purposes, had legal

---

[14] A. Hughes, *Politics, Society and Civil War in Warwickshire, 1620–1660* (1987), 343.

force only if accepted by the subjects themselves, or at least by those held to be representing them in Parliament. While the executive did on occasion seek to evade or manipulate these formal requirements, that they were something more than mere rhetorical window-dressing is apparent from a glance at other parts of the British Isles, or English territories overseas, where the exercise of executive powers was generally far less inhibited.

In modern democracies on the Westminster model Parliament is regarded as the ultimate site of sovereignty, its authority validated by popular consent expressed at general elections. But in seventeenth-century England both the functional and symbolic roles of government were vested in a single person, who did not merely reign, but actually ruled as well, if usually acting by delegated authority through a ministerial privy council, that 'great clearing house of government'.[15] Hence the daily business of politics centred on the person of the ruler and his or her household or Court, which remained always in being, unlike Parliament. The monarch enjoyed significant independent powers, or prerogatives, including the right to call, adjourn, prorogue or dissolve Parliament, to veto parliamentary legislation, to appoint bishops, judges, and ministers, and to conduct his or her own foreign policy.

Yet substantial authority and prestige also attached to the (until 1689) occasional sessions of the representative assembly, or Parliament. In this respect England increasingly stood almost alone against a general trend towards monarchical absolutism among the states of Western Europe. Equivalent representative assemblies elsewhere had either ceased to meet, like the French Estates-General, or else met only irregularly and exercised little effective independent authority, like the *cortes* of the various Spanish kingdoms, or indeed the parliaments of Ireland and Scotland. Besides its jealously guarded legislative and fiscal functions, Parliament was generally agreed to be a vital link between ruler and subjects. All the latter were supposedly present at sittings of its two constituent chambers, the House of Lords and the House of Commons, either in person, or by 'procuration and attorneys'.[16] But beyond this unhelpfully vague general proposition, no consensus existed as to Parliament's proper role in government. Its original functions had been largely judicial, and in some respects Parliament remained the nation's supreme lawcourt. Yet during times of political division and instability its law-making and taxing powers could also be used to block the executive's policies, and to press alternative courses upon a reluctant government. The resulting conflicts were aggravated by lack of an accepted external arbiter, and uncertainty about the precise boundaries of constitutional authority when executive and legislature were at odds. Neither civil war not its republican aftermath had settled this fundamental problem; it was not addressed, let alone resolved, at Charles II's restoration.

[15] D. Ogg, *England in the Reign of Charles II* (1956), 190.
[16] Sir Thomas Smith, *De Republica Anglorum* (1565), in G. R. Elton (ed.), *The Tudor Constitution* (1982), 241.

Meanwhile government still continued to be relatively personal, small-scale, and non-bureaucratic. No more than 1,200 individual holders of civil office can be identified in the administration of republican England from 1649 to 1660. While their numbers increased somewhat under the later Stuarts, civil servants remained relatively few by comparison with their bureaucratic counterparts across the Channel.[17] One main reason was that after 1660 English local administration largely reverted to the hands of unpaid local notables—substantial gentry landowners, lawyers, merchants, and business-men—who as Justices of the Peace (JPs) exercised a wide-ranging oversight of their social inferiors. The much-resented efforts of Charles I's privy councillors and Oliver Cromwell's major-generals to impose tighter supervision on these agents of local government were not revived at the Restoration. So the local bigwigs regained a large measure of autonomy in their dealings, both with those whom they ruled, and those in London who supposedly ruled them.

Formal rights of participation in this professedly anti-democratic system were largely reserved for men of property. Yet it was not only well-to-do males who concerned themselves with matters of government and politics. Below the propertied élite, service in minor parish offices, as churchwarden, constable, overseer of the poor or vestryman and on manorial, quarter sessions or assize court juries helped give even relatively lowly householders and husbandmen a sense of involvement and participation in public affairs. So did campaigning and voting in parliamentary elections, which in the second half of the seven-teenth century became more frequent, as well as involving a slightly larger pro-portion of the adult male population. Although women could not vote, stand for Parliament, or serve on ordinary juries or as local governors, they did hold some forms of quasi-public office at Court and as midwives, plague searchers, and hospital matrons. They might also simply make their views known, at home and abroad. Women were prominent in food riots and other popular protests against threats to the livelihoods of their families and themselves. Among the persons accused of speaking seditious words against the Stuart monarchy during Charles II's reign were nearly forty women (more than 10 per cent of those whose sex is known), while from 1679 the notable female play-wright Aphra Behn (1640–89) committed her polemical pen to the other, Tory, side of politics.[18]

The English prided themselves on enjoying a larger measure of inherited liberties and freedoms than less fortunate foreigners. But post-1660 govern-ments were hardly less authoritarian or intrusive than their interregnum pre-decessors, recognizing no civil rights to freedom of association, employment, movement, the press, speech, or worship. During Charles II's reign persons

[17] As late as the 1780s, fewer than twenty permanent officials staffed Britain's Foreign Office, as against more than seventy in its French equivalent: D. McKay and H. M. Scott, *The Rise of the Great Powers, 1648–1815* (1983), 210.

[18] T. Harris, *London Crowds in the Reign of Charles II* (1987), 193; S. H. Mendelson, *The Mental World of Stuart Women: Three Studies* (1987), 147.

absent from church on Sundays and those who violated the Sabbath by playing games, opening a shop, or travelling without a licence, who ate meat on Fridays, failed to denounce their neighbours' sins, refused to work for the (maximum) wage rates set by the JPs, wandered abroad from their parish of settlement, bore or fathered illegitimate children, told fortunes, published an unlicensed book, attended a prayer meeting, or pursued a trade without having first served the appropriate apprenticeship committed offences variously punishable by public penance, whipping, exposure in the pillory, fine, imprisonment, or trans-portation. Of course these provisions neither were nor could be uniformly enforced throughout the realm. Functions of social control and regulation were mostly discharged at the local level, by church, corporation, manorial, quarter sessions and other courts, and by (mostly unpaid) local officials who brought widely varying degrees of efficiency and enthusiasm to the task. One important exception was counter-insurgency intelligence. The Restoration monarchy took over secret service techniques pioneered against royalist con-spirators under Cromwell; by 1675 the secretaries of state were paying informers £4,000 a year for monitoring religious and secular dissidents.

As this last example suggests, insecurity, both perceived and real, was not the least significant continuity between the governments of republican and Restoration England. Whether the traumatic experiences of the 1640s and 1650s complicated or eased the task of Charles II and his ministers is another question. Certainly the strength of the reaction against the Commonwealth and all its works in 1659–60 can hardly be doubted. A craving to avoid any further upheaval, whether political, religious, or social, 'so matters might again fall into their old channel', as the young participant-historian Gilbert Burnet (1643–1715) put it, was both widely and deeply felt.[19] Such attitudes were not confined to the middling and upper sort, but shared by many of the common people, among whom enthusiasm for godly reformation had been far from universal. Besides facilitating a smooth return to monarchy in 1660, these con-servative sentiments retained considerable force into the 1670s and 1680s, when they were crucial to the government's successful handling of a major political crisis (see below, pp. 44–9).

Yet even disregarding the statutory restrictions of royal prerogative powers by the Long Parliament, which Charles II felt it expedient to accept in 1660, the lessons of the previous two decades clearly could be read in more ways than one. While the respectable classes generally recoiled in horror from any hint of a replay of 1641, let alone 1649, they also looked back with pride on the achieve-ments of English arms under Cromwell's leadership, in sharp contrast to the various military and naval débâcles presided over by Charles II. Together with these imperial and some institutional legacies (the end of extra-parliamentary taxation and prerogative courts, some slight administrative and legal reform,

---

[19] G. Burnet, *The History of my Own Time*, ed. O. Airey (1897), i. 151.

experience of a much-expanded executive role for Parliament), the turbulent events of the 1640s and 1650s had—not surprisingly—fostered new ways of thinking about government, politics, and the state, along with much else. By discussing the sources of political authority in analytically secular terms, the political philosophers James Harrington (1611–77) and Thomas Hobbes (1588–1679), together with a host of less distinguished controversialists and pamphleteers, had helped cloud the monarchy's charisma, and encouraged a more calculating approach to questions of allegiance. Despite the enthusiastic displays which greeted Charles II on his return to England, both he and his brother were to learn to their cost how little trust could be placed on personal loyalty, even to an anointed hereditary monarch.

Church and Dissent

Religion permeated everyday life in Restoration England. Christian belief and worship continued to provide an encompassing—if hardly uniform—framework of meaning for individuals, families, and communities, indeed for the entire social order. While some contemporaries expressed considerable anxiety about the spread of 'atheism', they generally meant by this term a lukewarm commitment to religious forms, not outright denial of the supernatural. The intellectual hegemony of Christianity was as yet largely unscathed. Despite widespread destruction of stained glass and church ornaments by Puritan iconoclasts during the 1640s, cathedrals and parish churches remained local landmarks, as well as significant administrative, cultural, and social centres. Religion was also an arm of government, a means of inculcating respect for authority, law, and order—although, as both recent and current events amply demonstrated, dissident religious beliefs could also motivate political dispute and opposion. In short, religious beliefs, institutions, and language continued to play a central if ambivalent role, as both cement and corrosive.

Whereas today only about 2.5 per cent of England's adult population admit to regular attendance at Church of England services, from 1661 onwards anyone over the age of 16 not frequenting divine service on Sundays faced the threat of fines and imprisonment. Compulsory church attendance was prescribed by invalidating a parliamentary measure of 1650, which had itself repealed various Elizabethan and Jacobean statutes imposing rigorous penalties on persons who refused to come to church. These 'recusants' included both Roman Catholics and radical Protestants conscientiously opposed to the doctrines and government of the state church created by Henry VIII's break with Rome. As re-established under Elizabeth, the Church of England was broadly Protestant in doctrine, but still administered by bishops and, in the eyes of some, retaining a number of 'popish' liturgical practices.

Most of those who had sought its further reformation along the lines of the Continental Protestant churches, termed Puritans by their opponents and 'the godly' by themselves, were prepared to work for change from within. But a zealous minority took the radical step of separating themselves off into covert groups of true believers, to worship according to God's truth as they found it. Such 'sectaries' or 'separatists', mostly relatively humble folk, were regarded with fear and suspicion by the more moderate or orthodox, and had suffered intermittent persecution until 1640. Meanwhile the commanding heights of the state church had been captured by an ambitious 'Arminian' party with the support of Charles I, who fully endorsed their authoritarian sacramentalism and anti-Calvinist theology.

Much to the horror of religious and social conservatives, the Long Parliament's strong anti-Arminian stance disabled the church's coercive apparatus and encouraged the sects to come into the open. Disagreement over the extent to which a fully reformed national church might tolerate these Baptists, Brownists, Familists, and other heterodox groups split the Puritan-Parliamentary forces. The more conservative 'Presbyterians', who wished merely to reform the government of the church by curbing the power of bishops, were outflanked by the 'Independents'. Their ecclesiastical ideal, strongly represented in the army, was a loose national federation of semi-autonomous congregations linked only tenuously to the state, with freedom of worship for all Protestants (except bishops and their supporters). Cromwell's subsequent attempts to establish a viable civilian republic were frustrated in part by growing opposition to even limited religious toleration, especially for radical plebeian movements and sects. These Baptists, Diggers or True Levellers, Fifth Monarchists, Muggletonians, Quakers, and Ranters shared little beyond belief in the autonomy of the individual conscience, a preference for lay preachers of both sexes over ordained clergymen, and championship of reform agendas directed against the interests of the propertied élite. Particularly alarming to a wide spectrum of respectable opinion was the mushroom growth of the Quakers, whose readiness to defy secular authority and social hierarchy in the name of the Lord was as yet unaccompanied by any commitment to pacifist principles. Fears that a breakdown of central government might allow such dangerous extremists even freer rein spurred a Presbyterian resurgence in 1659–60, as well as the return of the monarchy itself.

Although the young Charles Stuart had once solemnly agreed to support a Presbyterian church in return for military assistance from the Scots, his personal religious inclinations, to the extent that he had any, probably leaned towards the Catholicism of his French mother rather than the Anglican faith in which he had been brought up. But the evidence is inconclusive. In any case Charles and his advisers recognized that powerful anti-popish attitudes at all levels of society would negate his already slim chances of returning to England as king should he be thought to have embraced Rome. So the manifesto issued in his name from the Dutch town of Breda on 4 April 1660 diplomatically avoided any specific religious commitments, merely promising some tolerance 'in matters of religion which do not disturb the peace of the kingdom', pending parliamentary legislation 'for the full granting that indulgence'.[20]

While such legislation never materialized, at least not in Charles's lifetime, the fault lay less with him than his most vocal supporters. The bonfires and general festivities which greeted the king's successful restoration in the spring of 1660 signalled a massive reaction against all aspects of the defeated 'Good Old Cause'. The royalist poets Alexander Brome and Samuel Butler (author of the best-selling mock-epic *Hudibras*, which the ex-Cromwellian civil servant Pepys could not bring himelf 'to think … witty') caught the general mood when they jeered at the hypocritical zeal of the godly, and voiced a strong desire to hear no more of 'rules or reformation'.[21] Anglican clergy ousted from their benefices and royalist gentry laden with sequestration fines during the civil wars and Commonwealth had little intention of forgiving or forgetting the injuries which they and their cause had suffered. Fear, loathing, and resentment of all 'fanatics', the dominant tone of the Cavalier Parliament elected in 1661, ensured that the restored Church of England offered no accommodation to even the most moderate and respectable Presbyterian, let alone to Baptists, Congregationalists, and Quakers. After prolonged but fruitless negotiations between unbending Anglican bishops and increasingly dispirited Puritan divines, the Act of Uniformity in 1662 made worship according to a reissued version of the Anglican Book of Common Prayer mandatory throughout the land. Nearly a thousand clergy unable to declare 'unfeigned assent and consent to all and every thing contained and prescribed' therein were forced out of their church livings, joining another 700 ministers who had already been displaced.

Thus despite some conciliatory efforts by the King, his leading minister,[22] and a number of clergy who sought to moderate the intransigence of their more rigid colleagues, Anglican exclusiveness triumphed over moderate Protestant ecumenicism. 'Dissent' was cruelly if sporadically suppressed in many places (over 300 Quakers alone died in prison for their beliefs during Charles's II's reign).[23] But notwithstanding their own lack of internal unity, the Protestant Nonconformists were both far too numerous, and too well protected by sympathetic JPs, especially in larger towns, to be extirpated altogether. Henceforth English life would be marked by a deep cultural, political, and social divide, between Anglican 'church' and Nonconformist 'chapel'.

In retrospect the effective loss of the Church of England's monopoly status at the Restoration may be seen as part of a long-term institutional decline dating back even before the Henrician Reformation. Yet the established church remained a large, powerful, and privileged national institution. Besides

---

[20] J. P. Kenyon (ed.), *The Stuart Constitution, 1603–1688* (1986), 331–2.

[21] Pepys, *Diary*, 26 Dec. 1662, 28 Nov. 1663; A. Brome, *Songs and Other Poems* (1661, 1664), 109.

[22] Edward Hyde (1609–74), cr. earl of Clarendon 1661, had served as Charles II's chief adviser in exile, and lord chancellor from 1658.

[23] C. W. Horle, *The Quakers and the English Legal System, 1660–1688* (1988), 23.

commanding the formal adherence of the overwhelming majority of the population, it controlled most secondary schooling, as also the two universities of Oxford and Cambridge, and maintained an autonomous legal system (although the church courts' jurisdiction over doctrinal, moral, and sexual delinquencies was increasingly ignored by the laity). The 10,000 or so Anglican clergy comprised an élite of twenty-six bishops who sat alongside the temporal aristocracy in the House of Lords, the comfortably well-to-do deans and cathedral clergy, and an extensive mixed assortment of country parsons, city preachers, and poverty-stricken curates. Their lifestyles, ranging from princely to penurious, were supported from the church's vast but unevenly distributed landed endowments, and the fees and tithes payable by all parishioners, whether Anglicans or not. In short, the marginalization of Dissent left the Church of England impoverished in both human and spiritual terms, but still a good deal more than merely the leading English Protestant denomination. Above all the returning royalist gentry, the later nucleus of the Tory party, not only felt personal devotion to its doctrines and liturgy, but saw Church and Monarchy as mutually supportive institutions, the nation's best defence against a resurgence of religious fanatics, levellers, and republicans.

Culture and Ideas

The year 1660, according to the Worcestershire Presbyterian minister Thomas Hall, 'was a great year of combating with profane and superstitious persons'.[24] The saints' response to the restoration of church and king varied from outright resistance to partial or total compliance. Conspiracies, plots, and actual armed rebellion against King Charles evoked widespread alarm and savage repression. But most defiance took less violent forms, like the forthright avowal of the excluded Lincolnshire divine Robert Durant that he intended to continue preaching 'while any would come to hear him'.[25] Yet while large numbers of ministers and laymen did refuse to accept the Anglican church, there were also some very prominent conformists, like Edward Reynolds (1599–1676), the Presbyterian Oxford academic who accepted a bishopric in 1661. Moreover, the overwhelming majority of parish clergy simply acceded to the new religious settlement of the early 1660s, just as they had accepted the equally sweeping changes of the previous decades. Even for those who retained their former principles and high millenarian hopes, the urgency of the drive to make England a pattern of holiness to the world inevitably slackened. As conformist replaced zealot in positions of local power and influence, some measure of spiritual fatigue set in. With the enthusiastic reintroduction of maypoles and other symbols of traditional culture marking their failure to overcome popular

---

[24] Hughes, *Politics, Society and Civil War in Warwickshire*, 326.
[25] C. Holmes, *Seventeenth-Century Lincolnshire* (1980), 223.

resistance to moral reformation, the godly turned away in a mixture of sorrow and despair.

Yet defeat and introverted disillusionment do not adequately sum up the Puritan legacy to Restoration England. Despite the crushing of his hopes with the Good Old Cause, John Milton (1608–74) still thought it worth attempting to justify the ways of God to man in *Paradise Lost*, his great poetic epic first published in 1667. Numerous godly shibboleths, including insistence upon strict Sabbath observance, the use of a plain English style in preaching, and the dominance of the pulpit rather than the altar in ecclesiastical architecture, were absorbed by the Anglican church after 1660. The millenarian spirit, having sustained hopes of a new heaven and a new earth in the 1640s and 1650s, faltered with Christ's evident failure to return to rule in glory. But it was at least partly rechannelled into a secular utopianism, some of whose adherents looked to science, trade, and empire to build a bright future for the English people in this world. Mental attitudes and personal habits which Puritanism encouraged, or which at any rate often characterized the godly—a conscientious, hardworking, methodical, prudent, serious approach to the business of life, avoidance of ostentatious display, profligate expenditure, and other debilitating distractions—survived and flourished among the urban middling sort after 1660. Such character traits doubtless often contributed to individual success in the competitive world of commerce and industry, which in turn could tend to encourage somewhat ungenerous attitudes towards the less fortunate, including those in receipt of poor relief. England's economic achievements in the later seventeenth and eighteenth centuries cannot be explained simply in terms of the internalization of a Calvinist work-ethic, following the failure of the main Calvinist project, despite the prominence of Dissenters among early 'industrialists'. Yet the abandonment of attempts to impose a godly discipline on the nation at large after 1659 did contribute to the emergence of a culture in which the sphere of morality might readily contract to the individual's private conscience, while the Church effectively moved out of the market-place.

Since the Church of England as re-established after 1660 did not include all Protestants, religion remained what it had been over the previous two decades, a matter of consumer choice within legally defined limits, rather than automatic membership from birth of a national monopoly. This comparatively novel ideological pluralism encouraged debate and speculation over the merits of the various rival creeds and denominations, as well as a good deal of shopping around. It was not always feasible or realistic to draw a clear line between conformity and dissent, especially when many Dissenters practised 'occasional conformity' by receiving communion once a year according to the Anglican rites. In 1676 the rector of Frittenden, Kent, noted that his 315 parishioners included only two or three 'obstinate dissenters ... wholly refusing society with the Church of England'. However, there were also thirty-one 'Anabaptists or suspected thereof', two Quakers, two Brownists (or Independents), some thirty to forty 'neutralists between Presbyterians and conformists', a dozen 'licentious or such as profess no kind of religion', and another thirty or forty 'infrequent resorters to their parish church'.[26]

Apart from the evident looseness and permeability of these categories, the apparent extent of irreligion is noteworthy. Scepticism or apathy in matters spiritual may have reflected the continuing force of popular heterodoxy, especially as propagated by radical sects during the Interregnum; a principled rationalist rejection of the intellectual basis or historical authenticity of Christianity; impatience with theological and sectarian controversy; anti-clericalism; the fashionable post-1660 reaction against religious enthusiasm; or some combination of these. While local circumstances peculiar to Frittenden may also have been involved, indifference and resistance to the dictates of religion were frequently said to be increasing across the entire realm. Hence the title of John Eachard's successful *The Grounds and Occasions of the Contempt of the Clergy and Religion Enquired Into* (1670), even if the author's main pre-occupation was the economic and educational deficiencies of the Anglican clergy, rather than the 'decay of religion' arising as their consequence. Most of the institutional and personal shortcomings identified by Eachard (including non-residency, pluralism, simony, careerism, ignorance, poverty, pretentious-ness, and snobbery) would have been entirely familiar to would-be ecclesiast-ical reformers of the previous century and before. What kept his book in print, with a further ten editions before the century's end, was its wittily irreverent tone and mordant pen-portraits of such recognizable types as the 'profoundly learned' preachers, who 'bring in twenty poets or philosophers ... into an hour's talk: spreading themselves in abundance of Greek and Latin to a com-pany of farmers and shepherds', plus a general perception that both church and Christianity faced unprecedented intellectual and moral challenges.

The main intellectual threat was seen to come from rationalist materialism, especially in the mechanistic form purveyed by the reputed atheist Hobbes, who actually feared that he might be burnt as a heretic shortly after the Restoration. More generally the rise of science, the 'new philosophy', or what Robert Hooke (1635–1703), one of its more distinguished exponents, labelled 'physico-mathematical experimental learning', posed numerous challenges to conventional theological wisdom. Above all it offered an account of the nat-ural world which neither required nor left room for the traditional role of an activist God, who intervened directly in human affairs to reward the just and scourge sinners with plague and pestilence. While the origins of the scientific revolution of the seventeenth century are much debated, the extraordinary intellectual ferment of the 1640s and 1650s was probably more productive of schemes and speculation aiming at the utilization of knowledge than major scientific discoveries or inventions. From 1660, however, the influential Royal

[26] A. Whiteman (ed.), *The Compton Census of 1676* (1986), p. xxxix.

Society of London for Improving of Natural Knowledge brought together a mixture of academics, clergy, gentlemen-virtuosi, peers, courtiers, politicians, lawyers, merchants, and intellectuals, some of whom had been meeting informally over the previous decade, in both Oxford and London, to hear papers and discuss experiments. The Royal Society's first charter, issued by Charles II in 1662, described its aims as 'advancing the knowledge of nature and useful arts by experiment to the glory of God the Creator and application to the good of mankind'. Here and elsewhere members were insistent that their scientific investigations served to reinforce rather than undermine Holy Scripture and the teachings of revealed religion. They also carefully played down the radical antecedents of some of their number, banned political and religious debate from their meetings, and emphasized the value of 'a clear and deep skill in Nature' as an antidote to 'spiritual frenzies'.[27] The Royal Society did largely succeed in establishing the political and social respectability of science, even if many clergymen would have agreed with the young divine who wrote in 1681 that he preferred to consider 'the rain-bow as the reflection of God's mercy, than the sun's light'.[28]

By that time the work of the experimental chemist Robert Boyle (1627–91), and above all his younger contemporary, the great mathematician and physicist Sir Isaac Newton (1642–1727), was establishing a new intellectual paradigm which in time would entirely overwhelm orthodox Aristotelian cosmology and physics. In place of an earth-centred, heaven-surrounded, hierarchical, and qualitatively ordered cosmos, the Newtonian universe was infinite, yet serenely coherent and uniform. Its workings were governed by natural laws susceptible to mathematical enquiry, revealing in their exquisite rationality something of the purposes of their Creator, that 'Deity', who, as Newton wrote, 'endures for ever and is everywhere present, and by existing always and everywhere ... constitutes duration and space ... and knows all things that are and can be done'.[29] Although Newton's God was a somewhat remote figure, from the late 1680s the Newtonian world-view offered an acceptable middle path between atheistical materialism and the excesses of religious enthusiasm.

As the empirical study of nature became increasingly acceptable, magic and the supernatural were gradually marginalized. John Aubrey (1626–97), a foundation Fellow of the Royal Society, noted that superstition had declined since his childhood: 'the fashion was for old women and maids to tell fabulous stories nightimes, of sprights and walking of ghosts, etc. ... When the wars came, and with them liberty of conscience and liberty of inquisition, the phantoms vanished.' On another occasion Aubrey claimed that it was the growth of printing and spread of literacy which 'have frighted away Robin-goodfellow

---

[27] T. Sprat, *The History of the Royal Society of London* (1667), in *Seventeenth-Century England: A Changing Culture, i. Primary Sources*, ed. A. Hughes (1980), 330.

[28] Quoted M. Hunter, *Science and Society in Restoration England* (1981), 175.

[29] I. Newton, *The Mathematical Principles of Natural Philosophy*, tr. A. Motte (1729), ii. 390.

and the fairies'.[30] No doubt he exaggerated the extent to which popular animistic and magical beliefs had lost their hold, especially outside advanced metropolitan circles; the last legal conviction and execution of a person as a witch in England occurred at Hertford as late as 1712. Nor was it yet possible to draw a clear distinction between magic and science, especially while alchemy and astrology continued to command the adherence of such figures as Boyle and Newton (although the latter carefully refrained from publishing his extensive alchemical writings). Yet the sceptical trend was sufficient to alarm those who feared that any erosion of belief in the reality of a spiritual world would open the floodgates to outright atheism. Hence the determined efforts of such scholars as Meric Casaubon (1599–1671), and his younger contemporaries Henry More (1614–87) and Joseph Glanvill (1636–80) to collect irrefutable testimonies of supernatural occurrences with which to confound the doubters.

Another perceived threat to religion was general moral decline and pervasive sinfulness, regarded as both cause and effect of civil war, regicide, and the republic. Since morality was believed to be upheld by the teachings of religion, any apparent falling-away in standards of public or private behaviour was easily linked to the growth of irreligion. Yet despite the denunciations of contemporary preachers, and the conventional modern view of Restoration England as an era of unrestrained hedonism after the puritanical repression of the 1650s, there is little evidence that 1660 marked a general turning point of personal and sexual liberation. Indeed, while the ratio of illegitimate births may have been marginally higher between 1660 and 1669 (1.5 per cent) than it was in the 1650s (1.0 per cent), the century's highpoint for bastards (3.4 per cent) actually seems to have occurred during its first decade.[31]

But while the population at large may have gone about their not-so-wicked ways little affected by the end of the Puritan regime, things were very different at Court. There the King himself took the lead in gaming and wenching. A few bold preachers dared to denounce Charles's sexual promiscuity, but without discernible impact on his behaviour, which was frequently reported by Pepys in tones of prurient disapproval, somewhat incongruous in the light of his own marital infidelities. Of course the difference was that, especially after his marriage, the King's adulteries seemed peculiarly shocking in the public figure who headed both Church and State. Indeed Charles and his mistress Lady Castlemaine (1641–1709) were 'committing one of the great public adulteries of history', in a country where only twelve years before their conduct would have been punishable by death.[32] While public disapproval of its excessive severity soon made the 1651 Adultery Act ineffective, many of his subjects had no doubt that Charles's lewdness went too far in the opposite direction.

[30] *Aubrey's Brief Lives*, ed. O. L. Dick (1962), 12, 17.
[31] P. Laslett, *The World We have Lost Further Explored* (1983), 158.
[32] R. Hutton, *Charles II* (1991), 189.

Finally religion, or at least the Protestant faith—a distinction few of its adherents would have recognized—was challenged by 'popery'. The threat was hardly novel, but familiarity did not dull the fear and hostility Catholicism had long evoked, nor check the extravagance of anti-popish propaganda, with its nightmarish images of international Jesuit conspiracies promoting wholesale slaughter and subversion. The remaining English papists, although few in numbers (*c*.60,000) and overwhelmingly apolitical, were held guilty by association with the worst atrocities of the Counter-Reformation, and subject to ferocious if intermittently implemented penal legislation. Their position was not significantly improved by Charles's accession, despite his desire to repay the past kindnesses and loyalty of English Catholics with some measure of *de facto* toleration, although the anti-Puritan backlash did probably moderate pressure for rigorous enforcement of existing laws against papists. The eclipse of Spain as Europe's dominant military power may also have helped to contain English anti-Catholic fears, at least until Charles's desire for closer ties with Louis XIV's France began to arouse new anxieties in the early 1670s.

Enthusiasm or excessive religious zeal had been suspect long before the Restoration, and gentlemen were increasingly happy to leave abstruse theological points to the clerical profession. The sceptical Sir George Savile, marquis of Halifax (1633–95), suggested in 1684 that since religion and government were inextricably intertwined, matters religious should be so ordered as to 'keep men in a willing acquiescence ... without discomposing the world by nice disputes, which can never be of equal moment with the public peace'.[33] Perhaps such cool instrumentalism was a realistic prescription for relations between the Church of England and Protestant dissent, even if it ignored John Bunyan's Pilgrim and his desperate cry 'What shall I do to be saved?'[34] Yet Halifax underestimated the depth and nature of the gulf between popery and Protestantism, and the continued potency of religion as a divisive political issue. Indeed 'popery' was thought not to represent just a set of religious beliefs and practices (although many Protestants would have questioned whether Catholicism really was a religion properly so-called), but also an authoritarian ideology and political system entirely hostile to England's fundamental laws and liberties.

England, Britain, Europe, and the Wider World

Edward Chamberlayne, no mean chauvinist himself, claimed in 1669 that the notorious xenophobia of his fellow countrymen was actually confined to 'the lower sort of common people', reflecting their excessive 'wealth, insolence and pride' and 'rare converse with strangers'. Public abuse was the most obvious

---

[33] *Halifax: Complete Works*, ed. J. P. Kenyon (1969), 67.

[34] *The Pilgrim's Progress* (1678, 1684–5) of John Bunyan (1628–88), a Baptist tinker and lay preacher, became one of the most widely read books of all time; C. Hill, *A Turbulent, Seditious, and Factious People: John Bunyan and his Church* (1988).

form of hostility towards foreigners (although Bishop Thomas Sprat claimed that the cries of 'a Mounseur [i.e. Monsieur]' and 'French dogs' which were liable to greet newly arrived travellers on the streets of Dover reflected nothing more than 'the ill discipline of Dover School').[35] But the underlying attitudes expressed by such behaviour were far from confined to schoolboys and the lower orders. Those who had lived or travelled overseas as former royalist exiles in France and Holland, or young gentlemen whose fathers could afford to send them on a Continental Grand Tour, might be somewhat more broad-minded, if not outright proponents of the fashionable Francophilia which flourished in Court circles under those two half-French monarchs, Charles II and James II. But overseas travel was by no means limited to the élite: fishermen, merchants, sailors, soldiers, students, and servants of various kinds also ventured abroad in considerable numbers. Nor was contact with foreigners in England unusual, for townsmen at least, since substantial émigré communities of weavers and other craftsmen, originating mostly from France, Flanders, and Holland, had settled in London, Norwich, and other large urban centres, where they usually intermarried and brought up their children as 'native English'. In point of fact neither foreign travel, nor the experience of living in close proximity to foreigners at home, could be counted upon to moderate rather than reinforce the characteristic national contempt for the non-English.

Yet in various respects the English people interacted more closely with the inhabitants of Continental Europe than with the rest of the British Isles. Ireland, Scotland, and Wales shared some common elements of a Celtic cultural and linguistic heritage, and by 1660 all three could be regarded as conquered (if not yet, except for Wales, militarily secure) territories. There was, however, no common pattern to their constitutional, economic, and social relations with the dominant British kingdom. The principality of Wales and the kingdom of Ireland had both been assimilated to the English model of law and government, as well as receiving a local version of the Anglican church. The kingdom of Scotland, however, retained its distinctive legal system, administrative institutions, parliament, and national kirk. Scotland's loose association with England through the Union of Crowns at the accession of James VI and I in 1603 had even less impact on indigenous cultural, demographic, political, and social structures than the English absorption of Wales in the early sixteenth century. While the Cromwellian Protectorate temporarily incorporated Scotland (and Ireland) into a 'Commonwealth' under direct rule from London, the Scots generally—if somewhat naïvely—welcomed restoration of the Stuart monarchy as offering a return to national and parliamentary independence. Ireland, on the other hand, remained a colony of exploitation and settlement, whose native Catholic inhabitants had suffered large-scale expropriation of their lands by English and Scottish immigrants since the 1580s,

[35] Chamberlayne, *Anglia Notitia*, 60; [S. Sorbière and T. Sprat], *A Voyage to England ... as Also Observations on the Same* (1709), 108–10.

most recently and drastically in the wake of the Cromwellian reconquest. The resultant ascendancy of an ethnic and religious minority created a classical colonial situation. The Protestant Anglo-Irish élite controlled some two-thirds of the country's agricultural land, dominating the despised indigenous Catholic majority, and ultimately maintained in power by an army of occupation.

Ethnic and religious differences, plus centuries-old memories of conflict between England and her Welsh, Scots, and Irish neighbours (as well as more recent threats from both Ireland and Scotland), were further compounded by the relative inacessibility of the Celtic fringe. For London, and much of England, especially the more populous and prosperous southern and eastern counties, communications with France and the Low Countries across the Channel and the North Sea were generally easier and quicker than the overland routes to Wales or Scotland, or the perils of St George's Channel and the Irish Sea. By the same token, commercial and cultural relations between Glasgow, its western Scottish hinterland, and the Presbyterian settlers of Ulster in the north of Ireland were much closer than either enjoyed with London. Scottish students seeking to study abroad generally found the universities of Leiden or Utrecht more accessible, in both geographical and religious terms, than Oxford or Cambridge; Welsh ports like Neath and Swansea enjoyed closer maritime ties with Cork in Ireland or Bordeaux in France than with the cities of England's east coast. Nor did language yet provide a common bond—or medium for disagreement—except in the case of the Lowland Scots, who had spoken an English dialect since the Middle Ages. In the Scottish Highlands, Wales, and most of Ireland, the tongue of the common people continued to be Gaelic or Welsh, with English primarily the language of their chieftains, landlords, and rulers.

Outside the British Isles English was definitely a minority tongue. Although it was becoming easier to learn, as English grammars and phrase books began to be published in Europe for the first time, foreign ambassadors assigned to England generally had to rely on an interpreter, or conduct their business in French or Latin. Within England modern languages such as French, Italian, Spanish, and Dutch did not usually appear on the formal syllabus of grammar schools and universities, but were acquired from private tutors; the schoolmaster of Saffron Walden in Essex who advertised in 1674 his teaching of 'the Latin, Greek and French tongues' was thus something of an educational pioneer.[36] While French increasingly replaced Latin as the language of international culture, diplomacy, and tourism, a group of soldiers en route to serve with Louis XIV's army in 1671, finding that they could not make themselves understood in 'the little broken French we had learnt in England', were constrained 'to seek out such as could speak Latin'.[37] English ambassadors serving

[36] D. Cressy, 'The teaching profession', in W. Prest (ed.), *The Professions in Early Modern England* (1987), 131.

[37] 'Captain Henry Herbert's Narrative of his Journey through France with his Regiment, 1671–3', ed. J. Child (Camden Miscellany, 30; 1990), 301.

abroad were not markedly more conspicuous for their linguistic abilities; most could get by in Latin and French, but not Dutch or Spanish, while the difficulty of finding anyone capable of negotiating in German was explained by the fact that even 'Arabic and Chaldee are better known in our universities and country'.[38]

Opportunities for learning or improving French and other 'polite tongues' helped justify the growing practice of sending young gentlemen abroad on a Grand Tour, often carrying with them what has been called 'the first true guide-book in the English language', Richard Lassells' *The Voyage of Italy* (first published in 1670, with many subsequent editions).[39] Such travellers usually went to and from Italy, the wellspring of classical antiquities and Western civilization, by way of France, the leading contemporary source of fashionable dress and manners, also fast emerging as Europe's foremost diplomatic and military power. France's rise to geopolitical as well as cultural preeminence was a relatively recent development, facilitated by mobilization of the country's immense natural resources under a succession of dominant monarchs and their powerful ministers, coupled with the simultaneous decline of an overextended Spain. Cromwellian England had played a minor part in this process, allying with France against Spain in the closing stages of their long armed struggle. This intervention in Continental power politics was very costly and not perceived at the time as particularly rewarding (although the territorial gains included Jamaica, the first English colony appropriated by force from another European state and subsequently England's major West Indian possession). But like the earlier Anglo-Dutch war (1652–4), it amply demonstrated the formidable European, and indeed global, potential of the Commonwealth's large modern navy. How and on whose behalf that force would be employed by the restored Stuart monarchy was a matter of considerable interest to policy makers throughout Europe, as also to many of Charles II's own subjects.

Control and conduct of foreign policy was perhaps the most jealously guarded royal prerogative. But despite Charles's determination to manage England's overseas dealings in person, issues created by his tortuous diplomatic manœuvrings could not be quarantined from domestic politics and public opinion. Relations with France, the Netherlands, and Spain involved a host of commercial, cultural, and ideological considerations on which various constituencies and pressure groups adopted widely differing positions. In general terms, jealousy of the Dutch as colonial and trading rivals, tinged in Court circles with a distaste for their republican constitution and Calvinist religion, gave way during the 1670s to rising apprehensions that the expansionist France of Louis XIV might pose a still more fundamental threat to England's vital interests. Indeed France now inherited Spain's mantle of Counter-Reformation leadership, together with the status of most-feared bogy nation, embodiment

[38] P. S. Lachs, *The Diplomatic Corps under Charles II and James II* (1965), 55.
[39] E. Chaney, *The Grand Tour and the Great Rebellion* (1985), 120.

and champion of devilish popish designs against the laws, liberties, and Protestant religion of the English people. These ideologically charged sentiments were superimposed upon the traditional hostility felt for England's largest and closest Continental neighbour, an ill will so pronounced as to lead a newly appointed French ambassador to conclude in 1663 that 'The English naturally hate the French'.[40]

At this point, however, it was still the Dutch, rather than the French, who seemed to pose the most serious challenge, especially to English trade and territorial possessions outside Europe. The European discovery of the Americas, and of a sea route to Asia via the Cape of Good Hope, at the end of the fifteenth century had inaugurated an era of unprecedented commercial expansion and colonial exploitation. Although Spain and Portugal asserted monopoly rights to the fruits of their discoveries, they could not prevent the North Atlantic powers of England, France, and the Netherlands from venturing across the Atlantic and into the Indian Ocean. By the beginning of our period English colonies, forts, and trading posts were established in the Caribbean (Jamaica, Barbados, and half a dozen other smaller islands); along the eastern seaboard of North America from the subtropical Carolinas and Virginia north through Maryland and the New England confederation to Newfoundland; on the west coast of equatorial Africa; in India (Madras, Surat, and from 1661 Bombay, part of the dowry brought by Charles's Portuguese Queen); and at Bantam in Java. A few non-Europeans, mainly African servants, were even to be seen on the streets of London; Pepys hired a 'blackamoore' to cook for his family, 'who dresses our meat mighty well, and we are mighty pleased with her'.[41]

England's extra-European possessions were even more heterogeneous, in terms of population, economic basis, and mode of government, than the constituent kingdoms of the British Isles. But by the Navigation Act of 1651, which the Convention Parliament confirmed in 1660, all were incorporated into a single commercial network, designed to ensure that their trade was carried only in their own or English ships and that their most valuable products (notably sugar, tobacco, and cotton), were exported only to English ports. This legislation also provided that a strategic range of goods imported into England from Europe must be carried either in English vessels or those belonging to the country of origin. The Dutch and their dominance of maritime commerce were the real target of these somewhat complex measures. Possessing the largest and most efficient merchant navy in Europe, which enabled them to undercut rival freight rates by 30–50 per cent, the mercantile rulers of the Netherlands not surprisingly regarded the attempt to exclude all foreign competition from trade with England and her colonies as a hostile act. While commercial tensions were only partly to blame for the first Dutch War (1652–4),

---

[40] J. J. Jusserand, *A French Ambassador at the Court of Charles II* (1892), 126.

[41] *Diary*, 5 Apr. 1669.

which was mainly fought in European waters, the second (1665–7) resulted from naval and military clashes between Dutch forces and English slave traders along the Guinea Coast of Africa, and the capture by the English of the Dutch American colony of New Amsterdam (promptly renamed New York, after the king's brother James, duke of York).

Until a series of naval disasters culminated in the humiliating destruction of the anchored English fleet, this second Anglo-Dutch conflict may have enjoyed some measure of popular support, if probably less than was claimed by Court mouthpieces like the Poet Laureate John Dryden (1631–1700). Dryden's *Annus Mirabilis: The Year of Wonders, subtitled An Historical Poem ... Containing The Progresses and various Successes of our Naval War with Holland*, concludes with a prophetic vision of London, reborn like a Phoenix from the ashes of the great fire which devastated the old city in the summer of 1666, emerging as the 'famed emporium' and centre of the world's trade. Thus the discredited religious millenarianism which had depicted England as a second Israel, God's peculiarly chosen nation, the destined site of Christ's second coming, was succeeded by a secular forecast which envisaged England replacing the Netherlands as the destination of 'the wealth of all the world'.[42]

[42] Cf. C. Hill, *Some Intellectual Consequences of the English Revolution* (1980), 58–9.

2

SETTLEMENT DEFERRED

Restoration, Accommodation, Demobilization

The monarchy's reinstatement in 1660 was far from inevitable. In modern parliamentary democracies oppositions proverbially do not win elections: governments lose them. Likewise the Stuart restoration would not have occurred if the various anti-royalist forces had been able to overcome their mutual antagonisms and combine against the common enemy. But Oliver Cromwell's death in September 1658 removed the one person capable of both controlling the military and managing the parliamentary republicans. An officers' coup six months later, which effectively deposed his son Richard from the Protectorship, plunged the country into prolonged political chaos, with army factions and civilian politicians struggling for ascendancy. Even so, Sir George Booth's attempted royalist uprising in August 1659 attracted little support outside his native Cheshire, and was easily crushed by a combination of professional troops and county militias.

What then made it possible for Charles II to reclaim his kingdom only eight months later? Above all, the intervention of English forces based in Scotland under General George Monck (1608–70). This phlegmatic career soldier had been appointed by Cromwell to his Scottish command, after serving Charles I against the Scots and Parliament, and then Parliament against the Irish and the Scots. In late October Monck announced that he had been called by God 'as a true Englishman, to stand to and assert the liberty and authority of Parliament'.[1] By the time his army finally crossed into England on New Year's Day 1660, the 'Rump' of the Long Parliament was again sitting in the House of Commons. Within three weeks of his arrival in London its members had been persuaded to readmit those surviving MPs, overwhelmingly royalist in sympathy, whom the army had forcibly 'secluded' back in 1648. Because they easily outnumbered the sitting members of the Rump, this move opened the way for a final dissolution of the Long Parliament nearly twenty years after it had first met. New elections were then held for a free Parliament or 'convention' (so called because not summoned by the King), which on the first day of spring, May Day 1660, formally voted for unconditional restoration of the monarchy.

Contemporary accounts of the previous three months' manœuvrings between Monck and other high-ranking commanders, the junior officer corps, the Rump, the City of London, and the secluded members, among others,

---

[1] *A Collection of Several Letters and Declarations Sent by General Monck* (1660), sig. A2.

clearly indicate that this outcome was anything but a foregone conclusion. Monck's long-term objectives when he set off for London were quite mysterious to contemporaries and are little clearer today; the taciturn reserve for which 'Honest George' became famous quite possibly reflected as much puzzlement as deviousness. Yet the political skills which helped him retain the loyalty of his own troops, and neutralize those forces seeking to check the drift back to monarchy, might well have proved less effective had he been consciously committed to a royalist restoration from the outset. Coming to the English political scene as a relative outsider and unknown quantity, Monck benefited from the massive unpopularity of both army rule and the Rump. His position was also strengthened by the growing demoralization of commonwealthsmen, radical Puritan activists and all others who still retained a lingering faith in the 'Good Old Cause'. Economic recession, exacerbated by an exceptionally hard winter and skyrocketing food prices, intensified fears of impending social chaos. Dread of mutinous unpaid soldiers, not to mention 'anabaptists, quakers and atheists', sectaries and 'fanatics' of all descriptions doubtless encouraged many to look to Charles Stuart, as the puritan clergyman Ralph Josselin put it, 'out of love to themselves not him'.[2]

More immediately, what clinched the King's return was the failure of the leading republican general, John Lambert (1619–83), to check the mounting royalist tide. Following his dramatic escape from the Tower of London just before the Convention Parliament met, Lambert sought to summon a general rendezvous of troops to Edgehill in Warwickshire, where the inconclusive opening battle of the civil wars had been fought. Yet far from sparking a national anti-monarchist uprising, this move attracted little support from his erstwhile comrades in arms, and was quickly crushed by forces loyal to Monck. Lambert might have been more successful if those who had previously fought against Charles I and his son, or otherwise served their enemies, had expected no quarter from the vengeance of the returning royalists. But printed broadsides signed by prominent royalists were already announcing their abhorrence of 'all animosity and revengeful remembrance', and a firm resolve to let bygones be bygones, in the event that monarchy should be restored.[3]

The same accommodating, conciliatory tone characterized the monarch's own statement of terms, issued from his court in the Netherlands and published in London on 1 May. Charles's 'Declaration of Breda' was reassuringly vague, offering something to almost everyone: a general amnesty and pardon (except for persons excluded by Parliament), 'liberty for tender consciences' in religion (to be confirmed by act of Parliament), parliamentary settlement of claims for royalists' lands granted or sold by parliamentary order, and full satis-

[2] *The Diary of Ralph Josselin, 1616–1683*, ed. A. Macfarlane (1976), 457–8.
[3] *A Declaration of the Gentry of the County of Salop. who were of the Late King's Party* (1660); cf. *A Declaration of the Gentry of the County of Kent* (1660): British Library, Thomason Tracts 669 f. 24 (1, 74).

faction of all army arrears of pay (a promise which could only be financed with Parliament's assistance).[4] Such regal condescension had the desired effect, sweeping aside all thought of conditional restoration, and ensuring that when the King came into his own again, he did so without strings attached.

Charles was proclaimed in London on 8 May. Two weeks later he set sail for Dover with his court on the naval flagship hitherto known as the *Naseby*, now hastily re-christened the *Royal Charles*. Extraordinary scenes, both of spontaneous popular jubilation and carefully orchestrated public rejoicing, accompanied his progress towards London. Charles entered the capital on 29 May, his thirtieth birthday. The royalist John Evelyn recorded the joyous scene: 'the ways … strewed with flowers, the bells ringing, the streets hung with tapestry, fountains running with wine … I stood in the Strand and beheld it, and blessed God; and all this without one drop of blood, and by that very army, which rebelled against him'. Charles himself, less overwhelmed, reportedly remarked 'smilingly' that it must be 'his own fault he had been absent so long; for he saw nobody that did not protest, he had ever wished for his return'.[5]

Cavaliers, Conspirators, Dissenters

Republican disunity made restoration possible. But those who welcomed Charles II's return with bonfires and bells were themselves hardly of one mind. Triumphant cavaliers whose personal allegiance to Church and King had survived long years of defeat and persecution felt no affection towards Presbyterians whose royalism seemed at best calculated and whose acceptance of episcopacy was no more than grudging. Such differences of experience and outlook were compounded by long-standing structural problems. The respective powers of monarch and Parliament, and the character of the national church, having already provoked twenty years of civil strife and instability, remained unresolved and deeply divisive issues for the remaining quarter-century of Charles II's reign, and its coda, the brief four-year tenure of his brother James.

Internal security was the top priority for Charles and the government-in-exile which returned with him. Even if the political loyalty of the armed forces could have been relied upon, which it most definitely could not, the financial case for demobilization was overwhelming. Indeed the prospect of relief from taxes levied to support the New Model Army provided in itself a powerful argument for monarchy. Considering the fate of previous attempts to downsize or disband the military, the process went surprisingly smoothly, eased by loans from the City of London to meet arrears of soldiers' pay. Besides paying off most naval officers and seamen, Charles initially retained just over three

[4] J. P. Kenyon (ed.), *The Stuart Constitution, 1603–1688* (1986), 331–2.
[5] *The Diary of John Evelyn*, ed. E. S. de Beer (1955), ii 246; Edward Hyde, earl of Clarendon, *History of the Rebellion and Civil Wars in England*, ed. W. D. Macray (1888), vi. 234.

thousand troops (the 'guards'), drawn from his own, Monck's, and the former republic's regiments. For the time being this personal force could be plausibly represented as a prudent insurance against assassination attempts. Only later did it come to be viewed as a sinister move towards a standing army, poised to overthrow the laws and liberties of England.

While in hindsight all the plots against the monarchy which proliferated during the 1660s might seem doomed to failure, contemporaries could not be so sure. Certainly the government felt obliged to take every precaution against a republican coup, especially following the abortive but bloody London insurrection of the Fifth Monarchist lay-preacher Thomas Venner and his small band of soldiers for King Jesus in February 1661, and the more dangerous (because widely supported) Northern risings of 1663. So the restored regime purged the ranks of local government, both rural JPs and urban corporations, recruited informers to spy on dissidents, revived press censorship (the Licensing Act 1662) and restrictions on the mobility of the lower orders (the Act of Settlement 1662). Finally, although the Act of Indemnity and Oblivion passed by the Convention Parliament in the summer of 1660 sought to 'bury all seeds of future discords and remembrance of the former' under the amnesty promised in the Declaration of Breda, some fifty persons were expressly excluded from its provisions. Over the next two years a series of show trials and executions, together with gruesome ritual dishonourings of the exhumed corpses of Cromwell and others associated with the regicide of Charles I, served both to propitiate the loyalist lust for vengeance and send a dreadful warning to potential opponents of the new regime.

Royalist calls for revenge redoubled in May 1661 with the assembly of a new 'Cavalier' Parliament (as it was quickly dubbed, following the overwhelming electoral success of outright royalist candidates, at the expense of the Presbyterians who had dominated the Convention). Yet no general reign of terror ensued. Wholesale reprisals against erstwhile rebels would have been neither feasible nor prudent, as Charles himself recognized, given the vital role in his return of so many former enemies to his father and himself. Even the personnel of the new government represented a pragmatic—if at times uneasy—compromise between republican past and monarchical present. Thus the veteran Edward Hyde, created earl of Clarendon in 1661 in recognition of many years' service as chief royal political adviser, rubbed shoulders on the privy council with Anthony Ashley Cooper (1621–83), who in the 1640s had deserted the Crown to fight for Parliament. Ashley Cooper was also ennobled in 1661, rewarding his subsequent belated conversion to the royalist cause. The judiciary, other holders of high civil office, and the army and navy officer corps similarly included an assortment of returned royalists mixed with survivors from the Commonwealth and Protectorate.

In institutional and legal terms it was equally difficult to turn the clock back to a pre-war status quo. The appointment of judges with life-tenure during good behaviour, rather than at the King's pleasure, continued—if only until 1668—a practice adopted under pressure and reluctantly by Charles I in 1641. All Acts of the Long Parliament to which the royal martyr had assented automatically retained the force of law, although the statute excluding bishops from the House of Lords was repealed in 1661. The Triennial Act's provision for automatic issue of election writs after more than three years without a Parliament was replaced in 1664 by a toothless declaratory version lacking this machinery. The conciliar courts abolished in 1641 remained defunct, with the partial exception of the Council in the Marches of Wales, and despite desultory discussion about reviving the Court of Star Chamber. The Long Parliament's ordinance abolishing the Court of Wards became part of a financial package designed to minimize future friction between Crown and Parliament by guaranteeing Charles what then seemed a more than adequate annual income of £1.2m., derived from the repossessed royal estates, a range of customs duties, and a consumption tax or excise, levied indiscriminately upon the sale of beer, wine, and spirits, chocolate, coffee, and tea.

The final extinction of wardship (the Crown's lucrative feudal right to administer estates inherited by minors) removed an unpopular and arbitrary tax on the landed gentry and aristocracy. This de facto conversion of feudal tenures to freehold title also encouraged long-term agricultural investment, especially since the same security was not granted to lowly copyhold tenants. But in other respects questions of land ownership and title were among the most contentious issues facing the new regime. The decision to return to its original owners all royal, church, and private real estate which had been directly confiscated by Parliament or Protectorate aroused little public dissent. But many ex-royalists had expected or hoped that they might also be able to regain lands sold to pay off political fines imposed during the 1640s and 1650s. Failure to provide even token compensation for such forced sales exacerbated the government's manifest inability to satisfy myriad seekers after place or pension, who bombarded Whitehall with petitions recounting at length the losses they had purportedly suffered in the royal cause. Hence the increasingly embittered complaints that the Restoration had brought indemnity for the King's enemies and oblivion for his friends (cf. above, p. 37). Such frustrations undoubtedly aggravated the pervasive hostility towards 'fanatics' which characterized the Cavalier Parliament, and helped make the religious settlement it endorsed (see above, p. 22) far more exclusive and intolerant than Charles II himself might have preferred.

Charles II and the Crisis of 1666–1667

The third Stuart monarch may well have been the best-loved king in English history. Charles acknowledged seventeen royal bastards and certainly enjoyed the affections of many more women than his thirteen known mistresses. No apparent effort was made to conceal the King's extramarital activities from his subjects. Indeed Dryden's famous pro-government verse satire *Absolom and Achitophel* (1681) refers to Charles as 'Israel's monarch', who

> after Heaven's own heart
> His vigorous warmth did variously impart
> To wives and slaves, and wide as his command
> Scattered his Maker's image through the land.

Yet, ironically enough, Charles's marriage in 1662 to a Portuguese princess was childless, an omission of real consequence, both for the country and himself. Nor was this the only respect in which the 'merry monarch' (or 'slippery sovereign', as his biographer Ronald Hutton prefers) failed to exploit opportunities for enhancing the Crown's authority which presented themselves at the beginning of his reign. Charles's refusal to subject his wife to the indignities of divorce proceedings in order that he might remarry and beget an heir did spare her the ultimate marital humiliation, but the nation was to pay a heavy price for this rather uncharacteristic act of royal compassion.

Historians disagree as to how different Charles II's prospects in 1660 were from those which faced his father thirty-five years before. Marxists and Whigs tend to argue that the monarchy never fully recovered from the traumatic experiences of military defeat, regicide, and parliamentary government during the 1640s and 1650s. But modern revisionists point out that the legacy of those two decades cut both ways. The well-to-do and respectable could no longer suppose that civil war would not threaten their own powers and privileges. So they showed considerable reluctance to provoke a serious political breakdown which might lead to armed conflict, which tended to counterbalance Charles's personal reluctance either to go on his travels again, or to risk a repetition of his father's fate.

If Charles had consciously decided to expand the monarchy's powers and freedom of action, following the example of his French cousin Louis XIV, the means lay close to hand. The military forces which the king maintained, both within the country and close by (the Royal Barracks in Dublin were reputedly the largest in Europe), could be used either to overawe parliaments or to support the collection of non-parliamentary taxes. Even if some legislative restrictions upon the royal prerogative remained in force from 1641, the Crown still retained enormous powers of patronage, plus total theoretical autonomy in conducting foreign policy and appointing ministers. Most of the pulpits in the land, once again controlled by the Church of England, preached the absolute theological necessity of submitting without resistance to the commands of a divinely anointed king. Last—and in a personal monarchy far from least—Charles II was without doubt a far more astute, intelligent, likeable, and effective political operator than his father had ever been.

Yet apart from survival, and enjoyment, the restored king seems to have set no clear goals for himself or the monarchy. Nor did his first minister appear anxious to help enhance royal power, as Cardinals Richelieu and Mazarin had recently done in France. On the contrary, Clarendon's entire political career had been devoted to advocating legality and moderate courses, while he seemed no more able to formulate and pursue a long-term political strategy than his royal master. The result was not just drift, vacillation, and lost opportunities, but a gathering crisis which substantially fulfilled the political philosopher James Harrington's prophecy in 1660, that if Charles were to call 'a Parliament of the greatest cavaliers in England, so they be men of estates ... let them sit but seven years, and they will all turn Commonwealth's men'.[6]

Relations between the restored monarch and his subjects had soured as early as June 1662, according to Pepys, who observed that while Charles and his queen were 'minding their pleasures at Hampton Court' outside London, 'all people' were 'discontented'. Some (former royalists) felt insufficiently rewarded for their loyalty, others ('fanatics of all kinds') resented the loss of religious liberty, which was blamed on the King, however unfairly. The haughtiness of the bishops, the recent vengeful execution of the republican politician Sir Henry Vane (despite a prior royal undertaking that his life would be spared), and the new hearth tax were also causing much 'clamour'. Particularly aware of the financial constraints under which his beloved navy was labouring, Pepys lastly noted the likelihood of 'wars abroad ... when we have not money to pay for any ordinary layings-out at home'.[7]

The prolonged colonial skirmishings which eventually led to formal declaration of war against the Dutch early in 1665 were begun by state-licensed corporations, such as the slave-trading Royal Africa Company, a major investment vehicle for courtiers and members of the royal family. These semi-piratical activities inevitably provoked Dutch reprisals, which in turn gradually involved the state's naval resources. Despite mounting concern about extravagance at Court and the Crown's ballooning deficit, there was no difficulty in persuading Parliament to vote money on an unprecedented scale (£2.5m. over three years) for an all-out maritime war against Europe's major financial and trading power. But the unlikely amalgam of aristocratic anti-republican sentiment, long-standing commercial jealousies, and jingoistic popular anticipation of military successes comparable to those won by the Cromwellian regime did not survive a string of bloody yet inconclusive naval battles in 1665–6. War weariness grew with diplomatic isolation and commercial disruption resulting from the conflict itself. Public disquiet was compounded by agricultural recession, the disruptive effects of what only later came to be recognized as England's last epidemic of bubonic plague in 1665, and the great fire which next year burnt down most of the old City of London.

A significant opinion shift may be reflected in the general tendency to blame popish—rather than Protestant Dutch—arsonists for this terrifying

<hr />

[6] *Aubrey's Brief Lives*, ed. O. L. Dick (1962), 209.
[7] *Diary*, 30 June 1662.

conflagration, vividly described both in Pepys's diary and Dryden's *Annus Mirabilis*. But the government itself was responsible for the next disaster, the humiliating destruction by Dutch naval raiders of the pride of the English war fleet (including the *Royal Charles*) at anchor in the Medway in June 1667. True, parliamentary reluctance to supplement the funds already voted for war, even with the proviso that their expenditure should be supervised by an independent audit commission, had prompted drastic cuts in military and naval expenditure. Yet the scale of the disaster and the public fury which it aroused, once panic fears of invasion had subsided, made any such mitigating circumstances irrelevant.

Clarendon, already widely unpopular, was the obvious scapegoat. Charles ostentatiously distanced himself from this upright but coldly proud and stuffy lawyer-statesman, whose public career had been devoted to the house of Stuart (and whose eldest daughter Anne was married to Charles's brother). First dismissed from office, then impeached by Parliament and finally forced into perpetual banishment, Clarendon spent the remaining seven years of his life in France. There he completed, together with a self-justificatory political memoir, what is incomparably the finest participant-observer history of his tumultuous times. Meanwhile his former master turned to new men and new courses. As another distinguished author and one-time royal councillor wrote after the King's death, Charles II tended to treat his ministers much like his mistresses: 'he used them, but he was not in love with them'.[8]

Unstable Alliances, 1668–1677

A visitor to England in 1668 viewed King and Parliament as trapped in an uneasy relationship of mutual conflict and dependence: 'it is impossible', he concluded, 'that they should not make themselves intolerable to each other, and that both should not think of freeing themselves forever from such a necessary and troublesome subjection'.[9] Although coloured by coffee-house gossip and the contemporary Continental cliché of English political instability, Count Magalotti's judgement was not far off the mark. For all his wit and charm, Charles, like his grandfather James before him, remained an extravagant and often feckless ruler. Parliament, however fundamentally loyal, always required careful managing, and could easily turn downright obstructive, especially in the face of the King's hankering for a more tolerant religious regime. Most members of the two Houses did not consciously seek to restrict the royal prerogative or to enhance their own powers. Disputes between Commons and Lords were indeed frequent and on occasion (notably a jurisdictional row between the two Houses over the law case *Shirley* v. *Fagg* in the mid-1670s) no less disruptive than parliamentary clashes with the executive. But the combination

---

[8] *Halifax: Complete Works,* ed. J. P. Kenyon (1969), 255.
[9] *Lorenzo Magalotti at the Court of Charles II,* ed. W. E. K. Middleton (1980), 19.

of genuine uncertainties about Crown and Parliament's respective constitutional rights, the administration's inadequate control over the proceedings of either House, the monarchy's growing cash-flow problems, the Court's dubious moral reputation, deeply held differences of opinion as to the desirable extent of liberty in religious matters, and the ominous growth of French power in Europe inevitably provoked conflict, and speculation about extreme solutions.

Even before Clarendon's removal the King had freely exercised his undoubted prerogative of appointing ministers and accepting counsel from whomsoever he chose, including personal enemies of the Chancellor, such as the archetypal cavalier Sir Henry Bennet (1618–85), later earl of Arlington, and the idiosyncratic duke of Buckingham (1628–87), Charles's boyhood companion. Clarendon's fall encouraged Charles to take a still more active role. That outcome proved no more permanent than the better relations between government and Parliament which followed peace with the Dutch and a new pact (the Triple Alliance) with Holland and Sweden directed against the territorial ambitions of Louis XIV's France. But Charles and his loose-knit ministerial junta did succeed in extracting a greatly enhanced vote of taxes from the parliamentary session of 1669–70. This unexpected fiscal generosity sprang from intensive lobbying of individual MPs, plus the government's acceptance of a renewed anti-Dissenter Conventicles Act, which seemed to signal renewed commitment to upholding the Church of England.

Yet all the while Charles was playing a double game. His protracted personal negotiations with Louis XIV eventually produced a formal treaty between the two monarchs, signed at Dover in 1670 by two Catholic ministers, Arlington and Thomas Clifford (1630–73) but concealed from the other three members of the notorious ministerial 'Cabal' (as it was somewhat misleadingly labelled at the time, after the initials of its members, who otherwise had little in common). That Buckingham, Ashley Cooper, and Lauderdale[10] remained in the dark was not merely because Charles habitually played his political cards close to the chest. It also reflected the potentially explosive nature of the whole undertaking, especially the King's pledge to 'reconcile himself with the Church of Rome as soon as the state of his country's affairs permit[s]'.[11]

Charles II's innermost religious convictions, if any, remain a mystery. Perhaps they were accurately represented by this in-principle commitment to Catholicism. Yet he was also well aware of the strength of anti-popish sentiment in England. While the treaty left him free to decide when to announce his conversion, it committed Louis to providing a significant financial subsidy immediately, followed by further injections of cash to assist preparations for the joint attack upon Holland which was the other main aspect of the deal. The full contents of the Treaty of Dover remained unknown during Charles's lifetime.

[10] John Maitland (1616–82), a former Presbyterian who administered Scotland 1660–80, was cr. duke of Lauderdale in 1672.

[11] D. Ogg, *England in the Reign of Charles II* (1956), 344–6.

But any alliance with absolutist, expansionist, popish France would inevitably provoke mistrust and suspicion, both within and outside Parliament. Such anxieties were heightened, just before the outbreak of the third Anglo-Dutch war in twenty years, by the King's proclamation of a Declaration of Indulgence (1672). This measure invoked the royal prerogative to suspend all penal laws against religious non-conformists, Catholic recusants as well as Protestant Dissenters. Apart from its disturbing constitutional implications—in terms of the Crown's powers to annul parliamentary legislation by unilateral fiat, and thus effectively overturn statute law—the Declaration was widely condemned, not least by leading Dissenters, as encouraging the spread of popery.

The next parliamentary session, delayed until early in 1673, saw Charles, under intense financial and political pressure, withdraw the Declaration. Indeed he now accepted a new penal law designed to exclude Roman Catholics from public office. The Test Act required all government officials and military officers to receive the Anglican sacrament of Holy Communion and to disavow the fundamental Catholic doctrine of transubstantiation. Among those who consequently resigned their posts was the Lord High Admiral, Charles's younger brother James, duke of York. This proof that the notoriously authoritarian heir to the throne, who after Anne Hyde's death in 1670 had married an Italian Catholic princess, was himself a papist, cast a very different light on joint Anglo-French hostilities against the Protestant Netherlands. Long-standing commercial jealousies were now balanced by fears that the continued advance of Louis XIV's diplomatic and military juggernaut threatened the very survival of the reformed religion in Europe. Skilfully heightened by Dutch propaganda, these anxieties combined with a lacklustre military performance to make the war unpopular. They also encouraged a string of abortive parliamentary initiatives designed to secure the country against both popery and arbitrary government.

Charles was persuaded to conclude a separate peace with Holland in 1674, as part of yet another policy switch. The government's new 'Anglican' or 'cavalier' stance, rejecting the French alliance abroad while denying religious toleration to both Catholics and Dissenters at home, was orchestrated by Sir Thomas Osborne (1631–1712), a Yorkshire country gentleman whose rise to political prominence signalled the eclipse of the Cabal. Soon raised to the peerage as earl of Danby, Osborne sought both to improve the Crown's financial position and to consolidate a dependable pro-Court party in Parliament. Charles never wholeheartedly supported these initiatives, especially the anti-French stance, and indeed continued to receive cash payments from Louis throughout the period of Danby's ministry. But they did help frustrate the political activities of Ashley Cooper, created earl of Shaftesbury in 1672, who after dismissal from office the following year had become a prominent spokesman for the loose-knit 'Country' (i.e. non-Court) grouping of MPs which provided an ineffective opposition to the regime on the few brief occasions when

Parliament sat between 1674 and 1678. Outside Parliament the mid-1670s saw a steep rise in political writings hostile to the government, despite the press censorship and other attempts to restrict the circulation of inflammatory pamphlets, such as the poet-MP Andrew Marvell's anonymously published *Account of the Growth of Popery and Arbitrary Government* (1677).[12] Increasingly concerned at the prospect of a Catholic succession, and the government's suspicious reluctance to disband troops supposedly raised to assist the Dutch against France, public opinion was galvanized in the autumn of 1678 by revelations of an elaborate Jesuit conspiracy to murder the King and subjugate his loyal Protestant subjects.

Popish Plot, Reaction, and Proscription

The reality of what now appears to have been a wholly fictitious 'popish plot' was at first almost universally accepted, even if the principal intended victim 'did think it some artifice and did not believe one word of the plot'.[13] Despite a series of seemingly corroborative events, including the discovery of incriminating correspondence in the papers of a former secretary to the Duke of York, and the (still mysterious) murder of the magistrate who had taken the initial allegations, there were certainly glaring gaps and inconsistencies in the charges promoted by the lantern-jawed university drop-out, defrocked vicar, homosexual adventurer, charlatan and perjurer Titus Oates (1649–1705). But Charles plainly appreciated the potential political dangers of refocusing attention on his brother's Catholicism, and hence the issue of the succession. These were reinforced by a disgruntled ambassador's disclosure that the government's apparent anti-French posture of the last few years had not prevented the King seeking and receiving very large cash subsidies from Louis XIV. Oates's plausible salesmanship, embroidered by his dupes and emulators, gave new urgency to long-standing (and not wholly irrational) fears of English Protestants facing resurgent Counter-Reformation Catholicism. But the plot essentially took off because it fitted the political and psychological needs of all who had come to mistrust the general direction and style of Charles's government. As one member of the Commons declared, he did not believe the plot because 'Mr Oates' said it was true, 'but because it is probable to be true, therefore I believe it'.[14]

The central issue around which the crisis of the years 1678–81 crystallized was whether the duke of York should or could be allowed to succeed to the throne after his elder brother's death. Of course this was not merely a matter of James's personal fitness to rule, even if his alleged 'heady, violent, and bloody' temperament (as it was characterized by a document in Shaftesbury's papers)

---

[12] T. Harris, *London Crowds in the Reign of Charles II* (1987), 92.
[13] *Memoirs of Sir John Reresby*, ed. A. Browning (2nd edn., 1991), 153.
[14] Quoted K. H. Haley, *The First Earl of Shaftesbury* (1968), 484.

might appear to symbolize the underlying threat of popery and arbitrary government to true religion and English liberties.[15] But how serious was that danger and how best to counter it? Opinion on these questions was deeply divided, both within and outside Parliament. This division precipitated a new stage in the development of English political institutions, as previously fluid factional alliances of MPs and peers coalesced into two more or less distinct blocs, each backed by a rudimentary extra-parliamentary organization. The terms 'Court' and 'Country', applied to the royal government's supporters and opponents respectively as far back as the 1620s, had been revived again in the later 1660s. But during the political ferment of the three brief parliamentary sittings (March–July 1679, October 1680–January 1681, and March 1681) which followed Charles's long-awaited dissolution of the Cavalier, Long, or Pensioner Parliament in July 1679, 'Court' and 'Country' were for the first time supplemented by the more distinctive and ideologically specific labels of 'Tory' and 'Whig'.

Both were originally insults. Tory, derived from the Irish *Toraidhe* (bandit, cattle thief, outlaw), was applied to supporters of Charles II's refusal to countenance any alteration to the line of succession by excluding the duke of York. Besides objecting to the blasphemous subversion of a divinely ordained hereditary line of descent, Tories believed that if James's claim to the throne were blocked by Act of Parliament, none of the prerogatives of the Crown, nor indeed the private property rights of the subject, would be safe from parliamentary interference. And once Parliament in effect determined the succession, Parliament rather than monarch would be sovereign, and England would have become a republic, in fact if not in name. To term those holding such views Tories was to associate them with the Irish papist rebels whose atrocities against Protestant settlers in 1641 were part of the standard anti-Catholic repertoire. In point of fact most Tories were fiercely committed to upholding the Church of England's privileged monopoly against both papists and Protestant Dissenters. But in the tense and excitable atmosphere from late 1678 onwards such partisan smears became the basic currency of political exchange.

From the Court side of politics the natural riposte was to claim that supporters of exclusion and more effective parliamentary checks on the alleged absolutist tendencies of the royal executive were republican fanatics and/or puritanical rebels, like the Scots Presbyterian 'Whiggamores', or Whigs, who staged a major armed revolt against Lauderdale's autocratic regime in the summer of 1679. Those to whom this label was applied were not necessarily Nonconformists themselves, although Presbyterians, Baptists, Congregationalists, and Quakers tended to provide the backbone of organized support for the Country, exclusionist cause outside Parliament. Moreover, the aristocratic leaders of the Whig's parliamentary campaign sympathized with

---

[15] W. D. Christie, *A Life of Anthony Ashley Cooper First Earl of Shaftesbury* (1871), ii. 314.

Dissenters' pleas for a limited measure of religious toleration at the expense of the episcopal Church of England, not least in reaction to the unwavering support which Charles could count on throughout the crisis from the Anglican bishops sitting in the House of Lords.

Here lay one critical opposition weakness. Despite their success in three hard-fought elections to the Commons, the Whigs never managed to control the Lords, who in 1680 rejected the only exclusion bill to pass all procedural stages in the Lower House. A second crucial difficulty was to decide who should succeed to the throne if York were excluded. The choice lay between the

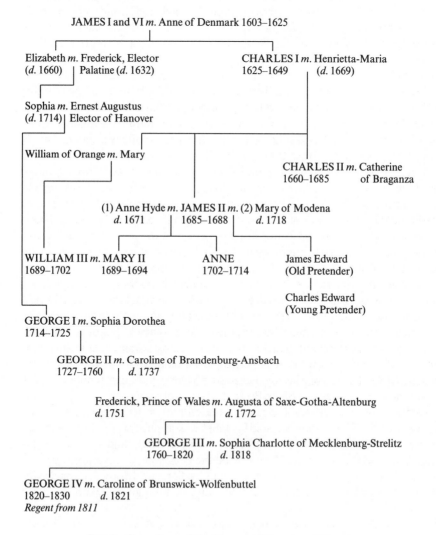

FIG. 2. Genealogy of the Houses of Stuart and Hanover

king's first-born but illegitimate son, James duke of Monmouth (widely touted as 'the Protestant Duke'), and Mary, York's elder daughter by his first wife, who had been brought up a Protestant and was married to William of Orange, the Protestant Stadtholder (or military commander) of the Netherlands.

Unfortunately, Monmouth's succession would fly in the face of the ancient common-law rule that bastards had no rights of inheritance. It could also be assumed that as a married woman Mary would be entirely subservient to her husband, a grandson of Charles I, who was not only a foreigner but allegedly no less domineering than his father-in-law. Divisions between the rival supporters of each candidate were naturally exploited by the Tories, while the objections to both led some prominent earlier opponents of the Court, like George Savile, marquis of Halifax, to reject the exclusionist case altogether, in favour of attempting to limit James's powers before he came to the throne.

If Charles had lost his nerve, these problems would not necessarily have proved fatal to the Whig cause. But besides his considerable political skills, and the charisma which still clung to the person of even this anointed monarch, the King also held a vital tactical trump card, in his power of calling and dissolving parliaments. True, that card retained decisive value only so long as the Whigs chose to play within the constitutional arena, rather than defying the Crown and appealing directly to the people. Yet for all their success in mounting large-scale popular demonstrations, especially in London, where the Green Ribbon Club, the most prominent of numerous oppositionist extra-parliamentary associations, staged huge 'pope-burning' processions on 17 November, Queen Elizabeth I's accession day, and helped co-ordinate election campaigns, petitions, and printed propaganda in favour of exclusion, the Whig leadership held back from that fateful confrontation. The Tory slogan ''41 is come again' implied that the Whigs were intent on exploiting popular insurgency just as their roundhead predecessors had done; but the differences between 1641 and 1681 far outweighed any apparent similarities.

Three may be mentioned. First, although religious bigotry lay at the heart of the crisis, the potency of politico-religious fervour had much diminished.[16] In particular, there is little sign of the radical puritan preachers whose apocalyptic sermons had fuelled demands for further reformation in Church and State in 1640–1. Political propaganda of a more secular cast was now disseminated mainly by printed broadsides, pamphlets, or tracts, media whose impact was both less urgent and more readily contradicted by published statements of an opposing viewpoint. Secondly, whereas Charles I's Long Parliament was secure from dissolution without its own consent, Charles II could avoid ministerial impeachments and other embarrassments by proroguing or dissolving parliamentary sessions. In March 1681 he summoned the last of his Parliaments to Oxford, royalist headquarters during the civil war, its university still a

---

[16] The distinction is well illustrated by the claim of the notorious Whig rake Lord Lovelace, that 'he was for a Protestant Duke and no Papist and God damn him he was for the Protestant religion': Haley, *Shaftesbury*, 592.

bastion of Church and King Toryism. Assured of yet another sizeable French subsidy, Charles chose to dissolve that body after a week's debates had demonstrated that the Whigs were unwilling to compromise on exclusion. The opposition responded not with a bang but barely a whimper, despite a rumoured 'design to have seized the King and restrained him 'til he had granted their petitions'.[17] Even those MPs and peers who had defied a proclamation by coming armed to Oxford left peaceably, under the surveillance of 600 royal life guards. The third difference, then, is that both Charles and his opponents had learned the lessons of the recent history to which the propaganda of both sides continually appealed. The Whigs, no less fearful than the Tories of sliding into civil war, did not allow themselves to be pushed over the precipice by crowd violence, while the government never lost control of events for want of the military resources to check an armed uprising.

Moreover, by 1681 the tide of public opinion—insofar as historians can trace such an evanescent phenomenon—seems to have turned in the Crown's favour. Scepticism about the plot and the motives of its promoters was now widespread. Tory demonstrations (where effigies of 'Jack Presbyter', rather than the pope, were burnt), newsletters, pamphlets, and petitions represented the King as true guardian of the protestant Church of England, the rule of law and the subject's liberties, against self-interested fanatics intriguing to re-establish 'their old beloved Commonwealth principles'.[18] Shaftesbury, plainly the most able and dangerous of these Machiavellian figures, was indicted for high treason. Acquitted by a sympathetic London grand jury (packed by the City's Whig sheriffs for the purpose), the man whom Dryden immortalized as 'the false Achitophel ... Sagacious, bold and turbulent of wit' prudently chose to spend the last years of his life in exile. Other aristocratic exclusionists were less careful, or fortunate. In 1683 Arthur Capel, earl of Essex (1631–83), William, Lord Russell (1639–83), and the important republican theorist Algernon Sidney (1622–83), each of whom may well have progressed from merely talking to actually planning rebellion with like-minded London radicals, were indicted for conspiring to assassinate Charles and his brother on their way home from the Newmarket races (the 'Rye House plot'). Essex purportedly committed suicide in the Tower; Russell and Sidney were convicted and executed, the latter on the dubious basis of arguments found among his papers which justified the subject's right to resist a tyrant.

These chilling acts, along with other political show trials, formed part of a general crackdown on political and religious dissent. Penal laws against Protestant Dissenters were strictly enforced, Whigs purged from commissions of the peace, and borough corporation charters recalled by legal writs of Quo

17 *Memoirs of Reresby*, 222.
18 *His Majesties Declaration To all His Loving Subjects, Touching the Causes & Reasons That moved Him to Dissolve the Two last Parliaments* (1681); M. Knights, *Politics and Opinion in Crisis, 1678–1681* (1994), Pt. II.

Warranto, to ensure that key local government offices in cities and towns with parliamentary representation were held by Anglican loyalists. Meanwhile a boom in foreign trade, and hence the customs' revenues, supplemented by French subsidy, enabled Charles to dispense altogether with Parliament for the last years of his reign, and to maintain sizeable standing armies in both England and Ireland.

James II, 1685–1688: A Threat to Church and State?

So when James Stuart, duke of York, finally succeeded to the English throne on 6 February 1685, his inheritance appeared a good deal more secure and substantial than the kingdom regained by his elder brother a quarter-century before. After four years of Tory reaction, the demoralized radicals, republicans, and Whigs were powerless to resist. Despite—or because of—the military precautions made possible by Charles's prolonged final illness, the popish monarch was proclaimed without 'disorder or tumult', if also without 'any shouts of joy'.[19] Many doubtless derived a measure of assurance from James's widely publicized declaration 'that he would defend the government of England both in Church and State as by law established'.[20] For those who did not, a desperate alternative was offered by Monmouth, whose ill-fated attempt that summer to raise the West Country 'for defence and vindication of the Protestant religion' succumbed to crushing defeat in the last pitched battle fought on English soil, at Sedgemoor outside Taunton, the Somerset clothing town long notorious as a stronghold of Dissent.[21]

This final blast on the trumpet of the Good Old Cause, like its equally disastrous Scottish counterpart led by Archibald Campbell, earl of Argyll (*c.*1638–85), showed that, however little they might care for James's religion, the landed gentry and aristocracy had no stomach for the personal and political risks inherent in rallying to such self-proclaimed champions of Protestantism. The prolonged 'bloody assizes' which followed Monmouth's capture and summary execution were presided over with vindictive enthusiasm by Lord Chief Justice George Jeffreys (1648–89), fully supported from afar by his sovereign. Over a thousand rebels—overwhelmingly common people, small farmers, urban artisans, and craftsmen, but also including Alice Lisle, the 70-year-old widow of a civil war regicide—were convicted. Of these some 250 were actually executed by public hanging, drawing, and quartering, and a further 800 transported to the West Indies. The judicial carnage and its appalling aftermath, of decomposing human remains stuck up on poles for public view, left Somerset 'like a shambles', and even James's most committed supporters somewhat ill at ease.[22]

[19] *Bishop Burnet's History of His Own Time* (1724), i. 620.
[20] Reresby, *Memoirs*, 353.
[21] *EHD, 1660–1714*, 119; R. Clifton, *The Last Popular Rebellion: the Western Rising of 1685* (1984).   [22] Clifton, *Last Popular Rebellion*, ch. 8.

The reaction to these events helps explain why the brief second session of James's Parliament in November 1685 was markedly less tractable than the first (May–July). Although still dominated by Tory—or at any rate, non-Whig—loyalists, thanks to the Court's determined electioneering, the House of Commons now proved unwilling to vote the large sums requested by James to maintain the army at around 16,000 troops, twice the size of the force he had inherited from his brother. Part of their reluctance derived from the King's speech opening the session, which made it clear that James intended to continue commissioning Catholics as army officers, contrary to the explicit provision of the Test Act. Having already been voted the same revenues for life his brother had enjoyed, mounting frustration at what he quite correctly took to be the questioning of his good faith and intentions by members of both Houses prompted James to prorogue Parliament after less than two weeks. It would not meet again while he held the throne.

In expressing his personal disbelief in the existence of a popish plot, Charles II had reportedly observed with perceptive tactlessness that 'No one would kill me, Jamie, to make you king'. Lacking his brother's charm and political astuteness, this ageing, bluff, military man, 'sincere, humourless and rather stupid', was committed to an agenda which went far beyond mere hedonism and personal survival.[23] James believed that he had been designated by God to restore his church in England. He may also have thought that, if Roman Catholics were to gain freedom of worship and the right to hold public office, the people as a whole, or at least those of any political significance, could not but come to recognize the error of their schismatical Protestant ways. Mass national conversion to Rome, following his own example, would then be a mere formality.

Yet some formidable legal and political obstacles stood between James and this desired end. Individual Catholics could only be appointed as privy councillors, lords-lieutenant, magistrates, army officers, heads of university colleges, and so forth if they had received a royal dispensation from compliance with the Test Act, which was specifically designed to keep all but Anglicans out of such positions. After half of the twelve common-law judges were sacked and replaced by more compliant colleagues (judicial security of tenure had not survived the first decade of the Restoration), the court of King's Bench in the collusive lawsuit *Godden* v. *Hales* (1686) upheld the Crown's prerogative right to dispense with penal laws in particular cases. However, wholesale suspension of the offending legislation was a more attractive administrative and ideological proposition, especially since the principle could easily be extended to all penal laws in matters of religion, whether directed against Protestant or Catholic non-conformists. True, the House of Commons had resolved in 1672 that such use of the suspending power was illegal. But Parliament was not sitting when

---

[23] M. Ashley in H. E. Bell and R. L. Ollard (eds.), *Historical Essays 1600–1750 presented to David Ogg* (1963), 202.

James promulgated his first Declaration of Indulgence in April 1687. By its means the King sought to redraw the map of English politics, with the aim of establishing a strategic alliance between Catholics, Protestant Dissenters, and the Crown, against the dominant Tory-Anglicans. This political realignment would in turn make possible the election of a new Parliament, with a majority of MPs prepared to repeal the Test and other penal laws, thereby establishing genuine religious toleration in England.

James's strategy, developed in conjunction with Father Edward Petre (1631–99), his Jesuit confessor, and the flexible Robert Spencer, earl of Sunderland (1640–1702), formerly a Whig exclusionist and shortly to declare himself a convert to Catholicism, assumed that, however much the Tory gentry might resent any erosion of the existing position of the Church of England and its adherents, they would never be prepared to compromise their fundamental constitutional principles by active resistance to God's anointed monarch. This assessment may well have been correct. But James was clearly taken aback at the stubborn opposition of the Anglican clergy, under the leadership of the veteran archbishop of Canterbury, William Sancroft (1617–93) and the bishop of London, Henry Compton (1632–1713), who in April 1688 were indicted for seditious libel, together with five episcopal colleagues. The bishops' offence had been to petition the King not to insist upon ministers of the Church of England reading a reissued Declaration of Indulgence from their parish pulpits, on the grounds that no man should be forced against his conscience to proclaim such a legally dubious document in the House of God.

This clerical reaction was fuelled by a potent mixture of high principle and material self-interest. James had publicly promised on numerous occasions to maintain the Church of England. But what exactly did he mean, and how much—if anything—were his promises worth? Even if his objective was nothing more than a level playing-field in matters religious, clergy of the Established Church who faced the prospect of direct competition from Dissenting ministers and popish priests might well fear erosion of their existing incomes, power, and community standing. On the most generous interpretation of his motives, when James thus challenged the dominance of the Anglican church, he was also threatening the worldly prospects of every Anglican clergyman. By the same token, Tory landholders who had been displaced as JPs by upstart Dissenters and obscure papists, army officers cashiered from their (purchased) regimental commissions for expressing doubts about the desirability of religious toleration, and university dons ejected from their valuable fellowships when they refused to appoint Catholics to head Oxford and Cambridge colleges—all had ample personal grounds, as well as principled cause, for fear and resentment.

Such animus inevitably affected attitudes towards James's general catholicizing drive, a campaign which became markedly more ambitious and tactless as his brief reign progressed. For instance, from the arrival in November 1685 of Count d'Adda, the Pope's personal envoy, James insisted that he should be treated as an official representative of the Vatican. Eighteen months later, when Rome promoted the Count to an archbishopric with special responsibility for heretical countries, the courtier duke of Somerset refused to participate in a state reception for him, on the grounds that any commerce with the Holy See was treasonable. James reportedly responded that as King he was above the law, and dismissed Somerset from his service with 'high displeasure'.[24] Incidents like this aroused comment and concern well beyond the narrow confines of the Court. Meanwhile many gentlemen had the uncomfortable experience of being 'closeted' by the King or his agents, seeking their agreement to support repeal of the penal laws if they were elected to Parliament. One such was Roger North (1653–1734), a leading Tory lawyer and office-holder, who after politely but steadfastly resisting the combined pressure of both James and Chief Justice Jeffreys, hastened home to write down a verbatim account of what he termed 'the most important act of my whole life'.[25]

What made all such episodes particularly ominous was the general international background against which James's policies tended to be interpreted, following a major Counter-Reformation initiative of his French cousin. In October 1685 Louis XIV had unilaterally revoked the Edict of Nantes, a treaty made at the end of the sixteenth-century Wars of Religion, under which French Protestants enjoyed some limited religious freedom. Over the next few years around 50,000 Huguenots, mostly skilled artisans and merchants, escaped well-publicized brutalities including enforced mass-conversion to Catholicism, by fleeing as refugees to the Netherlands and England. Their presence (especially in London and the south-east) reinforced the conviction that Roman Catholicism, absolute monarchy, and religious persecution were synonymous.[26] And while James publicly expressed his support for collections to relieve the Huguenots' sufferings, he did not condemn the Revocation itself.

William of Orange and the Protestant Wind

James's promotion of papists and popery caused dismay and disquiet among those same Anglican Tories who had most adamantly opposed his exclusion from the line of succession to the throne before 1685. What alone made the political situation bearable for these Church-and-King loyalists was the knowledge that James could not live for ever, and the confident expectation that after his death the throne would pass to his daughter Mary. Her marriage to Charles I's grandson William, ruler of the independent principality of Orange, had been one of Charles II's few genuinely popular foreign policy initiatives. The Stuarts were not famed for longevity, and James had already reached his fifty-

[24] *Burnet's History of His Own Time*, 716–17.
[25] F. M. J. Korsten, *Roger North (1651–1734): Virtuoso and Essayist* (1988), 223–6.
[26] J. F. Bosher, 'The Franco-Catholic danger, 1660–1715', *History*, 79 (1994), 21.

second year when he became king. Morever, since their marriage in 1673 he and his young Italian wife Mary of Modena had failed to produce a living heir, their five children having all died very young. So committed adherents of the Church of England had some reason to hope that James's objectionable catholicizing policies were only a passing phase. For their part, most Dissenters accepted Halifax's warning that the offer of religious toleration was no more than a cynical short-term political stratagem on the part of James and his co-religionists: 'You are therefore to be hugged now, only that you may be the better squeezed at another time.'[27]

The news of Queen Mary's pregnancy in late 1687 evoked responses which divided along predictable denominational lines. Whereas the Catholic dramatist Aphra Behn wrote 'A Congratulatory Poem to Her Most Sacred Majesty', James's two Protestant daughters, the Princesses Mary and Anne, expressed downright disbelief.[28] Their underlying fear was that if, as Catholics were already confidently predicting, the baby proved to be male, his sex would automatically give him precedence in the line of succession over his elder half-sisters. Moreover, a Prince of Wales would certainly be brought up a papist, thereby guaranteeing the continuation of the pro-Catholic measures inaugurated by his father. When Mary of Modena did produce a fine son on 10 June 1688, the Court and his parents' co-religionists throughout Europe joyfully celebrated Prince James Edward Stuart's safe, albeit slightly premature, arrival. Dryden, now converted to Catholicism, hailed the event as 'Britain's Revival', while to the head of an Irish religious order in France 'this dear darling of Heaven' was indeed 'the Messiah of Great Britain, whose cradle is the tomb of heresy and schism'.[29] However, street ballads and gossip countered that it was all too good to be true, drawing attention to a supposed lack of credible (i.e. non-Catholic) witnesses among the sixty or so persons who attended the birth, and claiming that the purported infant prince was actually an impostor, smuggled into the queen's bed-chamber in a warming-pan. Even the sober Tory gentleman John Evelyn described the birth as 'very surprising', since the queen's confinement had not been expected until the following month.[30]

The tension which generated these accusations and suspicions was further tightened at the end of the month by the dramatic trial of the seven bishops (above, p. 51) in the court of King's Bench. The bishops had already aroused unprecedented demonstrations of popular support on their journey to the Tower. But the 'Not Guilty' verdict, after the jury had been out all night, touched off an extraordinary outburst of national rejoicing, with bonfires, bells, 'huzzas and shouts for their lordships' delivery so great', according to one

---

[27] 'A Letter to a Dissenter' (1687) in Halifax, *Works*, ed. Kenyon, 106.

[28] S. H. Mendelson, *The Mental World of Stuart Women* (1987), 179.

[29] D. Ogg, *England in the Reigns of James II and William III* (1955), 201.

[30] R. J. Weil, 'The politics of legitimacy: women and the Warming-Pan Scandal', in L. G. Schwoerer (ed.), *The Revolution of 1688–1689: Changing perspectives* (1992), 65–82.

observer 'that it looked like a little rebellion in noise, though not in fact'.[31] Next day a bipartisan group of seven aristocrats, including Bishop Compton and the former Tory minister Danby, as well as the leading Whigs Edward Russell (1653–1727) and Henry Sidney (1641–1704), whose brother Algernon had been executed as a traitor in 1683, signed a letter urging William of Orange to come to England in order to defend the people's 'religion, liberties and properties'. They claimed that the level of dissatisfaction 'with the present conduct of the government' was so high that 'nineteen parts of twenty of the people throughout the kingdom ... are desirous of a change ... and would willingly contribute to it'.[32] These last assertions were plainly exaggerated—how could they know?—but as it turned out William had no intention of relying upon them.

In fact, it seems certain that William had resolved to lead an army of invasion against his Catholic father-in-law several months before the birth of the boy child who would, if not prevented, eventually become King James III—in other words, well before his envoys procured the famous invitation of the 'immortal seven'.[33] William had long been following events in England, with particular concern for his own and his wife's claim to the throne, as well as the role which English military and naval forces might play in either resisting or assisting what he regarded as Louis XIV's long-term plans for European supremacy. His decision to intervene was motivated by a mixture of fear and opportunity. The fear was that James would provoke civil war, in which the popular and republican forces might triumph; alternatively, if James and his purported son succeeded in establishing a Catholic monarchy, England could join with Louis XIV's France to destroy the remaining Reformed churches in Europe. Either outcome would obviously be fatal to his own and Mary's dynastic interests. The opportunity arose from the complexities of European power politics, which now engaged sufficient French troops in the Rhineland to prevent Louis blocking an invasion of England. The simultaneous escalation of a French tariff war against the Dutch helped persuade the seven usually disunited provinces of the Netherlands that backing William's plan to bring England into a European coalition against France provided their best chance for commercial and national survival.

Organization of the invasion proceeded through the spring and summer of 1688 as secretly as possible, aided by Holland's massive financial resources and the reluctance of both James and Louis to believe that William could be seriously contemplating an armed expedition against his father-in-law. In September, when it became obvious that this was indeed his intention, James initiated a wholesale restoration of Tory gentry purged from the commissions of the peace, and the town charters which had been forfeited during his drive to build a compliant parliamentary majority. He also dissolved the almost

[31] *Memoirs of Reresby*, 501.   [32] *EHD, 1660–1714*, 120–2.
[33] S. Baxter, *William III* (1966), ch. 17.

certainly illegal Ecclesiastical Commission (established in 1686) with which he had attempted to discipline recalcitrant Anglican clergy, reinstated the fellows of Magdalen College, Oxford, who had been dismissed for refusing his papist nominees, and sacked Sunderland, chief author of the attempted Dissenter–papist electoral coalition. But this desperate last-minute reversal was plainly too little, too late, to re-establish his credibility with the Tory–Anglican establishment. It did nothing to deter the various English conspirators now planning a series of provincial risings to coincide with the Prince's landing. Nor did it influence the army officers meeting in their self-styled 'Treason Club' at the Rose Tavern in Covent Garden, who had close links with Lieutenant-General John Churchill (1650–1722), the Tory soldier-courtier whose wife Sarah was Princess Anne's trusted confidante.

Delayed by autumn storms, William finally sailed at the end of October, with some 500 ships carrying around 21,000 troops, among them numerous English and Scots volunteers, plus four Anglo-Dutch brigades in the service of the Netherlands.[34] Bad weather, which first drove his ships back into harbour, changed to an easterly 'Protestant Wind', before which William's armada ran down the Channel, while the English fleet was still laboriously tacking out of the Thames estuary. By the time they emerged, William had begun disembarking his troops at Torbay in Devon on the evening of 5 November, Guy Fawkes Day, that potent anniversary of another great Providential deliverance at the beginning of this tumultuous century.

[34] J. I. Israel and G. Parker, 'Of Providence and Protestant Winds', in Israel (ed.), *The Anglo-Dutch Moment* (1991), show that the hitherto-accepted figure of 14,000 soldiers is too low.

PART II

Post-Revolutionary England
1689–1715

3

GLORIOUS REVOLUTION?

Revolutionary Practice and Principles

One reason why the events following hard upon William of Orange's landing came to be known as the *Glorious* Revolution was that—in England at least—they involved almost no armed conflict or loss of life.[1] This remarkable contrast to Monmouth's recent invasion, let alone the mid-century civil wars, resulted largely from James II's failure to make a determined military stand against the numerically inferior forces commanded by his nephew and son-in-law.

Physically debilitated, stricken by recurrent nosebleeds (here indeed the Revolution was far from bloodless), apprehensive for the safety of his family as well as himself, perhaps also fearful that William's safe arrival signified a loss of heavenly favour, James vacillated. His decision to turn back towards London from Salisbury on 23 November without giving fight merely hastened his already demoralized army's disintegration. Lieutenant-General Churchill, the King's former military protégé and commander at Sedgemoor, now headed a stream of officers and men defecting to William's camp. As the Prince moved slowly onward from Exeter, with declarations of support coming in from all over the country, James's military and political position collapsed. Having dispatched his wife and son to France, the King attempted to follow them incognito on 11 December. Some observant Kentish fishermen penetrated his disguise, and he was returned to London. But after the occupation of Whitehall Palace by detachments of Dutch guards, James was finally permitted and indeed encouraged to leave the country for the last time just before Christmas.

Gatherings of peers, and of surviving MPs from the parliaments of Charles II, reinforced by City aldermen and councillors, thereupon invited William to act as interim administrator of the realm, pending a new constitutional settlement. He agreed. In late January 1689 a 'Convention' Parliament (so-called after the precedent set in March 1660, the last time no king had been available to issue election writs) assembled at Westminster. After little more than a

---

[1] Gilbert Burnet (1643–1715), the clerical Whig exile who accompanied William's invading army, mentions two skirmishes, one in Dorset where 'some were killed of both sides', and another at Reading, where 'one of the Princes' officers was shot. He was a papist, and he was the only officer that was killed in the whole expedition' (*Bishop Burnet's History of His Own Time* (1724), i. 798). No bigot, Burnet would hardly have intended the implication that the death of a Catholic was immaterial; his social bias is more typical of his age and class.

week's intense debate and negotiation, it was agreed to offer the Crown jointly to William and Mary, but with full executive authority vested in William for life. They were proclaimed King and Queen of England on 13 February in the Banqueting House at Whitehall, after the presentation of a 'Declaration of Rights' which enumerated James's misdeeds and Parliament's 'ancient rights and liberties'.[2]

As this sketch indicates, there was no cataclysmic institutional or social upheaval. Nor did current usage of the word 'revolution' necessarily imply anything more than return to a previous state, such as the annual cycle of the seasons. But the impact of 1688–9 on contemporary and later ideas about government and politics is one main reason why these events amounted to a great deal more than a mere dynastic reshuffle.

As noted in Chapter 1 above (pp. 19–20), the traumatic events of the 1640s and 1650s aroused considerable interest in the origins, nature, and limits of political authority. Traditional accounts had depicted the realm as a divinely constructed organism, of which the monarch was head and the people limbs, or envisaged an immemorial ancient constitution allocating complementary rights and duties to ruler and subjects. But in 1651 Thomas Hobbes published his *Leviathan*, a path-breaking analysis of 'the matter, form and power of a commonwealth'. Hobbes postulated an all-powerful government rightfully commanding the subjects' obedience, thanks to their prior agreement that even such an authoritarian regime was preferable to an anarchic 'state of nature', where life must be, in Hobbes's memorable phrase, 'nasty, brutish, and short'. Because the Hobbesian state, or 'civil society', drew its legitimacy from rational human decision rather than historical precedent or Providential design, it might easily appear to validate any government which managed to seize and exercise *de facto* power. The author and his views were accordingly anathematized by Anglican clerics and royalists, the former particularly disliking Hobbes's refusal to derive the authority of kings directly from God, thus treating political theory as a science of society, not a branch of theology.

Sir Robert Filmer (d. 1653), the leading theoretical exponent of hereditary divine-right monarchy was, none the less, a layman. Filmer's posthumously published *Patriarcha, or the Natural Power of Kings Asserted* (1680) claimed that the absolute earthly dominance which God had bestowed on Adam in the Garden of Eden descended to all subsequent monarchs, who were literally Adam's successors, fathers of their people. Hence they must be obeyed without resistance, as the Fifth Commandment obliged children to obey their parents. Although written before the civil wars, Filmer's *Patriarcha* only appeared in print at the height of the Exclusion Crisis, being immediately taken up by supporters of the embattled monarchy. But it also attracted rebuttals, notably from John Locke (1632–1704), a former Oxford academic turned physician and

---

[2] E. N. Williams (ed.), *The Eighteenth-Century Constitution* (1960), 26–30.

political operative, who served as Shaftesbury's aide throughout the 1670s, subsequently following him into exile. Locke remained in Holland (defying the government's attempts to extradite him for suspected treasonable conspiracy) until after the Revolution, when he returned to England and a distinguished career as philosopher and public intellectual.

Locke agreed with Hobbes in seeing government as essentially a human arte- fact. But quite unlike Hobbes, or Filmer, Locke wished to impose clear limits on the powers of human rulers, and to leave open the possibility that the gov- erned might legitimately resist or even withdraw their allegiance from a despot. Hence he depicted all government as dependent upon the prior agreement of free, equal, and independent individuals 'to join and unite in a community', and be bound by constitutional arrangements acceptable to the majority. Whatever form these might take, whether monarchical or republican, the people only had a duty of obedience so long as the regime continued to provide the basic conditions of 'comfortable, safe, and peaceful living', for the 'preserva- tion of their lives, liberties and estates'. If a king, for example, 'sets up his own arbitrary will in place of the laws' enacted by representatives of the people in their 'legislative' (or parliament), the government was effectively dissolved, and the whole community free to choose themselves a new ruler.[3]

Although mostly written in the aftermath of the Exclusion Crisis to refute Filmer's *Patriarcha*, Locke's *Two Treatises of Government* had obvious relev- ance to the current political situation when it first appeared in print in 1689. Tories particularly disliked the notion that James II's departure had created a vacancy in government or on the throne. For adherents of strict hereditary divine-right monarchy, such an interregnum was literally impossible—'the king is dead, long live the king'. The constitutional fiction of James's voluntary 'abdication' sought to accommodate these scruples. Yet recent events plainly did involve a body with some claim to be considered the 'legislative' con- sciously rejecting one ruler and determining his replacement. True, Locke's em- phasis upon the equality, liberty, and innate natural rights of all men (and indeed women, if only by implication) was too reminiscent of the dangerous doctrines of Levellers and other civil-war radicals for most contemporary politicians to stomach. Nor did Lockian theories of government provide the main polemical justification for the Revolution in its immediate aftermath: arguments derived from history, law, and pragmatic or Providential necessity seemed more prudent to most defenders of the new regime.[4] Yet the coherence and force of his conception of government, and the closeness with which it fitted what the events of 1688–9 were increasingly seen to represent, helps ex- plain why Locke has long been regarded as *the* philosopher of the Revolution, and how his ideas on the original contract and the sovereignty of the people came to inspire new generations of radicals in the following century.

---

[3] The standard edition of Locke's *Two Treatises of Civil Government* is by P. Laslett (1960).

[4] J. P. Kenyon, *Revolution Principles* (1977), chs. 1–4.

Crown and Parliament

Locke might have made a more direct impact on political discourse in the 1690s if those who solicited William's intervention, or declared for him after his landing, had not consistently sought to play down the extent and significance of their technically treasonous actions. Deeply concerned to avoid another civil war, these persons of rank, property, and influence were anything but wild-eyed revolutionaries. Many whose fathers had fought for the royalist cause in the 1640s were now deeply embarrassed to discover that attachment to the Protestant Church of England outweighed their loyalty to God's anointed monarch. Even the Whigs, who by and large rejoiced at James's departure and greeted William as a deliverer, had no intention of allowing plebeian anti-Catholic rioters to seize control—let alone radical republicans like the veteran Commonwealth politician Edmund Ludlow (1617?–92), who now emerged from exile in Switzerland to make a brief but ominous appearance in London. These common aims of restricting popular participation, stressing continuity rather than change, and moving as quickly as possible to restore something like political normalcy, inevitably gave the events of 1688–9 a conservative and minimalist character.

This becomes particularly apparent when we consider how relations between Crown and Parliament were affected. Historians disagree as to whether the framers of the Declaration presented to William and Mary and incorporated in the Bill of Rights (as the 1689 statute by which the Declaration was formally enacted is known), consciously sought to impose significant limitations on the Crown. Some who did were undoubtedly dissuaded or outmanœuvred by more cautious colleagues. Yet, whatever the overall balance of intentions, the fact remains that while both documents make great play of condemning previous royal actions as illegal, they incorporate few novel or extensive restrictions on the royal prerogative, and no mechanisms for enforcing those which were introduced.

Many provisions of the Bill of Rights were vague constitutional clichés, or statements of good intent, as for example that 'Parliaments ought to be held frequently', that elections 'ought to be free', and that taxes should only be levied with express parliamentary consent. But others settled long-standing disputes between Crown and Parliament in the latter's favour. Thus both the purported royal prerogative of suspending laws, and the 'pretended power' of dispensing with laws 'as it hath been assumed and executed of late' were declared illegal, although the implied qualification presumably still left William free to dispense individuals from the penalties attached to non-compliance with laws in some cases. Perhaps the most serious limitation imposed by the Bill of Rights was to ban the raising or maintenance of an army in time of peace without parliamentary consent. But even this provision, which reversed statutes of 1660 and 1661 giving Charles II unfettered control of the armed forces, was found to have little practical value when attempts were made to invoke it during the late 1690s, due in part to the difficulty of distinguishing a standing army (illegal) from a bevy of military garrisons (legitimate). And the Bill of Rights wholly ignored the Crown's far-reaching executive powers to select ministers, to summon, prorogue, and dissolve parliaments at will, and to conduct foreign policy without reference to Parliament, although the use and abuse of these prerogatives had caused huge controversies during the previous two reigns.[5]

Ad hoc, unsystematic, vague, and lacking any general statement of philosophy or principle, the Bill of Rights is hardly an impressive revolutionary manifesto, especially by comparison with later documents like the American Declaration of Independence (1776), or the French Declaration of the Rights of Man (1789). While William and Mary were presented with the Declaration of Rights (from which the Bill derives) before being formally offered the Crown, that public offer was not conditional, and William made no reference to the Declaration in his brief speech of acceptance. Nor did the Bill itself enjoy the reserved status of a constitution or fundamental law; notwithstanding the bold assertion that it 'shall stand, remain and be the law of this realm for ever', there was and is no legal provision to prevent its amendment or repeal by any future Parliament.

A few more constraints on the powers of the Crown were enacted after 1689. The Triennial Act (1694) converted a vague provision of the Bill of Rights into the precise requirement that no more than three years should pass without a Parliament, and that no Parliament should remain in existence for more than three years. (The aim, hardly fulfilled, was to reduce the effects of ministerial and Crown patronage on the independence of MPs.) Fears that the courts might again be used to silence political enemies prompted the Trial of Treason Act (1696), which provided procedural safeguards, including legal representation and a copy of the charge, for persons accused of treason, who henceforth could only be convicted on the independent testimony of two witnesses. In 1701, the last year of William's reign, 'An act for the further limitation of the Crown and better securing the rights and liberties of the subjects', generally known as the Act of Settlement, spelled out the line of succession beyond James's daughter Anne. It also specified that any future monarch must be or become a member of the Church of England, and might neither leave the realm nor engage it in foreign wars without parliamentary approval. Further provisions required that all business properly the province of the privy council be transacted there, that foreign nationals neither be made privy councillors nor hold offices under the Crown, and that no such 'placemen' could sit in the Commons. A further clause specifying that judges should henceforth hold their places during good behaviour (rather than at the royal pleasure) and be removable only by address of both Houses of Parliament formally enacted what had actually been William's practice since 1689, and a long-standing Whig demand

5 Williams, *Eighteenth-Century Constitution*, 23–33.

before that. These measures are sometimes regarded as the capstone or final act of the Glorious Revolution. However, such an extension of its chronological boundaries inevitably diminishes the distinctive character of the events within them, especially since (as we shall see) the legislation of 1694 and 1701 was largely a response to William's actions, not those of James.

Nevertheless, when all is said and done, 1688–9 did mark a real watershed in Crown–Parliament relations. The annual sessions of Parliament which began in the first year of the new reign, and have continued to this day, were the most obvious functional—and symbolic—change. In view of the long preceding period of personal royal rule (effectively from 1681, with only a brief interruption in 1685), it seems quite improbable that the shift from Parliament as occasional event to Parliament as permanent and regular organ of government would have occurred without William's intervention. Nevertheless, this innovation cannot be directly attributed to any specific constitutional measure, but at least initially reflected William's ongoing need for parliamentary votes of taxation in order to keep English forces at war with France.

More broadly, except in the increasingly unlikely event of a successful counter-revolution, 1688–9 had definitively foreclosed the possibility of establishing some form of absolutist monarchy in England. Shutting off this potential line of development, which had been a far from remote option in the 1680s, and hence decisively confirming Parliament's legislative sovereignty, effected a real shift in the constitutional balance of power, for all the official rhetoric emphasizing continuity and restoration of the status quo. True, the Crown retained very substantial authority and influence, even if the divine-right principles of non-resistance and passive obedience still invoked by Church of England preachers well into the following century upheld the supreme power of monarch-in-parliament, not God's Anointed alone. Sorting out new working arrangements between Crown and Parliament after 1688 was also, as we shall see, a difficult and lengthy business; nor did William (or Mary) show any desire to abandon the monarchy's remaining prerogatives.

It may be a historian's typical error to place most weight on a close reading of the documentary traces of the 'Revolution Settlement' (an abstraction in itself), while overlooking the psychological impact of the events which generated those documents. Yet perhaps the clearest indication that a real change had occurred appears when we compare the terms of the coronation oath laid down by Parliament in 1689 with the form of words used by James II in 1685. He was then asked to 'grant and keep and by your oath confirm to the people of England the laws and customs granted to them by the kings of England'. But William and Mary had to swear that they would 'govern the people of this kingdom ... *according to the statutes in Parliament agreed on, and the laws and customs of the same*'.[6] The Declaration and Bill of Rights did represent a hasty

6 Ibid. 37–9.

compromise, vague in places and timid in others; but the very circumstances of their compilation made it unlikely that future relations between Crown and Parliament would ever be the same again.

Law, Liberty, and Toleration: How Much and for Whom?

Throughout the eighteenth century, especially after 1714, the 'late happy Revolution' was celebrated as the seedbed of those just rights and liberties which distinguished the fortunate English from French 'slaves', and all other less fortunate peoples.[7] Above all the Revolution supposedly established what we know today as the rule of law, together with a number of important personal freedoms. How far were these claims justified?

Although the concept of the 'rule of law' is relatively modern, a distinction between government constrained by law and arbitrary or despotic regimes was entirely familiar to the seventeenth century. By 'declaring the Rights and Liberties of the Subject' (to quote from its full official title) the Bill of Rights sought to ensure that all future governments were lawfully based. Henceforth no monarch would be able to bypass Parliament's legislative machinery or otherwise manipulate the law and the lawcourts. The most distinguished twentieth-century Whig historian regarded these provisions, together with the enactment of judicial tenure during good behaviour in 1701, as representing 'the triumph of the common law and lawyers over the king, who had tried to put prerogative above the law'.[8] Nevertheless, while judges were no longer removable by kings, they continued to be appointed, promoted, and superannuated on the basis of political acceptability as well as legal attainments.

Moreover the legal system as a whole remained complex, dilatory, ruinously expensive, and generally biased against the poor. Indeed it can be argued that only the well-to-do gained anything from the Revolution. In this view, the majority of the population, enjoying few of the 'liberties'—or, as we would say, privileges—associated with property ownership, such as the right to vote in parliamentary elections, were severely disadvantaged by the fact that from 1689 the landed and mercantile élites gained effective control of the political process, which they naturally used to further their own material ends. (Whether the Restoration monarchy possessed the means or desire to prevent landlords and merchants grinding the poor is another question.) On another tack, however, many of the subject's rights traditionally associated with the Revolution were actually of much greater antiquity (like trial by jury, and the prohibition of non-parliamentary taxation); in 1689 they were merely reasserted as ancient liberties endangered by recent royal encroachments. Others were primarily of

---

[7] Anon., *An Excursory View of the Present State of Men and Things* (1739), 15.

[8] G. M. Trevelyan, *The English Revolution, 1688–1689* (1938), 133; cf. D. F. Lemmings, 'The independence of the judiciary in eighteenth-century England', in P. Birks (ed.), *The Life of the Law* (1993).

institutional rather than individual significance (such as the principle of parliamentary freedom of speech), while others again developed only sometime after 1688–9 (like the much enhanced freedom of the press from government censorship or control, which followed Parliament's non-renewal of the Licensing Act in 1695).

A final reason for scepticism about the benefits conferred by the 'Glorious Revolution' arises from the anti-Catholic bigotry embodied in the concept of liberty endorsed by the parliamentary settlement of 1689. Following the customary identification of arbitrary power and popery as two sides of the same coin, James II was formally alleged to have 'endeavour[ed] to subvert and extirpate the Protestant religion and the laws and liberties of this kingdom'. So when what became known as the Toleration Act[9] permitted Dissenters who took oaths of loyalty to William and Mary to worship more or less freely (a reward for having largely resisted James's attempts to win their support), no such concession was extended to Roman Catholics—let alone Jews or Protestant Nonconformists who rejected the doctrine of the Trinity (Arians, Socinians, and Unitarians). Indeed the Bill of Rights went so far as to impose a religious test on the monarchy, asserting that 'it hath been found by experience that it is inconsistent with the safety and welfare of this Protestant kingdom to be governed by a popish prince'. All non-Anglicans continued to suffer under the various discriminatory measures which excluded them from government employment, entering the learned professions, or graduating from university; they were also required to pay local church taxes, even while contributing to the support of their own ministers and chapels or meeting houses.

Historians and the Revolution

There is no historiographical consensus about the meaning and significance of the events of 1688–9. Besides deploring its narrow class and sectarian bias, historians on the left are inclined to see this so-called Glorious Revolution as no more than a conservative postscript to the authentic English Revolution of the 1640s and 1650s. Conservatives, on the other hand, have (perhaps naïvely) praised James's commitment to religious toleration, questioned William's motives, and regretted the sufferings which the Revolution meant for those who remained loyal to James, all the while doubting whether 1688 wrought any truly fundamental changes to the essential English institutions of monarchy, aristocracy, Parliament, and established Church. These negative assessments are in part a reaction to the triumphalist Whig orthodoxy of the eighteenth century, and its subsequent repackaging in T. B. Macaulay's classic *History of England* (1848–53) and the work of his grand-nephew G. M. Trevelyan.

---

[9] Officially entitled 'An Act for exempting their Majesties protestant subjects, dissenting from the Church of England, from the penalties of certain laws': Williams, *Eighteenth-Century Constitution*, 42.

However, the flood of historical scholarship associated with its recent tercentenary has seen some more positive assessments of the Revolution, together with growing appreciation of its complex and diverse nature.

It now seems clear that, despite England's crucial role, the events of 1688–9 cannot be understood from an English perspective alone. Both the rationale and timing of William's intervention are only fully explicable within a European (or even global) context, just as the balance of power in Europe was profoundly affected by his successful harnessing of English military and economic resources for the struggle against Louis XIV. Events in England had a still more immediate impact on the neighbouring kingdoms of Scotland and Ireland. There James II had employed authoritarian Catholic ministers to implement his policies; the same domineering style of centrally directed rule was evident in the English settlements along the North American seaboard, where James continued his brother's agenda by suppressing colonial representative assemblies and attempting to merge the separate colonies into a Dominion of New England, under a Crown-appointed Governor-General with extensive fiscal and legislative powers.

James's flight to France gave the Scots Presbyterians their chance to seize the political initiative, declare that their erstwhile monarch had 'forfeited' his throne, and negotiate an uncompromising settlement with William, which finally excluded bishops from the kirk and significantly enhanced the Scottish Parliament's independence of royal control. In the summer of 1689 a coalition of conservative episcopalian Lowlanders, Catholics, and Highland clansmen staged what would be the first of many armed attempts to restore James and his successors; these Jacobites (from the Latin 'Jacobus' = James), unable to capitalize on their initial victory at the pass of Killiecrankie, were gradually dispersed over the next two years by a mixture of bribery and force, including an infamous Campbell massacre of the MacDonald clan at Glencoe in 1692. But these were mere skirmishes compared to the full-scale warfare which erupted in Ireland from December 1688, when the Catholic majority rose in support of James, their religion, and the hope of freedom from the Protestant English yoke (see below, Ch. 4.). While conflict between James II's opponents and supporters in Ireland and Scotland produced unparalleled bitterness and bloodshed, the Revolution was everywhere a divisive event. Pro- and anti-Williamite parties emerged even among the white settler populations of Barbados, Jamaica, and the Leeward Islands, as well as in the North American colonies, although, unlike the campaigns of the Irish and Scots Jacobites, their struggles had no impact on the eventual outcome in England.

If the 1688–9 Revolution was indeed an event in world and not just English history, its course and consequences, both immediate and longer-term, were by no means wholly willed or foreseen. Of course the objectives of many key participants were and remain uncertain. William's influential public declarations, before and during the invasion, that he had no ambition to seize the throne for himself, may or may not have been truthful; likewise the later avowals of Churchill and Danby that their sole purpose was to force James to hold elections for a free Parliament. Even when the aims of particular agents seem clear enough (for example, there is no doubt of William's desire to extend toleration to Roman Catholics as well as to Protestant Dissenters, and indeed to comprehend most of the latter within a more broadly based Church of England), they were frequently frustrated (in that case, by parliamentary resistance). Nor did the outcomes of 1688–9 remain static and unchanging. Most of the legal and political 'liberties' endorsed by the Bill of Rights were more likely to be of interest to the propertied elite than the lower orders; some indeed were explicitly limited by social rank, such as the right of 'subjects which are Protestants to have arms for their defence *suitable to their conditions*' (italics added).[10]

It may be granted that the Revolution was primarily the work of, and specifically benefited, a narrow and self-interested oligarchy. There is some evidence of popular support for William's mission, but then James received a very favourable reception from the London crowd on his forced return to the capital just before he finally got away to France. Yet the fact that later generations of lower-class radicals and reformers could successfully appeal to 'Revolution principles' and specific Bill of Rights provisions in the face of government attempts at their suppression must rank among its real, albeit unintended, consequences. Furthermore, whereas the Toleration Act was plainly not intended to ease the papists' lot, its effective abolition of the crime of recusancy (refusal to attend weekly Anglican church services) meant that, provided they behaved with discretion, Roman Catholics generally enjoyed the same *de facto* freedom of worship under William and his successors as did Protestant Dissenters.[11]

In conclusion, the political crisis precipitated by the Dutch invasion and James's flight was resolved in an inegalitarian, patriarchal, sectarian, and undemocratic fashion. Yet that is no good reason to regard the events of 1688–9 as positively inglorious, or less than revolutionary. It would be absurdly anachronistic to blame the late seventeenth century for failing to meet standards which are not universally accepted, let alone implemented, even today. Many who lived through those years certainly believed with Bishop Burnet that they had witnessed 'great and unusual transactions', 'an unexpected revolution'.[12] That this was the first revolution of modern times to be so described, and that its defining documents, the Declaration and Bill of Rights, have continued to provide a template for constitutions and political manifestos to the present day, suggests that they were not wholly mistaken.

[10] See J. L. Malcolm, *To Keep and Bear Arms: The Origins of an Anglo-American Right* (1994).

[11] J. Bossy, 'English Catholics after 1688', in O. P. Grell, J. I. Israel, and N. R. N. Tyacke (eds.), *From Persecution to Toleration* (1991), 369–87.

[12] Burnet, *History of His Own Time*, 618; G. Burnet, *Sermon before the Prince of Orange, Dec. 1688* (1689), quoted J. R. Hertzler, 'Who dubbed it "The Glorious Revolution"?', *Albion*, 19 (1987), 582.

4

THE RAGE OF PARTY

Political Assumptions, Ideologies, Structures

The circumstances of William and Mary's accession could only strengthen the contemporary belief 'that there have been more shakes and convulsions in the government of England than in that of any other nation'.[1] Nor was there much initial reason to think that this latest development would prove more successful than previous attempts to establish a stable constitutional and political order, in 1660, 1657, 1653, and 1641. Not until after—some would say long after—the defeat of James II's plans to regain his throne with French assistance, and then the death in 1714 of his daughter Anne, the last Stuart monarch, did the permanence and longer-term significance of 1688–9 become clear. Over the intervening quarter-century William and Mary, and Anne, together with the Revolution settlement which they embodied, faced the threat of Jacobite efforts to restore first James II and then his son ('James III', otherwise known as the Old Pretender). In the face of incessant factional and party conflict they also struggled to maintain the support of ministers, Parliament and public opinion for an expensive, protracted, and often highly unpopular war against Louis XIV's France.

Neither William nor Anne had any wish to be downgraded to constitutional figureheads, reigning without ruling. Nor were they. Yet the consequences of 1688–9, together with the demands of war finance, and certain personal characteristics of the two monarchs, tended to constrain their executive authority and correspondingly enhance Parliament's role in government. This last was symbolized in institutional terms by the advent of annual parliamentary sessions, coupled with the legislature's indispensable role in authorizing taxation, and the monitoring of expenditure by the Commons' Commissions of Accounts. Despite considerable frustration on both sides during William's reign, and determined efforts to extend restrictions on the royal prerogative in the late 1690s, the relationship of Crown and Parliament was generally one of mutual dependence, rather than serious confrontation. Given the lack of enthusiasm for a republic or a popish prince among the parliamentary classes and political nation at large, in the last resort there was little realistic alternative. Likewise the monarchs themselves fully recognized that their regal power and status ultimately rested on parliamentary approval, rather than birth or Divine decree.[2]

---

[1] W. Kennett, *A Compassionate Enquiry into the Causes of the Civil War* (1704), 17.

[2] G. Holmes, *British Politics in the Age of Anne* (rev. edn., 1987), 187.

Parliament's new prominence in the governance of the realm helps explain why bitter Whig–Tory conflict was the defining characteristic of politics between the Glorious Revolution and 1714. In conjunction with rivalry for the places and profits to which a seat in the Commons increasingly provided access, the parties continued to clash over Church–State relations, foreign policy, and the succession, much as they had done since the late 1670s. However, their differences now also involved sharply divergent interpretations of the meaning of 1688–9, often presented in a historical language which exploited and exacerbated ideological and personal divisions dating back to the 1640s. Thus the first printing of Clarendon's *History of the Rebellion* (1702–4) was envisaged by its Tory promoters as a contribution to the current struggle against Whigs and Dissenters. Likewise Tory election slogans in 1710 called for 'No Rump Parliament', and exhorted voters to 'Save the Queen's White Neck' (recalling the fate of Anne's grandfather some sixty years before).

Party strife was pervasive: 'all … the nation … is Whigs and Tory', wrote one observer in 1691.[3] While Parliament was the chief forum for displays of party loyalty, what Queen Anne's physician disparaged as 'Party-heat' also infected church and chapel, local government both urban and rural, the lawcourts, the militia, clubs, coffee-houses, newspapers and periodicals, theatres, business and financial institutions, and the professions.[4] After the (admittedly not very effective) 1662 Licensing Act which had authorized pre-publication censorship of the press was allowed to lapse in 1695, partisan political journalism and pamphleteering exploded. From 1702 the first English daily newspaper, the *Daily Courant*, supplemented existing newsheets and weekly journals which regularly brought political controversy and debate to a wide audience in London and the provinces. As many as 44,000 weekly copies of the nine newspapers published in the capital were being printed by 1704, with a total readership perhaps five times that size, at a time when London's population numbered under half a million. Occasional pamphlets, tracts, and broadsides dealing with particular political issues also achieved enormous circulations. When a fiercely anti-Whig sermon produced a controversial state trial in 1710, something like 100,000 printed copies of the sermon circulated, and nearly 600 individual pamphlets and other works were provoked by the trial itself.

The increased frequency of parliamentary elections, especially after the 1694 Triennial Act, further exacerbated party divisions. Over the twenty-six years between 1689 and 1715, no fewer than twelve general elections were fought, only one fewer than between 1715 and 1800. The English and Welsh electorate now numbered more than 300,000 adult males (comparable as a proportion of the total population to its mid-nineteenth-century size). Nor was participation in the drama and excitement of politics restricted to those relatively few men who possessed the parliamentary franchise: thus according to one report from

---

[3] H. Horwitz, *Parliament, Policy and Politics in the Reign of William III* (1977), 98.
[4] *The Diary of Sir David Hamilton, 1709–1714*, ed. P. Roberts (1975), 10.

a by-election at Leicester in December 1707, 'not a chambermaid, prentice or schoolboy ... but what is warmly engaged upon one side or the other'.[5] Popular partisanship was further encouraged by the fact that, unlike the highly organized bodies which dominate modern political life, both parties were merely informal groupings of like-minded individuals, membership of which involved nothing more than personal identification as Tory or Whig. Hence party politics were by no means confined to elections for the national Parliament, but spilled over into contests for place and influence in and over local government, charities, schools, the lawcourts, and most forms of social and sporting life.

The loose, unstructured nature of late seventeenth- and early eighteenth-century party politics confused contemporaries and makes difficulties for historians. While almost all politicians had an acknowledged or reputed party identification, their commitments ranged in strength from the barely nominal allegiances of the veteran parliamentary managers Sunderland and his contemporary Sidney Godolphin (1645–1712) to the extreme and inveterate partisanship of 'honest Tom' Lord Wharton (1648–1715), a notorious libertine, political songwriter, and electoral operator in the Whig interest. Furthermore, William III's accession caused the national political landscape to be gradually redrawn, with the Whigs no longer automatically cast as the party of opposition, speaking for 'Country' against 'Court' and its adherents. These older terms continued to be used, and necessarily so, since the positions taken by self-styled Whigs and Tories after 1688 often seemed at odds with their presumed party principles: in 1701 a politician complained that the 'ideas which belong to those old party names' had been abandoned by the Tories, for 'those who keep up their faction, by retaining the name of Tories, and running down Whigs, have nothing but the bare name of their party, and are that very thing which they run down'.[6]

Such ambiguities and contradictions have encouraged attempts to analyse parliamentary politics under William and Anne in non-party terms. In one view, derived from L. B. Namier's immensely influential analysis of *The Structure of Politics at the Accession of George III* (1929), political life after 1688 was dominated by competition for the fruits of office and power, rather than a contest of rival creeds or ideologies embodied in party labels. This interpretation depicted individual alignments in the political conflicts of post-Revolutionary England as determined not by party ties (which, supposedly, retained little more than rhetorical value), but more material bonds and pressures. These included kinship, education, locality, and, above all, personal clientage, or dependence on a faction or grouping run by a leading politician, or the Court. Thus apparent inconsistencies in the voting behaviour of individual MPs were identified and supposedly accounted for, as likewise more complex parliamentary manœuvres which occasionally saw supposed Whigs

[5] *The Correspondence of Jonathan Swift*, ed. H. Williams (1963), i. 62.
[6] J. Somers, *Jura Populi Anglicani* (1701), p. ix.

and Tories combine in opposition to a (far from united) ministry. However, closer analysis of division lists in both Houses, and poll books recording electoral behaviour, has shown that the overwhelming majority of peers, MPs, and electors divided consistently along party lines (although a substantial minority of voters also 'floated', changing votes from one poll to the next). In short, the Whig–Tory division, if sometimes complicated and overlaid by Court–Country splits, turns out to be the best guide we are likely to have to the chaotic twists and turns of political behaviour and issues, within as well as outside Parliament, during the quarter-century after 1688.[7]

War and Peace, 1689–1701

King William's evident lack of interest in establishing a close and cordial relationship with his new subjects was largely reciprocated. The 'morose temper of the Prince of Orange' attracted unfavourable comment even before the Convention Parliament resolved that he and the Princess Mary 'might be declared King and Queen of England, etc.'[8] If the uncharismatic William's brusque and distant manner was hardly endearing, his Calvinist religion, Dutch nationality, and fondness for his fellow countrymen proved even less popular. While the English-born and pious Anglican Mary could hardly be criticized on those grounds, her public demeanour was nevertheless faulted in the opposite direction, as excessively cheerful considering 'so sad a revolution, as to her father's person'.[9] It also came to be believed and resented that William had always sought to usurp the throne, not from any concern for English interests, but the better to pursue his European agenda. The first accusation is plausible, if impossible to verify; the second seems largely justified, although in William's defence it might be noted that the prospects for English Protestantism in a Europe dominated by Louis XIV would not have been bright.

The most intransigent opponents of the new regime were those whose consciences and previous commitments to James II dictated that they refuse even the modified oath of allegiance laid down in the Bill of Rights, which carefully omitted any reference to William and Mary as *rightful* monarchs. Beside a very few MPs and peers, these 'non-jurors' (literally, non-swearers) initially included eight bishops, headed by the respected Sancroft, who had previously led resistance to James's Declaration of Indulgence, and about 400 other clergymen, all of whom consequently forfeited their church benefices and livelihoods. This display of integrity by the non-jurors undoubtedly strengthened resolve among the less scrupulous majority to resist any further compromise of

[7] See J. V. Beckett, 'Stability in politics and society, 1680–1750', in C. Jones (ed.), *Britain in the First Age of Party, 1680–1750* (1987), 1–8.

[8] Evelyn, *Diary*, 29 Jan. 1689; W. A. Speck, *Reluctant Revolutionaries* (1989), 109.

[9] Burnet, *Bishop Burnet's History of His Own Time* (1724), i. 825. Mary evidently overreacted to her husband's request that she show no hint of resentment at being excluded from ruling in her own right; *Memoirs of Mary Queen of England, 1689–1693*, ed. R. Doebner (1886), 11.

the Church of England's tenets, as well as providing a principled core of support for Jacobite attempts at reversing the Revolution.

Nor was positive enthusiasm for the new sovereigns much in evidence. William's authoritarian record as Stadtholder of the Netherlands aroused concern, even among those who publicly hailed him as the country's liberator. They had some reason, given this half-Stuart monarch's reported statement that 'he would, since he had been called to the throne by God, maintain the authority reposed in him', and not become a mere 'Doge of Venice'.[10] Yet despite these brave words, William's grasp on that throne was far from secure, especially after his father-in-law's landing in Ireland with a small French army in March 1689. The victory achieved over James's overwhelmingly Catholic force at the River Boyne fifteen months later, still an event of enormous symbolic resonance in modern Ireland, effectively ended Jacobite hopes of launching a successful counter-revolution from that country. But Irish armed resistance continued, with the aid of French reinforcements, until another crushing defeat at Aughrim in July 1691. Meanwhile France's temporary naval supremacy in the Channel held out until May 1692, when a combined Dutch–English fleet reversed the humiliating defeat they had suffered off Beachy Head in mid-1690, just before William's triumph at the Boyne. Jacobite conspiracies and plots intensified after Mary's death in 1693, and as late as 1696 Louis XIV conditionally agreed to provide ships and troops for another invasion attempt, linked to an elaborate scheme for internal risings and William's assassination.

The uncertain future gave English politicians a strong incentive to hedge their bets or 'reinsure', maintaining discreet links with James's court in exile at St Germain outside Paris against the possibility of his future restoration. By the same token William was obviously best advised to avoid becoming the prisoner of any one faction, but to maximize his potential support by moderation and non-partisanship, even to those who had previously served his father-in-law in positions of trust. These tactics also suited William's private preference for the Tories as proven friends to monarchy, and his suspicion of the Whigs as at best semi-republicans. Yet although his first ministries included a number of prominent Tory figures from previous reigns, including Halifax ('the Trimmer'), Danby, and Daniel Finch, earl of Nottingham (1647–1730), by 1696 William found himself forced back into Whig one-party government, as his person and policies became increasingly unpopular.

Formal declaration of war in May 1689 marked the beginning of England's emergence from her intermittently pro-French and anti-Dutch, but essentially isolationist stance of the past thirty years. Allocated a leading role in the 'Grand Alliance' with Austria, the Netherlands, and various smaller European states which William had constructed as a barrier to French ambitions, this

---

[10] Horwitz, *Parliament, Policy and Politics*, 42.

Nine Years War involved the country's troops and ships in massive military operations, of unprecedented scale, and enormous financial cost. Since Parliament had carefully avoided voting permanent revenues to the new rulers at the outset of their reign, William would in any case have needed to seek parliamentary appropriations to meet the ordinary expenses of peacetime government. But now his military demands far exceeded any previous wartime expenditure, and could only be met by extraordinary measures, including a nominal 25 per cent direct tax on landed property, plus huge government borrowings (see below, Ch. 5). The Tory squires and country gentlemen, suspicious of standing armies since Cromwell's time, bore the brunt of the land tax. They disliked William's reliance on Dutch administrators and generals almost as much as they detested the mushroom rise of 'Dutch finance', and the associated 'monied interest' of bankers, brokers, and stock-jobbers who clustered around the newly established Bank of England. They were also horrified by the King's evident willingness to countenance the removal of all civil disabilities from Protestant Dissenters, thereby further downgrading the status of the Anglican church.

As the war continued on both land and sea without decisive outcome, it became clear that William's best chance of maintaining England's military commitment in the face of growing Tory opposition was to rely on the Whigs to secure annual parliamentary votes of supply and the passage of other government business. The middle years of his reign accordingly saw a Whig leadership cohort move into government, confronting Tories whose mistrust of executive and monarchy was now expressed in terms remarkably similar to the anti-Court rhetoric deployed by their Whig rivals a few years back. Thus the Tories supported classic 'Country' bills providing for the exclusion of civil and military office-holders or 'placemen' from the House of Commons, and barring royal dismissal of judges. Only use of the royal veto prevented these measures becoming law, and in 1694 William had to accept the Triennial Act, designed to stop the Crown accumulating a dominant following in a Parliament unchanged by elections.

The ministers of the 'Junto' (as the knot of Whig leaders was commonly known, from a Spanish word for council) managed to survive the conclusion of a peace, or truce, with France in 1697. But since that treaty of Ryswick recognized William as King of England, the case for military demobilization seemed overwhelming, except to William, anxious to maintain pressure on Louis in delicate negotiations over the imminent dismemberment of the Spanish empire. Despite royal threats of abdication, a major pamphleteering and parliamentary campaign against standing armies eventually forced the reduction of England's land forces to less than one-tenth of their wartime strength. Further humiliation for the ailing King came with the Act of Settlement (1701), in some respects more accurately characterized by its formal title, 'An Act for the Further Limitation of the Crown and Better Securing the Rights and Liberties of the Subject'. Having named the Protestant Electress of Hanover, James I's ageing granddaughter, as next in line to the throne after Princess Anne (whose last surviving child, the 11-year-old duke of Gloucester, had died in 1700), the statute proceeded to debar any future monarch from either involving the country in foreign wars or departing its shores without parliamentary consent.

Yet this exercise in xenophobic vindictiveness was not quite the end of the story. Renewed anxiety about Louis's ambitions and the prospect of a united Franco-Spanish empire crystallized that autumn when James II died and his son was proclaimed at Versailles as James III, rightful king of England. Understandably alarmed for the Protestant succession, a newly elected Parliament hastily approved all the military expenditure foreshadowed by William in a long and unusually eloquent opening speech, which focused on the need to sink party differences in the face of 'the common danger' arising from Louis's territorial designs. But such unwonted bipartisanship did not even outlast the King, who died in March 1702 after falling heavily from his horse.

Queen Anne and a Church Militant, 1702–1710

The accession of James's younger daughter was greeted with particular enthusiasm by those still uneasy about the violence done to the hereditary principle in 1689. Anne enjoyed the advantages of being native-born of English parents and brought up as an Anglican; her Danish husband Prince George was an amiable Protestant nonentity. These considerations helped compensate for a lack of political experience on the part of this 37-year-old mother of five (none of whose children survived to adulthood, although she was pregnant at least eighteen times). So did the support of her confidante Sarah Churchill (1660–1744), whose soldier husband John became Duke of Marlborough at Anne's accession. Anne's gracious manner and distinctive 'sweetness of pronunciation' (the result of early elocution lessons from one of her uncle's actress friends) left a favourable impression at her first public appearances as Queen. Her determined if slightly contradictory declaration that, while she knew '*my own* heart to be entirely English [italics added]', she would maintain William's commitment to the French war, was also well received.[11] From the beginning of Anne's reign conscious attempts were made to revive the public ceremonial life of the royal court centred on the monarch's person, including the quasi-religious healing ritual of 'touching for the King's evil', which had been discontinued in 1688. Parallels with the glorious achievements of the last Queen regnant, Elizabeth I, were also much in vogue, although, as she could hardly claim to be England's virgin bride, Anne was instead eulogized as the matronly mother of her people.[12]

[11] E. Gregg, *Queen Anne* (1984), 152.
[12] R. O. Bucholz, *The Augustan Court: Queen Anne and the Decline of Court Culture* (1993).

The highest hopes for the new reign were held by the Tories. Anne's hereditary birthright was strong enough to persuade even most Jacobites that the Pretender was merely her rightful heir. Nor did she conceal her devotion to the Church of England. Members of the 'Church' party (a revealingly common synonym for Tories) confidently expected that with Anne as Supreme Governor the Established Church of England would regain ground it had lost since religious pluralism was legalized in 1689. Convinced that religious disunity affronted God, threatened national security as well as the salvation of the people, and disrupted the peace of local communities, their concerns included the unexpected scale of the proliferation of dissenting congregations, meeting houses, and educational establishments since the Toleration Act; evasion of the legal provisions against the holding of public office by Dissenters, thanks to their practice of 'occasional conformity' by receiving Anglican communion once a year; and the growing ineffectiveness of the church courts. All these unsatisfactory developments had been characterized by the High Church spokesman Dr Francis Atterbury (1662–1732) as 'a settled contempt of religion and the priesthood', producing a concomitant spread of blasphemy, corruption, crime, heresy, and vice.[13]

Widespread throughout the Church (and by no means confined to clerics), such anxieties were felt most strongly by the often economically hard-pressed rank-and-file parish clergy. These disgruntled parsons found themselves increasingly at odds with the Latitudinarian or Low Church bishops whom William had promoted, precisely because of the latters' Erastian willingness to accept the dominance of the State in ecclesiastical matters. In 1701 the burgeoning High Church party had gained an institutional forum, thanks to the grudging revival of Convocation, the Church's parliament, which William had suspended in 1689. There the vehemence of the initial attack upon the hierarchy encouraged both High and Low churchmen to cement political alliances with the Tories and Whigs respectively.

But Anne would not willingly become the prisoner of either clerical or political party. Despite some initial gestures of support for the High Church cause, including the establishment of a fund based on church revenues originally seized by Henry VIII to supplement the incomes of poorer clergymen (Queen Anne's Bounty), she and her middle-of-the-road leading ministers were primarily interested in effective prosecution of the war with France. Yet Tory commitment to the Grand Alliance and its military efforts to prevent a union of the French and Spanish crowns was rarely more than carping and half-hearted. Chauvinist suspicions that most benefit went to ungrateful foreigners while England bore a disproportionate share of the financial and military burden prompted Tory politicians to advocate a 'blue-water strategy' of naval warfare in the Caribbean and Mediterranean, rather than the large-scale Continental

---

[13] F. Atterbury, *Letter to a Convocation Man* (1697), 2.

operations to which English land forces were committed in unprecedented numbers, especially after the strategic and commercial treaties with Portugal negotiated by Sir Paul Methuen (1672–1757). But when in 1704 desperation to push a statute outlawing occasional conformity through the Whiggish House of Lords led the Tory-dominated Commons to 'tack' the measure to the following year's land tax bill, even some of their own number rejected this subordination of the national military effort to party political feuding. The Queen also reluctantly allowed herself to be persuaded that continuation of the war necessitated greater dependence on the Whigs. Despite her own strong preference for a non-partisan administration, by 1708 the ministerial Whig Junto was back in office. Wharton, John Lord Somers (1651–1716), Charles Montagu, first earl of Halifax (1661–1716), and young Robert Walpole (1676–1745) shared power with the veterans Godolphin and Marlborough (the latter combining command of the allied forces and high-level diplomacy during the summer campaigning season with a leading role in domestic politics over the winter months).

Working closely with another gifted soldier and statesman, Prince Eugene of Austria, Marlborough's organizational and strategic genius saw the French defeated in a series of set-piece battles (Blenheim 1704, Ramillies 1706, Oudenarde 1708, Malplaquet 1709). Yet none of these famous—and bloody— victories was decisive, in the sense of forcing Louis to sue for peace on terms acceptable to the allies, who were indeed far from united on this or any other issue. Years of inconclusive and hugely expensive marches, countermarches, and sieges produced a general war-weariness from which not even the Queen and the Whigs were immune, while simultaneously boosting the stocks of the High Church/Tory party.

The immediate occasion of the Whigs' fall from office was the impeachment and trial of Dr Henry Sacheverell (*c.*1674–1724), a bumptious Oxford don turned London preacher. On 5 November 1709, a date customarily reserved for commemorating the nation's previous escapes from popery in 1605 and 1688, Sacheverell delivered an outrageously provocative sermon before the Tory Lord Mayor of London in St Paul's Cathedral. Far from respecting convention, Sacheverell used the occasion to mount a furious attack on Dissenters, Latitudinarians, occasional conformists, and Whigs. He even went so far as to assert that any who failed to accept the 'subject's obligation to an absolute, and unconditional obedience to the supreme power, in all things lawful, and the utter illegality of resistance upon any pretence whatsoever' (classical High Church and non-juror doctrines, scarcely compatible with belief in the legitimacy of the Revolution) were no better than traitors to both Church and State.[14] However, the exasperated ministry's decision to make an example of this turbulent priest by impeaching him for 'high crimes and misdemeanours'

[14] H. Sacheverell, *The Perils of False Brethren, both in Church, and State* (1709), 19.

before the Whig-dominated House of Lords (jury trial for seditious libel in the ordinary common-law courts being less likely to produce a conviction) turned Sacheverell into a popular Tory hero and martyr. Unruly crowds of plebeian supporters chanting 'High Church and Sacheverell' daily accompanied the Doctor to Westminster Hall. They managed in one night's rampage to demolish six of London's most prominent Nonconformist chapels and to threaten the Bank of England, before being dispersed by the Queen's Guards, miraculously without loss of life. Sacheverell also attracted the adulation of fashionable Tory ladies and their escorts, while his defence counsel adeptly exploited every possible loophole in the prosecution's case.

The outcome was legal victory but political disaster. Sacheverell's derisory sentence, a mere three-year's suspension from preaching, indicated that even within the Lords the balance of power had shifted against the Junto. Popular jubilation at this slap in the face for the Whigs and their allies spread across the country. Although Sacheverell's effigy was hung from a signpost in Nonconformist-ridden Nottingham, elsewhere his triumphal post-trial progress attracted cheering crowds, civic receptions, and lavish aristocratic hospitality. These demonstrations of support suggest that Sacheverell and the Tories had tapped an authentic vein of discontent. Dissatisfaction with the long-continued war and its associated economic and human hardships, exacerbated by recent harsh winters and harvest failures, was associated with deep-seated mistrust of Dissenters, financiers, and foreigners, and nostalgic yearning for the simpler 'Church and King' order of an (idealized and imaginary) pre-Revolutionary England. Translated into votes, aided by an army of black-coated electioneering clergymen, these sentiments inflicted a crushing defeat on the Whigs at the polls held in the autumn of 1710. The Junto had already resigned. Robert Harley (1661–1724), an experienced politician who had drifted away from the Whigs since the beginning of Anne's reign, took on the political management previously handled by Godolphin and Marlborough; the latter's wife had quarrelled with the Queen some years before and the Duke himself was shortly to fall from royal grace, and office.

Jacobitism and the Protestant Succession, 1710–1715

Anne was delighted to be relieved of the 'Five Tyrannizing Lords' of the Whig ministry. But she remained determined that both her person and government would continue to stand above the strife of party, declaring that 'though I have changed my ministers I have not altered my measures; I am still for moderation and will govern by it'.[15] This was not exactly what the triumphant Tories had hoped to hear, especially the 150 or so MPs who met weekly as members of the October Club, a pressure group seeking full-blooded reaction and proscription

---

[15] G. S. Holmes, *The Trial of Dr Sacheverell* (1973), 272.

of their enemies in Church and State, both centrally and locally, along the lines of the last years of Charles II's rule. But apart from the passage of a long-delayed act against occasional conformity in 1711, the High Church programme made disappointingly slow progress, at least so far as the extremists of the Tory-dominated House of Commons were concerned. Instead the main priority of Harley (now ennobled as earl of Oxford) was to pursue a satisfactory end to the war, through prolonged and tortuous negotiations, both with England's allies and the French. And well before a cluster of nine separate peace treaties was ready for signing at Utrecht in April 1713, the focus of domestic politics had shifted back to the fundamental problem of the succession.

Anne's health deteriorated markedly from the middle years of her reign, with more frequent and debilitating attacks of gout. (Her personal physician could only beg her to avoid the 'disquiet' which supposedly worsened the disease, adding unhelpfully 'for if she happened to die it was very probable that the nation would be in blood'.)[16] This gloomy prognosis reflected widespread fears that a significant portion of the political nation would resist by force the Act of Settlement's provisions for the ageing Lutheran Electress of Hanover and then her son Georg Ludwig to inherit the throne after Anne's death. Their preferred candidate was, of course, James Francis Edward Stuart, the Prince of Wales, or Old Pretender.

The degree and extent of support for the Jacobite cause both within and outside Parliament is very difficult to judge. It was usually a covert and always a potentially treasonable allegiance. Expressions of emotional attachment, often alcohol-induced, to 'the King over the water', or 'the little gentleman in black velvet' (the mole whose burrow caused William III's horse to stumble) cannot be equated with the principled commitments of non-jurors and Roman Catholics, or even the murky Jacobite underground of agents, couriers, plotters, and spies. However, it seems that the electoral landslide of 1710 brought to Westminster around fifty convinced Jacobite Tory MPs, who regarded 'James III' as rightful King-in-waiting and were committed to work for his restoration.[17] While the Pretender's Catholicism was obviously a, if not the, major obstacle, there was always some possibility—no one knew quite how much—that he might be persuaded to become a Protestant in order 'to enjoy his own again' (to quote an old royalist song, which experienced a distinct revival after 1710). Such hopes—or fears—prompted numerous ministers and politicians to establish discreet contact with the Jacobite Court at St Germain over the next five years.

But while there may have been a few Whig Jacobites, there were many more Tory Hanoverians. In other words, the Tories were less strongly opposed to a Hanoverian heir-apparent than the Whigs were united against a popish Pretender. Whig fears of Tory intentions to subvert the 'free and Protestant

---

16 *Diary of David Hamilton*, 54.
17 D. Szechi, *Jacobitism and Tory Politics, 1710–1714* (1984).

constitution' nevertheless grew apace after their second swingeing general election defeat in 1713. Both Oxford and Henry St John, Viscount Bolingbroke (1678–1751), his younger, headstrong, fast-emerging rival (who had incautiously allowed himself to be seen with the Pretender in Paris the previous year) were indeed in touch with 'James III'. But those contacts were not necessarily maintained with a view to furthering his return, as distinct from keeping all their own possible options open, and him quiet.[18] When James finally let it be known in March 1714 that he was not prepared to abandon his religion in order to gain his father's throne, these discussions collapsed. With Oxford out of favour at Court, Bolingbroke now launched a desperate bid to unite and entrench the Tories, with himself at their head, as a High Church but pro-Hanoverian governing party. The attempt failed, despite the passage of a long-awaited Schism Act to outlaw Dissenter schools, mainly because Anne was not prepared to give Bolingbroke the backing and high ministerial office which Oxford had enjoyed. Her death on 1 August 1714 effectively sealed the Tories' political fate for the next half-century.

However unwelcome the prospect of another foreign monarch (a Lutheran to boot), and however widespread positive belief in, or sympathy for, James Stuart's hereditary claim to the throne, overthrowing the Protestant succession by force was never going to be easy. As the smoothness of the transition to a new dynasty emphasized, entertaining vaguely Jacobite sympathies was one thing, taking decisive action based upon them quite another. But the Tories' patent ambivalence had sufficiently damned them in the eyes of the newly proclaimed King George I, whose hostility was reinforced by the fully fledged Jacobite rebellion which erupted in Scotland next year. Although planned in co-ordination with English dissidents, the disgruntled earl of Mar (1675–1732) broke out the Pretender's standard too early, and the Pretender himself reached Scotland too late, with insufficient men and money. South of the border it was only in Northumberland and Lancashire (notoriously the most popishly affected county in England), that any significant rallying to arms occurred, and even there the rebels quickly surrendered after their defeat at Preston. Perhaps better leadership—and luck—might have produced a different outcome; but it is certain that the failure of what became known as the Fifteen (although in Scotland it lasted into the following year) immeasurably strengthened both the Whigs and the new dynasty.

[18] J. H. and M. Shennan, 'The Protestant Succession in English Politics, April 1714–September 1715', in Ragnhild Hatton and J. S. Bromley (eds.), *William III and Louis XIV: Essays, 1680–1720 by and for Mark A. Thompson* (1968).

5

WAR AND THE STATE

Revolution, Diplomacy, and War

Between 1699 and 1703 Joseph Addison (1672–1719), a rising Oxford don and budding man of letters, travelled around Europe in order to prepare himself for future employment as a diplomat. From Italy Addison addressed to his Whig patron Charles Montagu, Baron Halifax (1661–1715), a verse letter which suggests that the beauties of the local landscape were largely negated by its oppressive political system. Although bleaker and colder, 'Britannia's Isle' is the home of that 'Liberty' which 'makes the gloomy face of nature gay'. According to Addison, liberty's benign influence extended well beyond the nation's shores:

> 'Tis Britain's care to watch o'er Europe's fate
> And hold in balance each contending state
> To threaten bold presumptuous kings with war
> And answer her afflicted neighbours' prayer.

However lamentable the poetry, the extent of the recent transformation in England's relationship to her European neighbours could hardly be better illustrated. Comparisons between English freedom and Continental—or more specifically, French—slavery had been a commonplace, at least of English authors, since medieval times. But before 1689, except perhaps in the brief Cromwellian interlude, it would have been preposterous to assert for England, or Britain, the role of arbiter in Europe's quarrels. Such a claim was still contentious, especially for many Tories, distrustful of foreign entanglements. Yet it could now be seriously advanced because the British state was no longer necessarily considered a marginal player in international power politics.

Here the Revolution did mark a decisive watershed. The mid-seventeenth-century civil wars, while following hard upon Scottish invasion and Irish rebellion, saw no direct military intervention from Continental Europe. But the events of 1688–9 were triggered by Dutch William's landing, and in turn had enormous repercussions on Europe, and indeed the whole world.[1] First, England's post-1660 role as a French dependency or satellite was decisively repudiated. This policy switch resulted no less from Louis XIV's diplomatic

[1] See esp. J. I. Israel (ed.), *The Anglo-Dutch Moment: Essays on the Glorious Revolution and its World Impact* (1991), 31 and *passim*.

and military support for James II's efforts to regain his crown, than William III's determination to lock England into a coalition of European powers aimed at checking further expansion of French arms and influence.

Secondly, this geopolitical realignment initiated a long-drawn-out sequence of Anglo-French wars, both in Europe and increasingly across the globe (a conflict which has been termed the second Hundred Years War, although it actually extended over a century and a quarter). Of course there was nothing wholly new about English rulers joining European alliances, or English troops fighting on the Continent. But the duration, geographical scope, and sheer magnitude of the commitment of men and money to war with France between 1689 and 1713, and in subsequent clashes down to the battle of Waterloo, were entirely novel. Both the scale and overall success of this military effort established England (strictly not Britain until 1707, although the term was used earlier, as Addison's lines indicate) in the first rank of European powers, despite her relatively small population and previous peripheral status. From the outbreak of what is variously and confusingly known as the Nine Years War, King William's War, the War of the Grand Alliance, the War of the League of Augsburg, and the War of the British Succession (1689–97), down to the French Revolutionary and Napoleonic Wars (1793–1815), England was continuously involved in European affairs through diplomatic activity and foreign alliances, even when not engaged in physical combat, for the most part in opposition to France. In short, the country functioned as a leading member of what contemporaries termed the European 'states system', rather than being marginalized by internal distractions and military impotence. How did this remarkable transformation come about?

The Sinews of War

Warfare has always been expensive. However, the general adoption of firearms and gunpowder during the sixteenth century led to massive growth in the size of armies and navies, and a quantum leap in the costs of equipping and deploying them. Governments struggled to raise the necessary funds from taxes and loans, in the process frequently immiserating their subjects and bankrupting themselves. One main reason for England's relative lack of engagement in Continental power politics before 1689 was mere inability to mobilize financial resources on a scale comparable to those commanded by the leading European powers, France and Spain.

English military expenditure had been traditionally a shared responsibility —and source of friction—between rulers and Parliaments. James II was more fortunate than his brother in this regard; the standing or professional army of some 6,000 men which he inherited soon grew to around 20,000, and reached a total of well over 30,000 troops by November 1688.[2] Such an impressive (and

---

[2] J. Childs, *The Army, James II and the Glorious Revolution* (1980), 4.

to many highly sinister) rate of expansion was feasible because of the lavish financial provision Parliament made for James in the aftermath of Monmouth's and Argyll's rebellions. Not surprisingly, William's Parliaments were less open-handed. Although the actual sums they voted to supply the Crown's needs were far larger than James ever received, these moneys did not come without strings attached. Most MPs seem to have recognized their predecessors' mistake in giving revenue grants for life to the previous two monarchs, and hence effectively forfeiting their influence through the power of the purse; as one remarked, 'When Princes have not needed money, they have not needed us.'[3]

The eventual financial package took almost a decade to work out, but principles of accountability and control were built in from the start. In 1689 the Crown's basic annual entitlement was set at only £1.2m., the same amount promised to Charles II almost thirty years before. This sum was some £200,000 short of the amount now required to cover peacetime government expenditure, even without any allowance for accumulated royal debts, on which the interest payments accounted for at least another £200,000 per annum. Moreover, those customs duties known as 'tonnage and poundage', the main source (other than various excise duties and hereditary royal revenues) from which this sum was to be raised, were granted to William and Mary for only a fixed term of four years in the first instance. All revenues (whether hereditary or otherwise) were earmarked for specific categories of expenditure, and government budgetary discretion was further restricted by the Commons' demand that any ministerial requests for additional 'supply' come before them with detailed estimates of how the money sought was intended to be spent. Finally, parliamentary Commissioners of Accounts were appointed to monitor the use made of all appropriated funds, and, as it was hoped, reduce corruption, embezzlement, and waste, besides facilitating the very large increases in revenue required 'for carrying a vigorous war against France'.[4] While none of these measures was wholly novel, never before had they been employed in so concerted and systematic fashion.

But apart from ensuring that financial pressures would oblige the Crown to observe the Bill of Rights' provisions for frequent Parliaments, William urgently needed sufficient funds to defend the realm against the threatened onslaught of James and his French allies in Ireland, and subsequently to pursue the war on the Continent, as well as to cover the government's non-military expenses. Whereas James II's total yearly income had never exceeded £3m., annual military spending alone reached £8.1m. in 1696, and peaked during the following decade at £10.2m.[5] Raising such astronomical sums demanded additional borrowings and taxation on a quite novel scale.

[3] H. Roseveare, *The Financial Revolution, 1660–1760* (1991), 87.

[4] C. Roberts, 'The constitutional significance of the financial settlement of 1690', *HJ* 20 (1977); J. A. Downie, 'The Commissioners of Public Accounts and the formation of the Country Party', *EHR* 91 (1976).

[5] D. W. Jones, *War and Economy in the Age of William III and Marlborough* (1988), 29.

During the 1690s experiments with various cumbersome and unpopular consumption and poll taxes (including levies on hackney coaches, hawkers, births, marriages, burials, and bachelors) were gradually relinquished in favour of a regular annual Land Tax, assessed at a rate of between 5 and 20 per cent (according to the government's immediate needs) upon the yearly value of all property, real and personal. As its name suggests, landowners were by far the major contributors; businessmen and merchants escaped virtually unscathed, since landed property was more visible and easily assessed (by unpaid panels of local notables) than other forms of wealth. A single flat-rate excise or sales tax, as advocated by the economic and political pamphleteer Charles Davenant (1656–1714) among others, would have been even more lucrative and less readily evaded. But numerous objections were voiced to any such impost: it would fall disproportionately heavily on the poor, create a vast centrally controlled bureaucracy, and place excessive power in governmental hands, since once imposed it would hardly be discontinued. Thus while indirect taxes, both customs duties (levied on imports and exports), and excise (a sales tax on specified commodities, including alcoholic beverages, tea, coffee, and chocolate, salt and spices, candles, soap, newspapers, and some textiles) contributed about 50–60 per cent of Crown revenues before 1715, the balance came from the directly assessed Land Tax—not the least reason for the war's growing unpopularity among the landed interest.[6]

The average annual taxation yield of around £4m. during William's reign was twice what James had been able to raise. But government still faced a large gap between income and outlays. The traditional way of making up that difference was by raising, or extorting, short-term loans from the City of London, the big chartered trading companies, and wealthy private individuals, like Sir Stephen Fox (1627–1716), who acquired a huge personal fortune as paymaster to the forces under Charles II. Lending money to the Crown could be profitable, but was always a risky business, since the number and frequency of repayments often depended more on the individual creditor's standing at Court than any contractual terms. Sir George Downing (d. 1684), a persuasive former diplomat who served as secretary to the Treasury from 1667 to 1672, was one of many who had been anxious to reduce both the lender's risk and the consequent high interest rates payable on government borrowings. He advocated long-term loans, secured on the proceeds of specific taxes or other revenue sources, through a national or public bank, modelled on the highly successful Bank of Amsterdam (most seventeenth-century financial innovations followed Dutch or occasionally French precedents). He also proposed a new bureaucratic role for the Treasury as financial watchdog over all government departments, thus reducing the need for borrowings through tighter control of expenditure. Downing's dream of a 'national Exchequer bank' did not survive

---

[6] J. V. Beckett, 'Land Tax or Excise: the levying of taxation in seventeenth- and eighteenth-century England', *EHR* 100 (1985).

his royal master's unilateral repudiation of payments due on £1.3m. worth of government securities in December 1671. This 'Stop of the Exchequer' inevitably damaged the monarchy's already fragile credit rating; a more positive if unintended outcome was the government's later solemn agreement to pay its financier creditors their regular annual instalments of interest from earmarked taxation revenues, thus originating what later became a permanent, funded 'National Debt'.

But if Charles II's reign had not been wholly devoid of initiatives in banking and public finance, England still lagged far behind the republican Netherlands, not least because adequate security for lenders meant holding the government to terms likely to conflict with the monarch's private interests. Little more could be done until relations between Crown and Parliament were renegotiated at the Revolution. Indeed William III's initial military campaigns were financed much as Charles II's Dutch wars had been, by a mixture of *ad hoc* taxes and short-term loans raised at an escalating premium over the legal maximum interest rate of 6 per cent. Despite greatly enhanced tax yields, the doubling and then tripling of government expenditure soon created a yawning deficit. Various ingenious schemes to bridge the gap were advanced, mainly in the form of annuities and lotteries offering a guaranteed income flow secured on specific taxes in return for a long-term loan of capital. It was Addison's patron Charles Montagu who put the first such proposal through the Commons in 1692.

Two years later Montagu backed a City syndicate, headed by the Scottish entrepreneur William Paterson (1658–1719) and incorporated by Act of Parliament as 'The Governor and Company of the Bank of England'. This body loaned the government £1.2m. raised from 1,268 well-to-do investors whose 8 per cent annual interest was guaranteed by Parliament. Although they paid in gold and silver coin, the Bank used their money to back the issue of readily negotiable paper notes, creating a fund of credit which significantly enhanced its total capital and hence its continuing ability to lend to the Treasury. The success of Paterson and his bank, coming after previous failures to establish precisely this kind of 'Dutch finance' under Charles II and James II, plainly reflected a new climate of confidence. Long-term public borrowings during King William's War have been described as experimental, tentative, relatively small in amount, and relatively expensive to raise. Yet by the end of Queen Anne's still more costly war nearly £16m. (or roughly half the total sum borrowed by the government) had been raised on a funded long-term basis, with regular interest payments guaranteed by Parliament from the proceeds of taxes.[7] Besides making it possible to confront Louis XIV by land and sea without the crushing taxation load which burdened that monarch's unfortunate subjects, the mobilization of credit after 1688 enlisted the material self-interest

[7] P. G. M. Dickson, *The Financial Revolution in England, 1688–1756* (1967), 47; Jones, *War and Economy*, 70–1.

of a growing body of investors in the public funds in support of 'Revolution Principles'.

The State's Servants

Creating effective military and naval forces from the proceeds of loans and taxes was scarcely less difficult than raising the money in the first place. Both demanded the services of administrators, bureaucrats, or civil servants, those whom contemporaries termed 'persons in office', or placemen. Their proliferation after 1688 paralleled the expansion of the military forces, and evoked similar nervousness among politicians and public opinion at large. Both were feared as placing too much power in the hands of government, and threatening the independence of Parliament (see above, p. 74).

The Civil Service which William and Mary inherited had already undergone some expansion and modernization in the 1680s, based upon such mid-century innovations as vesting committees rather than individual office-holders with responsibility for major administrative areas. These trends continued during the French wars, when full-time employment in the revenue-raising departments, notably Customs, Excise, Treasury, and Exchequer, more than doubled, despite William's abandonment in 1689 of the hearth tax and its small army of collectors. The overall size of the bureaucracy possibly trebled, from around 4,000 in 1689 to over 12,000 permanent officials by the mid-1720s.[8] These figures exclude the lawcourts, and the royal household (perhaps the only shrinking area of government employment over this period), as also the numerous part-time or temporary employees of Customs, the royal dockyards, and the Post Office.

It is not yet clear how far the multiplication of public servants in later Stuart England was accompanied by a general enhancement of administrative efficiency. Patronage (and to a lesser extent parentage and purchase) still played a crucial role in recruitment to offices under the Crown. Since such posts were generally held for life, with no mandatory retirement age, it was not uncommon for men to spend three or even four decades slowly working their way up the promotions ladder; a possible record for bureaucratic longevity was set by one Edward Webster, who managed to clock up no fewer than sixty-four years as a Treasury clerk between 1691 and 1755. On the other hand, the introduction of entrance examinations may have helped ensure some minimal level of competence among Customs officers; on-the-job training by informal apprenticeship perhaps had similar effects in other departments. The growing possibility of making a lifetime career in His or Her Majesty's service, with relatively little risk of sacking for party political reasons, perhaps attracted more able candidates, besides encouraging specialization and the establishment of efficient

[8] J. Brewer, *The Sinews of Power: War, Money and the English State, 1688–1783* (1989), 65–9; G. Holmes, *Augustan England: Professions, State and Society, 1680–1730* (1982), 254–6.

administrative routines. However, such developments were more noticeable in the newer revenue offices, and the Admiralty and Navy Board, than in older departments like the (literally) medieval Exchequer, despite that hidebound institution's slightly surprising role in managing the State Lottery set up in 1694. Although the French practice of creating and selling offices for revenue purposes was never established in England, father-to-son (and sometimes to grandson) inheritance of office, payment by a percentage of receipts rather than wages or salary, private use of public moneys, and the employment of deputies to undertake any real work associated with sinecure posts remained widespread.[9]

The armed services, which accounted for around two-thirds of the annual wartime budget, also expanded rapidly from 1688 onwards. While the employment of foreign mercenaries and differences between paper enrolments and actual troops mustered in the field complicate the statistics, by 1694 Parliament was setting aside funds to support some 93,000 soldiers, two-thirds supposedly recruited within the British Isles. Towards the end of the War of the Spanish Succession English taxpayers were supporting a land force of nearly 171,000 men, as well as 48,000 marines and sailors.[10] Even if most of these troops were actually foreign nationals fighting under allied command, an enormous logistical effort was still required to maintain English armies of 50,000–60,000 men in campaigns extending as far afield as Spain and the Danube. Moreover, given that there may have been fewer than half a million men aged between 16 and 60 years available for military service, and bearing in mind the rank-and-file soldier's unflattering contemporary reputation, together with high turnover rates from death in battle, disease, and desertion, it is no surprise that finding sufficient cannon fodder was a constant struggle.

In his hugely popular play *The Recruiting Officer* (1706), George Farquhar drew on recent personal experiences as a Lieutenant of Grenadiers recruiting in Shrewsbury to depict some of the wiles employed to induce Shropshire yokels to join the colours. Farquhar's expansive Sergeant Kite is a far more benevolent figure than the real-life Michael Tooley, provost-marshal of the Coldstream Guards, who in the early 1690s was detaining up to 200 unfortunate 'volunteers' at a time in his London crimping house, before shipping them off to Flanders. Besides convicted felons and debtors, from 1704 JPs were authorized to conscript all able-bodied men without 'any lawful calling or employment' as soldiers, so long as they lacked the vote (and hence could be regarded as both socially and politically expendable).[11] This provision put

[9] Holmes, *Augustan England*, ch. 8, and Brewer, *Sinews of Power*, ch. 3, take a slightly rosier view.
[10] J. Childs, *The British Army of William III, 1689–1702* (1987), 102–3; Jones, *War and Economy*, 10–11.
[11] 2 & 3 Anne c. 19, *An Act for Raising Recruits for the Land Forces and Marines*; Childs, *British Army of William III*, 111–12; G. M. Trevelyan, *England under Queen Anne: Blenheim* (1930), 218–19.

army recruiting on a similar basis to the compulsory 'impressment' of merchant seamen for the navy. Naval conscription had long been justified as unavoidable, since few warships were kept fully manned in peacetime, and only experienced sailors had the skills required to take them to sea, while the appalling conditions, brutal discipline, and assorted perils of naval service made it an even less attractive prospect than the army, especially for ordinary ratings.

Yet—with the possible exception of those unfortunates who found the prospects of adventure and prize money insufficient compensation for being compelled to sail its ships—as an institution the Royal Navy enjoyed far greater popularity and prestige than the army. The redcoats were still widely regarded with a mixture of fear and loathing which went back to Cromwellian days, reinforced by the plausible neo-Harringtonian, Country, and Tory view that a standing army was always a potential threat to the subjects' liberties. Such objections could hardly be levelled at the navy, which was indeed widely recognized as the country's main defence against foreign invasion, as well as the guardian of its burgeoning overseas commerce. The naval establishment grew considerably in size, complexity, and administrative sophistication during the second half of the seventeenth century, a process to which Samuel Pepys made a major contribution in his succesive posts as Clerk of the King's Ships, Surveyor-General of the Victualling Office, and eventually Secretary of the Admiralty, between 1660 and 1688. The extensive infrastructure of dockyards, ordnance, victualling, hospitals, and other facilities required to maintain the fleet made the navy by far the most expensive arm of government, acccounting for at least 20 per cent of annual peacetime public expenditure. Between 1688 and the latter stages of of the War of the Spanish Succession, the total number of English warships may have risen from around 173 to 313 (taking no account of authorized privateers, the privately owned vessels licensed to prey on enemy merchant shipping). Still more significant was the growth in ship size and firepower, particularly the larger proportion of vessels carrying 60 to 100 guns and purpose-built to take their place in the line-of-battle artillery duels which dominated naval tactics from the 1660s onwards. By 1715 Britain had 119 line-of-battle ships (up from only 83 in 1690), while the navy's total tonnage was nearly twice that of France, and about a third larger than it had been at the outset of the Nine Years War. The new mode of fighting at sea, and the increased numbers and size of battle-fleets, required better co-ordination between individual ships than ever before, encouraging the development of standard signal codes and sailing manœuvres, detailed in printed copies of the *Sailing and Fighting Instructions* carried aboard each vessel.[12]

The wartime fleet was manned by over 40,000 sailors. The thousand or so officers set over them could only gain promotion to the rank of lieutenant after

[12] M. Duffy, 'The foundations of British naval power', in M. Duffy (ed.), *The Military Revolution and the State, 1500–1800* (1980); J. B. Hattendorf, 'The struggle with France, 1698–1814', in J. R. Hill (ed.), *The Oxford Illustrated History of the Royal Navy* (1995).

three years of probationary service, including one as a midshipman, followed by an exacting Navy Board examination of their navigational and seafaring skills, which when introduced in 1677 became 'the first such test in the history of the British armed forces'.[13] Because naval commissions were not available for purchase, navy officers tended to be drawn from a wider social background than their military counterparts; but tensions between 'tarpaulins' who had worked their way up through the non-commissioned ranks and 'gentlemen' officers who owed their initial positions to patronage rather than seafaring experience waned steadily from the 1660s onwards. Prolonged warfare after 1688, plus administrative changes which facilitated continuity of employment (particularly the institution of half-pay service as a form of peacetime retainer) also helped make the navy an increasingly attractive career choice for young gentlemen of respectable family. Their opportunities for honour and profit expanded as England began to acquire offshore naval bases (Gibraltar, 1704; Minorca, 1714), and a permanent global maritime presence.

Great Britain as World Power

Besides giving England a new prominence in Continental Europe, the French wars consolidated her dominance of the neighbouring kingdoms of Scotland and Ireland. Since James VI of Scotland became the first Stuart ruler of England in the early seventeenth century, a more complete integration of the two realms had been frequently advocated from both sides of the border. But what one political commentator characterized as 'the hatred and hostility that ever was between the English and the Scots' was reinforced by deep-seated economic, social, and religious differences, which seemed to present insurmountable barriers to closer union.[14] Anglo-Scots divisions were if anything heightened by the Revolution and its aftermath. William III paid little attention to his northern kingdom, where loyalty to the exiled House of Stuart became a talisman of Scottish nationalism and Anglophobia, exacerbated by commercial and colonial rivalries, Anglican–Presbyterian sectarian bitterness, and English political insensitivity. Even a revival of the 'Auld Alliance' between France and Scotland seemed distinctly possible after Anne's accession, especially when formal negotiations for a union collapsed.

The Edinburgh Parliament thereupon enacted provisions for a separate national foreign policy and line of succession to the Scottish throne (Scotland had not been consulted over the Act of Settlement). Westminster retaliated with an Aliens Act (1705), which imposed a trade embargo and seizure of all Scottish assets in England if the Hanoverian settlement were not accepted and union negotiations reopened. With this ultimatum and the further threat of military action in the background, a new set of commissioners embarked upon

---

[13] I. Roy, 'The profession of Arms', in W. Prest (ed.), *The Professions in Early Modern England*, (1987), 201.

[14] H. Neville, *Plato Redivivus* (1681), ed. C. Robbins (1969), 142.

a further round of talks. The resulting treaty, accepted only after long and divisive wrangling within and outside the Scottish parliament, was for both parties clearly an act of necessity rather than inclination. Fearing a Jacobite takeover if Scotland retained its independence, the Whig government agreed to open England's domestic and colonial markets to Scottish merchants and make a substantial payment towards the costs of economic integration. Retaining their own church and lawcourts, but abandoning legislative and political autonomy, the Scots received representation in both Houses of the newly named Parliament of Great Britain when the Union was promulgated in 1707. The treaty soon became intensely unpopular in Scotland, where it was widely thought to have been first corruptly secured, then perverted, by scheming English politicians. But the successive failures of a French invasion attempt in 1708, the subsequent home-brewed Jacobite rising in 1715, and its disastrous Spanish-backed sequel in 1719, suggested that the single sovereign state of Great Britain would be even more difficult to dismember than it had been to bring into existence.[15]

London's domination of Britain's other kingdom was enhanced after 1688 for similar reasons, if by different means. The military reconquest of Ireland between 1689 and 1691 completed a process of colonial subjugation. The relatively lenient terms which William granted the defeated Jacobites under the Treaty of Limerick were soon superseded, as Dublin's Protestant-dominated Parliament enacted a comprehensive code of anti-Catholic penal laws, which the English Parliament unquestioningly endorsed. Further land confiscations confirmed and completed the work of the Cromwellian settlement; five-sixths of the country was now held by the Protestant English and Scottish settler minority, who constituted about a quarter of Ireland's population. The flight of Catholic aristocrats and the 'wild geese'—some 12,000 Jacobite officers and men who chose exile and enlistment with the French rather than swear allegiance to William—further facilitated a Protestant monopoly of political and economic power. The cowed, disarmed, and leaderless indigenous Catholic majority provided no seedbed for Jacobite counter-revolution. On the contrary, Ireland remained secure and relatively trouble-free so far as England was concerned well into the second half of the eighteenth century (see Chs. 7 and 14 below). No closer constitutional relationship was deemed desirable or necessary, so long as Poyning's Law continued as it had done since the late fifteenth century to require English approval of all legislation presented to the Irish Parliament, while surplus Irish manpower was readily available for English military purposes, and Irish exports were effectively excluded from English markets.[16]

[15] B. P. Levack, *The Formation of the British State: England, Scotland, and the Union, 1603–1707* (1987); P. W. J. Riley, *The Union of England and Scotland* (1978).

[16] D. W. Hayton, 'The Williamite revolution in Ireland, 1688–91', in Israel, *Anglo-Dutch Moment.*

Yet dominance of the British Isles was at most a necessary rather than a sufficient condition for England's emergence from peripheral isolation to rival French military pre-eminence in Europe. While William III's bilateral negotiations with Louis XIV between 1698 and 1700 on the dispersal or partition of the Spanish empire might seem to symbolize that transformation, matters were clouded by the nationality and personal role of the architect of the Grand Alliance, and the somewhat inconclusive outcome of the Nine Years War. The issue was put beyond doubt in the subsequent War of the Spanish Succession, both by Marlborough's battlefield and diplomatic triumphs, and the scale of British gains at the peace of Utrecht (1713–14). Besides finally accepting the Protestant Hanoverian succession and repudiating the Stuart Pretender, Louis XIV renounced any French claim to the throne of Spain and gave up to Britain the Caribbean island of St Kitts, together with Hudson's Bay, Newfoundland, and Nova Scotia in North America. In a separate treaty Spain ceded Mediterranean toeholds on Gibraltar and Minorca which had already proved of immense strategic importance to Britain, as well as invaluable rights of commercial access to the Spanish colonies of South America.

In recent years historians have become increasingly interested in the causes and consequences of England's move from the sidelines to became a major international presence after 1688. Obviously the differing capacities and priorities of individual statesmen and military leaders were of crucial importance. But why were the enormous resources of men, money, and ships deployed against the French by Marlborough and William not available to their predecessors? Much of the answer doubtless lies in the changed relationship of Crown and Parliament in post-revolutionary England, and the fact that both this and the Protestant religion would have been imperilled by a French victory. The continued economic and especially mercantile growth of the later seventeenth and early eighteenth centuries (further discussed in the next chapter), also encouraged—and enabled— the extension of British military and naval might against burgeoning French commerce and colonialism. Yet the maritime and trading pre-eminence of the seventeenth-century Netherlands was translated into stagnation and decline, not geopolitical hegemony, during the eighteenth century. How was Britain able to move in the opposite direction?

One possible explanation lies in the growth of what has been termed 'the fiscal-military state'. Historians have traditionally depicted eighteenth-century England as relatively undergoverned and lightly taxed, at least by contrast to the absolutist, bureaucratic, and centralized monarchies of Continental Europe. However, the hitherto unimaginable scale upon which British military and naval forces were deployed from 1689 onwards arguably demanded a new and much more powerful state apparatus, seemingly different only in degree, not kind, from its European counterparts.[17]

[17] Brewer, *Sinews of Power* (1989), 250; id., 'The eighteenth-century British state: contexts and issues', in L. Stone (ed.), *An Imperial State at War: Britain from 1689 to 1815* (1994), 61–5.

It has been too easy for all but specialists to overlook these complex and interlocking administrative, financial, and military developments in post-revolutionary Britain. Even so, a word of caution may be in order. The scale and effectiveness of government activities are easily exaggerated, not least because they tend to be comparatively well documented in extensive official archives. We should not forget that the armies of William III and Marlborough were still recruited, clothed, and armed at the expense of their regimental officers (who in turn had bought their commissions), and provisioned in the field by private contractors. As noted above, the state's servants were anything but uniformly competent in the discharge of their duties; near-disasters like the great recoinage crisis of 1696–7, when an ambitious attempt to improve the quality of circulating currency nearly caused both the Bank of England and arrangements for feeding the British army in Flanders to collapse, may also serve to remind us that the post-revolutionary financial world was not simply the modern City of London minus computers. Nor did the fiscal-military state exist merely as an end in itself. Not least among the interests and individuals whom it served were those businessmen who generated the trade surplus which both enabled and required England to project its forces across the seas.

6

TRADE AND THE TOWNS

Commercial Revolution

The year 1688 is less obviously an economic than a constitutional and political turning point. By establishing parliamentary sovereignty and the rule of law, the Revolution gave property owners a degree of security *vis-à-vis* the state which may well have been a desirable or even necessary precondition for further economic development over the medium to long term, including the financial innovations discussed in the last chapter. Nevertheless, the events of 1688–9 plainly had less immediate and obvious impact on the economy than on, say, Crown–Parliament relations.

This distinction might seem particularly clear in the case of the 'commercial revolution', since the great expansion of English overseas trade is usually thought to have begun around the mid-seventeenth century and continued into the 1770s and beyond. Of course chronological precision in such matters is difficult, if not impossible. Some contemporaries attributed the first 'enlarging of our commerce and the improvement of navigation' to Elizabeth I's active encouragement of maritime trade during the second half of the sixteenth century.[1] Bolingbroke, who shared this view, also discerned a 'new vigour' in matters commercial after 1660, while at the same time identifying 'new difficulties' in the form of Dutch and French competition, together with 'depredations abroad and ... taxes at home, during the course of two great wars' after 1688.[2]

Yet 1689 did see one real watershed in the history of English overseas trade, when 'for the better encouragement of the manufacture as well as the growth of wool' Parliament voted by a narrow margin to end the Merchant Adventurers' traditional monopoly of exporting woollen cloth to Europe.[3] This emasculation of the oldest surviving chartered trading company marked the end of a formative era. English overseas commerce had once been largely conducted by members of self-governing merchant guilds, who paid the Crown for exclusive trading rights in specific commodities and markets. But these companies were increasingly felt to be both redundant and restrictive, even before the Navigation Acts of 1651 and 1660 established—at least in theory—a closed

---

[1] J. Child, *The Great Honour and Advantage of the East-India Trade to the Kingdom, Asserted* (1697), 6.

[2] J. St John, Viscount Bolingbroke, *The Idea of A Patriot King* (1749), in *Works*, ed. D. Mallett (1754), iii. 105.

[3] 1 W. & M., c. 32, cl. 12, in *Statutes of the Realm* (1821), vii.

system of national monopoly or protection of trade between England, her colonies, and Europe. Only the East India, Hudson's Bay, and Levant companies, each involved in 'distant and dangerous' trades to Asia, Canada, and the Eastern Mediterranean, requiring expensive convoys of heavily armed ships and fortified trading posts, survived into the eighteenth century.

The decline of the trading companies from economic tigers to London dining clubs, although effectively achieved by political means, also mirrored the remarkable growth and diversification of English overseas commerce between the late sixteenth and the early eighteenth centuries. While textile exports to Europe remained the mainstay of English trade over this entire period, the lighter, coloured and patterned 'new draperies' were sold not only in the traditional commercial centres of Flanders and north-west Europe, but increasingly to Spain, Portugal, Italy, and other Mediterranean markets. The most rapidly growing branches of English trade involved still more distant markets and sources of supply, in the Americas, the East Indies, and Africa. These oceanic trades now supplied English and European consumers with extra-European luxury commodities, including tobacco, sugar, spices, and Chinese and Indian textiles (calicoes, chintzes, and silks), returning to the New World manufactured goods, provisions, and human capital, in the shape of indentured white servants and transported convicts from Britain, and black slaves from Africa. In 1700 London still dominated the nation's overseas trade, handling an estimated 70–80 per cent of all English exports and imports. But the rise of an Atlantic rim economy was already benefiting the westward-facing 'outports' of Bristol, Liverpool, Whitehaven and Glasgow, few of whose merchants belonged to the London-based trading companies.

Much scholarly energy and ingenuity has been devoted to reconstructing overseas trade statistics for the later seventeenth century from the surviving customs records. This is a complex and continuing task. Since pre-1696 figures are available for London alone, the contribution of trade through the outports before that date can only be estimated. Cargoes entering and clearing ports were not always inspected, their valuation was somewhat hit-and-miss, and obviously excluded smuggled goods (even if this last omission may not have mattered much until the level of duties, especially for French wines and spirits, rose sharply with the onset of war in 1689). The records also take no account of 'invisible' earnings and payments (for example, from marine carriage and insurance, tourism, and movements of bullion, the latter of crucial importance to the East Indies merchants). British involvement in the 'country' trades of Asia (between China and India, for example) is ignored, likewise the sale in the New World and the Mediterranean of fish caught off Newfoundland by English fishermen. The most lucrative example of a 'triangular' trade involved English ships sailing first to the Guinea coast of Africa with a cargo of cloth, ironware, spirits, and trinkets to exchange for slaves, who were then transported across the Atlantic (the 'middle passage', on which the death rate ran around 23 per cent in the 1680s). Those who survived were sold in the West Indies, and North America, whence the merchants finally sailed home with cargoes of sugar, molasses, rum, tobacco, and naval stores, largely destined for re-export to Europe. John Cary (*fl.* 1687–1720), a Bristol West-India merchant, enthused that 'the trade to Africa, whereby the planters are supplied with negroes for their use and service' not only increased the colonies' value to the mother country, but was itself 'all profit … indeed the best traffic the kingdom hath'.[4] Such stunningly amoral attitudes provoked, as yet, virtually no dissent or protest.

The 'increase of shipping' which the preamble to the Navigation Act proclaimed as its chief purpose provides an indirect measure of the expansion of overseas trade after 1660. The tonnage of English-owned merchant ships clearing English ports nearly doubled (from *c.*125,000 to some 200,000 tons) between the 1630s and the 1660s, increasing again to around 340,000 tons on the eve of the Revolution, before falling slightly (with privateering and other losses in the Nine Years War) to about 325,000 tons at the beginning of the eighteenth century. Yet even then the English merchant fleet was still perhaps only half the size of the Dutch, with a sizeable proportion of its tonnage actually built in the Netherlands, reflecting the superiority of Dutch shipwrights and shipyards. Indeed Dutch primacy in Europe's seaborne trade was maintained until the 1740s, although by then Britain had clearly surpassed Holland as the leading global trading power.

Later in the century Adam Smith (1723–90), whose *Wealth of Nations* (1776) effectively founded the modern discipline of economics, launched a comprehensive attack upon what he called the 'mercantile system' or national trading monopoly created by the Navigation Acts. According to Smith, the whole complex network of commercial protection had done little more than enrich British merchants (who in any case inevitably enjoyed a near-monopoly of trade with Britain's colonies) at the expense of British consumers and manufacturers. Like his modern intellectual descendants, Smith believed in the efficiency and equity of free market forces, neither constricted nor distorted by government action. Yet while the two decades of French wars which followed James II's deposition did bring huge shipping losses and massive commercial dislocation, even more severe short-term difficulties were experienced by England's main trading rivals, the Dutch and French. Indeed the immediate impact of war on British commerce and manufacturing was by no means wholly negative: for instance, the huge expansion in the numbers of men under arms throughout Europe created unprecedented opportunities to export English cloth for uniforms, especially when continuing military campaigns in the Netherlands and Germany severely disrupted textile production from England's traditional industrial competitors. In the longer term, the Utrecht peace settlement

[4] J. Cary, *An Essay towards Regulating the Trade, and Employing the Poor of this Kingdom* (1719), 52–3.

confirmed British access to important new markets and sources of raw materials, notably in Portugal and Spain (and their South American colonies), as well as much of French North America.

Merchant pressure groups exercised greater influence on government policy after 1688, when annual parliamentary sittings of several months became the norm. True, the merchants did not speak with a single voice, while the policy makers and politicians they lobbied were as much concerned with the power and prestige of the state as the profits of overseas traders. Yet they shared a common understanding that the volume of world trade was more or less finite; in this (as they saw it) zero-sum game, a larger share for any one country could only be gained at the expense of its competitors. Given that the heart of international commerce in the later seventeenth and early eighteenth centuries was indeed armed aggression, not the supposedly level playing field beloved of modern economic rationalists, the appeal of this belief—however wrong-headed it may now seem—is easy to understand.

Middling Orders

Overseas and inland trade expanded together during the commercial revolution. Distributing an ever-growing variety and volume of imported goods from the ports where they were landed to consumers throughout the country required an intricate network of carriers, dealers, pedlars, shipowners, and shopkeepers. Besides linking provincial urban centres, domestic trade was boosted by the continued expansion of London's population, manufacturing activity, and wealth. Internal commercial activity cannot be directly measured. Nevertheless, it is significant that dredging and other works doubled the length of navigable inland waterways during the second half of the seventeenth century, especially as the carriage of goods by river or sea was normally much cheaper and little slower than by land. Regularly scheduled road carrying services between London and the provinces also increased by at least 25 per cent between 1681 and 1705, despite the notorious disrepair of the highways, generally and not implausibly believed to be 'little, if at all, the better' than in Roman times.[5]

A relative lack of glamour, as well as problems of evidence, help explain why domestic trade has attracted less attention from historians than foreign commerce, despite its far larger value and volume. The gulf between that 'sober peaceable man' Ralph Guest of Myddle, Shropshire, whose 'employment was buying corn in one market town, and selling it in another' and great London tycoons like Sir Gilbert Heathcote (1651?–1733) and Sir Dudley North

---

[5] D. Gerhould, 'The growth of the London carrying trade, 1681–1838', *EcHR* 41 (1988), modifying J. A. Chartres, *Internal Trade in England, 1500–1700* (1977); N. Grew, 'The Meanes of a most Ample Encrease of the Wealth and Strength of England In a few Years' (*c*.1708): Huntington Library, Ms. HN 1264.

(1641–91), was not simply a matter of title and wealth.[6] Maritime trading, generally in armed ships, often to distant and inhospitable lands, risking attack from pirates and privateers as well as the natural hazards of the sea, still demanded adventurous and hardy spirits. Those who survived the voyages and residence overseas which constituted the major part of their apprenticeship were marked out by the experience. The 'mere merchant', engaged exclusively in foreign, wholesale trade, inevitably enjoyed a certain charisma denied to the stay-at-home artisan, manufacturer, or retail shopkeeper. Whereas women still occasionally gained craft apprenticeships and quite frequently carried on their husband's business or shop after his death, international commerce seems to have remained a wholly masculine preserve.[7]

In the mid-1690s Gregory King postulated two categories of 'merchants and traders by sea', the smaller and more prosperous consisting of 2,000 men enjoying annual incomes of around £400, while another 8,000 earned a mere £200 each.[8] Although both sets of (suspiciously rounded) numbers are probably underestimates, they warn us against generalizing from the four-figure incomes of London's wealthiest merchants (men 'greater and richer, and more powerful', according to the expansive Daniel Defoe 'than some sovereign princes'). Most traders who accumulated significant capital sums over their careers probably depended more on thrift than spectacular trading profits, and boosted their net worth by prudent dabbling in company stocks and government securities, insurance, shipping, and private moneylending. Maritime trade was not necessarily more lucrative than its inland equivalent, nor was the wholesaler clearly differentiated from the retailer, or 'such as carry on foreign correspondences' from the domestic trader. The Lancaster shopkeeper William Stout, a yeoman's son who set up as grocer, ironmonger, and tobacconist in 1688, averaged a clear annual profit of £100 over his first nine years in business; he then sold his shop to make a financially disastrous venture into foreign trade and shipowning, before returning to a mixed retail and wholesale business, combined with investments in occasional overseas voyages. Defoe also noted that 'the shopkeeper is sometimes a merchant adventurer, whether he will or not, and some of his business runs into sea-adventures, as in the salt trade … and again in the coal trade, from Whitehaven in Cumberland to Ireland'.[9]

[6] R. Gough, *The History of Myddle*, ed. D. Hey (1981), 183; R. Grassby, *The English Gentleman in Trade: The Life and Works of Dudley North, 1641–1691* (1994).

[7] Between 1711 and 1715, of fifty-three women creditors suing London bankrupts, the only two accorded the occupational label 'merchant' had male partners: P. Earle, *Making of the English Middle Class* (1989), 168.

[8] J. P. Cooper and J. Thirsk (eds.), *Seventeenth-Century Economic Documents* (1972), 780–1.

[9] Earle, *Making of the English Middle Class*, 34–51; R. Grassby, 'The rate of profit in seventeenth-century England', *EHR* 84 (1969); D. Defoe, *The Complete English Tradesman* (1726), ed. N. Mander (1987), 5, 7–8, ch. 22 ('Of the Dignity of Trade in England more than in Other Countries').

From the dizzy heights of London's plutocratic patriciate, down to the provincial obscurity of William Stout and his like, the expansion of mercantile numbers, prosperity and self-assurance during the later seventeenth and early eighteenth centuries closely matched the growth of trade itself. It was claimed —somewhat optimistically—in 1703 that, while trade 'formerly rendered a gentleman ignoble, now an ignoble person makes himself by merchandizing as good as a gentleman'. Shading off at the top into the landed gentry, whence many younger sons were recruited as apprentices, and in their lower ranks rubbing shoulders with artisans and petty shopkeepers, merchants albeit self-employed, worked for their livings, and this placed them firmly among the middle, or middling, sort. So did a common mode of occupational socialization and training by apprenticeship, the possession of a modicum of capital, and the urban associations which they shared with most members of the professions, old and new. The contemporary reality of this linkage is suggested by the 1714 characterization of clergy, lawyers, and merchants as 'three very great interests', contributing respectively 'unity', 'severity', and 'prosperity' to the political order.[10]

Against this positive assessment, professional men and, to a lesser extent, merchants, were frequently attacked as avaricious, dishonest, self-interested, and unproductive social parasites. Such complaints, hardly novel in themselves, were exacerbated by the strains of war and the land tax. The Tory-dominated Parliament of 1702 sought to spread the latter burden more widely by imposing a comparable levy of four shillings in the pound on the annual gains 'by their practices, or professions' of common and civil lawyers, physicians, surgeons, apothecaries, 'preachers and teachers in separate congregations [i.e. Dissenting ministers]; all brokers to merchants and all factors, and ... persons exercising any other profession whatsoever'.[11] As this heterogeneous catalogue suggests, 'profession' was an even vaguer term than 'merchant'. Broadly defined, it meant any job or occupation whatsoever. But the word was also used in a narrower sense, to denote callings which claimed superior dignity and worth to 'mechanical' or 'servile' trades, usually on the grounds that they demanded the exercise of mental rather than manual skills.

It was in this sense that the influential new periodical *The Spectator*, launched in 1711 by Addison and Richard Steele (1672–1729), a fellow-Whig who had previously founded the short-lived *Tatler* (1709–11), referred to 'the three great professions of divinity, law, and physic' as grossly overcrowded, thanks to over-ambitious parents, 'who will not rather choose to place their sons in a way of life where an honest industry cannot but thrive'—that is, in trade. 'How many men', demanded *The Spectator*, 'are country curates, that might have made themselves aldermen of London, by a right improvement of

---

[10] G. Miège, *New State of England under our Sovereign Queen Anne* (1703), quoted Earle, *English Middle Class*, 9; Anon., *Titles of Honour* (1714), 298.

[11] 1 Anne, c. 6, cl. 6, in *Statutes of the Realm*, viii. 10.

a smaller sum of money than what is usually laid out upon a learned educa-tion?'[12] Alongside the ballooning of such traditional educated callings, the later seventeenth and early eighteenth centuries saw the emergence of a host of nascent or would-be professional occupations, including those of actuary, banker, stockbroker and financier, engineer, estate steward, landscape gar-dener, musician, surveyor, and teacher, together with a very much expanded military 'profession of arms' and an enlarged body of civil, or public servants. Altogether, it has been claimed, in the half-century after 1680 the number of permanent jobs in the professions increased by around 70 per cent.[13]

In a more complex and prosperous economy, the growth of towns and the impact of war helped swell the numbers of professional persons, and the in-creased opportunities for individual advancement which the professions pro-vided may well have contributed in the long term to the relatively tranquil social equilibrium of Hanoverian England. More immediately, however, the career frustrations of the lower clergy, as also of the barristers, who encoun-tered a sharp decline in the volume of Westminster Hall litigation after 1680, added fuel to the flames of party and sectarian strife, and to the bitterness of confrontation between landed and moneyed interests between 1689 and 1714. The enlargement of the professional sector also tended to intensify those cul-tural, economic, and social divisions which increasingly distanced both the aristocratic landed elite and the genteel middling sort from the mass of their inferiors.

Urbanity: London and the Provinces

The fishermen and sailors who captured James II at Faversham on 11 December 1688 were prepared to release him 'if the City of London was will-ing', while the peers who sought to fill the vacuum left by James's flight ('for the preservation of the Kingdom and this great City') first met at the Guildhall with the city's governors to seek their prior approval.[14] The prominence of London's rulers on the national stage in 1688–9 reflected the capital's predom-inance, whether in cultural, demographic, economic, or political terms, in rela-tion to the country at large.

During the two centuries after 1500, the proportion of England's population living in London increased from around one person in fifty to one in ten or eleven. Over sixteen times bigger than the next most populous place in England (Norwich, with a mere 30,000 inhabitants), by 1700 London was a metropolis of some half a million people. Even Paris was no larger, although France's total landed area and population were both well over four times those of England. An equally telling contemporary comparison is conveyed by the full title of a

---

12 *Spectator*, no. 2, Friday 2 Mar. 1711.
13 G. Holmes, *Augustan England: Professions, State and Society, 1680–1730* (1982), 16.
14 R. Beddard, *A Kingdom without a King* (1988), 92–3, 195.

work first published in 1708: *Old Rome and London Compared, The First in its full Glory, and the Last in its Present State. By which it plainly Appears ... that* LONDON ... *exceeds it much in its Extent, Populousness and many other Advantages.*

London's rate of growth seems even more impressive when we consider that England's population as a whole increased by only about a quarter during the seventeenth century, whereas the capital itself notched up nearly a threefold expansion. Further, the notoriously unhealthy conditions and consequent savage mortality rates of metropolitan life meant that the ratio of births to deaths within London was too low even to sustain a stable population level. Exceptionally high levels of migration were required to compensate for the shortfall of baptisms over burials, and then to generate positive demographic growth. Late seventeenth-century London may have been absorbing around half the natural increase in the nation's population, besides substantial inflows of migrants from Ireland, Scotland, Holland, France, Germany, and even further afield. Not all who came to London settled there permanently; the substantial floating population of short-term visitors on business and pleasure, and the constant outward flow of emigrants makes it likely that at least one in six English adults had sampled metropolitan life.[15]

The intrepid traveller Celia Fiennes (1662–1741) breathlessly characterized her own home town at the beginning of Queen Anne's reign as 'London joined with Westminster, which are two great cities but now with building so joined it makes up but one vast building with all its suburbs'.[16] Thanks to aristocratic proprietors like the fourth earl of Southampton (1606–67) and entrepreneurial speculators like Dr Nicholas Barbon (d. 1698), development north of the Strand over the previous century had created a solid built-up area stretching as far as the village of Islington and the Oxford or Tyburn road bordering the newly fashionable West End estates and squares of Mayfair and St James's. South of the river the suburban parishes of Southwark were booming; dwellings and warehouses stretched almost without break from Vauxhall to Rotherhithe, and even more thickly on the opposite bank, from the Tower east through the crowded dockland suburbs of Wapping and beyond. The old medieval walled city, its timber and lath largely reconstructed in brick and stone after the Great Fire of 1666, remained a thriving financial, mercantile, retail, and manufacturing centre, albeit with a declining residential population. Seemly architectural settings for Anglican devotions were provided by rebuilding more than fifty parish churches in the Italianate style, under the supervision of the multi-talented Sir Christopher Wren (1632–1723); their spires and steeples punctuated the city's skyline, dominated by the dome of Wren's monumental St Paul's Cathedral.

---

[15] E. A. Wrigley, 'London's importance in changing English society and economy, 1650–1750', *P&P* 37 (1967).

[16] C. Morris (ed.), *The Illustrated Journeys of Celia Fiennes, 1685–c.1712* (1982), 222.

Contradicting long-held fears that London's prodigious growth must create an unmanageable urban chaos and impoverish the rest of England, the Tory Charles Davenant noted cautiously in 1695 that 'some people, who have thought much upon the subject, are inclined to believe that the growth of that city is advantageous to the nation'. Warming to his theme, Davenant asserted that 'not an acre of land in the country, be it never so distant ... is not in some degree bettered by the growth, trade, and riches' of London.[17] The capital's apparently insatiable appetite for fuel, labour, provisions, and raw materials was felt well beyond the Home Counties. From as far away as Wales, the North Country and the Scottish Highlands teams of drovers brought livestock to the Smithfield meat market, while by the late seventeenth century Northumberland's Tyneside collieries were shipping well over 600,000 tons of 'sea-coals' to London every year, for both domestic and industrial use. Besides encouraging more specialized and efficient production, London's demand stimulated employment in transport and other service industries, as well as boosting international trade—fully three-quarters of which passed through the port of London, to the considerable benefit of London's merchants, not to mention the dockers, lightermen, shipwrights, and associated workers who handled the vessels and their cargoes. On the other hand, and contrary to Davenant's optimism, market dominance on this scale could and did work against the interests of provincial suppliers, as well as, more obviously, the outport merchants.

While London's population was big, diverse, and rich enough to support an unparalleled concentration of luxury trades and services, London-generated fashions in the arts, building, dress, food, furniture, and leisure activities moulded and quickened consumption patterns across the whole country. Nowhere was this influence more apparent than in the provincial towns. In 1700 there were sixty seven urban centres in England with 2,500 or more inhabitants. Ten times as many could claim the title 'town' on legal or historical grounds, but their populations were often numbered in hundreds rather than thousands; only about thirty leading centres had more than 5,000 residents. Of course even these totals are very small by modern standards. But 'urbanity' depended upon a critical density of buildings, functions, and services, not just numbers of inhabitants. Thus besides provincial capitals like Exeter, Norwich, Shrewsbury, and York, more modest regional centres such as Basingstoke, Petworth, or Doncaster, together with newly fashionable resorts such as Bath, Harrogate, and Tunbridge Wells, offered a distinctively genteel quality of life to increasing numbers of residents and visitors. The century after 1660 saw many provincial townscapes reconstructed along classical lines, after the model of London's post-Fire rebuilding, and the laying out of formal gardens, walks, and residential squares like those of the capital. Fashionable public leisure activities—'assemblies' dedicated to dancing, card-playing and socializing, balls,

---

[17] Cooper and Thirsk, *Seventeenth-Century Economic Documents*, 809–10.

concerts, plays— proliferated, together with circulating libraries, clubs, coffee-houses, and facilities for outdoor sports, in the form of bowling greens and race courses.

These amenities attracted a diverse population in terms of age, class, gender, residence, and wealth, mingling representatives of the landed aristocracy and gentry with merchants, shopkeepers, and professional men, not to mention their wives, sons, and daughters. To this extent the 'urban renaissance' served a positive integrative function, privileging the virtues of polite and sociable behaviour over the claims of birth, rank, or politico-religious zealotry. Yet integration was a socially limited process; incorporating the genteel, perhaps even for some purposes the merely respectable, necessarily implied excluding those members of the populace who were neither.

The behaviour and condition of the urban poor attracted considerable attention from their social betters after 1688. Royal letters and proclamations called upon the clergy to 'preach frequently against those particular sins and vices which are most prevailing in this realm'. In 1691 Queen Mary made a particularly influential public appeal to the Middlesex justices for the enforcement of existing statutes against such offences as drunkenness, gambling, profanity, and Sabbath-breaking. Her strong personal commitment to the goal of moral regeneration encouraged the spread of 'societies for the reformation of manners', which originated in London but might soon be found in almost any city, town, or larger village of the kingdom. The main function of these moral vigilantes was to promote criminal prosecutions against blasphemers, drunkards, gamblers, prostitutes, and other social undesirables. Despite targeting the occasional token upper-class rake, their attention inevitably concentrated upon the labouring and unemployed poor. Meanwhile London and other urban magistrates were increasingly sentencing persons convicted of minor offences to terms of imprisonment with hard labour, rather than imposing the traditional penalties of branding or whipping.[18]

Attempts to establish houses of correction, workhouses, and municipal employment schemes in London, Bristol, and other cities similarly aimed at preserving social order and discouraging wrongdoing, in addition to relieving distress. Not so much breaking the cycle of poverty as reconciling the poor to their lot was the aim of the charity school movement, co-ordinated from 1698 by the London-based Society for Promoting Christian Knowledge (or SPCK). Ten years later more than 3,000 boys and girls were attending charity schools in London and Westminster alone. Yet besides learning to read their Bibles, and the duties of 'modest deference and humble deportment ... towards those whom the Almighty Providence hath placed in a superior station', it was also claimed that 'such as are best capable, are taught to write legibly, and cast

[18] 'Her Late Majesties Gracious letter ... for the Suppressing of Prophaness and debauchery', in *An Account of the Societies for Reformation of Manners in London and Westminster and other parts of the Kingdom* (1699); G. V. Portus, *Caritas Anglicana* (1912).

accounts tolerably, and thereby the better fitted for any future employment or vocation'.[19] An ordered social hierarchy, which also provided opportunities for individual self-betterment, was the ideal and to some considerable extent the reality of town life in early eighteenth-century England.

Economic Concepts and Calculations

Economics did not emerge as a more or less coherent and self-contained intellectual discipline until the last quarter of the eighteenth century. Yet by the 1690s a substantial body of printed pamphlet literature, accumulated over the past five decades, was informing public discussion of such topics as agricultural and industrial productivity, interest rates, money, taxation, and, above all, trade. A number of authors (including the developer Nicholas Barbon, and the merchant Dudley North) moved beyond what had become the standard preoccupation with securing a favourable national balance of foreign trade, or surplus of exports over imports, to explore the role of competition in boosting output and lowering costs, the complex interrelationships between wage rates, price levels and the operation of markets, and the importance of domestic consumption as opposed to overseas commerce. These writers followed the pioneering approach of Thomas Mun in treating economic matters as essentially autonomous, or at least analytically distinct from moral and religious issues. But they went further than Mun in identifying and even acclaiming acquisitive self-interest as the prime determinant of individual economic behaviour: 'The main spur to trade, or rather to industry and ingenuity, is the exorbitant appetites of men, which they will take pains to gratify ... did men content themselves with bare necessities, we should have a poor world,' North enthused.[20]

Aimed primarily at influencing government, Parliament, and to a lesser extent informed public opinion, economic debate was concerned with immediate policy issues. The French wars exacerbated inflationary pressures, especially those on basic foodstuffs (bread and beer) resulting from a series of poor harvests in the 1690s. They also caused considerable dislocation to trade, with some traditional European markets, and more widely, as the result of both official naval operations and privateering (the practice of licensing private ships to attack enemy vessels in return for a share of the booty). Potentially most serious was a balance of payments problem, linked to the growing shortage and effective debasement by 'clipping' of silver coin, which simultaneously threatened to paralyse both the military campaign abroad and economic activity at home. In confronting these and related problems the administration not only received much unsolicited advice from journalists, lobbyists, pamphleteers, and politicians, but initiated consultations with leading academics and

---

[19] R. Moss, *The Providential Division of Men into Rich and Poor* (1708), 16, 22.
[20] D. North, *Discourse upon Trade* (1691), quoted J. O. Appleby, *Economic Thought and Ideology in Seventeenth-Century England* (1978), 169–70.

intellectuals, including the philosopher John Locke, the scientist Isaac Newton (who actually became Master of the Mint in 1699), his Oxford mathematician colleague John Wallis (1616–1703), and the polymath Christopher Wren, as well as merchants and financiers who had published on economic matters, such as Josiah Child and Charles Davenant.

Their input was crucial to the establishment in 1696 of 'His Majesty's Commissioners for promoting the trade of this Kingdom, and for inspecting and improving His Plantations in America and elsewhere', better known subsequently as the Board of Trade, as a specialized administrative committee under the privy council, and to the risky if ultimately successful recoinage operation carried out between 1695 and 1697.[21] Locke's involvement in this complex undertaking reflected his long-standing interest in monetary theory; in 1691 he claimed to have identified certain 'laws of value' which governed economic life, comparable to the physical or natural laws discovered by his friends Newton and Boyle. His exposition of the quantity theory of money, which holds that prices reflect the amount of currency in circulation, was nevertheless overshadowed as an intellectual feat by 'the first full equilibrium analysis in the history of economic theory' which Dudley North published in 1692, depicting the reciprocal relationship between national stocks of gold and silver bullion and circulating coin as a wholly self-governing mechanism, demanding neither involvement nor regulation by the state.[22]

Yet for all their importance in the history of economic thought, these conceptual developments had little impact on contemporary policy. Despite increasingly sophisticated arguments for free trade and an unregulated market economy at the turn of the century, those years also saw the enactment of a comprehensive legislative programme designed to protect English manufacturing and maintain the economic dependence of the colonies. Here indeed originated that 'mercantile system' later denounced by Adam Smith, in a clear victory for anti-French chauvinism, narrow sectional interests (especially the woollen textile industry), and the financial needs of government, over the dictates of advanced economic thought. And while 'the first special statistical department ever created by any Western European state' dates from the appointment of Edward Culliford as Inspector-General of Exports and Imports in 1696, political arithmetic hardly lived up to the high expectations of its founding fathers by becoming an indispensable tool of government after 1688.[23]

Politicians, economic pamphleteers and political arithmeticians all had their own different agendas. True, Robert Harley showed an interest in Gregory

[21] P. Laslett, 'John Locke, the great recoinage, and the origins of the Board of Trade: 1695–1698', in J. W. Yolton (ed.), *John Locke: Problems and Perspectives* (1969).

[22] W. Letwin, *The Origins of Scientific Economics: English Economic Thought, 1660–1716* (1963), 191.

[23] R. Davis, 'The rise of protection in England, 1689–1786', *EcHR* 19 (1966); Appleby, *Economic Thought and Ideology*, ch. 9. G. N. Clark, *Science and Social Welfare in the Age of Newton* (1937), 138.

King's demographic and economic computations, with their obvious potential for raising taxation revenue; accurate actuarial (life expectancy) calculations were also of considerable relevance when much public income depended on the sale of annuities, although less so under Queen Anne, when most government funding came directly from the Bank of England and the great trading companies. But politicians did not command the bureaucratic resources necessary for the comprehensive national population census advocated by the political arithmeticians.

They also recognized that such an exercise would be hugely unpopular, whether from fears of its fiscal consequences or biblically derived 'superstition of numbering the people'.[24] Nor were King and his associates, let alone the more numerous contemporary economic commentators, mere disinterested searchers after objective social-scientific truth. On the contrary, just as merchants and country gentlemen assiduously pushed their own vested interests in print, so King's pessimistic Tory-Country outlook led him to exaggerate the damage wrought by King William's war on the nation's resources, and to urge boosting the population by fiscal incentives for larger families and taxes on the unmarried.

Yet the influence of those who claimed to have found a more systematic and rational approach to economic issues in the post-Revolutionary decades strengthened pre-existing tendencies to distinguish the material from all other aspects of human existence, while questioning or rejecting traditional ethical and religious restraints upon individual acquisitiveness. This outlook found its most notorious contemporary expression in Bernard Mandeville's satirical poem *The Fable of the Bees* (1714 and numerous subsequent editions). According to Mandeville (1670?–1733), a Dutch physician who had emigrated to London in the 1690s, attacks on vice and immorality failed to recognize that national prosperity was crucially dependent upon

> Millions endeavouring to supply
> Each other's Lust and Vanity.

In this sense 'Fraud, Luxury, and Pride' were indeed public virtues, since

> Bare Vertue can't make Nations live
> In Splendour.

—which was, of course, precisely to what the nation, or a large part of it, did increasingly aspire.[25]

---

[24] Cooper and Thirsk, *Seventeenth-Century Economic Documents*, 790–8; C. Brooks, 'Projecting, political arithmetic and the act of 1695', *EHR* 97 (1982). The reference is to King David's disastrous census of the Israelites (1 Chronicles, 21: 1–17).

[25] M. M. Goldsmith, *Private Vices, Public Benefits: Bernard Mandeville's Social and Political Thought* (1985).

PART III

Great Britain
Liberty and Property, 1707–1745

7

THE STATE OF THE UNION

Defoe's England

The British Isles were and are divided not only by St George's Channel and the Irish Sea, but also by long-standing cultural, economic, ethnic, and religious differences. Hence the formal political unity of England, Wales, and Scotland after 1707 hardly obliterated local loyalties, let alone created an immediate sense of British nationhood. But besides constituting perhaps the largest free trade area in the world, the Union was sustained by a common language and Protestant religion, factors conspicuous in their absence from the essentially colonial relationship between Britain and Ireland.

English self-satisfaction blossomed in the early eighteenth century. 'I do not think there is a people more prejudiced in its own favour,' wrote a Swiss visitor in 1727: 'They look on foreigners in general with contempt, and think nothing is as well done elsewhere as in their own country.' Hardly novel, that comforting conviction was strengthened by a sense of 'the many struggles which the people of this nation have had, to rescue their almost oppressed liberties and religion', until (according to a Whiggish writer in 1719) 'we are arrived at such a height of prosperity under the auspicious reign of our present august monarch, that we are become the envy of the neighbouring states ... and the terror of those that are our enemies'.[1] Economic and military success supplied further vindication of England's unique constitutional and political arrangements. The popular catch-cry 'Liberty and Property' encapsulated the belief that 'both foreigners that live here, and natives, have great reason to be thankful to Providence'. These blessings were held to be a distinctive privilege reserved for the English—or, after 1707, the British—peoples:

> Let Gallic Slaves Despotic Power obey;
> Justice and Liberty, in Albion sway.[2]

The odd dissident suggestion that praise of 'our excellent constitution above all others ... is little more than a jingle of words' was effectively drowned out by self-congratulatory rhetoric.[3] So long as an absolutist, Catholic, Stuart

---

[1] *A Foreign View of England in the Reigns of George I and George II: The Letters of Monsieur César de Saussure to his Family*, tr. and ed. M. van Muyden (1902), 177; H. Care, *English Liberties*, ed. W. Nelson (1719), sig. A2.

[2] W. Bulstrode, preface to R. Bulstrode, *Miscellaneous Essays* (1715), p. xxx; Anon., *An Excursory View of the Present State of Men and Things* (1739), 15.

[3] T. Baston, *Observations on Trade and a Public Spirit* (1728, first pub. 1716), 67, 105.

restoration appeared the only realistic alternative, the political and social order stemming from the Revolution settlement was likely to be widely regarded as the lesser of two evils, notwithstanding the satirical attacks of authors such as John Gay (1685–1732) and Jonathan Swift (1667–1745).

For a more positive, indeed almost wholly unqualified endorsement, and overview, of early Hanoverian Britain we need only turn to Daniel Defoe's *A Tour thro' the Whole Island of Great Britain* (1724–7). An exceedingly prolific author, Defoe's diverse publications included what is arguably the first English novel, his enormously successful *Life and strange and surprising Adventures of Robinson Crusoe* (1719). Born in 1660, the son of a London butcher, Daniel attended a dissenting academy and then set up as wholesale merchant, trading all over Europe and to New England. He fought for Monmouth, supported the Revolution, went bankrupt twice, and became an active political journalist during the 1690s, winning enormous acclaim in 1701 with a rollicking send-up of national pretensions to ethnic purity, especially on the part of anti-Williamite Tories:

> These are the Heroes who despise the Dutch
> And rail at new-come Foreigners so much;
> Forgetting they themselves are all deriv'd
> From the most Scoundrel race that ever liv'd …
> A True-born Englishman's a Contradiction,
> In Speech an Irony, in Fact a Fiction.

Henceforth Defoe paid his debts and earned his living as a professional writer, thanks to the publishing boom which followed the end of press censorship in 1695, together with the continued growth of literacy and affluence among his own middling sort. During Anne's reign he also worked as undercover political agent for Robert Harley; trips around the country and to Scotland canvassing public opinion, together with his earlier travels as a merchant, provided an exceptionally wide base of knowledge on which to build what his preface to the *Tour* characterizes as 'a description of the most flourishing and opulent country in the world'.

Unlike most predecessors in this genre, which combined guidebook, gazeteer, road-map, and topographical survey, Defoe was determinedly present-minded. He also stressed the hectic pace of change: 'the improvements that increase, the new buildings erected, the old buildings taken down: new discoveries in metals, mines, minerals; new undertakings in trade; inventions, engines, manufactures … these things open new scenes every day.' So in recounting purportedly personal reactions to what he had encountered on his travels (some of his material came from earlier writers), Defoe generally dwelt more upon contemporary economic and social conditions than antiquities and local legends. And while appreciating the 'beauty, and magnificence' of fine modern houses and gardens along the reaches of the Thames near London, 'which give a kind of character to the island of Great Britain in general', he showed little respect for the unimproved beauties of nature. The Lake District struck him as 'all barren and wild, of no use or advantage either to man or beast', especially since the closure of the copper mines established there in Elizabethan times. Far preferable was the West Riding of Yorkshire, where thanks to a thriving textile industry 'the country appears busy, diligent, and ... infinitely populous'. The rich pastures of the Dorset downs, the orchards of the Vale of Evesham, and Norfolk's mixed farming country also won his approval. But Defoe's greatest enthusiasm was reserved for prosperous manufacturing and trading towns, like 'Great Marlow, noted for its malt and meal market, for corn and paper mills, for its mills for brass ... its thimble-mill and mill for pressing oil from rape and flax seed', or the port of Liverpool, 'one of the wonders of Britain', 'increasing every way in wealth and shipping'.

Defoe depicts England as a land of great regional diversity, and marked economic specialization, especially, but not only, in the provision of food and fuel for London. While conscious of an underlying contrast between 'the whole South of the Trent ... infinitely fuller of great towns, of people, and of trade', and the relatively underdeveloped North, he confidently asserted the certainty, and desirability, of continued material development 'in a nation pushing and improving as we are'. Of course, Defoe's boosterism and high regard for enterprising men of business were hardly shared by all his potential readers. But the evident popularity of the *Tour* (at least seven further editions appeared in the half-century after its first publication) suggests that such attitudes struck a receptive chord with many contemporaries.[4]

Wales

Whereas Scotland is treated as a separate entity in the final three chapters of Defoe's *Tour*, his more cursory account of Wales is incorporated in an earlier description of England's midland and western counties. The difference in treatment was not accidental. Wales had always lacked a national parliament, and indeed any centralized political institutions. Because the Welsh derived their sense of corporate identity from a common language and history (or mythology), rather than allegiance to a Welsh state, their sixteenth-century political incorporation had been a relatively untraumatic experience, especially since the Tudor monarchs could claim Welsh descent. While the English might jeer or sneer at Welsh diet, dress, and speech, on the whole they were perceived as faintly comical cousins rather than dangerously alien foreigners, 'nothing like as treacherous as the Irish or as fanatical as the Scots'.[5]

[4] It is in this sense that Trevelyan claimed Defoe, rather than Swift, as the 'typical man of his age': cf. J. C. D. Clark, *English Society, 1688–1832* (1985), 43–4.
[5] G. A. Williams, *The Welsh in their History* (1982), 189–201; P. J. Jenkins, in *HJ*, 32 (1989), 388.

Defoe refers to Wales as 'dry, barren, and mountainous', and notes the omnipresence of 'tokens of antiquity'. Yet that somewhat negative image is continually qualified; in Brecknock ('or, as the English say, "Breakneckshire"') the mountains furnish 'yearly great herds of black cattle to England'; South Glamorgan 'is a pleasant and agreeable place, and very populous', with the port of Swansea 'a very considerable town for trade', and Neath, 'where the coal trade is also considerable'; even Haverford 'a better town than we expected to find, in this remote angle of Britain; 'tis strong, well built, clean, and populous'. The famous lead mines of Cardigan are revealingly characterized 'as perhaps the richest in England', while north of Denbigh the 'most pleasant, fruitful, populous, and delicious Vale, full of villages and towns ... made us think ourselves in England again'.

In Defoe's eyes, then, Wales was hardly an unproductive wilderness, for all its intimidating mountain ranges. While overlooking some major new developments, like the burgeoning iron industry of South Wales, he also tended to understate the extent to which Welsh standards of living and wealth fell behind their English counterparts. Thus the good quality of Welsh provisions and inns are particularly emphasized, along with the friendliness of the locals: 'Welsh gentlemen are very civil, hospitable and kind; the people very obliging and conversible.' Despite the discreet and tolerated presence of Catholic pilgrims and priests at the pre-Reformation shrine of St Winifred in Denbighshire, Wales was evidently no longer one of the 'dark corners of the land', as it had been characterized by zealous Protestants in the sixteenth century. The country's 400,000 or so inhabitants were still mostly Welsh-speaking, but several generations of evangelical activity, most recently channeled through the SPCK's charity schools, and the distribution of Welsh-language bibles and devotional literature, had propagated the teachings of reformed Christianity through all levels of society. The spread of Protestantism and retreat of Catholicism had important political consequences. Wales was a royalist stronghold during the civil war and Chief Justice Jeffreys by no means the only prominent Welshman among James II's advisers. Yet while semi-secret bands of Jacobite gentry in north and south Wales (the 'Cycle of the White Rose' and 'Society of Sea Serjeants') drank ritual toasts to the Pretender well into the eighteenth century, their members overwhelmingly declined to hazard life, fortune, and religion for the Stuart cause.[6]

Because the mountains impeded internal communications and accentuated regional differences, Wales lacked either a capital or even large towns; instead the northern Welsh counties looked to Chester as their major economic and social centre, while Bristol served a similar function for South Wales. Many Welsh market towns were growing in size and complexity during the later seventeenth and early eighteenth centuries, but these neighbouring English cities proved

[6] P. Monod, *Jacobitism and the English People, 1688–1788* (1989), 295–6; G. H. Jenkins, *The Foundations of Modern Wales* (1987), 308–12.

particularly attractive to the gentry families who had traditionally dominated Welsh politics and society, in the absence of a sizeable landed nobility. Still more gentry flocked to London, on business, pleasure, or both, together with sizeable contingents of cattle drovers, milkmaids, merchants, pedlars, law students, and domestic servants. By the early eighteenth century at least fourteen London coffee-houses were catering for predominantly Welsh clienteles, including both visitors and settled immigrants like Thomas Jones (d. 1731), the barrister-founder of the 'Honourable and Loyal Society of Ancient Britons', a body of pro-Hanoverian London-based Welshmen who met for an annual sermon and dinner under the patronage of the Prince of Wales.[7]

But if the Welsh still boasted descent from the original inhabitants of the British Isles, the indigenous Celtic culture and language of Wales were in retreat, especially among the increasingly Anglicized gentry. The impending displacement of a whole customary way of life was symbolized by the general substitution of English for Welsh baptismal names, and the gradual disappearance of the bards who had once played a key role in transmitting the traditional oral culture. Scholars such as the Oxford-based polymath Edward Lhuyd (1660–1709) and the historian Henry Rowlands (1655–1723) accordingly sought to retrieve 'almost lost accounts and antiquities ... out of the deep obscurities of time', and to record popular customs and folklore. Their efforts foreshadowed a remarkable revival of interest in Welsh history, language, literature, and music later in the century. Meanwhile the reception of metropolitan attitudes and values continued apace, a process which tended to widen the gap between the culture of the elite and that of the population at large, while simultaneously integrating Wales ever more closely with England, and Great Britain.[8]

Scotland

Having been ruled by an absentee monarch since 1603, Scotland lost its Parliament in 1707, and its privy council the following year. In the highly centralized political structure of Great Britain which the Union brought into being, North Britain was a decidedly junior partner, her subordinate status largely a function of demographic and economic weakness.

Calculations based on a hearth tax levied in 1691 suggest that Scotland's total population may then have reached around 1.25 m., or about a quarter that of England and Wales combined. The six devastating 'dear years' of repeated harvest failure from 1695 saw numbers shrink by a further 10–15 per cent, due to famine, malnutrition, and starvation on a scale long unknown in England. When Scottish demographic growth did resume, the rate of increase up to the

[7] H. Rowlands, *Mona Antiqua Restuarata* (1766, first pub. 1723), 1; R. T. Jenkins and H. M. Rammage, *A History of the Honourable Society of Cymmrodorion* (1951), 6–14.

[8] P. Morgan, 'From a death to a view: the hunt for the Welsh past in the Romantic period', in E. J. Hobsbawm and T. Ranger (eds.), *The Invention of Tradition* (1983).

middle of the eighteenth century was comparable to that experienced in England. Yet the quota of forty-five Scottish MPs allocated by the Treaty of Union was well below one-tenth of the grand total of 558 members returned to Westminster after 1707 (and only sixteen 'representative' Scots peers, elected by their fellow nobles, had seats in the the Lords). But even if reliable population estimates had been available to contemporaries, because the franchise and representation in both countries were firmly based on adult male property-holders, rather than mere numbers, the Scots could hardly have argued for 20–25 per cent of the seats in the House of Commons. Indeed, considering both Scotland's relative poverty, and ingrained English contempt for 'beggarly Scots', the final allocation was not ungenerous.

On a brief day-trip from Carlisle into Dumfriesshire in 1698, Celia Fiennes encountered 'very poor people' living in dirty and primitive dwellings without chimneys, 'just like the booths at a fair'; finding their insanitary habits and conspicuous 'sloth' equally repugnant, she chose to bring some smoked fish back to England for dinner, rather than endure the dubious hospitality of a Scottish landlady.[9] Defoe, who probably knew the country as well as any Englishman of his time, having played a part in securing passage of the Treaty through the Edinburgh Parliament in 1706–7, claimed to provide a balanced account 'of Scotland in the present state of it, and as it really is'. His attitude is essentially patronizing rather than contemptuous, emphasizing Scottish potential to attain English standards of economic performance, if only 'they had the same methods of improvement, and the Scots were as good husbandmen as the English'.

Defoe described a largely agricultural society, where communal farming of open fields and the lack of enclosed pasture for cattle severely restricted productivity. There was little industry (apart from the manufacture of linen and some woollen cloth), and not much trade, except at Dumfries, Dundee, and Glasgow, 'a city of business', whose merchants successfully exploited their recently gained access to England's American colonies. Otherwise the Union's immediate economic impact was to lure the nobility and gentry from their estates to London, and to swamp Scottish markets with English manufactured imports. However, with characteristic optimism Defoe insisted that the long-term prospects were bright, especially if the landed proprietors recognized their responsibilities by 'erecting manufactures, employing the poor, and propagating the trade at home'. Even the Highlands might one day enjoy 'a visible prosperity'; Defoe tentatively suggested that their inhabitants had recently become somewhat 'less wild and barbarous', despite the continued survival of the clans under their chieftains and lairds.

In some respects Defoe overstated Scotland's economic and social backwardness. Even if the benefits of Union took time to show themselves, recent

---

[9] C. Morris (ed.), *The Illustrated Journeys of Celia Fiennes, 1685–c.1712* (1982), 173–4.

research highlights a widespread commitment to agricultural improvement in the later seventeenth century, together with new-found vitality among Scottish merchants, who were 'entering the Atlantic trade, fructifying enterprise and stimulating social mobility within Scotland itself'.[10] Yet Defoe was undoubtedly better disposed to think well of the Scots than most of his fellow countrymen. When a young gentleman announced 'that he hated the name and sight of a Scotchman, because it was the genius and nature of that nation to be tricking cheating rogues', one of his companions thought him 'too general in his invectives' but still agreed that 'they have more generally a disposition to play the knave than the English'.[11] The hostility was mutual; Defoe and his companions found it politic to pretend that they were French when travelling on the Gaelic-speaking north-west coast.

Although the Reformation had inevitably weakened traditional Franco-Scottish ties, the Presbyterian kirk did not dominate the entire country. It was precisely in the Highlands and north-east, where Catholicism and the Episcopal Church remained strong, that the French-backed Jacobite cause exercised its strongest appeal. Among Protestant states the Netherlands, rather than England, was arguably the major external cultural influence on Scotland for several decades before and after 1707. Beside copious imports of printed books, maps, and newspapers, the Dutch provided training in medicine and Roman law to large contingents of Scottish students, while the liberal theology of the great Hugo Grotius (1583–1645) remained influential among Scots Calvinists well into the eighteenth century.

So continuing cultural differences as well as ancient ethnic enmities fuelled Anglo-Scottish antagonism and misunderstanding. North of the Border resentment naturally focused on the Union itself, as a shameful betrayal—or corrupt sale—of national independence ('ane end to ane old song'), compounded by subsequent snubs and humiliations at the hands of English politicians. Their high-handed refusal in 1711 to admit Scots peers who also held British titles to the House of Lords, and the Toleration Act of 1712, which restored lay patronage of ecclesiastical livings and legalized the position of the Episcopalian clergy, much to the displeasure of the Presbyterian majority, aroused particular resentment. Yet as this last instance emphasizes, Scotland was anything but a united society speaking with a single voice. Jacobite efforts to overthrow both the Union and the Hanoverian Succession in 1708, 1715, 1719, and 1745 failed for many reasons, but above all because hostility towards rule from London did not outweigh the divisions separating Scottish Catholics, Episcopalians, and Presbyterians, and the reciprocal mistrust between Highlander and Lowlander.

---

[10] E. Richards, 'Scotland and the uses of the Atlantic Empire', in B. Bailyn and P. Morgan (eds.), *Strangers within the Realm* (1991), 77–9.

[11] *The Diary of Dudley Ryder, 1715–1716*, ed. W. Matthews (1939), 227.

In point of fact London soon found Scots affairs and personalities sufficiently impenetrable to require the attention of a 'manager' or 'minister' in the shape of Archibald Campbell, earl of Islay and later third duke of Argyll (1682–1761), who from 1725 until his death furthered both government policy in Scotland and Scottish interests with the English administration. Islay's long and powerful career provides one example of the kind of opportunities which the Union created for ambitious Scots, some of whom exercised their talents in the London-based professions, and a great many more further afield, in the army and the colonies. Apart from thus creating vested interests in its own perpetuation, the Union inevitably facilitated greater English cultural penetration of Scotland. Thus reprinted copies of English weekly journals like the *Spectator* brought the cult of civility and the language and mores of metropolitan society to an increasingly Anglicized and urbanized Scottish ruling élite. Yet the cultural traffic was never solely one-way. Whereas Scots students were advised in 1715 that some knowledge of English law was 'very requisite to a compleat lawyer, in our united state', the 1721 edition of a standard English legal dictionary included various terms from Scots law 'necessarily introduced into the state-law of Great Britain' since 1707, 'being thereby in a manner naturaliz'd, and adopted into our mother tongue'. Thus even in the sensitive area of legal institutions, which were formally excluded from the Treaty of Union, a process of interaction and partial assimilation had evidently begun.[12]

Ireland

While Ireland retained both a national Parliament and a substantial demographic lead over Scotland throughout the eighteenth century, it also remained much the more dependent of the two societies. The kingdom's subordinate status, springing from both ancient and recent history, was underlined by England's lack of response to requests from the Irish Parliament before and after 1707 for a formal act of union or incorporation. Any possible doubts as to the nature of the relationship were settled by the passage in 1720 of a Declaratory Act, 'for the better securing the dependency of the kingdom of Ireland upon the crown of Great Britain'. This statute, the ill-famed '6th of George I', affirmed both the authority of the Westminster Parliament to legislate for Ireland, and the incapacity of the Irish House of Lords to supersede its English counterpart as a final court of legal appeal for Ireland.[13]

The Declaratory Act was a warning shot directed at the effective political nation of early eighteenth-century Ireland, that minority of Anglicans (or more strictly, adherents of 'the Church of Ireland as by law established'), later known as the (Protestant) 'ascendancy'. Reliable statistics are lacking, but in

[12] *Law, Religion and Education Considered* (Edinburgh, 1715), 96; *Les Termes De La Ley* (London, 1721), preface.
[13] *EHD, 1714–1783*, 683.

the 1730s the dispossessed and disenfranchised Catholics may have comprised around three-quarters of the total population. Presbyterians, many of Scottish origin, and a few other Protestant Dissenters (notably Huguenots and Quakers) made up perhaps a further 10 per cent, with their main strength in the northern province of Ulster. The minority remnant of Anglo-Irish 'Church' nobility, gentry, clergy, and lawyers who alone could exercise public office or sit in Parliament held a somewhat equivocal view of their own identity. To the Catholic native Irish and the Presbyterian Irish-Scots they presented themselves as Englishmen abroad, but in their dealings with the government in London, and its intermittently resident representative, the Lord-Lieutenant, as 'West British' or Irish patriots.[14]

Housed in resplendent new premises on Dublin's College Green from 1739 onwards, the Irish Parliament showed similar ambivalence in its roles as the ascendancy's forum and mouthpiece. Aping Westminister legislative procedures and party rhetoric, its members were not always easily managed by the administration housed in Dublin Castle. They proved particularly troublesome in the disputes which led to the Declaratory Act, and subsequent protests over 'Wood's halfpence', the copper coins minted for circulation in Ireland by an English entrepreneur, who had paid George I's mistress £10,000 for the contract, without consulting Irish needs or wishes. But recognition that their landed estates and political privileges were in the last analysis guaranteed by English military force, notably the 12,000 troops permanently garrisoned in Ireland, together with well-rehearsed group memories of the last great papist insurrection of 1641, severely constrained Anglo-Irish demands for national political autonomy.

Apart from recognizing the country's strategic importance, and exploiting patronage opportunities provided by the Irish Church and civil administration, most English politicians showed little interest in or knowledge of Ireland. As was bitterly observed at the height of the coinage crisis by the Irish-born Jonathan Swift, who had suffered much humiliation and disappointment in his efforts to make a career in England, 'Our neighbours ... have a strong contempt for most nations, but especially for Ireland: they look upon us as a sort of savage Irish, whom our ancestors conquered several hundred years ago.' Although without any immediate sequel, apart from the repeal of Mr Wood's coinage patent, Swift's popular *Drapier's Letters* attacking English attitudes and policies towards Ireland demonstrated the political potential of appeals to a growing sense of colonial nationalism. Similar sentiments and resentment also underlay the widespread contemporary tendency to blame England for Ireland's notorious poverty and economic backwardness.[15]

[14] Cf. R. Foster, *Modern Ireland, 1600–1972* (1988), ch. 8; T. C. Barnard, 'Crises of identity among Irish Protestants, 1641–1685', *P&P* 127 (1990).

[15] *A Letter to the Whole People of Ireland* (1724), in *Satires and Personal Writings by Jonathan Swift*, ed. W. A. Eddy (1932), 311; D. Dickson, *New Foundations: Ireland, 1660–1800* (1987), 66–70, 77–9.

Some Irish historians regard that accusation with scepticism. L. M. Cullen has pointed out that such measures as the Woollen Act of 1699, which forbade the export of Irish-manufactured cloth, were pushed through the Westminster Parliament by pressure groups (in this case Bristol merchants assisted by the powerful West Country clothing interest), and therefore hardly reflect a deliberate government policy of suppressing Irish development in order to protect English economic interests. The extent to which the Irish economy was actually damaged by English restrictions is also questionable. Although the legal inability of Irish merchants to import such commodities as tobacco directly from the British-American colonies undoubtedly was to their disadvantage (as it was also to their Scottish counterparts before 1707), it is not clear that Irish consumers suffered any commensurate loss, nor that restrictions on the export of Irish glassware to England significantly slowed the growth of the domestic Irish glass industry. Similarly, the problems which the Irish woollen cloth trade faced in the early eighteenth century probably had more to do with domestic recession than the infamous English legislation of 1699.[16]

A small economy poorly endowed with natural resources is always vulnerable to pressures exerted by larger and more powerful neighbours. But there were some Irish economic bright spots; this period saw real growth in the nascent linen industry (strongly encouraged from both London and Dublin, where the Linen Board was established in 1711 to assist its development) and in the export of provisions (salt beef and butter) for use at sea and in the American plantations. Overall exports and imports both stagnated during the first third of the century, but thereafter entered a period of sustained and fairly rapid expansion. Population also continued to grow throughout the eighteenth century at a higher rate than in either England or Scotland, for reasons which remain obscure, even if the spread of a subsistence potato monoculture was doubtless one of them.

Yet in other crucial respects Ireland's relative backwardness cannot be doubted. Outside the splendours and sociability of metropolitan Dublin, whose 130,000 or so residents made it the second largest city in the British Isles by the 1750s, the booming port-cities of Cork and Belfast, and a few smaller urban centres, the country remained poor, remote, undercapitalized, and thinly settled. The use of barter was widespread, thanks to a perennial coin shortage, Ireland's rudimentary banking facilities, and the prevalence of subsistence farming. Farming practices which struck English observers as extremely primitive, and the low agricultural productivity which went with them, were commonly attributed to a mixture of ethnic and religious conservatism. There was also an obvious lack of incentives for improvement in a tenurial system dominated by absentee landlords, who delegated the leasing of their increasingly subdivided estates to grasping middlemen. The specific impact of the penal

---

[16] L. M. Cullen, *An Economic History of Ireland since 1660* (1987), chs. 2–3.

laws, which allowed no Catholic to hold a lease for longer than thirty-one years or even to own a horse worth more than £5, were probably less damaging than the cultural and sectarian gap between English-speaking Protestant proprietors and Gaelic-speaking popish tenants, not to mention the cumulative impact of more than a century of communal conflict, invasion, intermittent warfare, land confiscations, and forced resettlements.

Of course individual and regional variations abounded; while parts of King's and Queen's counties, in Dublin's hinterland, and the Presbyterian north-east struck observers as relatively well cultivated and prosperous, wolves still roamed the remote south-west during the early years of the eighteenth century. We should not overlook the existence of positive initiatives for change, such as those furthered by members of the Dublin Society, established in 1731 to promote Irish agriculture and industry. Yet the general impoverishment of rural Ireland is undeniable. It is impossible to say how conditions generally compared with those endured by, say, the French or Spanish peasantry. But Bishop William Nicolson claimed never to have seen 'even in Picardy, Westphalia or Scotland' such 'dismal marks of hunger and want' as when he travelled through Ulster in the summer of 1718.[17]

The continued episodes of famine, mass starvation, and accompanying epidemic illness well into the eighteenth century, most notably in the late 1720s and 1740s, are also very striking. In 1741, long remembered as *bliadhain an air*, 'the year of the slaughter', the philosopher George Berkeley (1685–1753) wrote of 'whole villages entirely dispeopled'; another observer claimed that a third of the 'common people' had perished from hunger or disease.[18] Such a human catastrophe, possibly on a scale not exceeded even by the great famine of the mid-nineteenth century, makes it less surprising that the Jacobite rising of 1745 left Ireland almost entirely unmoved.

[17] W. E. Lecky, *History of England in the Eighteenth Century* (1878–90), ii. 216.
[18] M. Drake, 'The Irish demographic crisis of 1740–41', *Historical Studies VI*, ed. T. W. Moody (1968), 101–24.

8

FROM PARTY STRIFE TO ONE-PARTY RULE

The Elector of Hanover, King George I

The first two Hanoverian kings are traditionally dismissed as boorish foreigners, who lacked (in Macaulay's words) 'those personal qualities which have
often supplied the defect of a title'.[1] However xenophobic, this judgement does
point to a fact of prime importance. As prince-electors of Hanover, ruling a relatively small and recently emerged state in north-west Germany, George I and
II never focused exclusively on matters British. This geopolitical schizophrenia
tended to marginalize their status within the British polity, and accentuate their
dependence upon the ministers who formally served but in many respects actually managed them.

Of the two, George I was the more capable and prepossessing; his inability to
read, speak, or understand English on first arriving in the country is somewhat
offset by evidence of a later fondness for Shakespeare's plays, and the English-
language notes in his own handwriting on ministerial memoranda. George was
54 when he succeeded to the throne; long separated from the wife who had
cuckolded him (albeit accompanied to England by a quasi-official mistress), he
shunned crowds and soon began a Hanoverian tradition by falling out with his
son and heir. When political necessity dictated, George could overcome his
preference for the quiet life by entertaining on a grand scale and to considerable
effect. Indeed his recognition of the need to woo public support during an extended quarrel with the Prince of Wales lasting from 1717 to 1720 partially
contradicts George's supposed lack of interest in England and English affairs.
Somewhat unimaginative (on the very eve of his accession to the throne a visiting British diplomat was struck by how little he knew 'about our constitution'),
his respectable tastes in music and the visual arts were insufficient to save him
from the erudite Lady Mary Wortley Montagu's put-down: 'In private life he
would have been called an honest blockhead.'[2]

However, nationality apart, the main objections to Georg Ludwig—soon
Anglicized to plain George—were that he ascended the throne solely by virtue
of the Act of Settlement, thus excluding nearly sixty claimants better qualified

[1] 'The Earl of Chatham', in *Works of Lord Macaulay* (1866), vii. 213.
[2] R. Hatton, *George I: Elector and King* (1978); W. Coxe, *Memoirs of the Life and Administration of Sir Robert Walpole* (1798), ii. 42; *EHD, 1714–1783*, 100.

on hereditary grounds, most notably the English-born (if half-Italian) 'James III'; that he was a Lutheran, not an Anglican (except when in England); that he had no intention of totally abandoning Hanover on becoming king of Britain; and that he did little or nothing to hinder the political eclipse of the Tory party. According to a popular contemporary ballad, 'When George in pudding time came o'er', the Vicar of Bray, that infinitely adaptable but most recently High Church clergyman, changed his tune yet again, 'And so became a Whig, Sir'. Such opportunistic conversions were not uncommon from 1714 onwards.[3]

The King and his German advisers felt little sympathy for the Tories as a group, blaming them for England's desertion of Hanover and the other allies by making a separate peace with France in 1713. Even so, George may initially have hoped to govern through a mixed-party administration, albeit with a preponderance of Whigs. But as his two predecessors had already discovered, however desirable in theory, party rancour made such coalitions extraordinarily difficult in practice. Two prominent pro-Hanoverian Tories who were asked to join the administration shortly after the King's landing in September 1714 actually declined, claiming that their party deserved not token representation but equality with the Whigs. Such delusions of grandeur did not survive the overwhelming defeat of the demoralized and divided Tories in the general election held early next year, and their progressive purging from all government office, both central and local, including the armed forces and the county commissions of the peace. Bolingbroke's subsequent flight to join the Pretender in France, Oxford's imprisonment and impeachment on a charge of high treason, and the disastrous débâcle of the Jacobite rising that autumn, directly implicating a small number of Tory MPs and peers, set the seal on the Whigs' unprecedented and total political triumph.[4]

The victors moved swiftly to consolidate their electoral achievement, and the proscription of the Tories. Among the first legislation of the new Parliament was a Riot Act, provoked by a rash of anti-Dissenter, anti-Whig and pro-Jacobite street protests in London, Bristol, and the Midlands. Henceforth groups of more than twelve persons failing to disband within an hour of being called upon to do so by a magistrate were guilty of a capital offence and those dispersing them by force were indemnified for any resultant injuries or deaths. At the same time troops were mobilized to keep order in the streets. Loyalists like the young Thomas Pelham-Holles, duke of Newcastle (1693–1768) also organized counter-demonstrations, in the form of pope-burning, anti-Pretender processions, based on the Whig 'mug-houses' (political clubs whose members drank their copious loyal toasts in beer-mugs emblazoned with images of King George).

The Whigs never entirely suppressed all 'rebellious riots and tumults', let

[3] The Vicar also averred that 'George my lawful King shall be, | Except the times should alter'. Cf. J. H. Plumb, *The Growth of Political Stability in England, 1675–1640* (1969), 163–9.
[4] L. Colley, *In Defiance of Oligarchy: The Tory Party, 1714–1760* (1982), 50, 179–81.

alone non-violent protests, like the wearing of white roses on the Pretender's birthday. But they dealt a still more damaging blow to the long-term political prospects of their opponents with the Septennial Act of 1716, which extended the maximum life of parliaments, present and future, from three to seven years (unless interrupted by the reigning monarch's death). Given the Whigs' overall poor showing at the polls since the 1680s, postponement of the next general election until 1722 conferred a real and immediate political advantage, by allowing ample time for the seismic shift of ministerial power away from the Tories to be reflected in the distribution of electoral patronage. More than doubling the length of each parliamentary term also enhanced the value of seats in the Commons, and hence the electoral benefits of influence and cash, neither of which the Whigs now lacked. Rushed through Parliament, supposedly in order to prevent the Jacobites exploiting electoral turmoil, 'to stir up the people to not only riots, but even a fresh rebellion', the Septennial Act betrayed an old Whig principle, by drastically reducing the electorate's direct influence on Parliament, while simultaneously easing the transition to a more tranquil political era.[5]

The Venetian Oligarchy Inaugurated[6]

The prime exponent of the new politics of Hanoverian England was a large-framed, tough-minded politician named Robert Walpole, who first followed his father into Parliament in 1701 at the age of 25. The following year Walpole switched from the tiny Norfolk constituency of Castle Rising to the prosperous neighbouring port of King's Lynn, which he would represent for the next forty years. From the start Walpole identified himself with the Whigs, after his father's example and that of other kinsfolk and connections among the Norfolk squirearchy. His energy, intelligence, and consummate parliamentary skills were recognized both by his own party and by the nominally Tory ministry of Anne's early years, which first brought him into office in 1705. Walpole had revelled in, and profited from, the complexities of financial administration as secretary at war and treasurer of the navy, besides taking a prominent role in the Sacheverell prosecution. The subsequent Tory reaction saw him not merely lose office but face charges of corruption and embezzlement, which led to a brief spell of imprisonment in the Tower. Emboldened rather than cowed by the experience, he continued to attack Harley's regime as insufficiently committed to 'Revolution Principles' and the Hanoverian succession.

At Queen Anne's death Walpole regained a place in government. But his political career was temporarily blocked by senior members of the Whig Junto, from whom he actually split in 1717 by resigning as chancellor of the exchequer

---

[5] J. P. Kenyon, *Revolution Principles* (1977), 182–8, 203– 4; but see also Ch. 12 below.

[6] The young Benjamin Disraeli's partisan view of the 18th-c. Whig magnates as a 'Venetian Oligarchy' was propounded in his novel *Sybil* (1835), ch. 3.

and moving into parliamentary alliance with a heterogeneous assortment of discontented 'Country' Whigs and leaderless Tories. For nearly three years his formidable abilities were devoted to harassing both the persons and policies of the ministry. This stance involved Walpole in the risky game of siding with the Prince of Wales, Georg Augustus, whose father had expelled him from the family home of St James's Palace. The danger of irrevocably alienating the King was aggravated by Walpole's criticisms of the size of the army, of the purported sacrifice of British international interests to those of Hanover, and of improvement in the legal status of Dissenters—all Tory positions, scarcely consistent with either the Whig tradition or Walpole's own previous stance.

Political salvation came with the bursting of the South Sea Bubble, a financial catastrophe of hitherto unimaginable proportions. The South Sea Company, established in 1711 ostensibly as a Tory-backed joint-stock venture trading with the Spanish colonies in the Americas, enjoyed valuable trading privileges, including the 'Asiento', or monopoly of supplying the colonists with African slaves, granted to England at the peace of Utrecht. However, the Company's directors were less interested in commercial enterprise than high finance. Seeking to surpass the Bank of England as a financial institution, they devised an ingenious and apparently lucrative scheme to take over the huge post-war national debt. Parliament's acceptance of their complex proposals early in 1720 touched off months of frenzied speculation in the company's shares, and those of numerous even more dubious ventures hastily floated in order to exploit the prevailing get-rich-quick mentality. Walpole was among those who plunged heavily, but had the good fortune to dispose of most of his own holding of South Sea stock before the speculative bubble burst in the late summer of 1720, thereby escaping the devastating losses suffered by large numbers of investors.[7] As the mania subsided and the claimed losses mounted—according to the Lancashire shopkeeper William Stout 'at least twenty thousand people of all ranks' were ruined, and 'its supposed some millions of money lost and carried away by foreigners'— a frenzied search for culprits, redress, and vengeance began. The administration's greatest worry was the direct involvement of numerous MPs, ministers, courtiers, and members of the royal family, up to and including the King, many of whom had received discounted South Sea stock in return for promoting the company's interests in various more or less dubious ways.[8]

Having been brought back into office (although not the inner ring of cabinet ministers) just before the Bubble burst, Walpole's qualifications to sort out the mess were his apparent distance from these shady transactions, and an unrivalled understanding of public finance. He was also fortunate in that three of the implicated ministers died within six months of the collapse, while Charles

[7] J. Carswell, *The South Sea Bubble* (1960).
[8] *The Autobiography of William Stout of Manchester*, ed. J. D. Marshall (1967), 81; J. Trenchard and T. Gordon, *Cato's Letters* (1733; first pub. 1721), i. 75.

Spencer, earl of Sunderland (1674–1722), with whom Walpole had quarrelled in 1717, was forced to resign as first lord of the treasury. Replacing Sunderland at the head of the administration early in 1721, Walpole went on to establish a record for continuity in office as head of government which still stands in Britain.[9] Given the rapid turnover of governments and ministers during the previous three decades, his twenty-one years as first or 'prime' minister was a remarkable achievement. How did he do it?

Walpole's political opponents had a simple one-word answer—corruption. His regime—dubbed the 'Robinocracy'—was widely depicted as exemplifying all the most objectionable developments which had afflicted English public life since 1688, especially so far as the Tory landed gentry were concerned: Dutch finance, the monied interest, a standing army, European military entanglements, the land tax, proliferating placemen, and wholesale venality. Together, their baneful effects had supposedly enabled 'The Great Man', 'Bluff Bob', 'Bob Booty', or 'The Skreenmaster' (a reference to Walpole's presumed role in screening or whitewashing those responsible for the Bubble) to use purchased voices and votes in order to overthrow the constitution. So the poet Alexander Pope (1688–1744) portrayed the Robinocracy (according to his friend Swift 'the worst times and peoples, and oppression that history can show') as cause and symptom of deep-seated national degeneracy:

> Statesman and Patriot ply alike the stocks
> Peer and butler share alike the Box,
> And Judges job, and Bishops bite the Town
> And mighty Dukes pack cards for half-a-crown
> See Britain sunk in lucre's sordid charms[10]

Yet for all its artistic and moral force, this line of attack may be better evidence of Walpole's success at alienating the intellectuals than a plausible explanation of his political longevity. It would in fact be difficult to demonstrate that the political nation became significantly more corrupt (however we may define that term) under the early Hanoverians than it had been under the later Stuarts, especially since most of Walpole's tools of parliamentary management went back well before 1715. Moreover, any such interpretation tends to absolve Walpole of either blame, or credit, for his achievement—he can hardly be held responsible for universal venality—while failing to explain why his successors were unable to repeat it. Nevertheless, the image of 'Robin' as 'Grand Corrupter' was sufficiently persistent and pervasive to justify a closer look at the political system he operated.

---

[9] For Westminster democracies generally it was beaten only by Sir Thomas Playford's twenty-seven years as premier of South Australia, 1938–65.

[10] I. Kramnick, *Bolingbroke and his Circle* (1968), 69; J. A. Downie, 'Walpole, "the Poet's Foe"', in J. Black (ed.), *Britain in the Age of Walpole* (1984), 172.

Parliamentary Management

The means Walpole used to bend both Houses of Parliament to the government's will were hardly novel. The possibilities for using judicious manipulation of Crown patronage to build a party of 'king's friends' had been amply demonstrated in the later seventeenth century, by Danby and Sunderland among others. Systematic attempts to manipulate electoral outcomes were of still greater antiquity, although additional tools recently devised for the purpose dated respectively from 1696 (the Last Determinations Act) and 1710 (the Qualifications Act). These statutes were used to restrict the numbers of both enfranchised electors, and candidates, thereby tending to reduce the frequency of expensive contested elections. However, Walpole's unprecedented success as parliamentary manager largely reflected his ruthless and systematic approach to the distribution of favours in return for political support. The long duration and completeness of his ascendancy, and the effective political sidelining of the Tories, enabled him to achieve a patronage monopoly unmatched since, and no more popular than, that exercised by the first duke of Buckingham under the early Stuarts. This achievement was undoubtedly facilitated by the much augmented patronage resources at his disposal, both places (thanks to the post-1688 growth of the central bureaucracy) and cash (especially the 'secret service' funds, controlled but not accounted for by Treasury). Significant new opportunities for dispensing these material favours were also created by the appearance at Westminster from 1707 onwards of a relatively impoverished contingent of Scottish politicians.

Parliamentary management through electoral manipulation and patronage was necessary to ensure the effective conduct of government business. To this end modern parliaments are effectively controlled through the party system, which dominates the entire political process; MPs depend on party endorsement for their seats, and must in general vote as the party dictates. But eighteenth-century political leaders could not rely on party discipline to constrain their followers. Neither Whigs nor Tories possessed the means or the will to operate in this fashion. Indeed neither was a political party in the modern sense of a national election-fighting organization with an explicit manifesto or programme and a formal membership structure. Hence (and especially after 1714) party labels were no reliable guide to parliamentary behaviour, which was dictated primarily by personal considerations, including family connections and ties of friendship, as well as the reciprocal obligations of clients and patrons. In any case, a significant minority, both within and outside Parliament, were proud to be identified as independents, aloof from either party.

A full House of Commons would have consisted of 558 MPs, 489 returned from English and the remainder from Welsh and Scottish constituencies. However, actual attendance during parliamentary sessions was well under half or a third of that nominal total. Most members (who were unpaid) sat either for counties or boroughs, although the universities of Oxford and Cambridge were also each represented by two MPs. The 'forty-shilling freeholders', that is to say, adult males possessing landed property worth at least £2 per annum, returned the two 'knights of the shire' for each of the forty English and twelve Welsh counties. Borough franchises, by contrast, varied widely. Something close to a householder or adult male suffrage prevailed in a few large urban constituencies like Southwark and Westminster, with over 5,000 qualified electors; but there were a good many more closed or 'pocket' boroughs, tiny decayed hamlets where the vote was restricted to the occupants of a small handful of 'burgage' properties. The smaller the constituency, in general the more easily (and relatively cheaply) its representation was controlled; over a third of all boroughs had fewer than 100 electors.

Most parliamentary elections were actually not contested. Even the closely fought general election of 1722 saw contests for only half the English and Welsh seats; by 1747 the proportion had dropped to one-fifth.[11] The growing expense of fighting an election after passage of the Septennial Act deterred potential rivals, and encouraged the making of private deals in order to avoid a contest; such arrangements were facilitated by the fact that most boroughs returned not one but two members. These trends enhanced the importance of wealthy and influential political operators like the duke of Newcastle or later Sir James Lowther (1736–1832), men who controlled or at least influenced a number of boroughs, and whose stables of MPs usually, although not invariably, respected the preferences of the 'friends' who had secured their election. In the last analysis, however, governments changed not as the result of general elections, but because ministers no longer enjoyed the monarch's favour. To put it another way, electoral outcomes generally reflected consequential adjustments to the flow of Crown patronage, rather than initiating them.

The House of Lords, with twenty-six bishops who from the mid-1720s mostly sided consistently with the government, and fewer than 200 lay peers, many infrequent attenders, was generally more malleable than the much larger and less sedate Commons. Hence Walpole's wholly unexpected decision in the early 1720s to accept a peerage for his elder son rather than himself had enormous strategic consequence, by permitting his continued direct involvement with the business and personnel of the Commons. There he relished the role of simple country squire, reading his gamekeeper's letters and munching Norfolk apples during debates. Yet even the fastidious Philip Stanhope (1694–1773), a later political enemy who had sat in the Commons for ten years until his elevation to the peerage as earl of Chesterfield in 1725, conceded that Walpole's powers of exposition and persuasion made him 'both the best parliament-man, and the ablest manager of Parliament, that I believe ever lived. An artful rather than eloquent speaker, he saw, as by intuition, the disposition of the House,

---

[11] F. O'Gorman, *Voters, Patrons, and Parties: The Unreformed Electorate of Hanoverian England, 1734–1832* (1989), 108.

and pressed or receded accordingly'.[12] While many who voted with the government were bound to Walpole by various favours—offices, jobs, pensions—extended to themselves, their patrons, kinsmen, or dependants, his active presence in the House helped maintain and reinforce these ties of obligation, as well as providing ample opportunity to work on MPs who remained relatively detached from the Court and ministry.

So although Walpole exploited the political potential of Crown patronage more successfully than any previous minister, his long hegemony did not in fact merely depend upon the outright purchase of parliamentary votes. At the same time, his ability to manage Parliament, and especially to secure substantial increases in the civil list revenues voted to both George I and George II, plainly helped predispose those monarchs in his favour. He only retained that confidence, without which his parliamentary ascendancy would have been almost irrelevant, by adept and careful management of his royal masters (not to mention their mistresses, and George II's long-suffering Queen Caroline). Finally, his adoption of moderate, even Tory-leaning policies defused a number of potentially inflammable issues which might well have split Walpole's ministry and alienated many of its supporters. Thus Nonconformist campaigns in the 1730s for repeal of the Test and Corporation Acts were deflected, for fear of a hostile High Church reaction; the gentry and aristocracy gained substantial relief from the land tax burden, thanks to increased consumption taxes; an Anglo-French alliance was linked to the maintenance of peace in Europe, as well as the isolation of the Pretender; trade and manufactures were encouraged by reducing export levies, and providing protection for particular commercial lobbies, such as merchants trading with the West Indies. A cautious, pragmatic, unambitious approach to government fitted well with Walpole's self-characterization as 'No saint, no Spartan, no reformer', one whose 'great maxim in policy' was to 'submit to old inconveniences rather than encourage innovations'.[13]

Opposition, War, and Walpole's Fall

The authority of the 'Great Man' increased with the passing years. When his brother-in-law and former political colleague Lord Townshend (1674–1738) resigned from the post of secretary of state in 1730, Walpole added effective supervision of foreign policy to his existing responsibilities for the nation's finances and control of Crown patronage. His predominance as 'Sole'—not merely 'Prime'—minister aroused inevitable resentment, aggravated by his opulent and unashamed enjoyment of power.

Even the Prince of Wales, who succeeded as George II at his father's death in 1727, would gladly have dispensed with the man whom he had previously

[12] Chesterfield, *Characters of Eminent Personages of his Own Time* (1777), cited in A. F. Scott (ed.), *The Early Hanoverian Age, 1714–1760* (1980), 140.
[13] Quoted P. Langford, *The Excise Crisis* (1975), 147.

'called rogue and rascal'.[14] Yet unlike most former royal favourites and first ministers, Walpole triumphantly survived this dangerous transition, partly by offering the new King a substantial increase in his civil list income, and also through his excellent relations with the new Queen, Caroline of Ansbach, who exercised considerable influence over her difficult and graceless husband. George's unpopularity with his subjects rivalled and possibly exceeded that of his father, and for similar reasons. The inactivity of the Pretender and his supporters since the early 1720s was gradually reducing the credibility of a Jacobite alternative to the Hanoverian 'usurper', but Walpole's own public image was not improved by the widespread dislike of his master, which the frustration of hopes that he would 'give no protection to Robin' doubtless aggravated.[15] Meanwhile the various fruits of patronage lavishly bestowed on Walpole's family and friends, together with incidents like the 1725 impeachment and conviction of Lord Chancellor Macclesfield for selling offices in his court, reinforced perceptions of pervasive corruption.

In 1726 Bolingbroke, returned from exile in France but not restored to his seat in the Lords, joined with the renegade Whig William Pulteney (1684–1764) to launch a new weekly journal, *The Craftsman*. This vehicle of an emerging parliamentary and out-of-doors opposition purported to expose the 'craft' or fraud, which, according to its first number, 'has crept into the camp as well as the court; prevailed in the church as well as the state; has vitiated the country in the same manner that it has poisoned the City, and worked itself into every part of our constitution'. Thus began a campaign which sought to mobilize public opinion in defence of familiar 'Country' concepts and values against an overpowerful executive, Whig oligarchs, and the moneyed interest. Walpole's person and policies were also attacked and lampooned in newspapers, pamphlets, broadsheets, ballads, cartoons, and prints, as well as on stage, most famously in John Gay's *The Beggar's Opera* (1728), which depicted him variously as highwayman, fence, and crooked gaoler. In response the ministry mounted its own public relations campaign, spending more than £50,000 during the 1730s to subsidize at least eight London newspapers, whose writers busily refuted claims that Walpolian corruption threatened parliamentary independence, the ancient constitution, or the subjects' liberties.[16] Attempts were also made to suppress extra-parliamentary criticism by prosecuting authors, editors, and printers, interfering with the circulation of their journals through the government-controlled Post Office, and legislating in 1737 to impose pre-performance censorship on all theatrical productions.

Yet while angering Walpole, and scarcely improving his public image, something more than a floodtide of printed abuse and ridicule would be required to

[14] *Lord Hervey's Memoirs*, ed. R. Sedgwick (1952), 34.

[15] *Robin's Panegyyrick. Or, the Norfolk Miscellany* (n.d., c.1729), 108.

[16] S. Targett, 'Government and ideology during the Whig Supremacy: the political arguments of Sir Robert Walpole's newspaper propagandists', *HlJ* 37 (1994).

erode his political supremacy, firmly based as it was on the twin pillars of royal favour and parliamentary dominance. Even in 1733, when a well-organized industry campaign against the proposed replacement of cumbersome customs duties on wine and tobacco with a more efficient excise or consumption tax led to violent London riots and a steep decline in the government's usual comfortable majorities, withdrawal of the offending legislation quickly restored Walpole's parliamentary numbers, if not altogether his psychological edge. This incident demonstrated that while around a third of MPs were ministerial dependants or placemen, their votes could not be considered rock-solid for the government on every occasion. Nor was Walpole able to rely on party loyalty, since the parliamentary Whigs always included an assortment of 'Country' dissidents, like Pulteney and his followers, who consistently spoke and voted against government measures.

Nevertheless, even when combined with the 130–150 Tory MPs who continued to be returned, especially for the freeholder-based county constituencies, and some larger urban electorates not readily controlled by aristocratic patrons or oligarchic corporations, these opposition groupings were usually far outnumbered by Whigs of a broadly pro-ministerial disposition. The ability to mobilize their potential support, by a mixture of cajolery, persuasion, and pressure, was Walpole's ultimate parliamentary–political weapon. Electioneering had much less importance; there were only four general elections during his entire term in office (in 1722, 1727, 1734, and 1741), and the preponderance of Whig-controlled borough seats meant that even in the last of these, held a year before his fall, the anti-Walpole forces failed to win a Commons majority.

Walpole might well have remained in office until his life or health gave out, but for two domestic events and one international development. In September 1737 history repeated itself when George II ordered his son and heir out of St James's Palace; Prince Frederick moved to Leicester House, quickly gathering a caucus of opposition politicians around him. Two months later his mother Queen Caroline died. The removal of Walpole's most influential ally at Court, and the heir apparent's emergence as a focal point for both Tory and 'Patriot' Whig dissidents, were politically unsettling. But rapidly worsening relations with both Spain and France were still more serious, in that they threatened what Walpole had spent his entire ministry trying to avoid—a domestically divisive and inescapably expensive European war.

Walpole's lack of martial fervour derived from concerns about the impact of war on trade and taxes, plus the risk of foreign assistance for a Jacobite rising, reinforced by his own experience of the cost and divisiveness of the long campaign against Louis XIV. But his reluctance was eventually overcome by a combination of diplomatic considerations and domestic pressures. These latter originated with the South Sea Company (now shrunk to a purely commercial role) and independent merchants trading with the Spanish Americas from London and Bristol under the terms of the peace of Utrecht, backed by a number of his own ministers and an increasingly aggressive public opinion. The administration's apparent weakness in the face of armed confrontations between Spanish coastguards and British merchant ships proved a political godsend to the opposition. One of the witnesses and victims of alleged Spanish atrocities whom they produced has given his name to the 'War of Jenkins's Ear', upon which Walpole reluctantly embarked in the autumn of 1739.

Inconclusive hostilities against Spain, mainly in the Caribbean, gave way next year to general European tensions over the territories of the Austrian Habsburgs. Bourbon France and Spain, with Prussia, gradually lined up against Britain and her (rather few) allies. Against a background of diplomatic confusion, military stalemate, continued opposition sniping, and growing differences with his ministerial colleagues, the ailing and tired Walpole fought his last general election in the spring of 1741. The outcome gave the ministry only a bare Commons majority over his opponents, who continued to gather support both before and after the first meeting of the new Parliament six months later. This haemorrhaging of votes from the government led to a series of defeats on relatively minor issues, which nevertheless made it clear that the 'Great Man' could no longer guarantee the passage of business through the House.

In February 1742 George II grudgingly accepted the necessity of Walpole's resignation, news which touched off widespread public rejoicings. Promoted to the peerage and untouched by the parliamentary committee of inquiry set up to investigate his alleged misdeeds, Walpole nevertheless continued to play a significant political role from behind the scenes until his death three years later. With his advice and encouragement the King frustrated Tory hopes of returning to power as members of a new 'Broadbottom' or coalition ministry. Carteret and Pulteney, the Whig leaders of the parliamentary anti-Walpole forces, were neutralized by being brought into office. The Tories' continued proscription, combined with French fears of encirclement by an Austrian–British–German coalition after George II's victory in mid-1743 at Dettingen, the last battle commanded by a British sovereign, generated elaborate plans for Jacobite invasion, which was blocked in 1744 by bad weather and the Royal Navy. The following summer saw an excessively impromptu landing in northwest Scotland by the 'Young Pretender', Prince Charles Edward Stuart, who carried with him 'little money, seven followers, and none of the French aid he had been repeatedly told was a *sine qua non* for a rebellion'.[17] Bonnie Prince Charlie nevertheless managed to raise a scratch army, which seized Edinburgh, where he held court at Holyroodhouse, the traditional Stuart royal palace. In November the Jacobites marched south into England, encountering little resistance, or assistance, on the way. The Young Pretender's arrival at Derby, a mere 132 miles (211 km.) from the capital, on 4 December, created considerable panic in London and 'great confusion' as far away as Norfolk, whence a

---

[17] B. Lenman, *The Jacobite Clans of the Great Glen, 1650–1784* (1984), 149.

clergyman's wife wrote to her sister, 'God knows what is to become of us nor where we are to go'.[18] But the support promised from both English Jacobites and France failed to materialize. There followed divided counsels, ignominious retreat, a terrible slaughter at Culloden, and the effective elimination of Jacobitism as a political force.

Crown and Parliament: Who Ruled Britain?

The '45 challenged both George II and the entire political order established over the previous three decades. For J. H. Plumb the defining characteristic of that era was a new-found stability, due to the consolidation of oligarchical Whig rule, pre-eminently the work of Sir Robert Walpole. In his classic account of *The Growth of Political Stability in England, 1675–1725*, Plumb traced the intensification of party political strife under the later Stuarts, and its rapid diminution after the accession of George I. However, it has been argued recently that in so far as early Hanoverian England was more politically stable than later Stuart England, the explanation is that the divisive political and religious issues which had provoked civil war in the mid-seventeenth century were settled once and for all at the Glorious Revolution. Yet both these viewpoints are challenged by those who play down the extent of change between the seventeenth and eighteenth centuries, pointing to the continued centrality of the Crown's political and administrative roles, and even suggesting that the monarchy 'reached an apogee of power under the first two Georges'.[19]

As with all controversies between historians, these divergent conclusions reflect differences of approach and values which are unlikely to be reconciled by any amount of evidence produced in support of particular viewpoints. Yet scholarship is cumulative, and advances in understanding often take the form of reaction to established orthodoxies. A stress on stability as the defining characteristic of the post-1715 or -1721 political world makes good sense if we compare the constant shuffling of ministers and administrations under William and Anne with the one-party rule and political longevity of Walpole (even if some ministerial instability did return after 1742). Another key indicator is the treatment meted out to those on the losing side of politics; the likelihood of facing impeachment or attainder, the Tower or the scaffold, fell quite markedly after 1714–15 (compare the proceedings against Walpole in 1711 and 1742). Yet it is also possible to exaggerate the political torpor of the early Hanoverian era, by overlooking the liveliness of popular radical, 'patriot', and oppositionist agitation in the press and on the streets, especially of London and the larger cities, the strength of sympathy for the Jacobite cause, and the

[18] A. Hartshorne (ed.), *Memoirs of a Royal Chaplain* (1905), 113.
[19] C. Roberts, 'The growth of political stability reconsidered', *Albion*, 25 (1993); J. C. D. Clark, *Revolution and Rebellion: State and Society in England in the Seventeenth and Eighteenth Centuries* (1986), 80.

continued political activity of the Tories, both at Westminster and in the provinces.

Of course much depends on what exactly is meant by 'stability'. Judged in terms of the likelihood of civil war, or a fundamental reconstruction of the political and/or religious constitution, let alone a social revolution from below, the Britain of George II appears significantly more stable than the England of Charles II. This difference may well be attributable in part at least to the long-term consequences of the Glorious Revolution. But Plumb's prime concern was with tracing and explaining changes in the nature and tempo of ministerial change and party political strife, not surveying the larger, more abstract, and somewhat more nebulous nature of Crown–Parliament relations.

For Plumb the rise of political oligarchy in the early eighteenth century followed the consolidation of landed estates in the hands of the greater gentry and aristocracy from the later seventeenth century onwards (see p. 149 below). One of his critics, who believes oligarchy was hardly more prevalent in the eighteenth than the seventeenth century, sees the post-1688 supremacy of Parliament over Crown as reflecting a long-term transfer of land from monarchy, Church, and peasantry to the landed ruling class who dominated the political nation. But another totally rejects any such causal relationship as Marxist or *marxisant* 'economic reductionism'. In this view the world of politics was a largely self-contained realm, more influenced by religious belief and such theological concepts as the divine right of kings than any socio-economic pressures. Accounts of the 'triumph of Parliament over Crown in 1688 [and] of Commons over Lords in *c.*1714–60' are also rejected as arrant Whiggery. On the contrary, after (as indeed largely before) 1689, King and Parliament are said to have worked together, both strengthened by a more powerful state and the greater efficiency with which the King's ministers managed the Parliament. Moreover, the early Hanoverian monarchs supposedly continued to play an active part in the business of government, just as the royal Court remained the focal centre of politics and political intrigue.[20]

While hardly less selective than the orthodox simplifications which it both caricatures and rejects, this conservative revisionism has the virtue of forcing us to think carefully about some fundamental issues. For example, how exactly did the relationships and roles of monarch, ministers, and Parliament differ before and after 1688? Sunderland under James II and Walpole under George II both depended upon a royal master's favour; but unlike his predecessor, Walpole also had to deal with regular meetings of Parliament, and could hardly expect to retain office indefinitely after losing control of the Commons. The basis of the titles and authority of the two monarchs was also very different: George II claimed neither to rule by divine indefeasible hereditary right, nor to possess the concomitant quasi-magical healing powers which the exiled

---

[20] Clark, *Revolution and Rebellion*, 2–4, chs. 3, 5.

'James III' continued to exercise.[21] George II could personally steer the foreign policy of Hanover, where he ruled as an absolute monarch; he enjoyed notably less autonomy in respect of British foreign relations, and certainly exercised far less individual authority than Charles II and his brother had done. Yet the simple dichotomy implied in the heading of this section is potentially misleading. 'Crown' and 'Parliament' were not mutually exclusive alternatives, or necessary antagonists, especially after the Glorious Revolution and, even more, the Hanoverian succession. Indeed, if anyone could be said to have ruled Britain in the early eighteenth century, it was surely the ministerial executive, whose power and very being depended precisely upon an ability to co-ordinate these two institutions.[22]

[21] Cf. the contemporary description of the king as 'a legal Prince', ruling 'by law, and not by Royal will', whose title came not from a 'fancied Line | But by the People's Choice, his Right's Divine': 'Philopatriae', *South Britain: A Poem* (1731), 21.

[22] The effectiveness of that co-ordination helps explain why after 1708 no monarch sought to exercise the royal prerogative to veto parliamentary legislation: cf. D. L. Keir, *The Constitutional History of Modern Britain since 1485* (1964), 297.

9

RELIGIOUS BELIEF AND PRACTICE

Church and Chapel

The influential French author Voltaire, whose extended London visit in the mid-1720s reflected a growing European interest in things English, depicted political and religious liberty as characteristic of this 'country of sectarists', where 'everyone is permitted to serve God in whatever mode or fashion he thinks proper'.[1] In point of fact, the Blasphemy Act of 1698 made denying the doctrine of the Trinity, the truth of Christianity, or the authority of Scripture punishable by up to three years' imprisonment. Those publishing theologically heterodox opinions also risked prosecution for blasphemous libel. Yet it must immediately be added that these legal provisions were rarely invoked, and attempts in the early 1720s to strengthen them failed to win parliamentary support. For all Hobbes's fears, no heretic had been executed in England since the early seventeenth century (although a 19-year-old theological student was hanged for heresy in Edinburgh in 1698). To that extent, Voltaire's central point holds good: by George II's reign religious diversity had come to stay.

The last serious attempt to revive a coercive Church–State alliance occurred during the Tory–High Church alliance of 1710–14, when anti-Dissenter legislation sought to stamp out occasional conformity and bring all forms of education under Anglican control.

Although these measures did not long outlast Queen Anne, notwithstanding the apprehensions of many parsons their Church lost relatively little ground to Dissent over the next thirty years. The licensing of nearly 4,000 Dissenting chapels and meeting houses between 1689 and 1710 had prompted Anglican fears of a Nonconformist population explosion. But this proliferation was evidently attributable to the mobility of congregations rather than the numerical expansion of their membership. In fact Dissenting numbers probably stagnated and possibly shrank across the whole denominational spectrum (Presbyterian, Congregationalist or Independent, Baptist, and Quaker) throughout the early decades of the eighteenth century, and especially after 1714, even as greater self-confidence became apparent in the architecture and siting of their places of worship.[2]

The Church of England dominated the more populous countryside, both village and manor house, as well as the cathedrals, universities, and grammar

---

[1] *Letters concerning the English Nation* (1733), letter 5.
[2] M. Watts, *The Dissenters: From the Reformation to the French Revolution* (1978), 382–93.

schools, whereas Dissenting chapels and meeting houses were found pre-dominantly (if never exclusively) in urban settings frequented by the (broadly defined) industrious middling sort. Protestant nonconformists could both vote and stand for Parliament, but their direct political representation was minus-cule; only twenty-five Dissenter MPs have been identified between 1715 and 1760, while the House of Lords was even more of an Anglican preserve. These figures reflect the continued drift to conformity of the landed elite since the mid-seventeenth century, as does the relatively small size of the four main dis-senting sects, whose adherents made up barely 6 to 7 per cent of the population in 1714. Their numerical weakness was compounded by internal disunity. Although Anglican High and Low factions remained locked in combat through the 1720s and beyond, the established state church was sustained by a mixture of inertia, privilege, and sentiment. Dissenters, by contrast, enjoyed no such national status, institutional structure, or historical tradition, despite the efforts of contemporary denominational historians like Edmund Calamy (1671–1732) and Daniel Neal (1678–1743) to create a usable past, at least for the more numerous and wealthier Presbyterians. Worse, long-standing doctrinal and socio-economic divisions inhibited co-operation among non-Anglicans; not until the early 1730s was England's first permanent extra-parliamentary political lobby group—the Protestant Dissenting Deputies—established to defend their common interests, although not those of the Quakers, who continued to rely on their own long-established committees for this purpose. Lacking both the status of martyrdom and the stimulus of per-secution, rejecting 'enthusiasm' and excessive zeal, Dissent was becoming com-placent, middle-aged, and respectable, concerned more with practical morality and personal piety than winning souls for Christ or building a New Jerusalem.[3]

The burden of civil disabilities still imposed by the Test and Corporation Acts may have helped generate a shared sense of labouring under an unjust yoke, but hardly excluded Protestant nonconformists from public life alto-gether. From 1726 a series of Occasional Indemnity Acts increased the difficulty of prosecuting non-Anglican office-holders, but well before that Presbyterian businessmen effectively dominated the towns of Bridport and Nottingham. In urban centres elsewhere their counterparts served as mayors, aldermen, councillors, overseers of the poor, turnpike commissioners, and so forth. Of course discrimination hardly required a statutory basis. The insist-ence of the Church-controlled grammar schools and universities that students should subscribe to the Anglican Thirty-Nine Articles is a case in point, al-though Cambridge University only imposed this requirement on those wishing to graduate with a degree (unlike Oxford, where subscription was required of all would-be students). Nor was it especially difficult for Dissenters to practise

[3] J. Walsh and S. Taylor, 'Introduction: The Church and Anglicanism in the "long" eighteenth century', in J. Walsh, C. Haydon, and S. Taylor (eds.), *The Church of England, c.1689–c.1833* (1993), 51.

law or medicine. So their undoubted prominence in business, trade, and industry throughout the eighteenth century most probably reflects not so much the unavailability of other career options, but rather a close correlation between Dissenting beliefs and membership of the urban social strata from which merchants and manufacturers were predominantly drawn.

Even if some contemporaries, and later historians, may have exaggerated their civil disabilities, Dissenters certainly did not enjoy legal equality with conforming Anglicans. Besides supporting their own chapels or meeting houses, ministers, and charities, they still had to pay the local church fees, rates, and tithes. Following Hardwicke's Marriage Act in 1753, Dissenters could only be lawfully married in a parish church by a clergyman of the Church of England, yet might be denied the right of burial in the local churchyard by an unsympathetic parson. Dissenters were still sometimes harassed in the ecclesiastical and secular courts, despite the generally more sympathetic attitude of the common-law judges. Given these circumstances, and the more ample career prospects which the Church could offer ambitious and well-connected young ministers, the continued desertion of both lay and clerical nonconformists, including men of the calibre of Thomas Secker (1693–1768), a future archbishop of Canterbury, is hardly surprising. Nor should we wholly discount the effectiveness of propagandists for the Established Church, with their claims that 'cool reason, sound judgment, and a diligent trial' must convince any wavering Dissenter that the Anglican liturgy 'minister[s] more real and solid benefit, than all the fancied advantages of separate worship'.[4]

If Dissent's apparent threat to the Church tended to drop away after 1714, fears of 'popery and arbitrary power' as an alien menace to 'our religion, laws, and liberties' were kept alive by the armed rebellion of 1715, subsequent revelations of Jacobite plots in 1717, 1719, and 1722, the planned French invasion of 1743, and the actual rising of 1745–6. A battery of ferocious penal laws, both old and new, seemingly banned Catholic worship and the presence of Catholic priests in England. Additional economic and social disabilities were imposed on convicted Catholic recusants, including a doubled rate of land tax, group fines, and property levies, as well as numerous restrictions on residence and travel. Yet enforcement was always patchy (as the jurist Blackstone commented, 'these laws are seldom exerted to their utmost rigour'), and despite some panic in the aftermath of the '15, the small Catholic community's continued existence was never seriously in doubt.[5] Indeed the traditional assumption of steady eighteenth-century decline has recently been stood on its head, by the claim that papist numbers actually grew by over 25 per cent from 1700 to 1770. However, even if that assertion proved to be correct (and it involves some exceedingly heroic assumptions), we would still only be talking about a

[4] H. Stebbing, *The Excellency of the Constitution of the Church of England consider'd* (1732), 19.
[5] T. Herring, *A Sermon Preach'd At the Cathedral Church of York* (1745), pp. iv, 33; W. Blackstone, *Commentaries on the Laws of England* (1765–9), iv. 56–7.

mere 60,000–80,000 persons, or just over 1 per cent of England's total population.[6]

Their continued self-identification as Catholics depended on a mixture of factors. These included geographical clustering in parts of the country which were either relatively remote or difficult to police (notably but not exclusively Lancashire, Staffordshire, the north-eastern counties, West Sussex, and London, with its sizeable immigrant Irish community); patronage and protection provided by small numbers of aristocratic and gentry families to their neighbours, tenants, and servants; and the ministry of a well-organized body of Catholic priests supervised by four vicars-apostolic, each responsible for one of the large missionary districts into which England and Wales had been divided under James II. Perhaps the very marginality of Catholicism helped its adherents maintain a degree of commitment to their faith which larger and more mainstream denominations, above all the Church of England, found increasingly hard to elicit.

Echoing Victorian critics, the Hanoverian Church was long portrayed as corrupt, materialistic, and spiritually moribund. This was essentially an indictment of the clergy, not least the bench of Whig bishops. Their number included Benjamin Hoadly (1676–1761), much execrated by non-jurors, High Churchmen, and Tories for his Erastian insistence on ecclesiastical subordination to the secular power, who never visited his Welsh diocese of Bangor during the six years he held the see, and the former naval chaplain Lancelot Blackburne (1648–1743), who while archbishop of York supposedly kept a mistress and acknowledged at least one illegitimate child. But there was nothing new about careerist, immoral, non-resident, and pluralist clergymen, and it remains to be shown that corruption, incompetence, and neglect were more widespread or acute among eighteenth-century clerics than their seventeenth- or sixteenth-century predecessors. Nor can Walpole and his 'Pope', Bishop Edmund Gibson of London (1669–1748), claim the dubious distinction of being the first politician and prelate to agree that high ecclesiastical office was properly reserved for men both of 'known affection to the Established Church', and 'well affected towards the administration of the state'.[7]

Recent research on the quality of pastoral care and the vitality of religious life in the eighteenth-century Anglican Church shows, unsurprisingly, enormous variations across the country and from parish to parish in such basic matters as the frequency of communion services and attendance at them. There were some positive general trends: for example, the improved educational qualifications of ministers (now overwhelmingly university-educated, with just a few curates still lacking this professional job ticket), and the alleviation of clerical poverty (thanks partly to Queen Anne's Bounty, a fund established

---

[6] E. Duffy, *Peter and Jack: Roman Catholics and Dissent in Eighteenth-Century England* (1983); J. Bossy, *The English Catholic Community* (1975); *EHD, 1714–1783*, 408–9.

[7] N. Sykes, *Edmund Gibson, Bishop of London, 1669–1748* (1926), 408.

under royal patronage in 1704 to subsidize the poorest beneficed clergy). At the same time, both these developments had the less desirable effect of further distancing the clergy from ordinary members of their congregations. Again, the Society for Promoting Christian Knowledge, and the Society for the Propagation of the Gospel in Foreign Parts, educational-cum-evangelical religious associations founded by pious Anglican laymen and ministers at the end of the seventeenth century, both seem to have lost much of their original impetus by the 1740s. Yet the SPCK continued to promote and co-ordinate the operation of hundreds of local charity schools, which taught poor children basic reading and writing skills within a strongly religious framework.

Excessive concentration on the clergy's moral and spiritual shortcomings can easily obscure the greatest problem facing the Augustan Church, that of adjustment to a new era of political dependence (on politicians, rather than the monarch) and radically diminished authority. The legal toleration of Dissent had subverted the religious uniformity, the identity of congregation and community, on which the church courts once relied when punishing people for offences against sexual morality and ecclesiastical good order (such as absence from church services). The ministerial suspension of Convocation in 1717, after its high-flying Lower House had condemned Bishop Hoadly for having 'dangerously undermined' the doctrine and authority of the Church, left Anglicans with no independent deliberative forum or legislative machinery.[8] But even these negative institutional changes were overshadowed by persistent challenges to the basic beliefs which the Church existed to profess.

Latitudinarianism and Freethinking

'Latitudinarian' first appeared in the early 1660s as a derogatory label applied by both returning High Church royalists and ejected Puritan nonconformists to a group of Anglican clergy at Cambridge University. These men had conformed under the Commonwealth and then accepted the restored episcopacy, but nevertheless sought to preserve as much Protestant unity as possible through a broad, inclusive, moderate religious settlement. Latitudinarians rejected Laudian authoritarianism, dogmatic Calvinist theology, enthusiasm, and Aristotelian scholasticism. Instead they emphasized reason, scripture, and the study of Nature by the experimental methods of the new science as the best means of understanding God's purposes. John Tillotson (1630–94), who became the immensely popular London preacher of a prudential, undogmatic 'natural religion' after losing his Cambridge fellowship in 1661, succeeded the non-juror William Sancroft as archbishop of Canterbury thirty years later. This latitudinarian triumph was much resented by the emerging High Church party, not least on account of Tillotson's suspected doctrinal heterodoxy.

---

[8] *EHD, 1714–1783*, 352–3.

Henceforth 'latitudinarian' tended to be used indiscriminately of both theological liberals or moderates, and clerical Whigs, those who would later agree with Hoadly that the Church was a mere human organization lacking any independent, divinely ordained rights or powers.

Under Tillotson, and his like-minded successor Archbishop Thomas Tenison (1636–1715), the latitudinarians continued to gain influence and preferment, further exacerbating party conflict within the post-Revolutionary Church. These clerical disputes about allegiance and toleration were accompanied and intersected by extensive theological controversy. A cluster of anti-Trinitarian heresies denying Christ's equal divinity with God, known variously as Arianism, Socinianism, and Unitarianism, had already acquired some eminent covert followers, including Milton, Locke, and Newton, besides a few more or less open clerical advocates. While anti-Trinitarian views continued to be propounded and denounced during the 1690s and beyond, a related but still more radical attack on orthodox theology developed in the writings of the anticlerical Deists and Freethinkers. Extending and popularizing Locke's *The Reasonableness of Christianity* (1695), John Toland's *Christianity not Mysterious* (1696) rejected any dogma which depended upon divine revelation as distinct from human reason, thereby reducing religion to a core belief in a supernatural Creator whose moral law, fully apparent in Nature, required no mediation by a distinct church or priesthood. By invoking rival versions of ecclesiastical and religious history, and comparing the doctrines of Christianity with those of Islam and Judaism, a highly subversive and original 'critique of religion as a cultural artifact or document' was formulated by Toland (1670–1722), Anthony Collins (1676–1729), and Matthew Tindal (1657–1733), among others.[9]

The flood of heterodox publications which followed the lifting of censorship in 1695 was hardly checked by the Blasphemy Act of 1698, even if William Whiston (1667–1752), Newton's successor as Professor of Mathematics at Cambridge, was expelled from the university, and narrowly escaped prosecution for the Arian views expressed in his *Primitive Christianity Revived* (1711). Thomas Woolston (1670–1733), yet another freethinking Cambridge don, actually died in the King's Bench Prison, where he had been incarcerated for publishing his ultra-sceptical *Six Discourses on Miracles* (1727–30). Yet these prominent victims of outraged orthodoxy were exceptionally unlucky, in that they represented only the tip of what was widely represented as an immense iceberg of anticlericalism, heresy, calculated amorality, and infidelity. In High Church eyes, latitudinarian 'natural religion' was a slippery slope, leading inevitably to Deism and worse, even if few as yet distinguished firmly between atheism as intellectual disbelief and atheism as immoral or God-defying behaviour. Questioning the spiritual basis of ecclesiastical authority was thought

---

[9] J. A. I. Champion, *The Pillars of Priestcraft Shaken: The Church of England and its Enemies, 1660–1730* (1992), 229.

by some to fall into the latter category. To deny that 'present ministers and preachers of the Gospel have their commission from Jesus Christ', thundered Dr Robert Moss, was 'no other than a covert way of undermining all religion and introducing the wildest libertinism, Deism and (if it were possible) downright atheism'.[10]

'Serving the Designs of Enthusiasm'[11]

The possibility of such a doctrinal domino effect cannot be wholly dismissed, but the extent of its impact, outside small metropolitan and university coteries of advanced thinkers, is less certain. The orthodox clerical majority hardly remained silent in the face of what they regarded as licentious impiety and gross error. Besides the annual public lectures established under the bequest of the erudite and pious natural philosopher Robert Boyle in 1691, 'for proving the Christian religion, against notorious infidels', a stream of sermons and treatises sought to refute the cynics and doubters on their own ground. At the level of public controversy these efforts were very successful. By the late 1730s the champions of Christianity, notably the non-juror mystic William Law (1686–1781), the bishop-philosopher George Berkeley (1685-1753), and the ex-dissenter Bishop Joseph Butler (1692–1752), seemed to have entirely routed the Deists (even if the latter's ideas subsequently turned out to have been 'not dead, but sleeping'[12]). The anti-Trinitarians, who were less easily disposed of, maintained their presence at Cambridge University and exercised growing influence on the large, relatively well-to-do Presbyterian wing of Dissent.

Yet if natural religion might sometimes lead to heresy or outright disbelief, a more likely outcome was the kind of bland or calculating piety epitomized by a sermon supposedly preached in 1740 'on the duty of getting a good estate and keeping a good reputation'.[13] (The preacher's model was doubtless Tillotson's still popular published sermons, which bore such titles as 'The Wisdom of Being Religious' and 'The Advantages of Religion to Society'.) In their anxiety to avoid any hint of the 'enthusiasm' or 'fanaticism' associated with civil war sectaries, the original Cambridge Latitudinarians and their eighteenth-century successors tended to the opposite extreme, of sober worldly rationalism. So according to Thomas Herring (1693–1757), yet another later archbishop of Canterbury, the Gospel provided 'a new discovery, that true religion did indeed consist in the practice of moral virtues'. While avowing that 'Christianity is more the religion of the heart, than the head', Herring nevertheless emphasized 'the reasonableness and simplicity of its doctrines, productive of an innocent, and useful, and pious life'. Human sinfulness and suffering, or Christ's

---

[10] R. Moss, *A Sermon Preach'd at the Parish-Church of St Laurence-Jewry* (1708), 8–9.

[11] H. Stebbing, *An Earnest and Affectionate Address to the People Called Methodists* (1745), 4.

[12] L. Stephen, *History of English Thought in the Eighteenth Century* (1902), i. 462.

[13] Wesley's *Journal*, quoted W. A. Speck, *Stability and Strife: England, 1714–1760* (1977), 106.

promise of eternal life, scarcely rate a mention; 'the sense of the mysterious and the numinous in religion' was, indeed, 'dangerously attenuated'.[14]

But not everywhere. Three months after Herring's sermon was delivered a 35-year-old Anglican minister listening to a reading from Luther's commentary on Paul's Epistle to the Romans felt 'my heart strangely warmed', and gained the assurance of personal salvation which had hitherto eluded him. John Wesley (1703–91) would spend the rest of his life—and he lived another fifty-three years—attempting to bring similar assurance to 'the people of all sorts'. This last phrase occurs in a letter written from Bristol less than a year later, one of several describing the extraordinary popular response to his open-air evangelism, which attracted huge audiences (sometimes up to 'six or seven thousand attentive hearers').[15] It points to the emergence of a new breed of evangelical mass missionary preachers, among whom George Whitfield (1714–70) easily topped the bill, drawing as many as 50,000 Londoners at a time to sermon-meetings on Kennington Common and Moorfields, the visible manifestation of a Protestant religious revival sweeping simultaneously across Britain, Continental Europe, and North America. Another characteristic of this same awakening was the particular province of John's younger brother, Charles Wesley (1707–88), who during his lifetime composed more than 5,500 hymns, a massive, enduring contribution to the expression of popular religious fervour.

The movement Wesley created and led (having parted theological company with Whitfield's Calvinism in 1741, the first of many such splits) derived its name from the 'methodical' preoccupation with their religious duties of four Oxford University students, who formed an association, derisively nicknamed the 'Holy Club', in the late 1720s. Religious societies, groups of devout young Anglican men meeting regularly for 'pious conference', having emerged in Restoration London, flourished during the post-Revolutionary decades. They reflected a concern for reformation and regeneration, both national and personal, which the ordinary worship of the established church seemed unable to provide. John Wesley's movement owed a good deal to these societies as an organizational model of lay ginger groups operating within and yet somewhat apart from the church. However, from the beginning Wesleyan 'bands' and 'classes' also included women, who took a leading role as organizers, preachers, and teachers. Another crucial influence was his High Church theological background, which eventually helped him embrace an Arminian belief in the universality of saving grace gained through faith, rejecting the strict Calvinist predestinarian division between an elect minority and the reprobate majority. Finally, during an otherwise unhappy missionary sojourn in the newly settled British colony of Georgia, Wesley came into contact with the Moravian

[14] N. Sykes, *From Sheldon to Secker* (1959), 150–1; T. Herring, *A Sermon Preached before the Incorporated Society for the Propagation of the Gospel in Foreign Parts* (1738), 10, 29; Walsh and Taylor, 'Introduction', 43.

[15] *The Letters of John Wesley*, ed. J. Telford (1931), i. 291, 296.

Brethren, a pietist Continental Protestant sect whose beliefs considerably influenced his own. It was also in Georgia that he first made use of lay assistants, 'field preaching', and extempore prayer, all later characteristic features of Wesleyan Methodism.[16]

Wesley and his fellow evangelists aroused suspicion and hostility well before they began open-air preaching; indeed it was their progressive freezing-out from church pulpits which eventually impelled them to take to the fields, so that the itinerant preacher addressing a public religious meeting anywhere but in church soon became a Methodist trademark. Clerical opposition was perhaps evoked less by the size or social mixture of the audiences attracted to such occasions, than the evangelicals' sweeping attacks on their own doctrinal and pastoral bona fides; 'does it not savour of self-sufficiency and presumption, when a few young heads ... set up their own scheme, as the great standard of Christianity?' asked Bishop Gibson. What made the spiritual ruthlessness, or arrogance, of Wesley and his colleagues particularly provoking was that it could not be dismissed as the product of plebeian illiteracy, even if the highly charged emotional atmosphere, fits, faintings, 'inspired tongues and itching ears' which accompanied their meetings seemed alarmingly reminiscent of the worst excesses of mid-seventeenth-century enthusiasm.[17] From the early 1740s, especially in rural areas, touring Methodist preachers were likely to be confronted by antagonistic, sometimes violent crowds, often orchestrated, or connived at, by the local parson, squire, or village notables. Popular hostility was also generated by hostile printed material, plus widespread fear (given colour by Wesley's non-juring connections and anti-Calvinism) that the Methodists constituted a papist fifth column, particularly dangerous at a time of threatened Jacobite invasion.

Wesley was certainly no mechanical fanatic or 'tub-preacher', but the highly educated son of a Tory parson, possessing great organizational skills, high intelligence, a beautiful, penetrating voice, and an indefatigable capacity for hard work. Still less was he a willing agent of moral, political, or social subversion, even if Methodism did help to liberate some of its followers, particularly women, and most notably Selina Hastings, countess of Huntingdon (1707–91), from communal and domestic constraints. Wesley might rather be regarded as an evangelical entrepreneur, who having discerned a huge market gap arising from the failure of both Dissent and the established Church to cater adequately for the spiritual needs of much of the population, went about methodically to supply the deficiency. He was no lonely pioneer in the business of saving souls; in the field before him were the charismatic Whitfield, and a major Welsh revival movement begun by Howel Harris (1714–73) and other

[16] J. Walsh, 'Religious societies, Methodist and Evangelical, 1738–1800', *Studies in Church History*, 23 (1986).

[17] Sykes, *Edmund Gibson*, 307–15; *Observations upon the Conduct and Behaviour of a Certain Sect* (1740), in *EHD, 1714–1783*, 390.

itinerant preachers in the mid-1730s. Other significant figures with similar concerns included the influential Northampton-based Independent minister Philip Doddridge (1702–51), and a number of evangelical Anglican clergy, including John Berridge (1716–93) and William Romaine (1714–95), who never joined the Methodist movement. What particularly distinguished Wesley from these contemporaries were his unusual longevity, coupled with a remarkable ability to keep his followers more or less together in what would eventually become—although not formally until after his death in 1796—a distinct religious denomination.

Confessional State or Secularizing Society?

It was frequently complained throughout the first half of the eighteenth century (and beyond) 'that Christianity in this kingdom is very much declining'. Not mere apathy or lukewarmness, but 'an open and a sort of fashionable contempt, of every thing that's serious and sacred' was deplored by Dr Thomas Gooch in 1712. Before his death in 1733 that exceedingly 'grave and Christian' judge Sir Thomas Pengelly despaired of the 'most shocking manner' in which the 'meaner sort of people breed their children; few have any religion themselves; how then can it be expected that they should instill it into their tender offspring?'[18] Such accusations were nothing new. From 1660 onwards Anglican clergymen had been obsessed with the supposed decline of Christian values, while clerical attacks on religious ignorance and indifference were commonplace throughout the preceding century. Yet in 1711 the Deist Matthew Tindal, confronting High Church claims of a 'late excessive growth of infidelity, heresy, and prophaneness', argued that a significant reduction in metropolitan crime and public disorder since 1688 contradicted the notion of a 'gradual defection from piety and virtue to irreligious ignorance'. A more orthodox contemporary thought that the spread of charity schools 'through all the parts of this kingdom' had 'dispelled the gross ignorance of the common people' with regard to matters of religion.[19]

So far as outright atheism is concerned, historians have been criticized as 'readier to explain the greater prevalence of unbelief after the Restoration than to demonstrate its extent'.[20] But the surviving evidence is both fragmentary and difficult to interpret. The volume of publications advancing atheist or freethinking positions grew noticeably from 1690 onwards. There was also some easing in the criteria of acceptability for public discourse by the 1720s, which

[18] Anon., *A Short Way with Prophaneness and Impiety* (1730), 4; T. Gooch, *A Sermon Preach'd before the Honourable House of Commons* (1712), 20; *Some Private Passages of the Life of Sir Thomas Pengelly, Late Lord Chief Baron of the Exchequer* (1733), 19.

[19] J. Spurr, *The Restoration Church of England* (1991), 19; M. Tindal, *The Nation Vindicated* (1711), 18; W. Bulstrode, in R. Bulstrode, *Miscellaneous Essays* (1715), p. xix.

[20] G. E. Aylmer, 'Unbelief in seventeenth-century England', in D. H. Pennington and K. V. Thomas (eds.), *Puritans and Revolutionaries* (1978), 41.

enabled Bernard Mandeville to argue openly that atheists need not be immoral persons. At the same time published refutations of atheism were also becoming more common, while the volume of religious publications in general remained very high: in 1721 there were said to be enough copies of printed sermons alone on the booksellers' stands 'in St Paul's Churchyard to build another cathedral'. On average nearly a hundred new sermons a year went into print during the first half of the eighteenth century. During this period books and pamphlets on religious topics (including bibles and prayer books) comprised about one-third of the total annual output of some 700 published titles; indeed it has been claimed that 'the evidence points to an almost astonishing interest in religious works generally and biblical criticism specifically'.[21]

Notwithstanding some uncertainties about the social geography and functional consequences of literacy in Augustan and early Hanoverian England (see below, Ch. 11), we may perhaps discern a growing polarization between sceptics and believers. Yet far too little is currently known about popular beliefs, as distinct from those of the educated reading public. The anticlerical journalist Thomas Gordon (1691?–1750) claimed in 1733 that genuine 'free-thinkers, that is, men who bring all things to the bar and trial of right reason' were few in number, whereas the 'mob and the many will always be orthodox, always true to the Church, and to holy-Days, and pious rioting'. Unfortunately, Gordon thought the reasons for this popular conservatism 'too apparent to need mention'. But they evidently included deference to 'authority and the priesthood', reminding us of clerical prominence in inciting crowd violence against both Dissenters and Methodists— not that popular hostility to the intrusive and self-righteous godly necessarily required such encouragement.[22] On the other hand, the geographical distribution of support for the Methodists and other evangelical preachers, plus the known shortages of church and chapel accommodation, especially in London and fast-growing provincial towns like Bristol and Newcastle, suggest that neither the established Church nor Dissent were doing much more now than they had in the seventeenth century to cater for the spiritual needs of the labouring poor, especially those at the very bottom of the socio-economic hierarchy, in isolated communities, or places experiencing rapid demographic and economic growth through industrialization.

Gordon's distinction between an enlightened few and the conformist majority parallels the widening gulf which some historians have perceived as opening up in the later seventeenth and eighteenth centuries between an elite written, and an oral popular culture. There seems little doubt that various beliefs and

[21] J. Trenchard, *A Collection of all the Humourous Letters in the London Journal* (1721), 41; T. R. Preston, 'Biblical criticism, literature, and the eighteenth-century reader', in I. Rivers (ed.), *Books and their Readers in Eighteenth-Century England* (1982), 98–9; P. Rogers (ed.), *The Context of English Literature: The Eighteenth Century* (1978), 51–2.

[22] [T. Gordon], *A Supplement to the Sermon … Addressed to a very Important and most Solemn Churchman* (1733), 32.

practices which survived among the rural labouring poor to be recorded by nineteenth-century collectors of 'folklore' had long since been discarded by many, perhaps most, of their urbanized socio-economic betters. Magic and sorcery provide the major case in point. Well before the felony of witchcraft was finally removed from the statute book in 1736, successful criminal prosecutions of accused witches had become impossible, thanks to the combined scepticism of judges, lawyers, and juries. But although no formal witch trial was held in England after 1712, popular superstition remained strong enough to bring about the lynching of an old woman as a witch in rural Hertfordshire in 1751, an act for which one of the ringleaders was himself later tried and executed. At the same time, routine resort to cunning men and women, astrologers, conjurors, fortune-tellers, divination, and self-administered sympathetic healing magic was by no means confined to plebeians, despite the condescending manner in which such practices were reported by the newspaper and periodical press. Nor did élite and popular culture inhabit absolutely separate worlds; to the end of his days John Wesley firmly believed in ghosts and witches, as well as the healing powers of electricity.

Popular beliefs and culture were not entirely fixed and stable, although in so far as magic's decline reflected marginally greater human control over a marginally less threatening environment (thanks to such innovations as newspaper lost-and-found advertisements, insurance, deposit banking, and improved fire-fighting techniques), the effects of these developments naturally tended to be felt first by literate urban property owners. Some fascinating recent research has mapped a gradually changing attitude towards suicide in early modern England. Traditionally viewed as a crime against God, instigated by Satan's direct prompting, suicide came increasingly to be regarded as an act of desperation committed by temporarily unbalanced individuals undergoing intolerable psychological stress. This shift from an explicitly religious to a secular diagnosis can be followed not only in the learned discussions of philosophers, physicians, and theologians, but also from the changing pattern of verdicts brought in by coroner's juries. During the seventeenth century the deceased was typically found to have committed the crime of self-murder, to have died *felo de se* (a felon by his/her own hand); but from the early eighteenth century onwards the verdict was overwhelmingly one of death *non compos mentis* (while of unsound mind). Coroner's jurors were small property owners from the lower ranks of the middling sort, 'cultural amphibians' who inhabited the worlds of both printed and oral culture. Their verdicts therefore provide us with a uniquely systematic perspective on the popular mentality, and an index to its gradual colonization by the more explicitly rational and secular attitudes characteristic of the educated élite.[23]

---

[23] M. MacDonald and T. R. Murphy, *Sleepless Souls: Suicide in Early Modern England* (1990).

It is perhaps not surprising that historians have reached seemingly contradictory conclusions about the nature and role of religion in early eighteenth-century England. Against the view that secularism was in the ascendant, as 'the fires of religion burned low', it has been insisted that the Hanoverian realm was a 'confessional state', where a 'Christian faith and moral code was the common possession of all social strata'.[24] The concurrent claim that Christian belief (not easily defined, then or now) was 'almost universal' at the beginning of the eighteenth century is not so much implausible as incapable of proof. After 1688, and even 1714, the established Church certainly retained a privileged role, formal status, and real parochial strength, constituting the central norm against which all other religious affiliations or denominations were measured. Nor was there as yet any widely acceptable secular ideology or humanist belief system to stand in place of Christianity. Yet the Hanoverian Church of England enjoyed nothing like the legal monopoly of worship exercised by its official counterparts in Austria, France, Russia, and other genuine 'confessional states' of Continental Europe. Nor can there be much doubt that under the early Hanoverians religion was increasingly concerned with individual rather than communal reformation, more a matter of willed decision than unconscious culture, and less integral to almost all aspects of life and thought than had been the case over the previous century and a half.

[24] T. W. Heyck, *The Peoples of the British Isles: A New History from 1688 to 1870* (1992), 105; J. C. D. Clark, *English Society, 1668–1832* (1985), 87.

10

PRODUCTION AND CONSUMPTION

The Landed Interest: Depression and Improvement

At the beginning of the eighteenth century England was still an overwhelmingly agricultural economy and society. It has been estimated—no precise measurement is feasible—that in 1700 agricultural production accounted for over 40 per cent of total national output, even excluding crops and livestock consumed on the farm rather than brought to market. Agriculture provided artisans and manufacturers with most of their raw materials: 'Wool, flax, silk, cotton, hides, leather, hair, fur, straw, wood'. Around three-fifths of the adult male labour force then found employment on the land. But because farm work was still essentially a family concern, nearly a million women and children field-workers easily outnumbered some 595,000 men. And for all the glamour, rapid recent growth, and frequent high profitability of finance and overseas trade, political rights and social status continued to be most closely linked to the ownership of land.[1]

Regional variations in soil-types, climatic conditions, and cultivation patterns complicate generalization about farming across the country as a whole. However, agricultural prices certainly stagnated during the first half of the eighteenth century, with those for most grains (wheat, barley, oats, rye) actually dropping slightly between the 1680s and the 1740s, despite several sudden jumps due to bad harvests and inflated wartime demand between 1688 and 1714. Only partially offset by rising prices for livestock, the overall downward trend was particularly marked during the 1730s and 1740s. In these decades of agricultural depression, it was claimed that the 'interest of our British landholders has been declining several years last past', while 'innumerable are the distresses of our farmers'.[2]

Stable or falling grain prices reflected a combination of weakened demand and increased supply. Whereas population growth had fuelled price inflation in the later sixteenth and early seventeenth centuries, the marked demographic slowdown from the 1650s to the 1720s checked domestic demand for the main food grains. Part of the resultant slack was taken up by export sales to Ireland

---

[1] P. Deane and W. A. Cole, *British Economic Growth, 1688–1959* (1967), 78. J. V. Beckett, *The Aristocracy in England, 1660–1914* (1986), ch. 2; *EHB* 45, 106–7; E. A. Wrigley, *Continuity, Chance and Change* (1988), 18.

[2] J. Thirsk, *England's Agricultural Regions and Agrarian History, 1599–1750* (1987); G. E. Mingay, 'The agricultural depression, 1730–1750', *ECHR* 8 (1956), 323; M. Overton, *Agricultural Revolution in England: The Transformation of the Agrarian Community, 1500–1850* (1996), 64.

and the Continent, which amounted to nearly one-third of the total wheat harvest at their mid-eighteenth-century peak, although in most years a far smaller fraction of cereal crops was exported. Total output of grains from English and Welsh farms may have risen by about 20 per cent—from 12,094m. to 14,653m. 'quarters' (about 2.9 hectolitres) between 1695 and 1750. Livestock populations and the associated output of animal products, together with fruit and vegetables, are even trickier to estimate. However, one recent attempt suggests that the volume of crops, meat, wool, hides, and dairy goods produced in England and Wales may have increased by nearly 50 per cent over the first half of the eighteenth century.[3]

How did these substantial productivity gains come about? Farmers and landowners, mostly engaged in commercial rather than subsistence agriculture, obviously sought increased yields to offset falling agricultural prices, thus protecting or even enhancing their incomes. But what enabled them to pull off a feat unmatched by their European counterparts (except the Dutch)? The output of arable crops can be increased by improved cultivation methods, or an increase in the land area cultivated, or both. While considerable tracts of arable in the Midlands were being converted to pasture for cattle and sheep, the area under cereal crops seems to have expanded by about 7 per cent during the first half of the eighteenth century. But as that increased acreage can hardly have accounted for even half the estimated rise in grain production, the balance must be attributed to more efficient or, as contemporaries would have said, 'improved' farming.

Historians once celebrated a dramatic 'agricultural revolution' around the middle of the eighteenth century, when new techniques of cultivation and animal husbandry gave a massive boost to farm yields. However, it is now generally agreed that agricultural innovation was a much more gradual, long-term process, extending well back into the seventeenth or even the sixteenth century, when new cash and fodder crops and various other techniques for enhancing soil fertility, mostly borrowed (like so much else) from the Netherlands, were first introduced to England. Widespread adoption of these measures in the later seventeenth century enabled farmers to augment and improve their livestock herds, and thus benefit from a generally stronger demand for beef, mutton, and wool than for grains, while also using the increased supply of animal manure to raise crop yields.[4]

Such initiatives were undertaken particularly, although not exclusively, by 'progressive' landlords and their tenants. The edging-out of small peasant cultivators on customary tenures by large-scale leasehold farmers employing landless agricultural labourers had also been in train since the sixteenth century. The process was frequently associated with the enclosure of open-field

---

[3] *The Agrarian History of England and Wales, v. 1640–1750*, ed. J. Thirsk (1985), ii. 444–54; *EHB* 100–3.

[4] J. V. Beckett, *The Agricultural Revolution* (1990); Overton, *Agricultural Revolution in England*.

villages and the consequent extinction or restriction of smallholders' grazing rights upon what had previously been common pasture land. It was accelerated after 1688 by the double impact of land tax and long-term stagnant or falling agricultural prices on those who lacked the resources to cushion themselves against a run of bad—or excessively plentiful—harvests. The selling-up or squeezing-out of cottager-copyholders and tenants at will, and even some smaller yeomen freeholders, was most noticeable in the arable and mixed farming areas of East Anglia, the South-East, and the Midlands, less apparent in the upland grazing regions of the North and West.

At the summit of the emerging (and in European terms, unique) three-tiered structure of English rural society stood, or sat, the landed proprietor. The late seventeenth and eighteenth centuries saw some expansion and consolidation of large landed estates, paralleling a simultaneous increase in the average size of individual farms. Historians are not agreed as to the underlying causes or extent of these trends, which were by no means uniform across the country. Two new legal developments—'equity of redemption' and the 'strict settlement'—may have assisted by respectively reducing the risks of raising loans on mortgage, and the ability of proprietors to alienate their family estates. Large-scale landholders generally found it easier to finance the expensive drainage, enclosure of open fields, and other works necessary to raise productivity and hence attract substantial tenants who would pay their increased rents promptly and not run down the farms they leased. But by no means all aristocratic landlords followed the example of the famous Viscount Charles 'Turnip' Townshend of Rynham in Norfolk, who after retiring from politics in 1730 (see above, p. 127) continued his earlier efforts to foster advanced agricultural practices, including the use of turnips as a field crop on his extensive estates. Indeed the policy of many noblemen, like the successive heads of the rising Leveson-Gower family in Staffordshire, 'was to let the farms of their estate and then have nothing more to do with them'. Yet the demonstration effect of prominent magnate pioneers in encouraging their tenants to adopt up-to-date farming methods cannot be entirely discounted, even if most active 'improvers' seem to have held more modest estates, numbered in hundreds rather than thousands of acres. Absentee landlords great and small often showed keen interest in the details of estate management, relying on a resident steward to represent their interests in dealings with the tenantry. 'Women of quality and estates' were also encouraged to 'be as well acquainted with the rentals of their lands, the situation, leases and condition ... as their husbands', even if it was not expected that they should interest themselves in the finer points of animal husbandry and crops.[5]

---

[5] J. M. Rosenheim, *The Townshends of Raynham: Nobility in Transition in Restoration and Early Hanoverian England* (1989); J. R. Wordie, *Estate Management in Eighteenth-Century England* (1982); D. R. Hainsworth, *Stewards, Lords and People: The Estate Steward and His World in Late Stuart England* (1992); H. J. Habbakuk, *Marriage, Debt and the Estates System: English Landownership, 1650–1950* (1995), M. Wray, *The Ladies Library* (1714), 20.

Finally, increased rural productivity was both demanded and enabled by England's relatively high level of urbanization, which fostered agricultural specialization to meet the food needs of town-dwellers, as well as the rural artisan and manufacturing population. A favourable intellectual and institutional climate also helped. The optimistic, pragmatic, utilitarian attitudes associated with the new science fostered systematic approaches to identifying and promulgating efficient agricultural practices. A legal and political order heavily tilted towards the interests of men of property was conducive to long-term investment in agricultural improvement. As state revenue needs were increasingly met by indirect consumption taxes, the share derived from the land tax gradually dropped. Although perhaps two-thirds of England had been enclosed by 1700, the early years of the eighteenth century saw landowners switching from negotiated enclosure agreements to the use of private Acts of Parliament, which made it easier to overcome local opposition from poor cottagers and tenants. Additional agricultural productivity meant not just greater output per acre, but greater output per worker; enclosed fields actually increased labour productivity by reducing employment, especially of women and children. In human terms, this shifted the burden of coping with the long run of low agricultural prices to those who could least afford it. More intensive cultivation of smaller farms by independent peasant proprietors and their families might perhaps have achieved the same growth in productivity per acre, without destroying the customary fabric of rural society, and making the poor 'strangers in their own land'.[6]

Manufactures and Manufacturing

Early in Queen Anne's reign the botanist and medical practitioner Nehemiah Grew (1641–1712) looked back to 'former ages', when 'our manufactory was very contemptible'. Houses were mostly thatched, not tiled, with windows 'of lattice for glass' (that is, small lead-lights, not large panes); plates, spoons, candlesticks, now usually of pewter or silver, 'heretofore were commonly made of wood', while 'we had not a sheet of white paper of our own making to write upon'. But 'the number of our manufactures, invented at home or brought to us from abroad, is exceedingly increased of late years'. Grew's contemporary, the Bristol merchant John Cary, was also struck by signs of growing efficiency and 'ingenuity': 'the glassmaker hath found a quicker way of making it out of things which cost little; silk stockings are wove; tobacco is cut by engines; books are printed; deal boards are sawn with mills; lead is smelted by wind-furnaces; all which save the labour of many hands'.[7]

---

[6] R. C. Allen, *Enclosure and the Yeoman: The Agricultural Development of the South Midlands, 1450–1850* (1992); E. P. Thompson, *Customs in Common* (1991), 184.

[7] 'The Meanes of a most Ample Encrease': Huntington Library, Ms. 1264; J. Cary, *Essay towards Regulating the Trade* (1719), 98.

Economic historians have recently been revising downwards the estimated rate of economic growth during the later eighteenth century. As the heroic stature of post-1750 economic expansion has tended to diminish, greater scholarly attention focuses on the nature and pace of industrial activity in early eighteenth-century England. (The dethroning of the classical concept of an eighteenth-century agricultural revolution, discussed in the previous section, was similarly accompanied by heightened recognition of advances in agricultural productivity during the century after 1650.) In this context some scholars speak of 'proto-industrialization'. Strictly speaking, however, that term refers not merely to the growth of rural cottage or small workshop manufacturing before the rise of urban industry, but to abstract, complex, and for present purposes unrewarding concepts of production for export, with the associated replacement of small independent craft workers by a proletarianized workforce.[8]

Although some of Grew's and Cary's examples (like printing, sawmills, and stocking frames) went much further back, the later seventeenth and early eighteenth centuries saw the introduction of new manufacturing enterprises using both imported and indigenous techniques (fine papermaking and lead crystal glass are two good examples). Incremental improvements to existing processes could bring cheaper prices, or wider choice, or both, especially for textile products and ceramics. There were also significant new departures in industrial organization and technology. Among these were what has been hailed as the first authentic factory, a huge water-powered silk yarn mill on the River Derwent employing a workforce of some 300 women and children, built for Thomas Lombe (1685–1739) between 1718 and 1721. Another major mechanical development saw steam-powered pumps to drain water from mine workings developed by Thomas Savery (1650?–1715) and much improved by his partner Thomas Newcomen (1663–1729), whose engines had spread both across the country and to Continental Europe before his death. Of at least equal and probably greater long-term significance was the discovery by the ironmaster Abraham Darby (1677–1717) at Coalbrookdale in Shropshire of a means to smelt iron ore using cheap and readily available coal, or coke, rather than the traditional, increasingly scarce and expensive charcoal. In 1733 the inventor John Kay (1704–79) applied for a patent to protect his mechanized 'fly' or 'flying' shuttle', claiming that by automatically returning the shuttle from one side of the loom to the other it could double a cloth weaver's daily output. From around this time opposition in the lawcourts and Parliament to the introduction of new 'arts, mills and engines, which save the labour of hands', on the grounds that they would lead to unemployment, social unrest, and inflated poor rates, seems to drop away noticeably.[9]

[8] M. Berg, *The Age of Manufactures, 1700–1820* (1985), 77–83; Wrigley, *Continuity, Chance and Change* (1988), 91–4.

[9] P. Mathias, *The First Industrial Nation* (1972); P. Mantoux, *The Industrial Revolution in the Eighteenth Century* (1934); C. MacLeod, *Inventing the Industrial Revolution* (1988), 161–5.

So early eighteenth-century manufacturing industry was far from moribund or stagnant. While the labour force still mostly worked from home, or in small artisan workshops, some tendency towards concentration in larger productive units was already apparent. Besides the Lombe silk mill and its imitators, there were the huge royal naval dockyards at Portsmouth and Plymouth, each with more than two thousand employees by 1750, and the sprawling Crawley iron-works near Newcastle upon Tyne. In London brewing had become a capital-intensive industry, and the big plants of Barclay, Truman, Whitbread, and the rest countered the threat to their market from cheap distilled spirits in the 1720s by introducing 'porter', the first true mass-production beer. Staffordshire also saw significant increases in the labour force, output, and physical size of individual potteries during the half-century before 1760.

The country's largest employer of labour (outside agriculture and domestic service), the textile industry, felt more sustained competitive pressures, from both European and Asian rivals. The result was lower consumer prices, and wages, despite successful lobbying for protective legislation which in theory excluded imported cottons and silks in the early eighteenth century. Meanwhile the rise of new regional centres, such as the thriving worsted manufacture area around Halifax in Yorkshire which fascinated Defoe, challenged the long-established pre-eminence of the western and East Anglian clothing counties. Considerable quantities of woollen cloth were still being produced in such urban centres as Exeter, Gloucester, Norwich, and of course London, the country's largest industrial centre. But a decentralized cottage, domestic, or putting-out system of production, in which raw material and sometimes tools or equipment were controlled by a capitalist entrepreneur, had long characterized most branches of cloth manufacture. Now the workers were increasingly dependent on piece-rate earnings from their trade, rather than treating it as a by-employment for slack times on the farm. A similar growth of specialized industrial employment occurred in the West Midlands and South Yorkshire hardware and metalworking trades, which likewise benefited increasingly during the early eighteenth century from the opening-up of new export markets (in this case for tools, guns, and domestic utensils) among British colonial settlements across the Atlantic.

Consumers and Consumerism

A take-off of North American demand for British manufactured goods during the 1740s brought the colonists closer to the broadly based consumer economy which had gradually emerged in England over the two previous centuries. Many new craft industries established from mid-Tudor times onwards, mainly in the countryside, produced a bewildering range and variety of household and personal goods, including textiles, clothing, tableware, crockery, mirrors, drinking glasses, ornaments, and trinkets. 'By the end of the seventeenth century', Joan Thirsk tells us, 'people had a choice of so many different qualities of linen for domestic use and personal wear that it was impossible to count them', while ready-made clothing, such as knitted stockings, haberdashery, even fruit trees and vegetable seeds, presented a 'magnificent range of choice'.[10]

An attractive, indeed profitably addictive range of extra-European imported products had also become widely available, in the form of chocolate, coffee, tea, sugar, and tobacco. All these 'groceries', originally rare and expensive luxuries for the elite, soon became relatively commonplace and affordable. Tobacco imports from Maryland and Virginia, amounting to less than 15,000 lb. (6,818 kg.) in 1615, reached 13m. lb. (5.9m. kg.) at the end of the century, plus nearly twice that amount re-exported to Europe. Smokers were by now paying less than a twentieth of the pre-1640 price for the noxious weed, which seems to have been consumed at all social levels, while alehouses provided both tobacco and china-clay pipes for their patrons. White sugar halved in retail price during the seventeenth century and then dropped a further 20 per cent by 1750, while less highly refined brown sugar was about a third cheaper. Total sugar imports for domestic consumption easily doubled from the 1660s to the century's end, then doubled again by the 1730s, when they were running at nearly 15 lb. (6.8 kg.) per person per year, although the well-to-do presumably consumed a good deal more than that, and their socio-economic inferiors a lot less.[11]

Besides its culinary uses, sugar was in demand to sweeten drinks, especially cocoa, coffee, and tea. Tea, the last of the caffeine drinks to arrive in England, soon became the most popular. Since the mid-seventeenth century coffee and cocoa had been taken (largely but not solely by men) in coffee- and chocolatehouses, popular commercial establishments (London alone had about 500 at George I's accession) which also provided food and alcohol, writing facilities, free newspapers, and periodicals.[12] Tea, however, was predominantly a domestic beverage, and consumed as much or more by women as by men. After 1713 the East India Company's regular shipments from Canton were supplemented by large quantities of smuggled tea; in 1745 a parliamentary committee estimated that 3m. lb. a year, at least three times the amount of legal imports, was being brought into the country by smugglers, including large gangs of Jacobite sympathizers operating in south-eastern England. According to the censorious clergyman Thomas Alcock (1709–98), a 'new species of expense crept in of late years among the lower sort is tea-drinking'; even paupers (as he claimed) 'have their tea once, if not twice a day', while along the coast, 'where by clandestine means [i.e. smuggling], tea is afforded cheaper, it is the ordinary

[10] T. H. Breen, 'An empire of goods: the Anglicization of British North America, 1690–1776', *Journal of British Studies*, 25 (1986); J. Thirsk, *Economic Policy and Projects: The Development of a Consumer Society in Early Modern England* (1978), 106.

[11] C. Shammas, *The Pre-Industrial Consumer in England and America* (1990), ch. 4; P. Clark, *The English Alehouse: A social history, 1200–1830* (1983), 134–5.

[12] S. Pincus, ' "Coffee Politicians Does Create": Coffeehouses and Restoration Political Culture', *Journal of Modern History*, 67 (1995).

breakfast of the meanest of the inhabitants'. Since many female domestic servants reportedly refused to work in any establishment where tea was not provided, Alcock gloomily predicted that when 'from servants they go to be poor men's wives', the same 'expensive appetites' would be 'propagated by example to the offspring'.[13]

When Nehemiah Grew commented in the mid-1700s on the replacement by metal of wooden eating and drinking utensils, pewter tankards and plates were already being supplemented in a few well-to-do households by fine china cups, plates, and saucers, plainly better suited than pewter to serving hot drinks. Surveys of probate inventories listing movable goods taken after their owner's death suggest that the 1720s saw a marked extension into the middling ranks of china, porcelain, tea and coffee pots, knives and forks, and glassware. The fine pottery market continued to be dominated by Asian 'blue and white' imports until the 1740s, but thereafter locally produced porcelain and other high-quality ceramics were increasingly competitive with the imported article. A more controversial case of import substitution followed the bitter struggle of the silk and woollen industries against the immensely popular calicoes and chintzes first imported by the East India Company in the mid-seventeenth century, culminating in a statute of 1721 which actually banned all cotton cloth from England. Although never fully effective, this draconian protective legislation left the nascent domestic cotton textile industry free to develop cotton–linen blends, printed with brightly coloured patterns copied from the Indian originals, to supply a demonstrated demand for colourful, light, and washable clothing and furnishing fabrics. Those unable to afford new garments, whether made up by a tailor or bought ready to wear, might still manage to outfit themselves with cheaper, serviceable, and not inevitably unfashionable second-hand clothing. A flourishing national market in used gowns, aprons, caps, jackets, breeches, shirts, stockings, and so forth, was serviced by a network of dealers, hawkers, pawnbrokers, and 'salesmen', the latter characterized in a careers handbook of 1747 as persons who 'deal in old clothes, and sometimes in new. They trade very largely.'[14]

This last example raises an important general question: how, and how widely, both in geographical and socio-economic terms, were standardized consumer goods distributed during the first half of the eighteenth century? Rising real wages, thanks to stable or falling food prices, may have provided many workers with increased disposable income, at a time when the commercial and professional middling sorts were generally enjoying considerable prosperity; on the supply side, the advent and increasing cheapness of the extra-European

[13] J. B. Botsford, *English Society in the Eighteenth Century as Influenced from Overseas* (1924), 62–9; P. Monod, 'Dangerous merchandise: smuggling, Jacobitism, and commercial culture in Southeast England, 1690–1760', *Journal of British Studies*, 30 (1991); T. Alcock, *Observations on the Defects of the Poor Laws* (1752), 47–8.

[14] R. Campbell, *The London Tradesman* (1747), 202.

groceries matched an ever-widening and more affordable range of standardized manufactured articles. Commodities and potential customers were brought together by retail shopkeepers, pedlars and stall-keepers, whose clienteles, premises, and stock-in-trade naturally varied very widely. The high-class emporia of London, with their plate-glass windows 'where the choicest merchandise from the four quarters of the globe is exposed to the sight', impressed natives and foreign visitors alike; according to Defoe, fitting-out even a London pastry-cook's shop in order to 'make a show to invite customers' could cost a cool £300.

Such glittering displays might prompt provincial envy, and sometimes imitation. But potential consumers outside London gained access to imported and domestic wares via more modest retail outlets, found in most towns, and even many villages, supplemented by the ubiquitous itinerant chapmen and hawkers. By 1750 the number of shops per head of population in England seems to have been greater than ever before, or indeed since. Village shops, often kept by cottagers and others of humble means, usually had a limited stock centred around groceries, cheese, and beer, items which tended to be bought frequently and in small quantities. Demand for consumer goods was presumably often generated by their mere availability. But historians have also pointed to the growing use of newspaper advertising, handbills, and other forms of printed publicity to arouse interest and generate sales. Although consumption patterns were not simply set by the gentry and then copied deferentially by their inferiors, a desire to keep up with changing fashions in clothing, furniture, and domestic fittings, and to emulate the appearance and tastes of social superiors, also moulded consumer behaviour.[15]

How far ownership and use of the new consumer items extended down the social hierarchy is not altogether certain. The inventory evidence on which we mainly rely omits the very poorest householders, as well as married women, and peters out after *c.*1725. It also provides inadequate detailed information about the possession of clothing and textiles. However, present indications are that while tea (and gin), tobacco, and some textile goods, like cotton handkerchiefs and gowns, enjoyed very wide circulation during the first half of the eighteenth century, consumer semi-durables such as knives and forks, glassware, prints, and window curtains were rarely found among the mass of the labouring and wage-earning population. They were also more common among town-dwellers than country folk, and independent craftsmen or professionals than the landed gentry.

But if the inroads of consumerism were uneven, they were far from inconsequential. The urban middle classes constituted a large and growing market for the products of domestic manufacturing industry, as well as extra-European

---

[15] M. van Muyden, *Foreign View of England* (1902; see Ch. 7 n.1), 81; D. Defoe, *The Complete English Tradesman* (1726); H. and L. H. Mui, *Shops and Shopkeeping in Eighteenth-Century England* (1989).

consumables. By enhancing domestic amenities, their purchases tended to re-inforce the emerging role of the household as a centre of interaction and soci-ability for family and friends, rather than a mere functional site for sleep and work. The emphasis upon decorative furnishings, and the rituals associated with tea-drinking, point to women's distinct and growing influence in the do-mestic sphere. Even the restricted consumption menu of the poor may have tended to undermine a prevailing 'leisure preference', by creating new wants which demanded additional income for their satisfaction. If so, workers could well have been encouraged to further efforts once they had earned the mini-mum necessary for subsistence, albeit at the risk of damage to the health of those who existed on only marginally adequate diets. Of course they are also likely to have been particularly susceptible to 'the appetite-abating and energiz-ing properties' of tobacco, sugar, tea and coffee.[16] Finally, steadily expanding consumerism held enormous potential for enhancing government revenue.

Government and the Economy

Between the establishment of an Anglo-Scots common market by the Act of Union in 1707, and the destruction of its Jacobite enemies at Culloden nearly four decades later, the share of British public revenue contributed by con-sumption taxes (excise and import duties) consistently rose. The proportion de-rived from direct taxation (mostly of land) correspondingly fell. This trend was constant, despite short-term anomalies largely attributable to the disruptions of war. Over the five years 1706–10, less than a third (£8m.) of total govern-ment revenues (£26m.) was paid in by the excise commissioners; in the period 1746–50 excise payments had more than doubled (to £16m.), comprising nearly half of a substantially larger (£35m.) total government income.

Notwithstanding official uneasiness voiced about taxing the necessities of the poor, the excise fell on a wide range of non-luxury manufactured com-modities, including candles, coal, salt, and soap, as well as beer, cider, leather, and malt. In addition tea and sugar, already fast becoming 'luxuries of the lowest ranks of people', attracted substantial customs duties. So the continued expansion of government revenues during the first half of the eighteenth cen-tury was achieved by regressive indirect taxation of the population at large, while the landed and mercantile élite, whose parliamentary representatives voted the necessary legislation, saw their own share of the taxation burden de-cline proportionately. Governments found it politically expedient to keep the rate of land tax as low as possible during peacetime, and not to enquire too closely into the relationship between assessed and market values of landed estates, relying upon a combination of increasing consumption levels and higher excise rates to maintain the steady upwards revenue trend. By eroding

---

[16] Shammas, *Pre-Industrial Consumer*, 297.

the disposable income of the wage-earning classes, this policy must have tended to dampen domestic demand, hence retarding the sales, and growth, of manufacturing industry, at least in the short run.[17]

Most of the funds raised were either spent directly on warfare, or paid the interest on moneys borrowed to fight wars. Even during the period of official peace between 1714 and 1739, expenditure on defence purposes stood at 39 per cent of the government's outgoings, while interest payments on the National Debt (incurred during the previous wars with Louis XIV) took no less than 44 per cent. In the years of declared war from 1740 to 1748, military and naval payments amounted to two-thirds of the total, and the Debt (held by British and Dutch financiers, propertied investors, and institutions) took up another quarter, leaving a bare 10 per cent for the purposes of civil government. But these wars were arguably justifiable on pragmatic grounds, both as part of an ultimately successful struggle for British control of markets and sources of raw materials in America, Africa, and Asia, and more immediately because of their invigorating impact across the whole economy. In general, increased demand for manufactured goods (especially metalware and textiles), supplies of coal, foodstuffs, timber, and labour probably outweighed the disruptive impact on trade and industry, especially since the main direct British military commitment in the 1740s was made by the navy rather than on land, where Austrian and German mercenaries did most of the fighting.[18]

Even if all or part of the money allocated to war had somehow been diverted to non-military purposes, the 'fiscal-military' state's rudimentary bureaucracy would have found considerable difficulty in spending it in a productive fashion. Hanoverian government was not merely decentralized, but 'polyarchic'— multi-centered—with power widely and almost randomly distributed among a bewildering array of agencies and individuals, including Crown, ministry, both houses of Parliament, privy council, the Church of England, the lawcourts, the Bank of England, and the East India Company. In addition a host of local authorities, from JPs and aldermen to turnpike commissioners and overseers of the poor, operated with little oversight or supervision from the centre. Politicians showed minimal concern for, indeed hardly any conception of, a co-ordinated national economic policy. The provision and upkeep of non-military socio-economic infrastructure—roads, bridges, harbours, schools, hospitals, prisons—were left to local, private initiatives, albeit increasingly facilitated by Act of Parliament. Industrial relations, law and order, and social welfare, especially the relief of poverty and unemployment, were also the prime responsibility of local authorities, operating under a mixture of custom and national legislative provisions.

[17] J. V. Beckett and M. Turner, 'Taxation and economic growth in eighteenth-century England', *EcHR* 43 (1990); cf. P. O'Brien, 'The political economy of British taxation, 1660–1815', *EcHR* 41 (1988). A. Smith, *The Wealth of Nations* (1776, 1904), ed. E. Cannan, ii. 401.

[18] O'Brien, 'Political economy', 2 (table 1).

The central government's relatively low domestic profile did not necessarily make for economic efficiency. For example, the Royal Mint's inability to keep sufficient silver coins in circulation for everyday transactions caused persistent difficulties to tradesmen and customers alike. The legal system's delays, expense, inflexibility, and uncertainty in handling commercial disputes were another constant complaint. A modern economic rationalist looking to eighteenth-century England as a model of small government might be even more disturbed by the persistence of customs and legislation restricting the free play of market forces, including laws designed to prevent profiteering in food-stuffs, price-fixing regulations (for bread, beer, and other basic commodities), apprenticeship, and poor-relief provisions. Far from any commitment towards commercial deregulation or free trade, the early eighteenth century saw further elaboration of agricultural and industrial protectionism on the foundations laid by the Navigation Acts, with an intricate array of bounties, tariffs, export prohibitions, and other restrictive measures partially codified by Walpole's customs reforms. In short, early Hanoverian England was not an unregulated free-market society, but rather characterized by a unique mixture of economic individualism and mercantilism with traditional collectivism, paternalism, and order.

PART IV

Empires Won and Lost
1746–1788

11

PEOPLE

Population Growth

England's population apparently did not surpass its mid-seventeenth-century peak of 5.3m. until the early 1720s. Population growth continued very slowly for the next twenty years or so, held in check by the severe if intermittent impact of harvest failure and epidemic disease (influenza, smallpox, dysentery, and typhus, but significantly not bubonic plague) between 1727 and 1730, and again in 1741–2. Then from *c*.1750 the yearly demographic growth rate steadily climbed above 0.5 per cent. By the last decade of the century it had reached the unprecedented level of 1.2 per cent, producing a total of some 8.6m. inhabitants in 1801.

That these figures are at best approximations is readily admitted. Neither the complex statistical model on which they are based, nor the numerous working assumptions required in order to convert a mass of parish register entries into computable demographic data, have escaped scholarly criticism. Yet both results and methodology seem positively robust when compared to anything currently available for Ireland, Scotland, or Wales. The Welsh may have numbered about 300,000 at the beginning of the eighteenth century, perhaps half a million by 1770, and 600,000 by *c*.1800. If so, their numbers increased much faster than those of the Scots, whose population seems to have been in the order of 1.25m. in 1700, only about 3 per cent more by 1750, and some 1.6m. at the end of the century. Ireland, by contrast, despite having fewer than 2m. inhabitants in 1700, and suffering very severe demographic losses during the first half of the eighteenth century, saw a doubling of population to about 5m. by 1800. The English rate of growth was nothing like so rapid, at around 70 per cent for the whole century. But it was roughly twice that of France over the same period, even if in 1800 the total French population (29m.) was more than three times larger.

Why did England's population expand so rapidly in the second half of the eighteenth century? The explanation may not lie in unique national circumstances, given the even higher growth rates experienced in Ireland, perhaps Wales, and certainly Finland over the same period. But it should take account both of England's long-standing relative prosperity and more recent economic diversity, as well as her extensive colonial possessions across the Atlantic and elsewhere. These attracted an estimated 300,000 British (overwhelmingly young and English) migrants in the course of the eighteenth century, an outflow which more than balanced the immigration of Scots, Irish, and Welsh seeking to better their fortunes, if only because the latter could and did return more easily to their native lands. Yet quite apart from the lack of effective border controls and hence comprehensive records of movement in and out of the country, immigration alone would not have been able to fuel a demographic expansion on the scale outlined above. Indeed Wrigley and Schofield postulate a net migration *loss* of over half a million people from England during the course of the eighteenth century.[1]

If England's population did not increase because more people were entering the country from abroad, it must have risen as a result of births exceeding deaths. Such excess could have followed (i) a decline in the death rate, (ii) a rise in the birth rate, or (iii) some combination of (i) and (ii). Wrigley and Schofield's preference for (iii) rests on their belief that the eighteenth century saw only slight improvement in mortality levels, but a decisive drop in the average age at which women first married (from around 26 to 23 years). Since contraception was minimal and illegitimacy rates low, although rising, a fall in the mean female age at marriage would have meant more children for each marriage, and hence a rising birth rate, especially since the proportion of women who never married was simultaneously diminishing.

However, the evidential and methodological bases for nominating increased fertility, rather than declining mortality, as the prime cause of the post-1750 population surge are somewhat contentious. To oversimplify, the family reconstitutions of twelve parishes upon which Wrigley and Schofield relied to demonstrate declining female age at marriage are flawed by problems of record linkage, and population mobility, especially among the poor and young. What is more, marriage licences, a source which Wrigley and Schofield did not exploit, actually point to a slight overall *rise* in female age at first marriage over the eighteenth and early nineteenth centuries. Recent studies of life expectancy across a wide range of occupational and social groups also suggest that average life spans may have increased by as much as ten years over the eighteenth century, as against the two to three years postulated by Wrigley and Schofield. Improved nutrition, and better standards of domestic hygiene stemming from the substitution of brick and tile for bare earth floors, plus the spread of inoculation against smallpox, could all have contributed to this outcome, which by itself might account for the total estimated growth of population in eighteenth-century England.[2]

The Common People

While historical demographers continue to debate the causes of England's post-1750 population surge, our main concern is with its consequences. In

[1] E. A. Wrigley and R. S. Schofield, *The Population History of England, 1541–1871* (1989), chs. 6–7; M. Anderson, *Population Change in North-Western Europe, 1750–1850* (1988), ch. 2.

[2] P. Razzell, *Essays in English Population History* (1994), chs. 7–8.

many parts of the world today continued population growth threatens not merely depressed living standards, but also a downward spiral of urban over-crowding, epidemic disease, famine, and socio-political breakdown. Later eighteenth-century England was spared such an outcome, but demographic expansion undoubtedly pressed closely on available resources, especially of food. Annual population growth rates between the 1760s and the end of the century as reconstructed by Wrigley and Schofield (0.5 to 1.21 per cent), generally exceed recent estimates of the yearly rate of increase in agricultural productivity (between 0.1 and 0.8 per cent); in other words, the pace of demographic growth was evidently outstripping the expansion of farm output.[3] Equally ominous, from mid-century real wages for the adult male workforce across the country ceased to rise, checking a trend which had been more or less continuous since Charles II's restoration. In general it seems that only some non-agricultural workers—typically in manufacturing and the building trades—received sufficient increase in their hourly or weekly rates of pay to compensate for the inflation in prices, particularly for food, which began from the 1750s. These fortunate individuals and their families were concentrated in the rapidly growing industrial areas of Yorkshire, Lancashire, the Midlands, and Staffordshire—broadly, counties above a line drawn from the River Severn in the west to the Lincolnshire Wash in the east. In the region south of that line, where somewhat over half the nation's population lived at mid-century, real wage rates either stagnated, or actually fell, as they did in London and the rural south-east.[4]

Yet neither national farm output data nor real wages statistics by themselves provide unambiguous evidence of a sustained general deterioration in living conditions between the defeat of the '45 and the eve of the French Revolution. Indeed there are some contrary indications. English agriculture, already perhaps the most productive in the world, diverted substantial quantities of grain from export markets to home consumption after 1750. While short-term rises in food prices seem to correlate quite well with upward movements of mortality rates before 1745, thereafter the relationship becomes inverse and almost imperceptible. In other words, even when the price of bread soared, most people were evidently still able to get enough to eat, or at least not so much less as to starve them to death. Nor was there a revival of the long-distance migration, typically from country to town in search of food and work, characteristic of hard times in previous centuries. Of course food shortages, hunger, and malnutrition were hardly banished from later Hanoverian England. Recent calculations suggest that in the 1780s adult members of the labouring poor may have existed on an average daily intake of 2,500 to 2,700 calories (mostly in the form of 'starchy staples'—grains and potatoes). Western nutritionists would today allocate 3,500–4,000 calories to persons engaged in hard physical exertion; the

---

[3] N. Crafts, 'The industrial revolution', in *EHB* 51.
[4] P. H. Lindert, 'Unequal living standards', in *EHB* 368–71.

difference may partly reflect a slower pace of work and smaller-framed workers then than now.[5]

Harvest failures leading to local shortages of grain and high bread prices provoked outbreaks of food rioting in the late 1740s, 1756–7, 1766 (the most widespread episodes), 1771–3, and 1782–4 (as they had also done earlier in the century, and would continue to do for another eighty years). These noisy protests by crowds of industrial workers, miners, and their wives often involved verbal and physical threats to bakers, farmers, millers, and corn-dealers, and mass attacks on their property. But far from posing a direct challenge to the authority of the Hanoverian state, the aim was to force local magistrates to do their duty, by ensuring adequate supplies of reasonably priced staple food-stuffs. Nevertheless, such outbreaks underline the precariousness of workers' budgets, especially when sharp price rises coincided with periods of recession and mass unemployment, as in the aftermath of the Seven Years War (1756–63), and the War of American Independence (1776–83).

Adult male wage rates were no more then than they are now identical to weekly adult male earnings, let alone total family incomes. (Statistical evidence about female wages or earnings has been neglected, but women's work seems consistently to have been paid at half to two-thirds the rate of comparable work by men.) Individual and family earnings were frequently eroded by sea-sonal or structural unemployment, and underemployment, sickness, and pay-ment in kind or truck (except where clothes, food, and lodging formed part of a live-in servant's income, and agricultural prices rose sharply, as they did dur-ing this period). Alternatively they might be augmented by working longer hours (assuming work was available), and supplemented by fruit and veget-ables grown in a cottage garden, corn gleaned after harvest, the grazing of live-stock, foraging for wood, and other common rights. Customary perquisites, like the farmer's sale of food to agricultural labourers in his employment below market price, the shipwright's 'chips', and the tailor's 'cabbage' (respectively, timber and cloth remnants), could also be significant benefits. Apart from such variables, hard to quantify as they are, calculations of average national real wages necessarily blur important regional and occupational variations, as well as short-term fluctuations in retail prices.

The difficulty of generalizing about the lot of the 'common people', or 'the poor' (increasingly interchangeable terms in contemporary usage) is not con-fined to the statistical realm. After all, we are dealing not only with the bulk of the population, but men, women, and children who followed many widely differing modes of life. A careers handbook of 1747 provides details of 'trades, professions, arts, both liberal and mechanic', including those of sailor, chimney-sweep, milliner, rag-man, bird-cage maker, weaver, brewer, glover, butcher, tailor, spangle, bangle and button-ring maker, bricklayer, and over

---

[5] C. Shammas, *The Pre-Industrial Consumer in England and America* (1990), ch. 5.

three hundred more, but not labourer, fisherman, miner, servant-in-husbandry, domestic servant, soldier, midwife, wet-nurse, or prostitute.[6] Gregory King's famous late seventeenth-century socio-economic analysis had classed together all 'common seamen', 'labouring people', 'cottagers', soldiers, vagrants, and paupers, who with their families he thought amounted to just over half the total population, as actual or potential recipients of parochial poor relief. In the late 1750s Joseph Massie (d. 1784) attempted to update King's figures. Although their socio-economic categories are not strictly comparable, and he made no estimate of the 'legal poor', Massie believed that some 941,000 families, 81 per cent of the total, had annual incomes of less than £50, or just under £1 a week. It has been suggested that £40–50 was the absolute minimum annual income required by those aspiring to respectable 'middling sort' status. By contrast an unskilled labourer in Lancashire received at mid-century 6 shillings, less than one-third of a pound, as his wage for a six-day week, although a skilled craftsman in a booming trade might earn upwards of £60 a year, and London wages were up to twice as high as those paid in the country. By the 1770s women farm-workers could also earn a shilling a day, but only at harvest time, and half that for the rest of the year; a live-in dairy maid received annual 'board wages' of £3 to £5.10s.[7]

Diverse and very numerous, the eighteenth-century 'labouring poor' (a term popularized by Defoe) nevertheless left relatively little evidence in their own words from which their attitudes, beliefs, experiences, and values might be reconstructed. Yet precisely these have been the central theme of some of the most imaginative and lively historical writing of recent times. Using official and legal records, ballads, folk literature, and newspaper reports, among other sources, the late Edward Thompson and his followers present a new kind of 'history from below', seeking to 'rescue ... from the enormous condescension of posterity' the aspirations and lives of the deprived and usually inarticulate.[8]

It seems unlikely that the aristocracy and gentry of Stuart England enjoyed a much closer and less exploitative relationship with tenants, servants, and other social inferiors than did their Hanoverian counterparts and descendants. However, rising agricultural prices and rents, booming foreign trade, lagging wages, and a regressive taxation régime during the second half of the eighteenth century doubtless exacerbated existing inequalities between the upper and middling classes and the bulk of the population, thereby eroding that 'gradual and easy transition from rank to rank' previously celebrated by some contemporaries.[9] The lure of polite respectability may have also contributed to a widening cultural divide between the labouring poor and their immediate

[6] R. Campbell, *The London Tradesman* (1747).

[7] B. Hill, *Eighteenth-Century Women* (1984), 195; E. W. Gilboy, *Wages in Eighteenth-Century England* (1934), 220–4, 281.

[8] E. P. Thompson, *The Making of the English Working Class* (1963, 1980), 14.

[9] Cited A. W. Coats, 'Changing attitudes to labour in the mid-eighteenth century', *EcHR* 11 (1958), 49.

social superiors. 'Proletarianization', the process whereby previously independent yeomen, husbandmen, and master-craftsmen became propertyless—and hence presumably more vulnerable—wage labourers is also relevant in this context. Indeed it has been suggested that the eighteenth-century population rise is largely attributable to widespread adoption of a proletarian pattern of earlier marriages, which could not have occurred in a predominantly small-holder and artisan economy (where the goal of economic self-sufficiency encouraged later marriages, and restricted fertility). Yet although the eighteenth century did see wage labour spreading, we lack firm evidence to plot the speed of its advance, whether within the agricultural sector or across the economy as a whole. Little more can be said than that between 1600 and 1800 a majority of agricultural workers were landless labourers: the proportion of proletarians to the working population as a whole may either have remained more or less constant, or indeed decreased during the course of the eighteenth century.

In Marxist models of historical change the advent of an exploited proletariat accompanies the triumph of capitalism over feudalism, as cash transactions replace customary and personal links between individuals, and previously self-sufficient families become wholly dependent on a male breadwinner's wage. The later eighteenth century certainly saw a buyer's market for labour, encouraging employers in both agriculture and manufacturing to attempt to curtail traditional rights and perquisites. Agricultural employment opportunities for women and children also declined, at least in the arable regions of southern England. But apart from the legal extinction of common grazing rights following enclosure—admittedly a major exception—the efforts of employers and property owners to restrict or abolish customary perquisites met with very mixed success. Thus despite a legal decision of 1788 that 'no person has at common law a right to glean in the harvest field', the age-old practice of gathering unreaped or fallen grain after harvest continued to contribute 'up to an eighth of annual household earnings and often more in households headed by widows' until the advent of mechanical harvesting in the nineteenth century.[10] Similarly, penalties for the embezzlement or customary appropriation of materials by workmen, especially in the domestic or putting-out system of manufacture, were sharply increased by the 'Bugging Act' of 1749, which imposed mandatory imprisonment and a whipping on convicted offenders, who were only liable to a fine under previous statutes. Yet the legislation made little practical difference, since before 1749 the vast majority of those convicted had been unable or refused to pay the fine, and so were whipped and imprisoned instead. Meanwhile the worsted cloth manufacturers of Bradford and Leeds published frequent newspaper advertisements listing the penalties for workers who retained any materials with which they had been provided, but still went on buying back large quantities of waste thread from weavers.

[10] P. King, 'Customary rights and women's earnings: the importance of gleaning to the rural labouring poor, 1750–1850', *EcHR* 44 (1991), 476.

Notwithstanding these various qualifications and reservations about the extent of structural deterioration in living standards and working conditions, rising prices and rapid population growth undoubtedly made for much harder times after 1750 than during the previous fifty years, especially in southern England. Despite national economic gains, 'the increase of wealth' (as one pessimistic commentator pointed out in 1757) 'is by no means equally divided or diffused: the trader reaps the main profit; after him the landlord ... but the common artificer, and still more the common labourer, gain little by the exorbitant advance of trade'. At least 113 disputes between workers and employers were reported in the twenty years after 1760, more than twice the number of the previous two decades; 1777 was the peak year for London, where three years later the week-long Gordon riots posed the most serious threat to public order since 1688, perhaps even 1659–60. National expenditure on poor relief tripled between the late 1740s and the early 1780s (from nearly £0.7m. to £2m., representing a rise of from 1 per cent to 2 per cent of national income). Even allowing for rampant price inflation and substantial population increase over that same period, the real per capita outlay on public assistance of the poor rose by more than one-third in one generation, not counting private charitable expenditures.[11] Occasional runs of unseasonably cold or wet weather with consequent poor harvests, and the recessions which followed the end of wars in 1764 and 1783, added further misery to living conditions which at best were often exceedingly grim.

The London magistrate and novelist Henry Fielding (1707–54), whose *Tom Jones* (1749) reveals his own wide knowledge of both high and low life, believed that it was ignorance, not lack of compassion, which explained why the poor were 'so often mentioned with abhorrence, and so seldom with pity'; their sufferings were, he thought 'less observed than their misdeeds':

But if we were to make a progress through the outskirts of this town, and look into the habitations of the poor, we should there behold such pictures of human misery as must move the compassion of every heart that deserves the name of human. What, indeed, must be his composition who could see whole families in want of every necessity of life, oppressed with hunger, cold, nakedness, and filth; and with diseases, the certain consequences of these—what, I say, must be his composition who could look into such a scene as this, and be affected only in his nostrils?[12]

Whatever the answer, many firmly believed that 'our poor' had brought all their troubles on their own heads, since they

can not only acquire a comfortable support by working only a small part of their time, but also the means of debauchery; and this is the reason why our common people both

[11] J. Brown, *An Estimate of the Manners and Principles of the Times* (1757), 192. C. R. Dobson, *Masters and Journeymen* (1980), ch. 2; P. Slack, *The English Poor Law, 1531–1782* (1990), 30–1.

[12] H. Fielding, *A Proposal for Making an Effectual Provision for the Poor* (1753), in [H. Fielding], *An Enquiry into the Causes of the Late Increase of Robberies and Related Writings*, ed. M. R. Zirker (1988), 230.

in town and country are so wicked, debauched, and profligate. The only way to make them temperate and industrious, is to lay them under a necessity of labouring all the time they can spare from meals and sleep, in order to procure the common necessities of life.[13]

Such attitudes may have softened somewhat after 1750, as money wages lagged behind rising prices and humanitarian sympathy for the sufferings of those in poverty was reinforced by fears of mass migration or social unrest if conditions continued to worsen. But as with growing criticism of the socially discriminatory game laws which sought to restrict hunting to the landed élite, the class bias of the legal system, especially the bloodthirsty criminal code, and the coerced recruitment of fishermen, merchant sailors, and poor landsmen by naval press gangs, these concerns had little or no immediate practical outcome.

Apart from apathy, lethargy, and self-interest, one main reason for lack of positive action to ameliorate the hardships of the poor was the acceptance of occasional rioting by the lower orders as a fact of life which posed no serious threat to the survival of the whole social order. Underlying that confidence was a widespread belief in the relative prosperity, and freedom, of the English people, as compared to the poverty and subjection of foreigners, especially the French. Obliging Anglophile visitors frequently endorsed the comparison; in 1765 the Frenchman Jean-Paul Grosley observed that London artisans earned twice what their equivalents were paid in France, 'eat and drink well, are handsomely clothed, and procreate accordingly'. Twenty years later a French duke's son reported enthusiastically from rural Suffolk that 'the labourer is not oppressed, is even treated with consideration by the upper class; the simple peasant, more comfortably off than ours, is well clothed, and eats meat every day'. Even if this young traveller's tale sounds a bit too good to be true, it testifies to the power of a national myth, besides possibly reflecting a genuine contrast with the condition of the French peasantry. The popular image of beef-eating, liberty-loving, albeit over-taxed John Bull may well have helped reconcile many of the poor to their lot, especially while their material reality did not deprive it of all credibility.[14]

'The Upper Part of Mankind'

By considering those variously styled the low, inferior, mean, many, base, plebeian, and poor, before the high, superior, great, few, gentle, noble, and rich, we have inverted contemporary priorities, and proprieties. Such an approach also runs counter to one modern image of the Georgian era as synonymous with aristocratic elegance, and the more considered scholarly notion of an 'age of aristocracy' embodied in a federation of great country houses, dominated by

[13] W. Temple, *A Vindication of Commerce and the Arts* (1758), 56.
[14] A. Parreaux, *Daily Life in the England of George III* (1969), 173; *A Frenchman's Year in Suffolk*, ed. N. Scarfe (1988), 78.

the personal leadership and values of the landowning élite. But despite the immense political power and social cachet wielded by this small body of superior and on the whole very rich persons, who by 1790 may have owned as much as a quarter of the cultivated land in England and Wales, the extent of their ascendancy is a matter of some controversy.

During the course of the entire eighteenth century, just 1,003 persons held English peerages; 43 were women peeresses in their own right, either by inheritance or creation, including the mistresses of the first two Hanoverian monarchs, who did not receive writs of summons to sit in the House of Lords. In 1700 there were 163 male peers (dukes, earls, marquises, viscounts, and barons). Numbers remained fairly static until after 1760, then rose to 267 by 1800, mainly as the result of new creations in the 1780s and 1790s. For most of the century English peers were outnumbered, if certainly not outranked, by their Irish and Scots counterparts, many in fact English-born; the former sat in their own national parliament, while after Union the latter elected a token sixteen of their steadily dwindling band to the House of Lords. Below the peerage came two further groups, title-bearing but legally unprivileged, the baronets and knights, who in 1760 comprised about 700 men, making around 1,089 titleholders in all.[15] We might add (following Joseph Massie's 1759 calculations) another thousand esquires (technically, male persons who had the right to display a heraldic coat of arms) and perhaps as many as 16,000 'gentlemen'. However, the formal birth and lifestyle requirements governing the two latter titles had been widely ignored even before the Court of Chivalry and College of Arms gave up attempting to police them in the late seventeenth century. By 1730, according to the lexicographer Nathan Bailey, 'all are accounted gentlemen that have money'. More accurately, it was the appearance of wealth which mattered, as the grubby and footsore German pastor Carl Moritz found when he walked into an inn in the Oxfordshire village of Nettlebed on a summer's evening in 1782 and was shown to the kitchen to eat with the domestic servants. Next morning he came downstairs wearing a clean shirt, whereupon he was served breakfast in the parlour and gratifyingly addressed as 'sir' rather than 'master', the latter form of address being reserved (as he noted) for 'farmers and common people'. By this time 'individual vintners, tanners, scavengers, potters, theatre managers, and professors of Divinity could all claim the status [of gentleman] publicly and without irony.'[16]

So below the tiny titular élite of peers, baronets, and knights, the upper reaches of eighteenth-century English society were very loosely defined. Membership depended on ascribed social categories rather than inherited and legally sanctioned ranks, especially for 'gentleman', the largest and loweststatus category. In this respect England differed markedly from Continental

[15] J. Cannon, *Aristocratic Century: The Peerage of Eighteenth-Century England* (1984).
[16] C. P. Moritz, *Journeys of a German in England in 1782*, tr. R. Nettel (1965), 125; P. Corfield, 'Class by name and number in eighteenth-century Britain', *History*, 72 (1987), 43.

Europe, where those legally entitled to noble rank were both absolutely and relatively more numerous: France had perhaps 120,000 nobles towards the end of the eighteenth century, and Spain no fewer than 700,000, or some 7–8 per cent of her total population. Further, only peers enjoyed any distinct legal privileges in England, and unlike even the poorest French *hobereaux* or Spanish *hidalgos*, these did not include immunity from taxation.[17] Another key difference was that the commercial and professional middling sort which interposed itself between England's upper and lower orders seems to have been relatively a good deal larger and wealthier than its Continental equivalents.

Much significance has been attached to the supposed ease with which wealth acquired in the professions, trade, or industry was translated into membership of England's uniquely 'open aristocracy'. By refreshing itself in this fashion, the landed élite supposedly disarmed potential challenges from below, besides holding out glittering prizes for entrepreneurial success, and facilitating the acceptance of broadly pro-business government policies. Yet the openness of the aristocracy, or at least of its most rarefied heights, can easily be exaggerated. It appears that all but 23 of the 229 individuals raised to the peerage during the eighteenth century already had close kinship or marriage connections with peers, or were transferring from Scots or Irish titles. From a slightly different angle, studying changes in the ownership of 362 large country houses in the three counties of Hertfordshire, Northamptonshire, and Northumberland between the mid-sixteenth and the late nineteenth century led Jeanne and Lawrence Stone to the conclusion that overall only one-fifth (although between 1760 and 1819 more than a quarter) of the owners of these mansions acquired them by purchase, rather than inheritance or marriage. Businessmen comprised just one-third of these purchasers overall (although 41 per cent between 1760 and 1819), the majority being smaller landed gentry 'trading up' from more modest properties.[18]

Of course these findings do not altogether settle the matter. Neither the powerful, but tiny, titular peerage, nor the owners of large country houses can be considered equivalent to the English aristocracy, or the nation's landed élite. However amorphous and ill-defined, that latter body certainly embraced a significant majority of the gentry (that is to say, the baronetcy and knightage), as well as many landowners whose houses fell below the minimum size necessary for inclusion in the Stones' data set. In short, while direct recruitment of nouveaux-riches from the middling sort to the rarefied social and economic heights represented by the House of Lords and county big houses was a relatively rare event (although some critics suggest that the Stones' own figures actually demonstrate a remarkably high uptake, both of newcomers in general and businessmen), mobility from counting house to (smaller) country house,

[17] I. Woloch, *Eighteenth-Century Europe: Tradition and Progress, 1715–1789* (1982), 80.
[18] Cannon, *Aristocratic Century*, ch. 1; L. and J. C. F. Stone, *An Open Elite? England, 1540–1880* (1984), table 6.2.

and hence membership of the ruling class, was a distinctive and significant feature of eighteenth-century English social structure. Nor should we forget that
because titles descended only to male heirs, younger sons from peerage families
necessarily found themselves in the Church, the law, and the armed services,
while they, their elder brothers, and their sisters intermarried with the gentry,
the City, and the professions, as well as mixing with them at the newly fashionable resorts of Bath, Buxton, Harrogate, and Tunbridge Wells. So even the
uppermost tier of the 'upper part' was, if not exactly 'open', at least far from
being an isolated caste.

These questions of social mobility and structure are interesting both in
themselves and for the light they shed on the influence of aristocrats and their
values in mid- to later eighteenth-century England. Contrary to revisionist
insistence on the continued cultural hegemony of an 'aristocratic ethic' in
England's pre-1830 *ancien régime*, a stream of criticism and denigration was
directed at the peerage from the 1770s onwards. Thus Thomas Delamayne's
anonymously published verse satire *The Patricians* (1773) comprehensively exposed the hollowness of aristocratic claims to hereditary merit and political
virtue, inviting readers to

> See the proud Peer, who no one science knows
> Save that of levées, equipage and clothes!

Aristocratic vices—notably duelling, gaming, and sexual libertinism—also attracted increasingly unfavourable comment from journalists, ministers, and
moralists during the last third of the eighteenth century.[19]

Contemporaries were not conscious of living in a *distinctively* aristocratic or
hierarchical age, but rather emphasized, sometimes disapprovingly, the commercial character of their society. Blenheim Palace, Harewood House, Holkham Hall, Woburn Abbey, and other splendid country houses, with their
immense landscape gardens laid out by the talented 'Capability' Brown (1715–
83) or his successor Humphrey Repton (1752–1818), still stand as impressive
monuments to the power and wealth of the aristocrats who built and occupied
them. But the middling sort also had substantial architectural achievements to
their credit in London and many provincial centres, including Bath's crescents,
terraces, and squares, and the Mansion House and Assembly Rooms at York.
Among those who commissioned and sat for portraits painted by fashionable
artists like Joseph Highmore (1692–1780), Richard Wilson (1714–82), Joshua
Reynolds (1723–92), Thomas Gainsborough (1727–88), and George Romney
(1734–1802), from whose works much of our sense of the elegance and grace of
eighteenth-century English life derives, were merchants, financiers, army and
navy officers, lawyers, clergymen, men of letters, and their families. Nor did the
aristocracy constitute the major market for the applied or decorative arts,

[19] P. Langford, *Public Life and the Propertied Englishman, 1689–1798* (1991), ch. 8; D. Andrew,
' "Adultery-a-la Mode": the law and attitudes to adultery, 1770–1809', *History*, 82 (1997).

including the furniture of Chippendale, the metalwork of Boulton, and Wedg-wood ceramics. The entrepreneurial potter Josiah Wedgwood (1730–95) indeed succeeded in achieving his ambition to become 'Vase Maker General to the Universe' by pursuing a remorseless public relations and advertising cam-paign which established fashionable acceptance of his wares, but only in order to exploit the vast domestic middle-class market.

Wedgwood firmly believed that 'Few ladies, you know, dare venture at any-thing out of the common style 'till authorized by their betters—by the ladies of superior spirit who set the ton.'[20] Emulation of aristocratic fashions and tastes was indeed endemic among the middling sort, as many foreign visitors noticed. During his stay in Hertfordshire in 1748 the Swedish agronomist Per Kalm recorded that it was 'not unusual to see a farmer's or another small personage's wife clad on Sundays like a lady of "quality", and her every-day attire in pro-portion'. Kalm also noticed that the fashion for wigs was not confined to 'the principal ladies'; 'farm-servants, clodhoppers, day-labourers, farmers, in a word, all labouring folk go through their usual everyday duties with perukes on the head', merely because it was 'the custom and mode'. But female or male eagerness to imitate their betters in matters of dress and interior decoration hardly implied unqualified deference to aristocratic leadership in every sphere of life. This was especially apparent in the realm of politics, despite marked in-creases during the second half of the eighteenth century in the numbers of Commons' borough constituencies controlled by peers, and the proportion of noble cabinet ministers. Thus many larger urban electorates successfully re-sisted elite electoral patronage, and developed or revived various forms of popular action, such as mass petitioning of Parliament, and the formal issue of instructions to their MPs. Even the forty-shilling freeholders in the county con-stituencies could turn nasty if they felt their vital interests were threatened, as Lord Coleraine found to his cost in 1763, when his support for a tax on cider caused a massive defection of Gloucestershire voters 'in all the vale and forest, great cider counties'.[21]

Childhood

During the second half of the eighteenth century infant and child mortality rates were at least twenty times higher than in most modern industrial societies. Overall nearly one out of every four babies born (22.2 per cent of girls, 23.5 per cent of boys) died before reaching 10 years of age; half these deaths occurred in the first twelve months. Unrecorded burials of new-born infants mean that

[20] N. McKendrick, 'Josiah Wedgwood: an eighteenth-century entrepreneur in salesmanship and marketing techniques', *EcHR* 12 (1960), 415.

[21] *Kalm's Account of his Visit to England on his way to America in 1748*, tr. J. Lucas (1892), 326; N. Rogers, 'The middling sort in eighteenth-century politics', in J. Barry and C. W. Brooks (eds.), *The Middling Sort of People* (1994).

these figures, derived from family reconstitutions, are certainly underestimates, which also fail to reflect substantial urban–rural and socio-economic differences in mortality rates. One reason why the rich generally had larger families of children than the poor was that their offspring had much better chances of surviving the critical first year of life. In London 63 per cent of all babies born between 1750 and 1769 died before the age of 5; over the next twenty years the figure improved to 51.5 per cent. This slight if welcome change for the better was also apparent at the national level, reflecting a long-term improvement in life expectancy which set in around the middle of the eighteenth century.[22]

These overall grim statistics have been invoked to explain what is sometimes characterized as the detached and unloving relationships of early modern parents and children. Thus it is suggested by Lawrence Stone that parents avoided close emotional involvement with their children as a form of psychological defence against the inevitable trauma of bereavement. However, generalized claims of parental aloofness seem exaggerated, and based on a narrow range of evidence. Some degree of outward formality in parent–child, and other interpersonal relations was certainly not incompatible with strong ties of affection between family members. Indeed parental concern and love, joined with 'suspension of belief in their children's frequently transitory existence' is eloquently expressed in innumerable seventeenth- and eighteenth-century autobiographies, diaries, and letters, for example those between Lady Caroline Fox (1723–74) and her husband Henry, first Baron Holland (1705–74). Moreover, the post-1660 period, when some contemporary observers (including John Aubrey and Clarendon) detected a growing informality in family life, actually coincided with a temporary jump in infant death rates, before their long-term post-1750 decline.[23]

The later seventeenth and early eighteenth centuries did see the dissemination of more child-centred and permissive attitudes, at least among the middling propertied classes. The insistence of Algernon Seymour, seventh duke of Somerset, that his own children remain standing in his presence must have begun to seem distinctly eccentric well before that 'proud Duke' died in 1750 at the age of 85. John Locke's *Some Thoughts Concerning Education* (which after its initial London publication in 1693 had a further nineteen English, thirteen French, and five Italian editions before 1761) spread the notion that children 'must be tenderly used ... must play and have playthings'. Far from breaking the child's will, which many besides John Wesley's mother regarded as a necessary prerequisite to any worthwhile educational endeavour, Locke advocated an upbringing which took account of individual personality, relying mainly on

[22] R. A. Houston, *The Population History of Britain and Ireland, 1500–1750* (1992), 49–51; Wrigley and Schofield, *Population History*, 248–50; M. George, *London Life in the Eighteenth Century* (1930), app. I.
[23] L. Stone, *The Family, Sex and Marriage in England, 1500–1800* (1977), 81–2 and pt. 4; L. Pollock, *Forgotten Children: Parent–Child Relations from 1500 to 1900* (1983).

the incentives of praise and the urge to emulation, rather than the threat of corporal punishment. Ninety years later a Prussian visitor noticed that even poorer English parents seemed to be 'kind and indulgent, and do not crush the spirit of the young with blows and curses so much as ours do'.[24]

Such enlightened attitudes were hardly universal. One reason for the horrific infant death rate in London during the first two-thirds of the eighteenth century was the rising number of foundlings or abandoned babies, orphans, illegitimate, and pauper children hastily passed on from parochial poor-law officers to 'nurses'. Having little financial incentive to keep their charges alive, these ladies frequently allowed and sometimes assisted them to die. The philanthropical sea-captain Thomas Coram (1668–1751), seeking to check this massacre of the innocents, established a foundling hospital with mixed private and government funding in 1739. But the scale of the problem far exceeded the capacity of any single institution. In 1763, after ten years of patient fact-gathering, lobbying, and pamphleteering by Jonas Hanway (1712–86), a concerned Coram Hospital board member, Parliament passed comprehensive legislation to regulate the nursing of poor infants, including the payment of cash rewards for all who survived the process. The average number of London burials thereupon dropped by some 2,100 a year.[25]

Education and Literacy

Orphans and other children supported by the poor rates could be compulsorily apprenticed from the age of 10, and were often much younger when they were handed over to employers in order to get them off the parish books. The fate of the London boy chimney-sweeps, forced into a particularly hazardous occupational slavery when as little as 4 or 5 years old, attracted considerable attention in the 1780s, culminating in an ineffectual attempt at statutory control of their working conditions in 1788. Yet otherwise the hitherto universal practice of sending young adolescents out to service in another household, the boys typically as apprentices in husbandry (i.e. farm labourers), the girls as domestic servants, was in slow decline. Apprenticeship remained by far the most popular form of vocational education, but apprentices increasingly stayed at home, rather than moving in under their master's roof and disciplinary control. Not only trades and relatively low-status occupations made use of formal and informal apprenticeships; for example, would-be lawyers typically learnt their craft by working as articled clerks or pupils in the chambers of experienced practitioners.

Education of a more general or academic nature was provided by a bewildering variety of private or at most semi-public institutions. The state discharged

[24] M. Girouard, *Life in the English Country House* (1978), 182; Moritz, *Journeys*, 68.
[25] George, *London Life in the Eighteenth Century*, ch. 1, app. 2; on Coram, see L. Colley, *Britons: Forging the Nation, 1707–1832* (1992), 56–61.

no educational role, apart from training future artillery officers and engineers at what became the Royal Military College, Woolwich, and a less successful naval academy at Portsmouth. In the absence of national systems of assessment, teacher training, or institutional certification, standards and achievements varied very widely. According to parental ambitions and resources, children might learn to read and write at home, with a governess or at their mother's knee. Alternatively they could attend a small local school, run by a 'dame', the curate, or perhaps even the village shopkeeper, like the good-hearted Thomas Turner (1729–93) of East Hoathly, Sussex, who in 1754 hired a fire-eater to perform for his students, and gave them 'five quarts of strong beer' to celebrate his birthday.[26] Some village and town schools founded by charitable bequest provided a free elementary education; in 1746 the pious mystic William Law (1686–1761) left funds to endow an existing school for girls in the Northamptonshire village to which he had retired five years before. Charity schools, maintained from public subscriptions, benefactions, and other local sources, provided very rudimentary training with a strong Church of England slant for the poorest children. They were promoted on a national basis by the SPCK since the 1690s, and their numbers seem to have peaked early in George II's reign after some 1,500 schools had been established, but picked up again in the 1770s. An ingenious and successful variant was the Sunday school, popularized although not originated by the Gloucester journalist Robert Raikes (1735–1811), where poor children were taught before or after attending church services. The national Sunday School Society established in 1785 to further the concept temporarily overcame denominational rivalries by enlisting the support of Anglicans, Methodists, and Dissenters. But most Sunday Schools resulted from local initiatives, predominantly by middle-class promoters, but occasionally as spontaneous exercises in working-class self-help.

English was the language of instruction in all these 'petty' schools, which most children might attend for perhaps four to six years, family finances and employment opportunities permitting. In order to learn Latin and Greek, the basis of the formal academic curriculum, and of polite culture, it was necessary to attend and often board at a fee-paying Church of England grammar school, or alternatively a Dissenting Academy. All such institutions were usually closed to the poor for economic reasons, and also to girls, whose only hope of acquiring the learned tongues was instruction at home. At the same time, and contrary to Locke's warnings about the moral, psychological, and social dangers of 'a mixed herd of unruly boys', the aristocracy and gentry were increasingly abandoning private home tuition for their sons to patronize a few fashionable 'public' schools which recruited pupils from all over the country. Westminister was especially favoured for the first two-thirds of the century, and thereafter Eton College. Even Warrington Academy, that 'Athens of the Nonconformist north' which appointed the brilliant young Presbyterian

---

[26] *The Diary of Thomas Turner, 1754–1765*, ed. D. Vaisey (1984), 9, 36.

minister and natural philosopher Joseph Priestley (1733–1804) to its teaching staff in 1761, initially offered a classical curriculum 'almost wholly adapted to the learned professions'—that is, suitable for would-be ministers, lawyers, and medical practitioners. The prestige of a classical education as a token of gentility flourished, doubtless encouraged by growing awareness, especially among the middling sort, that Greek and Latin were 'far from being of any real use to the generality of tradesmen and mechanics'. Priestley did introduce lecture courses on history and the laws and constitution of England to Warrington. But the more utilitarian subjects, including modern languages, mathematics, book-keeping, geography, and modern history, were generally best acquired from a private tutor, or at institutions with a specifically commercial and technical orientation, like the 'college of mathematics' established at Newcastle in 1760, and comparable institutions set up in other industrial centres. The vocational mission of these privately owned and operated schools was in a sense parallelled by the numerous day and boarding academies for young ladies found on the outskirts of London and many provincial cities, which professed to equip their charges with the feminine accomplishments—needlework, music, dancing, drawing, perhaps some rudimentary French or Italian, and a genteel carriage—all 'supposed to increase a young lady's chance of a prize in the matrimonial lottery'.[27]

It is impossible to estimate what proportion of the population attended school of any kind during the eighteenth century. However, surviving figures for male students entering tertiary education, as represented by Oxford, Cambridge, and the four inns of court, point to a dramatic drop in enrolments from their early seventeenth-century peak. The decline continued for well over a hundred years, and despite a partial recovery during the last third of the eighteenth century, student admissions in the 1790s still remained below their 1700s level.

TABLE 1 *Average annual tertiary education admissions, selected decades*

	Universities	Inns of court	Totals
1630–9	498	280	778
1700–9	283	167	450
1760–9	161	125	286
1790–9	203	164	367

Sources: L. Stone (ed.), *The University in Society* (1974), i. 91–3; D. F. Lemmings, private communication

The reasons for the post-Restoration slump are complex, and not fully understood. But parental dissatisfaction with both the quality of instruction and the lack of academic or pastoral oversight was undoubtedly a significant

---

[27] J. Locke, *Some Thoughts Concerning Education*, ed. J. Garforth (1964), 101; J. Collyer, *The Parent or Guardian's Directory* (1761), 20; J. Priestley, *Lectures on History and General Policy* (1793), sig. A3; M. Edgeworth, *Practical Education* (1798), i. 522.

factor. The legal inns had never provided any form of personal tuition, and from the 1680s onwards they also effectively abandoned all law-teaching by the traditional oral 'learning exercises'. The rakish Templar, far better acquainted with playhouses, gaming clubs, and ladies of the town than his law books or the courts, remains a familiar literary stereotype throughout our period.[28]

While London offered unrivalled opportunities for fashionable dissipation, undergraduate students at eighteenth-century Oxford and Cambridge could also enjoy an intensive social and sporting life. Peers of the realm were especially favoured, receiving their degrees without even a token examination, although this was probably not the chief reason for their increasing presence at the universities in the course of the eighteenth century. The political economist Adam Smith, who had studied at Glasgow University before winning a scholarship to Balliol College, Oxford, in 1740, characteristically explained the low academic standards of the English universities by the fact that the income of college fellows came wholly from endowments, whereas Scots academics, relying on fees paid directly by students, had a material incentive to take their scholastic duties seriously.

Another distinguished Oxford alumnus, the historian Edward Gibbon (1737–94), formed an equally unfavourable view of his alma mater, later characterizing the fourteen months he spent as a gentleman commoner at Magdalen College, Oxford, in 1752–3 as 'the most idle and unprofitable of my whole life'. Gibbon's experience was both usual but somewhat atypical, in that—unlike most undergraduates—gentleman or fellow-commoners (who paid higher fees in return for the right to wear a distinctive gown and dine with the dons at high table) were as yet not generally expected to study or conform to college discipline. Smith and Gibbon would probably have been little better impressed by Whig Cambridge than Tory Oxford, although the Cambridge curriculum did at least reflect the influence of Newtonian natural philosophy and the mathematical sciences. Cambridge also saw the introduction of a form of competitive assessment in mathematics from 1753, even if the proposals of academic reformers to establish annual examinations across the entire curriculum were crushed by their conservative colleagues. Desultory attempts to introduce lecture courses for law students at the inns of court during the second half of the eighteenth century met with equally little success.[29]

Yet it would be misleading to conclude on this negative note. The deficiencies of institutionalized tertiary education in eighteenth-century England (which should no more be exaggerated than minimized) directly affected only a small fraction of the male population. Even they did not lack alternatives, including the flourishing Scots and Dutch universities (popular both among Dissenters,

[28] D. F. Lemmings, *Gentlemen and Barristers: The Inns of Court and the English Bar, 1680–1730* (1990), ch. 4.
[29] A. Smith, *The Wealth of Nations* (1776, 1904), ed. E. Cannan, ii. 283–8; E. Gibbon, *Autobiography* (1796; 1962), 39–41.

and for medical studies), and the Continental Grand Tour. Educational opportunities, formal and informal, had never before been so diverse and widely utilized. Midway through the century national adult literacy rates, as measured by the ability to sign one's name, were running at about 60 per cent for males and a little under 40 per cent for women. These aggregate figures conceal wide variations, since literacy was closely correlated with occupation, social class, and place of residence. A marked town/country division is apparent. No fewer than 92 per cent of London bridegrooms and 74 per cent of their brides were able to sign rather than merely make their mark on the marriage register in the 1750s, as against only 46 per cent of men and 28 per cent of women marrying in the largely rural county of Bedfordshire. The six northern English counties of Cumberland, Westmorland, Lancashire, Northumberland, Durham, and Yorkshire had a slightly higher adult male literacy rate (64 per cent) than the national average in the 1750s. But north England stood on a par with lowland Scotland, whereas more than two-thirds of men from the Gaelic-speaking Scots highlands and islands were unable to sign their names. National male literacy shows no marked change for the remainder of the century, but a slight rise in female rates from the mid-1780s may be associated with the advent of the Sunday school movement.

Since handwriting was usually taught after and apart from reading, sometimes by a specialist writing-master, these statistics may well understate the extent of bare literacy. By the same token they do not necessarily indicate an ability to read or write fluently. Nor should it be assumed that the spread of literacy simply depended on the availability of schooling. Most people sought to learn to read or have their children taught to read only when the practical utility of reading was brought home to them. Religion remained a powerful incentive; among the Quakers literacy was universal. So was the experience of urban life, with its concentration of commercial and other transactions which either required or were facilitated by the ability to read and write. Newspaper advertising and announcements, street-signs, printed handbills and forms, woodcuts and engravings incorporating written captions or legends, broadsheets, chapbooks, novels, and pamphlets all worked to this end. A Russian visitor to London in 1790 reported that the maid who brought him a cup of tea in the morning 'discusses with me the novels of Fielding and Richardson'; an Irish clergyman fifteen years before observed with surprise how 'a whitesmith in his apron and some of his saws under his hand', entered a coffee-house and 'called for his glass of punch and the paper, both of which he used with as much ease as a lord'. It was indeed the potentially empowering effects of literacy which led some conservatives to oppose even Sunday schools as likely to unsettle the lower orders, although they thereby underestimated the potential of literacy to reinforce as well as to subvert the status quo.[30]

[30] R. Houston, *Literacy in Early Modern Europe* (1988), chs. 7–9; F. Wilson (ed.), *Strange Island* (1955), 130; *Dr Campbell's Diary of a Visit to England in 1775*, ed. J. L. Clifford (1947), 58.

Love and Marriage

From around the middle of the seventeenth century, according to Lawrence Stone, it came to be gradually accepted that an individual's rights to emotional fulfilment outweighed the collective interests of his or her family and broader kinship group. Hence it followed that marriage should be based on a couple's free choice and mutual affection, rather than—as hitherto—arranged by their parents with a prime view to dynastic economic advantage. Hence also increased closeness and emotional warmth between parents and children, rather than functional but unloving families dominated by patriarchal husbands and fathers. Stone's belief in the rise of what he terms 'affective individualism' and the 'companionate marriage' have been criticized as over-schematic, excessively optimistic, and fatally dependent on generalization from the relatively well-documented albeit wholly unrepresentative landed elite. Yet his case still carries considerable weight, and not only because no one else has better succeeded in making sense of this amorphous, complex, and important topic, on which the surviving evidence is neither comprehensive nor straightforward.[31]

While Stone may tend to exaggerate the absence of emotional intimacy between spouses, parents, and children in sixteenth- and early seventeenth-century England, his thesis is not effectively refuted by citing individual instances of apparently affectionate married couples, or the widespread concern of husbands to ensure that the material needs of their wives would be taken care of after their own death. Stone's case for 'a growing introspection and interest in the individual personality [and] a demand for personal autonomy' during the seventeenth and eighteenth centuries depends upon multiple indications of emergent self-awareness. These include the chronicling of private inner as well as public outer life by diarists like Samuel Pepys and Dudley Ryder, and novelists, including Daniel Defoe, Samuel Richardson (1689–1761), Laurence Sterne (1713–68), Sarah Fielding (1710–68), Charlotte Lennox (1720–1804), Fanny Burney (1752–1840), and many more; the realistic representation of appearance and character in portraits, sculptured busts, and funeral monuments; and a mounting concern with personal privacy, manifested both in domestic architecture (the provision of separate upstairs bedrooms for all family members, the exclusion of servants from family meals, and of apprentices from their masters' houses) and polite manners (involving among other things the provision of individual knives and forks at table, and greater emphasis on bathing and bodily cleanliness, including shaving the head as a deterrent to lice). Like the growing use of intimate forms of address between husband and wife (the replacement of 'Sir' and 'Madam' by Christian names), this evidence comes largely from and about the propertied classes, as Stone freely admits. His assumption that such attitudes and practices gradually trickled down the social hierarchy is open to doubt, but that hardly affects the

---

[31] Stone, *Family, Sex and Marriage*; cf. Sharpe, *Early Modern England*, ch. 2.

validity of his claims in relation to the gentry and middling sort. The sources from which a comparable history of the emotional life of the early modern masses might be written do not seem to exist, or if they do, have yet to be discovered and exploited by historians.

If marriages among the 'upper part' were indeed becoming less patriarchal and more companionable, we might expect to see changes in the status of wives, or even women in general, as part of the same process. Some gains were undoubtedly made. While Locke had endorsed male sovereignty in marriage, on the dubious grounds that the husband was 'abler and stronger', his contractarian rationalism guaranteed the wife certain basic rights not granted by existing English law, including control of her own property, and the possibility of separation or divorce with custody of their children. Building on these considerable if still theoretical concessions, the learned spinster Mary Astell (1668–1731) posed an embarrassing question at the start of the eighteenth century: 'If all men are born free, how is it that all women are born slaves?' Astell, arguably England's first feminist, advocated the establishment of a retreat where ladies 'convinced of the emptiness of earthly enjoyments' could study to overcome the 'narrow education' which she regarded as the real basis of her sisters' presumed natural inferiority to men, returning to the world as teachers in order to work among the rising female generation. Among her protégés and admirers was Lady Mary Wortley Montagu (1689–1762), who taught herself Latin and introduced the practice of inoculation against smallpox to England on her return from Turkey with her ambassador husband, whom she had secretly married in 1712. A professed feminist in her later years, Lady Mary would have sympathized with the anonymously published *Woman not inferior to Man* (1739), which argued for the intellectual equality of the sexes and asked 'why do the men persuade themselves that we are less fit for public employments than they?'[32]

The growing contemporary prominence of women as actresses (replacing boys on the stage from the 1660s), artists, composers and musicians, novelists, poets, and scholars, as well as consumers of literature and the arts, gave added point to the question, as did the generally sympathetic treatment of female aspirations and potential in the *Spectator*, the *Gentleman's Magazine*, and other widely circulating periodicals. Some men doubtless reacted like the sterotypical wealthy ex-merchant Sir Humphrey Henpeck in James Miller's popular play *The Man of Taste* (1735), who complains that his wife is 'wedded more to philosophy and poetry, than to me'.[33] This character would hardly have approved of the intelligent and learned ladies of the famous Blue Stocking Circle, including Elizabeth Vesey (1715?–91), the wealthy Elizabeth Montagu (1720–1800), and Mrs Frances Boscawen, whose admiral husband

---

[32] J. Locke, *Two Treatises of Civil Government*, ed. P. Laslett (1960) II, ch. 7; M. Astell, *Reflections upon Marriage* (1700), in B. Hill (ed.), *Eighteenth-Century Women* (1984), 248.
[33] J. Miller, *The Man of Taste* (1735), 9.

supposedly named the group after the unfashionable blue woollen stockings worn to its informal London gatherings by the botanist and author Benjamin Stillingfleet (1702–71). From the 1750s onwards the Blue Stockings sought with some success to mix fashionable society and the literary world, countering by their personal example traditional prejudices against the 'immodesty' or unpleasing 'masculinity' of women intellectuals and writers. They did tend to shrink from the assertive determination of less socially elevated females who wrote for a living, like the radical republican historian Catharine Macaulay (1731–91), or the novelist and translator Charlotte Lennox (1720–1804). But the moral and social legitimacy of female involvement in the public sphere as artists and writers won widespread acceptance in the second half of the eighteenth century, symbolized by Richard Samuel's frequently reproduced group portrait (*c*.1779) of the 'Nine Living Muses of Great Britain'. The need to improve the education of girls attracted considerable support, if less agreement as to what form that improvement should take. The claim by the scientific popularizer and travelling lecturer Benjamin Martin (1704–82) that 'it is now [1772] growing into a fashion for the ladies to study philosophy' (i.e. science) may not have been entirely wishful thinking. Criticism of the legal and social disabilities of women, and the inequity of the sexual double standard was also increasingly voiced. And even before the emergence of Methodist women lay-preachers, extensive evangelical missions were being undertaken by Quaker women like Deborah Bell (*c*.1689–1738), who 'visited many of the meetings of Friends in most parts of England, Wales, Scotland, and was twice in Ireland'.[34]

So it is hardly surprising that a judge's reported endorsement in 1782 of a husband's right to beat his wife, provided he used a stick no thicker than his thumb, provoked public outrage. On the other hand, some of what a tract of 1735 termed *The Hardships of the English Laws in Relation to Wives* were eased by eighteenth-century judicial decisions. For instance, the Anglicized Scot William Murray (1705–93), who as Lord Mansfield presided over the court of King's Bench for nearly thirty years from 1756, strategically extended the range of exceptions to the ancient common-law rule that a married woman had no separate legal personality or responsibilities, being wholly under the guardianship of her husband.[35] Unfortunately, little is known about the practical impact of these and other judgements, especially in the complicated area of women's property rights before, during, and after marriage. Likewise the widespread adoption from the late seventeenth century onwards of the conveyancing device known as the strict settlement, enabling landowners to prevent their potentially improvident heirs from gambling away the family estate, may

---

[34] B. Martin, *The Young Gentleman and Lady's Philosophy* (1772), 2; *A Short Account of the Labours and Travels in the Work of the Ministry of that Faithful Servant of Christ, Deborah Bell* (1776), p. xii.

[35] J. Oldham, *The Mansfield Manuscripts and the Growth of English Law in the Eighteenth Century* (1992), 1245–51, 1265.

have helped ensure that daughters received marriage portions, but at the same time could reduce their chances of inheriting the estate itself, in the interests of preserving a male line of descent. Which of these outcomes was more frequent, and significant, remains uncertain.

The law attached cash equivalents to sexual transgressions, by giving a father the right to sue his daughter's seducer, and cuckolded husbands a claim for damages against their adulterous wife's lover (in an action for 'criminal conversation'). This doubtless both encouraged and reflected a tendency to view women as the property of their male 'protectors' (those whom the Blue Stockings drily termed 'lords of Creation'). By no means all men shared the snobbish earl of Chesterfield's professed belief that women should be flattered and humoured but never taken seriously, since they were 'only children of a larger growth', who might possess wit, but lacked 'solid reasoning good sense'. Consistent with the elegant cynicism of the long series of letters of advice to his illegitimate son, published in 1774 after both father and son were dead, Chesterfield warned against openly avowing such sentiments. But it was rather his advocacy of sexual permissiveness and social dissimulation which provoked Dr Samuel Johnson (1709–84) to the damning dictum that Chesterfield's *Letters* taught 'the morals of a whore, and the manners of a dancing master'. Still more damaging to feminist aspirations than calculating 'Chesterfieldism' were the popular writings of the French novelist and *philosophe* Jean-Jacques Rousseau (1712–72), who made much of woman's distinctive qualities, 'formed to please the man'. His novel *Julie* (1761) and educational treatise *Émile* (1762), both widely available in English translations, championed the 'sentimental family' as the proper female sphere of action, supposedly designated by Nature herself, thereby providing up-to-date ideological rationalization for excluding women from all public political and productive life. Even thirty years after their first publication, Rousseau's views were a prime target of Mary Wollstonecraft's feminist *Vindication of the Rights of Woman* (1792).[36]

There are a few recorded instances of eighteenth-century women holding lesser local government office, such as church warden, constable, and overseer of the poor. Aristocratic ladies like Sarah Churchill, duchess of Marlborough, played a significant political role behind the scenes, at Court or as hostesses in their London and country houses, and occasionally managed an inherited constituency interest. Headed by the eccentric duchess of Queensberry (*c*.1701–77), a group of ten women, mostly titled, stormed the gallery of the House of Lords in 1738, defying attempts to exclude them from hearing a debate on war with Spain. The ebullient Georgiana Cavendish, duchess of Devonshire (1757–1806), acquired wide notoriety when she appeared in public with her sister to canvass for the Whig leader Charles James Fox (1749–1806) at the

---

[36] L. Stone, *Road to Divorce: England, 1530–1947* (1990), 83–95, 231–300; *Lord Chesterfield's Letters to his Son and Others*, ed. R. K. Root (1975), 66–7; *Boswell's Life of Johnson*, ed. R. W. Chapman (1953), 188.

hotly contested Westminster election of 1784. Nevertheless, the possibility of enfranchising women was barely mentioned by proponents of parliamentary reform, not least because most daughters and wives were presumed to be subject to the political influence of their fathers and husbands (but see also below, p. 279). A mixture of male dominance, female vapidity, and mutual social ambition was commonly blamed for the deplorable tendency of farmers' and tradesmen's daughters and wives to turn ladies of leisure, withdrawing from active involvement in dairy, market-place, or shop to a life of more or less genteel ease in the parlour. Those women who might hanker after active modes of life found a shortage of employment opportunities compatible with gentility, or even respectability, while in the south and east of the country work on the land for their poorer sisters was also contracting. The various branches of medical practice, not least midwifery, were or were becoming dominated by males, teaching was underpaid and very competitive, governesses notoriously enjoyed lower status than male tutors, and the various trades associated with needlework paid so poorly that parents were warned against apprenticing their daughters into what often proved a gateway to prostitution. The flourishing state of that industry, especially on the streets of London, was such that a German visitor who went for a walk down Fleet Street on a December evening in 1775 described himself as being beset every ten yards by 'lewd females ... even by children of 12 years old'.[37]

Such rampant vice graphically underlined the distinction between good and bad women, and the dangers awaiting all those who could not or did not find a man to protect and support them. Moralists and novelists harped on the crucial importance of women preserving their virginity before marriage and their chastity thereafter, despite all the persuasive wiles of men inflamed by libertine principles, pornographic literature, and pervasive sexual hedonism. Their admonitions were directed primarily to polite society; for the rural lower orders, especially in the first half of the century, a betrothal agreement, not necessarily even witnessed, following an extended courtship was at least as important a sexual and social rite of passage as the church marriage service. However, in 1753, seeking to eliminate clandestine under-age marriages, especially of heiresses with male adventurers or wealthy young men with servant girls, Lord Chancellor Hardwicke (1690–1764) persuaded Parliament to pass a statute which nullified all marriages except those of persons over the age of 21 or minors with parental consent, celebrated before witnesses by an Anglican clergyman according to the rites of the Church of England. The Hardwicke Marriage Act succeeded both in doing away with the scandal of secret and ill-recorded marriage ceremonies performed in the Fleet Prison by seedy parsons, and imposing a measure of parental control upon feckless teenagers from the

[37] B. Kenner (ed.), *The Women of England From Anglo-Saxon Times to the Present* (1980), ch. 8; Campbell, *London Tradesman*, 208–9; *Lichtenberg's Visits to England*, ed. M. Mare and W. H. Quarrell (1938), 65–6

propertied classes, although as the legislation did not apply in Scotland the border village of Gretna Green long continued to provide instant nuptials for determined elopers. In achieving these ends Hardwicke used the full power of Church and State to impose a rigid and relatively expensive set of formalities on all who wished to marry, rich and poor alike. He also arguably eroded the rights of jilted girls, who had previously been able to use their seducer's promise to marry as the basis of an action for damages (breach of promise of marriage) in the common-law courts. The readiness of Parliament to pass the Act also reminds us that the rhetoric of affective individualism was not necessarily incompatible with close attention to the material aspects of love and marriage.[38]

Minorities

The audience which journalists and pamphleteers addressed on such public issues was generally conceived of as heterosexual, masculine, propertied, Protestant, and English. Contemporaries increasingly saw male homosexuality as a distinct deviant sub-culture, mirroring the corruption and effeminacy which some feared must inevitably accompany the growth of national wealth and luxury. As we have seen, women were conventionally excluded from all but the most marginal roles in public life, along with paupers and Catholics. Foreigners (or 'strangers') were by definition alien and other. Yet since the early seventeenth century the country had been largely ruled by foreign-born monarchs, whose subjects now included an increasingly diverse immigrant component, together with Englishmen and others living across the seas.

The Irish constituted the largest group of foreign nationals in England. Many originally entered the country as seasonal harvest workers, then joined the relatively long-established Irish community in London, or more recent residential groupings in Liverpool, Manchester, and the industrial north-west. Their Catholic religion, combined with a willingness to undercut prevailing unskilled wage rates, and a tendency to congregate in urban ghettos, made them particularly unpopular with the English labouring poor. It seems to have been industrial rather than religious hostility which generated London street violence against Irish builders' labourers and weavers in 1736, although ethnic and sectarian motives came to the fore in the Gordon riots of 1780. An Irish clergyman visitor to London in 1775 noted that the shamrock was worn by few on St Patrick's Day, other than beggars and chairmen (the burly and often unruly figures whose sedan chairs functioned as pedestrian taxis); other menial occupations exploiting Irish physical strength and stamina (which Adam Smith attributed to their staple diet of potatoes) included those of ballast-man, coal-heaver, porter, and navvy or general labourer.

---

[38] D. Lemmings, 'Marriage and the law in the eighteenth century: Hardwicke's Marriage Act of 1753', *HJ*, 39 (1996).

Like other foreigners, native-born Irish generally had no legal parish of settlement, and hence no entitlement to poor relief. A charitable society in Norwich which sought to fill this gap assisted 111 destitute male Scots and twenty-nine Irishmen, together with their families, between 1778 and 1784. Community-based self-help risked reinforcing negative stereotypes of ethnic exclusiveness (hence the Norwich body, originally the Scots Society, prudently reinvented itself the Society for Universal Goodwill). Yet the very existence of such organizations indicates that by no means all Celtic immigrants joined the ranks of the working or unemployed poor. London's pre-eminence as commercial, entertainment, legal, literary, political, social, shopping, and tourism capital of the British Isles ensured extended visits from significant cohorts of Irish and Scots landowners, and their families, including younger sons seeking advancement, especially in the professions. James Boswell, the endearingly confused son of a Scots judge, provides a particularly vivid autobiographical account of his first vist to London at the age of 22, where he encountered men and women of all sorts, not a few fellow Scots, and 'the great Mr Samuel Johnson, whom I have so long wished to see'.[39]

Most Scots, like the 50,000 or so French Huguenots, and smaller communities of Dutch and Germans centred on London, were at least Protestants, although that fact alone hardly spared them from the unwelcoming chauvinism of their hosts. The Jews, whose numbers rose slowly but steadily after their de facto mid-seventeenth-century readmission to England in 1656, had little other than reputed wealth and commercial skills to recommend them, apart from fading millenarian hopes that their eventual conversion to Christianity would usher in the Second Coming. Few did convert, and many Ashkenazi (from Central Europe) were anything but affluent. However, the Sephardic community (originating from Portugal and Spain) included some wealthy financiers and merchants, like Samson Gideon (1699–1762), whose loan of over £1m. to the government in 1745 continued a tradition of Jewish financial support for the anti-Jacobite cause dating back to William III's reign. Another 'very rich Portuguese Jew' was the English-born banker Joseph Salvador (1716–86); in 1761 a visiting German noble, noting that such men were received at Court and mixed in the best society, commented that because English Jews did not wear beards 'they cannot be distinguished at all from other people'.[40]

Most Jews never achieved—and perhaps few aspired to—this degree of assimilation. Nor was anti-Semitism unknown in Hanoverian England, as popular reaction to the 1753 'Jew Bill' amply demonstrated (see below, p. 189). But Jewish chances of effective assimilation were generally better than those of Africans or Asians. While a few Chinese and Lascar seamen brought back on

---

[39] F. Eden, *The State of the Poor* (1797), ed. A. G. L. Rogers (1928), 257–8; *Boswell's London Journal, 1762–1763*, ed. F. A. Pottle (1950), 260.
[40] F. Kielmansegge, *Diary of a Journey to England in the Years 1761–1762*, tr. P. Kielmansegge (1902), 170.

East India Company ships lived in dockland London, black Afro-Americans constituted the country's main non-European ethnic minority. African slaves first arrived in the mid-sixteenth century, and with the growth of the slave trade after 1660 England's black population may have expanded to somewhere between 15,000 and 20,000 a century later. Mostly former slaves or slaves' descendants, they were typically shipped from the Caribbean or Southern colonies with their planter or slave ship captain owners; some freed and free blacks also entered the country as sailors, and even a few more as students, sent by well-to-do African families to acquire the benefits of an English schooling. Until the last two decades of the century advertisments offering slaves (often children) for sale or seeking the return of runaway slaves appeared regularly in London newspapers and those of Bristol and Liverpool, the other main slaving ports. At the same time, it was widely if inconsistently assumed that England's free institutions were incompatible with the degraded status of a slave, especially in the case of a baptized Christian. Chief Justice Mansfield cautiously declined to endorse this proposition in so many words when he held in 1772 that the black slave James Somersett could not be forced to leave England against his will, despite his master's wish to ship him back to Jamaica in irons. Nevertheless Mansfield's ruling was acclaimed as a major blow against the slaving interest, by both blacks and their growing band of supporters under the leadership of the determined civil servant Granville Sharp (1735–1813). Having managed Somersett's case, Sharp went on to build a coalition of Dissenters, evangelicals, and humanitarians committed to extinguishing slavery throughout the empire by legislative abolition of the slave trade.

The growing prominence of ethnic immigrant minorities counterpoised Hanoverian Britain's commercial, imperial, and maritime expansion, and the associated diaspora of English emigrants, sailors, merchants, soldiers, and rulers to Asia, Africa, America, and Australia. The 'strong partiality' of the English 'in favour of their country' still went hand-in-hand with considerable generalized contempt for other peoples and places. So the marginal cultural and legal status of the non-native born, like the black Ignatius Sancho (1729–80), a member of the duke of Manchester's household who nevertheless felt himself 'only a lodger, and hardly that' in England, reflected issues of national identity and civic participation which also troubled many colonists, especially in North America, as well as some Dissenters, Roman Catholics, and women.[41]

[41] *Dr Campbell's Diary*, 65; K. Wilson, 'Citizenship, empire, and modernity in the English provinces, *c*.1720–1790', *Eighteenth-Century Studies*, 29 (1995), 84.

12

POLITICS, POPULARITY, AND PATRIOTISM

The Old Corps: Pelham and Newcastle

Although not immediately recognized at the time, the failure of the '45 marked a major turning-point in English history. Henceforth the Stuart cause no longer seriously threatened the house of Hanover, the Revolution Settlement, and the Act of Union. As the Jacobite issue accordingly faded from view, and with it much of the significance of the traditional Whig–Tory divide, a rising generation of younger politicians began to address new issues of domestic and foreign policy created by a more diverse and forcefully expressed public opinion, as well as the continued growth of Britain's maritime power and imperial presence overseas.

An Anglo-German army and its artillery under the command of the man subsequently known as 'Butcher' Cumberland, George II's soldier-son, soon completed the military destruction of the Jacobites during and after the one-sided battle of Culloden Moor (April 1746). But the ineffectiveness of Jacobitism—in England, although not yet in Scotland—had already been demonstrated by the Young Pretender's dismal failure to recruit supporters on his march south, despite the large-scale commitment of English land forces to Flanders and consequent lack of troops to block his path to London. Fears lingered that 'this rebellion tho' stopped for a while is not yet over'. The strong showing of administration candidates at the general election called prematurely the following year reflects the persistence of such concerns, linked with a predictably powerful rallying of loyalist and patriotic sentiment. Yet the overwhelming confidence of those best placed to calculate the risks was apparent even before Culloden, in the renewal of high political faction-fighting temporarily interrupted by the Jacobite invasion, and the abrupt mass resignation of the entire ministry in February 1746.[1]

This extraordinary and unprecedented action gave notice from the 'Old Corps' of former Walpole supporters led by Henry Pelham (1696–1754) that they were only available to serve George II on the condition that they enjoyed his undivided confidence. In particular he must not attempt to use other ministers than themselves to pursue foreign policies of which they disapproved.

---

[1] *The Correspondence of the Dukes of Richmond and Newcastle*, ed. T. J. McCann, Sussex Record Society, 73 (1984), 224.

Having soon found he had little choice than to capitulate, George reinstated the Pelhams and grudgingly appointed the brilliant, moody, and erratic William Pitt (1708–78) to the post of paymaster-general. Pitt, younger son of a Tory country gentleman, but grandson of the fabulously wealthy and Whiggish nabob 'Diamond Pitt', who had acquired his huge fortune as Governor of the East India Company in Madras, first attracted attention in the later 1730s as a brilliant and biting parliamentary orator. His self-dramatizing stance as a 'Patriot', scathing anti-Walpole speeches, and characteristically contemptuous description of Hanover as a 'despicable Electorate' still rankled with the King. Paymaster-General Pitt consolidated his reputation for personal integrity by ostentatiously refusing the huge profits customarily enjoyed by occupants of that office. However, Pitt exercised little influence over policy, which for the next decade was essentially controlled by the bland but hardworking Henry Pelham, partnered by his fussy and diffident brother Newcastle, conceivably 'the strangest man in public life in eighteenth-century England'—despite formidable competition for that title—and an outstanding lawyer-politician, Philip Yorke, Baron Hardwicke, Lord Chancellor from 1737 to 1756.[2]

Besides negotiating a settlement which brought the stalemated European hostilities to a formal close in 1748 and secured French recognition of the Hanoverian succession, if no cessation of Anglo-French colonial rivalry, the Pelham ministry and its parliamentary supporters displayed mildly reformist tendencies in domestic matters. Before his death in 1754 Henry had carried out a major reorganization of public finance, including substantial reduction of the National Debt, a 25 per cent cut in the rate of interest paid on government borrowings, and administrative consolidation of various interest-bearing securities into a single stock (still today known as 3 per cent Consols). Opening up government loans to public subscription rather than confining them to an inner ring of Whig plutocrats, and repealing the contentious veto powers bestowed by Walpole on London's Court of Aldermen in order to curb opposition activities within the City helped secure acceptance of this package. Another courageous measure was adoption in 1752 of the Gregorian calendar, spurned as a popish innovation since the sixteenth century. The earl of Macclesfield, a keen amateur astronomer who promoted the removal of the eleven-day time difference between England and the Continent in the interests of enlightenment as well as efficiency, reportedly met calls when campaigning for his son's election to Parliament next year from 'country fellows to give an account, and restore the eleven days he's cheated the country of'.[3]

The considerable cultural disruption and practical difficulties flowing from this change were predictably dismissed as manifestations of clownish ignorance and superstition. More serious hostility was aroused by proposals for facilitating the naturalization of foreign Protestants, even though none actually

2 R. A. Kelch, *Newcastle, a Duke without Money: Thomas Pelham-Holles, 1693–1768* (1974), 7.
3 A. Hartshorne, *Memoirs of a Royal Chaplain* (1905), 187–8.

secured parliamentary majorities. The 'Jew Bill' of 1753, a similar proposition which did slip briefly into law, was hastily repealed once ministers realized the likely electoral impact of the popular anti-Semitic xenophobia it aroused. Also controversial if less politically damaging were Hardwicke's Marriage Act (pp. 183–4 above), a Gin Act (1751) which superseded earlier attempts to reduce consumption of spirits by confining retail sales to licensed premises, and the gruesome Murder Act (1752), which vainly sought to bolster capital punishment's deterrent effect by consigning the bodies of hanged murderers to the surgeons for dissection, or alternatively for gibbeting and public display. This desperate measure reflected widespread fears of moral collapse and mounting criminality in the late 1740s–early 1750s, as demobilized soldiers and sailors swelled the ranks of the unemployed, prompting a House of Commons committee to 'revise and consider' the whole body of criminal law. Taken together, all this legislative activity somewhat qualifies the conventional picture of mid-eighteenth-century governmental complacency and inertia, even if much of the law-making resulted from bills sponsored by individual members, rather than a coherent agenda of ministerial legislation.

William Pitt and War with France

Apart from the crisis of 1744–5, and the fierce but short-lived storm over Jewish naturalization, the Pelham 'Broadbottom' administration enjoyed relative tranquillity. The anti-Walpole parliamentary coalition of Tories and 'Country' or 'Independent' Whigs had not survived the '45. Party differences became increasingly blurred, as both the plausibility and threat of Tory–Jacobite links diminished, and the urgency of Tory calls for checks on unbridled executive power slackened. In 1748 it was suggested that Whig and Tory now bore 'so near a resemblance one with the other, that the difference between them is not worth the tossing up for'. Even the role of Leicester House as a haven for dissident politicians was suspended in 1751 by the unexpected death of Frederick, Prince of Wales, since the new heir to the throne, his son George, was at 13 still a little young to take up the opposition mantle usually worn by Hanoverian heirs apparent. Military involvement in Europe had largely ceased even before the peace treaty of Aix-la-Chapelle in 1748, so the potentially divisive side-effects of warfare were absent. Finally, the competent but unassuming Henry Pelham 'acquired the reputation of an able, and honest minister', and was altogether a far less divisive figure than Walpole had been.[4]

His death in March 1754 therefore shattered what had been a period of political quiescence: 'everything is thrown into confusion' according to Horace Walpole (1717–97), Sir Robert's gossipy younger son. The 'extraordinary scenes' observed by another politician directly involved in the post-mortem

[4] *De Toryismo, Liber: Or, A Treatise on Toryism* (1748), ii; *The Memoirs and Speeches of James 2nd Earl Waldegrave, 1742–1763*, ed. J. C. D. Clark (1988), 153.

jockeying for place arose primarily from the need to find a new government leader in the House of Commons.[5] The obvious candidates were Henry Fox, a persuasive debater whose clandestine marriage to a daughter of the duke of Richmond had, however, made him a fierce opponent of both Hardwicke and his Marriage Act, and William Pitt, the King's particular *bête noire*. Despite their personal rivalry Fox and Pitt, born respectively in 1705 and 1708, represented a new and significantly younger political generation than the 'Old Corps' followers of Hardwicke and Newcastle. That battle-scarred duo, who had both entered public life in the early years of George I, now showed understandably little desire to dilute their recently enhanced authority. Pitt and Fox accordingly moved into opposition, although the latter was bought off the following year with the post of secretary of state. Pitt had been long and painfully afflicted with what he and contemporaries unhelpfully called 'gout', a term used for almost any otherwise unidentified physical or psychological disorder. But now recently and happily married to Hester Grenville, daughter of a distinguished Whig family, he continued to denounce the administration from the back benches, in speeches of remarkable length, passion, and oratorical power. Their hyper-patriotic and enormously effective message was in substance little changed since the days when Pitt had attacked Walpole for showing insufficient commitment to defending England's legitimate national interests, and excessive concern for those of Hanover. What gave his words growing resonance, both within and outside Parliament, was the continued drift towards war with France.

By the 1748 peace treaty France had regained possession of various British conquests, including the fortress of Louisburg, strategically placed on Cape Breton Island to command the entrance to the St Lawrence River, and hence the northern end of the inland water system which runs through Canada to the Great Lakes, then via the Ohio and Mississippi Valleys to Louisiana, New Orleans, and the Gulf of Mexico. French determination to hold and strengthen this line against English colonists pushing inland from the Atlantic seaboard produced recurrent armed clashes. Taken together with the expulsion of French settlers from Acadia (Nova Scotia), continued Anglo-French tensions in India and the Caribbean, and British actions on the high seas against French naval and merchant shipping, these mounting skirmishes made the formal outbreak in Europe of a still undeclared war all but inevitable. It came with a successful French expedition against the strategically important Western Mediterranean island of Minorca, where Britain had maintained a naval base since 1708.

The loss of Minorca in mid-1756, and the failure of a Royal Navy fleet under Admiral John Byng to dislodge the French, were widely regarded as a massive

[5] *Horace Walpole's Correspondence*, ed. W. S. Lewis *et al.*, xx. 411 (Walpole to Horace Mann, 7 Mar. 1754); *The Political Journal of George Bubb Dodington*, ed. J. Carswell and L. A. Dralle (1965), 254.

national humiliation, unmatched since the Dutch storming of the Medway ninety years before. The administration and its policies came under fierce attack from Pitt and other parliamentary speakers, from a wide cross-section of the press, both metropolitan and provincial, and perhaps most ominously from some thirty-six parliamentary constituencies, which directed their representatives to demand an official enquiry into the Minorca débâcle. Under these pressures the ministry began to crumble. In November 1756 the King agreed, very reluctantly, to accept a new government whose dominant figure was Pitt, avowing—with characteristic overcharged rhetoric— 'I know that I can save this country, and that no one else can.'

Events did not immediately bear out this claim. Pitt's precarious parliamentary position was hardly improved by disabling attacks of gout, or his fruitless efforts to save the unfortunate Admiral Byng, who was court martialled, condemned, and eventually shot on his own quarter-deck as a scapegoat for Minorca. But if George II's adamant refusal to pardon Byng was apparently supported by public opinion 'out of doors', his dismissal of Pitt a few weeks later evoked another, albeit more contrived, storm of protest. Pitt's supporters in London and the provinces showered their hero with presentation gold boxes containing congratulatory testimonials and civic freedoms, in a campaign fully reported by the *London Evening Post*, the *Monitor*, and other sympathetic newspapers and journals. These depicted Pitt as a patriot martyr, fallen victim to the corrupt practices of Newcastle and the Old Corps. His parliamentary following was too small for him to form a ministry in his own right. But he did have on his side the weight of publicity, fears of 'a mutinous spirit, in the lower class of people', and backing from the Leicester House reversionary interest in the person of Lord Bute, a Scottish peer who enjoyed the favour of both Prince George and his widowed mother. Together these helped persuade other politicians, notably Newcastle, and eventually the King himself, that no viable government was possible without Pitt.[6]

The resultant Newcastle–Pitt coalition, in which Pitt ran the war, while Newcastle managed Parliament and patronage, turned out surprisingly well. The long-standing Anglo-Austrian alliance, originally directed against Louis XIV, had collapsed at the outbreak of hostilities. This diplomatic revolution saw the emerging military might of Frederick the Great's Prussia abandon France to line up with Britain, while in exchange Habsburg Austria overcame her traditional enmity for Bourbon France. Initial military reverses in Europe revived threats of a French invasion. But 1759 became a 'wonderful year', producing an unprecedented tally of military and naval victories, not only on the Continent but across the world. The list of British conquests included French Canada, the valuable Caribbean sugar island of Guadeloupe, and the West African slave-port of Goree, while French territorial ambitions in India were

---

[6] *Memoirs of Waldegrave*, 206.

effectively terminated by the military forces of the East India Company. On reading a newspaper account of 'our army in America, under the command of General Wolfe, beating the French army under General Montcalm, near the city of Quebec', the Sussex shopkeeper-diarist Thomas Turner rhapsodized: 'Oh, what pleasure it is to every true Briton to see with what success it pleases Almighty God to bless His Majesty's arms with, they having success at this time in Europe, Asia, Africa and America'. The nation's imperial triumph, foretold in millenarian visions for over a century, seemed on the verge of fulfilment.[7]

A New Reign, a New Politics?

George II's long-anticipated death in October 1760 did not signify merely a formal change of rulers. The conscientious, graceless, and naïve 22-year-old who now succeeded to the throne was the first English-born monarch since Queen Anne. Far from being another German prince who had fortuitously acquired some unruly offshore islands, George III identified himself as British to the boot-heels: 'Born and educated in this country, I glory in the name of Briton,' he informed his first Parliament. Since the new King, unlike his two predecessors, could hardly be depicted as an alien ruler imposed on the nation by a corrupt Whig oligarchy, the hitherto divisive conflict, apparent or real, between British and Hanoverian national interests disappeared from view, and with it a major tenet of both Toryism and Jacobitism. By supporting Pitt the Tories had already abandoned their distinctive parliamentary identity as a patriot, 'Country' opposition. Now royal removal of their proscription from office and honour at Court and in the counties at last finished off the old Tory party. The Whigs, for their part, had long since lost any coherence, other than as an anti-Tory grouping. Thus (as the path-breaking research of Lewis Namier demonstrated) instead of following a simple two-party pattern, parliamentary-political divisions under George III were as random as a tessellated pavement, reflecting the temporary alignments of individual politicians and their factions or personal followings, either as supporters or as opponents of the current administration.[8]

Brought up under the close supervision of his widowed mother, who could claim ample reason to detest her insensitive and overbearing father-in-law, the young Prince George William Frederick had imbibed a typical Leicester House oppositionist outlook, along with maternal admonitions to 'Be a King'. An impressionable late developer, George lacked self-confidence, and was much influenced by his (and his mother's) 'Dearest Friend', John Stuart, earl of Bute (1713–92). He seems to have decided that when he did become King he must right the wrongs done to his mother, the constitution, and 'this poor country' by his grandfather and the corrupt, self-interested, Old Corps Whig Junto. As

[7] *The Diary of Thomas Turner 1754–1765*, ed. D. Vaisey (1984), 191, 195.
[8] L. Namier, *The Structure of Politics at the Accession of George III* (1957).

'favourite and adviser', Bute's Scottish nationality, family name of Stuart, and supposed affair with the Queen Mother attracted much hostile comment, not solely from Whigs who purported to fear for the Revolution Settlement as well as their own pre-eminence. But they were the main source of hints that George's ambition 'to put an end to those unhappy distinctions of party called Whigs and Tories' cloaked a Court conspiracy to wind back the constitutional clock towards seventeenth-century-style absolutist monarchy. Most historians today follow Namier, rather than the Whig pamphlets and histories of the eighteenth and nineteenth centuries, in dismissing such suggestions as hysterical partisanship. Yet if only because the ministerial executive had acquired a large measure of control over both Crown and Parliament since 1714, let alone 1689, George's eager, diligent, and self-righteous attempts, in collusion with his inexperienced and self-important mentor, to recapture some political initiative were bound to provoke mistrust and resentment. Here was one reason for the difficulty which the new King experienced over the first decade of his reign in finding ministers who were both acceptable to him and capable of commanding a majority in Parliament.

Two other potentially disruptive features on the 1760s political scene must be mentioned. Pitt's rise to power a few years before had demonstrated how much influence 'popularity' could now exert on the world of high politics. Out-of-doors opinion had hitherto tended to be mobilized only sporadically, and against, rather than in support of, ministers or measures. The continued growth of the press helps explain why political issues of greater than local interest increasingly attracted more sustained attention, not only in London but across the British Isles. From 1695, when Parliament's failure to renew the Licensing (Printing) Act resulted in the lapse of pre-publication censorship, newspaper and magazine publishing had continued to grow by leaps and bounds. By 1760 Londoners had a choice of four daily newspapers, together with five or six which appeared three evenings a week; by 1783 there were nine dailies, ten bi- or tri-weeklies, and four weeklies. The provincial press also grew rapidly, although at first reproducing much copy from the metropolitan papers, many of which also circulated by post to rural subscribers. Even after the doubling of government stamp duty caused a sharp increase in the price of all periodical publications in 1757, around thirty-five country newspapers were being published by 1760. A rough indication of total circulation is that 9.5m. newspaper tax stamps were issued that year, rising to 12.6m. in 1775, when some London papers were selling 3,000–5,000 copies per issue; even earlier the *York Chronicle* had claimed a circulation of up to 2,500 copies, despite the competition of its rival, the *York Courant*.[9] Raw circulation figures were far exceeded by total readership. Not only coffee-houses, but clubs, inns, and taverns frequently provided a selection of current papers and magazines for their

[9] J. Black, *The English Press in the Eighteenth Century* (1987); G. A. Cranfield, *The Development of the Provincial Newspaper, 1700–1760* (1962).

customers. Exposure to the print media was also increased by the common practice of reading aloud, both in family and non-domestic settings, and by the wide availability of cheap printed caricatures and cartoons, which often carried a political message or reference.

Not all publications took a recognizable or distinctive political line, and some that did supported the administration; it was even asserted in 1764 that the press had become notably less partisan than in Walpole's time, because almost every London paper 'inserts indiscriminately the piece written for the ministry, as well as those against them'.[10] As this comment implies, much of the political content of newspapers and magazines took the form of contributions from correspondents, genuine or fictitious, canvassing issues of the day, rather than reports of domestic and foreign news. While the reader addressed in such pieces was usually by convention a 'polite' male person, educated and proper-tied, the audience they reached extended well beyond the ranks of those qualified either to stand as or to vote for MPs. It certainly included skilled artisans and small tradesmen, who would only have been enfranchised in a few larger urban constituencies, and women.

While the press helped mould attitudes to national political issues, public opinion could and did operate quite independently of parliamentary elections, as when Pitt acquired and retained office under George II. Indeed, since only about 4 per cent of the population held the right to vote, and most seats were uncontested, it might seem that elections played little part in Georgian political life. However, when the workings of electoral politics are closely scrutinized the picture which emerges is of an 'active and participatory experience' for a large and not wholly deferential cross-section of the community. Three main points stand out. First, the 269 English and Welsh constituencies ran the gamut from twenty or so truly venal boroughs, where parliamentary seats were effectively sold for cash, to a similar number of open boroughs, where the outcome of elections was not dominated by any patron but determined by a large, vocal, and politically conscious electorate. The largest category of constituencies (over eighty in all) recognized the right of a patron, typically a substantial landed proprietor, to nominate one or both of its two parliamentary representatives. But this was conditional on the magnate retaining the electors' goodwill by properly discharging his responsibilities and distributing the fruits of his patronage, whether in the form of custom for local artisans, shops, and businesses, jobs for their children and kinsfolk, charity for the poor and needy or support of civic improvements. In short, the propertied elite had to work hard to maintain their influence over most of the parliamentary seats they 'controlled'.

Secondly, although between 1754 and 1790 the national (English and Welsh) electorate was perhaps a quarter smaller than it had been in 1715, it still

---

[10] *Gentleman's Magazine*, Mar. 1764, 113.

included over one person in six of the adult male population (women did not get the vote in Britain until after the First World War); voter turnout in contested elections actually increased from the 1740s onwards. So although the franchise was plainly not distributed on democratic lines in the second half of the eighteenth century (very few contemporaries believed it should be), the right to vote was not uniformly restricted (except by gender), nor the preserve of a mere handful of propertied men.

Thirdly and last, just as political involvement was not limited to the enfranchised (petitions from boroughs to Parliament in the 1770s and 1780s were signed by roughly twice the numbers qualified to vote in those constituencies), so the political function of elections was not restricted to the selection of parliamentary representatives. The proportion of contested elections declined from around a third to a half at the beginning of the eighteenth century to about a fifth in the three general elections of 1747, 1754, and 1761. But it thereafter recovered to between a quarter and a third of all elections in the later eighteenth and early nineteenth centuries. Given the huge and mounting expense of fighting an election (each of the three candidates for the hotly contested county of Oxfordshire in 1754 spent £40,000), as well as general elite reluctance to engage in open conflict on the hustings, this is a surprisingly high figure. But even uncontested elections required the presence of the nominated candidates to canvass support among the voters, thereby displaying a commitment to the institution of Parliament, and the idealized independence of both electors and constituency. The customary electoral rituals, depicted by the popular artist William Hogarth (1697–1764) in a widely reproduced series of images—the candidate's entry to the electorate, the canvass of voters, the chairing of the returned member—constituted a public blending of aristocratic and plebeian mores which served a long-term integrative function, but also provided opportunities for destabilizing and violent protest on national as well as local issues.[11]

'Wilkes and Liberty!'

In every sense the most dramatic eighteenth-century manifestation of such popular political activity centred on the physically and morally unprepossessing figure of John Wilkes (1725–97)— 'that devil Wilkes' to George III, but 'the Patriot' to many of his subjects.[12] From a wealthy but non-establishment background as second son of a London distiller and his Presbyterian wife, educated by Dissenting ministers and at the University of Leiden, a loveless if lucrative

---

[11] This discussion has drawn heavily on F. O'Gorman, *Voters, Patrons, and Parties: The Unreformed Electoral System in Hanoverian England, 1734–1832* (1989); see also J. Black, *The Politics of Britain, 1688–1800* (1993), ch. 3.

[12] See P. D. G. Thomas, *John Wilkes: A Friend to Liberty* (1996).

arranged marriage brought Wilkes into Buckinghamshire landed society. In 1757, at a cost of £7,000, he won election to Parliament. Identified as a patriot follower of Pitt, he kept a low profile in the Commons, being better known as a high-living man about town, part of an aristocratic libertine circle, the 'Monks of St Francis' or Hell-fire Club, whose members mixed their wine and women with ritualistic anticlerical blasphemy.

It was political journalism that made Wilkes a celebrity. In satirical response to the *Briton*, a pro-government publication edited by the Scottish-born novelist Tobias Smollett (1721–71), Wilkes entitled the weekly essay-sheet which he began to co-publish in 1762 the *North Briton*, thus highlighting the administration's purported dominance by Bute and fellow Scots. By now the King's anxiety to end the war with France, which he regarded as an expensive and unnecessary distraction from urgently needed domestic moral reform and political regeneration, had procured the resignations of Pitt and New-castle, the dismissal of Devonshire, another leading Whig magnate, and Bute's appointment as first lord of the treasury, or prime minister. Peace was actu-ally signed in February 1763, but the terms of the Treaty—or, as opposition journalists would have it, 'Treason'—of Paris, especially the return to France of the West Indian islands of Guadeloupe and Martinique, continued to be attacked as a betrayal of the national interest by Pitt and his mercantile sup-porters.

The *North Briton* for its part depicted the peace as a renewed Franco-Scottish alliance and continued hammering the hapless Bute until the favourite re-signed, after less than a year at the head of government. Even then Wilkes's paper continued to denounce the terms Bute had negotiated; its forty-fifth issue for 23 April 1763 carried a slashing attack on references to the treaty in the King's Speech closing Parliament earlier that month. By apparently impugning the Crown's integrity as well as that of the ministry, no. 45 provided the new prime minister, Pitt's alienated brother-in-law George Grenville (1712–70), with what looked like a golden opportunity to silence Wilkes and other oppon-ents of the peace. Under a general warrant issued by the secretaries of state against the authors, publishers, and printers of no. 45 as 'a seditious and treasonable paper', Wilkes was arrested and imprisoned in the Tower.

General warrants, directed against unnamed or unknown authors, book-sellers, and printers, had been used as a kind of hunting licence by administra-tions attempting to retain some measure of control over the press ever since the non-renewal of the Licensing Act in 1695. But after suing out a writ of habeas corpus and invoking his privilege of immunity from arrest as an MP before the Court of Common Pleas, packed with supporters from the City of London, Wilkes was freed. It was these merchants, professional men, shopkeepers, and artisans as much as the judges to whom Wilkes addressed the claim that his cause concerned 'the liberty of all peers and gentlemen, and, what touches me more sensibly, that of all the middling and inferior set of people'. The 'many thousands' who escorted him home after his release chanted what would become 'the new slogan of militant radicalism, "Wilkes and Liberty!"' [13]

Characteristically unsatisfied with this victory, Wilkes launched proceedings for theft and wrongful arrest, which secured damages and judicial decisions against the legality of general warrants. He pressed his luck further by having the *North Briton* reprinted in book form, hoping to pay off his considerable debts, together with an obscene poem parodying Pope's *Essay on Man*. When a copy of this *Essay on Woman* obtained by the government was found to be attributed in part to the ultra-respectable bishop of Gloucester, the House of Lords condemned its real author for impiety, then joined with the Commons in voting no. 45 'a false, scandalous and malicious libel'. Wilkes had left the country on Christmas Day, ostensibly to visit his daughter in Paris; in his absence he was formally expelled from Parliament, then charged, prosecuted, convicted, and outlawed on charges of blasphemy and seditious libel.

Wilkes did not return to England until 1768, having obtained neither a pardon nor any official compensation for his sufferings in the 'cause of Liberty' from the three ministries which followed in quick succession after Grenville's dismissal in 1765. Believing himself betrayed by former friends and patrons, notably Pitt, no longer 'the great Commoner' since accepting a peerage as earl of Chatham, Wilkes decided that, 'like an old Roman', he would now appeal directly to the people. He accordingly nominated for Parliament in the large county electorate of Middlesex on the northern fringes of London. After jubilant crowds celebrated his runaway victory all over London and Westminster, breaking the windows of known opponents and chalking the number 45 on doors, buildings, and even the Austrian Ambassador's boots, Wilkes gave himself up to imprisonment on the old seditious libel charge. Numerous demonstrators gathered outside the King's Bench Prison across the river in Southwark to express their support. On 10 May 1768, the day of Parliament's opening, a Wilkite crowd variously estimated at from 15,000 to 40,000 people was dispersed by armed troops, who killed seven (including passers-by) and wounded more. This 'Massacre of St George's Fields' became a leading item in the brilliant publicity campaign Wilkes orchestrated from prison, linking his individual cause with that of English liberties along lines pioneered by the Leveller leader John Lilburne (1614?–57) more than a century before. But Wilkes could exploit a far larger range of print media, as well as various consumer goods, including coffee and tea pots, jugs, pipes, buttons, and medallions specially produced in his honour, with which to mobilize a socially and geographically diverse body of supporters. [14]

Expelled again from Parliament, this time on more dubious legal grounds, he was re-nominated for Middlesex, and re-elected unopposed; when this election was annulled, Wilkes stood unopposed again, and was once more rejected by

[13] G. Rudé, *Wilkes and Liberty: A Social Study of 1773 to 1774* (1962), 27.

[14] J. Sainsbury, 'John Wilkes, debt, and patriotism', *Journal of British Studies*, 34 (1995).

Parliament. At a fourth election the Court candidate was easily out-polled by Wilkes, but then formally declared member for Middlesex by a House of Commons which now appeared to be behaving as part of an arbitrary, self-perpetuating oligarchy, rather than the representative of the people. While these extraordinary events unfolded, Wilkite agitation spread well beyond London. Petitions seeking both the patriot's release and numerous political and social reforms were forwarded from nearly twenty counties and a dozen cities. 'The Society of Gentlemen Supporters of the Bill of Rights', a body of London business and professional men formed early in 1769, both to defend the liberties of the subject and to pay off Wilkes's debts, encouraged electors to 'instruct' their MPs to support Wilkes's reinstatement. Members of the Society also advocated various legal and political measures to protect the subject's rights against an authoritarian executive, to eliminate electoral bribery and corruption, and to secure a more 'full and equal representation of the people' in Parliament.[15] While he eventually became the first person to move (unsuccesfully) for parliamentary reform in the House of Commons, most of Wilkes's personal goals were both less ambitious and more easily fulfilled; but the constitutional issues he had been responsible for raising henceforth refused to go away.

[15] *The Letters of Junius*, ed. J. Cannon (1978), 404.

13

RULING INSTITUTIONS

Blackstone and the Rule of Law

Members of a Middlesex grand jury were informed by the magistrate Sir John Hawkins in 1770 that since Christianity was 'part of the law of the land', they had a duty to control 'that licentious and daring spirit, which leads men to deny ... or controvert its precepts, and by consequence to weaken, if not dissolve, the bonds of society'.[1] The interdependence of law and religion in upholding the established order of things was an eighteenth-century commonplace. Yet Hawkins and his listeners would also have been well aware of the disruptive potential of religious differences, and the decidedly mixed reputation of the law and its practitioners.

Nearly twenty years earlier a failed barrister turned Oxford don had announced a 'Course of Lectures on the Laws of England'. Whatever his deficiencies as practitioner, the classes offered by William Blackstone (1723–80) proved an enormous hit, both with undergraduates merely 'desirous to be in some degree acquainted with the constitution and polity of their own country', and those intending a career at the bar. Neither English university had previously taught English common law, which since the inns of court ceased to offer any form of legal instruction in the later seventeenth century could be acquired only via apprenticeship or private study. The fame of Dr—soon Professor—Blackstone spread far and wide. In 1762 a New York merchant noted the 'high character of a Professor at Oxford', who was said to have brought the law's 'mysterious business to some system, besides the system of confounding other people and picking their pockets'.[2] Three years later Blackstone's lectures began to appear in print as *Commentaries on the Laws of England*, soon to become, and remain, the most influential law book in the English language.

Blackstone's great achievement was to map the common law's tortuous complexities in a manner at once authoritative, clear, and elegant. The result was eulogized by a younger contemporary, the erudite lawyer-linguist William Jones (1746–94), as 'the most correct and beautiful outline that ever was exhibited of any human science'. While not wholly uncritical (of procedural complexities, for instance), Blackstone depicts England's constitution and laws as reflecting the natural order of the cosmos, yet also rooted in the distinctive

---

[1] J. Hawkins, *A Charge to the Grand Jury* (1770), Camden 4th ser. 43 (1992), 422, 427.
[2] *Letter Book of John Watts*, ed. D. C. Barck (1928), 13.

historical development of the English nation. Superficial flaws could hardly mar the fundamental soundness of such a construct. Blackstone indeed likened the law of his age to 'an old Gothic castle, erected in the days of chivalry, but fitted up for a modern inhabitant ... The interior apartments ... cheerful and commodious, though their approaches are winding and difficult'.[3]

Even some lawyers found this defence of the legal status quo a little hard to swallow, and denied Blackstone's claim to have discovered intellectual coherence in what was really no more than a formless jumble of precedents and rules. On the other hand his former student Jeremy Bentham (1748–1832), a barrister turned philosopher and social reformer, complained that Blackstone celebrated the law as it stood, rather than critically assessing its constituent parts against the utilitarian criterion of 'the greatest good for the greatest number'. These attacks barely dinted the popularity of Blackstone's work as an expository text. But they paralleled the ambivalence of broader community attitudes towards the laws of England.

On the one hand, it was widely proclaimed that 'government by law' was 'the glory of this constitution'. Even if the workings of England's legal system—assuming it was a system—might be perhaps 'in some respects imperfect', trial by jury and habeas corpus secured a degree of protection for individual liberties 'that is little short of perfection'.[4] Yet in more practical and less abstract terms the law's anomalies, complexities, delays, expense, and uncertainties were fiercely criticized throughout the eighteenth century. The poet Oliver Goldsmith put it succinctly: 'Laws grind the poor, and rich men rule the law.' Wilkites, among whose leadership lawyers were prominent, attacked abuses in legal administration as an extension of their political reform campaign in the 1760s and 1770s. Others followed Jonathan Swift's *Gulliver's Travels* (1726) in blaming the law's worst defects on its practitioners, 'bred up from their youth in the art of proving by words multiplied for that purpose, that white is black and black is white, according as they are paid'. The lawyer's 'unintelligible gibberish' and 'amazing tedious forms' supposedly confounded simple matters of right and wrong, enriching 'dignified rogues' at the expense of 'the helpless but honest'. A mock-epitaph captures one stereotypical view of the legal profession:

> Beneath this smooth stone, by the bone of his bone,
> Sleeps Master John Gill;
> By lies when alive this attorney did thrive,
> And now that he's dead he lies still.

[3] W. Jones, *An Essay on the Law of Bailments* (1781), 3–4; W. Blackstone, *Commentaries on the Laws of England* (1765–9), iii. 268.

[4] Anon., *The Law of Parliament in the Present Situation of Great Britain Considered* (1788), 5; *State Necessity Considered as a Question of Law* (1766), 6.

Junius, the anonymous political satirist of the late 1760s, expressed similar sentiments when he mockingly protested: 'do not injure me so much as to suspect I am a lawyer—I had as lief [rather] be a Scotchman.'[5]

It is true that lawyers have never been much loved, while complaints about the law's costs, delays, and injustices long antedate the eighteenth century. But a slump in the volume of civil litigation handled by the common-law courts, bottoming in the 1740s, may have encouraged practitioners to maximize their incomes by spinning out those suits which did come their way. Certainly the costs of going to law, particularly the level of fees charged by barristers and exacted by legal functionaries, rose very steeply between the later seventeenth and mid-eighteenth centuries. From 1729 attorneys and solicitors, the more numerous, lower-status practitioners, had been subject to a rudimentary registration requirement. But this parliamentary measure was no more immediately successful in curbing unethical practitioners than the attempts at professional self-regulation which followed the establishment around the same time of the 'Society of Gentlemen Practisers in the Courts of Law and Equity', a precursor of the modern solicitors' Law Society.

Nevertheless, attempts were made, especially just after George II's accession, and again in the aftermath of the War of Austrian Succession, to remedy various long-standing legal deficiencies. Parliamentary committees enquired into gaols and prisoners, fees charged to litigants, and the workings of the church courts; legislation required all legal proceedings to be conducted in English (rather than Latin and law-French), established local 'courts of requests' to adjudicate small claims, and enhanced the salaries and tenure of judges. The judges themselves played a significant role in moulding the law by the decisions which they handed down from the bench. Thus Lord Mansfield was largely responsible for creating a coherent body of commercial law, based on the practice of London's merchant community, during his thirty-two years as Chief Justice of King's Bench from 1756 to 1793.

Yet these scattered efforts did not amount to a sustained law reform programme. They certainly failed to tackle fundamental problems, of costs, delays, doctrinal inadequacies, and jurisdictional conflicts between the ancient common-law courts, the court of Chancery (which administered its own distinct code of equity), and the ecclesiastical courts, still exercising authority over marriage, divorce, and the probate of wills. Unsurprisingly, in the last quarter of the century the law's deficiencies began to be attributed less to the corruption of its pristine purity by unscrupulous men and modern luxury than to antiquated doctrines and obsolete structures, 'the customs and perplexity of barbarous ages'.[6]

[5] O. Goldsmith, 'The Traveller' (1764). [A Clergyman of the Church of England], *A Plain Argument* (1761), 29; R. Campbell, *The London Tradesman* (1747), pp. xxviii–xxix; *Memoir of Sir Simeon Supple* (1775), 39; J. Hackett, *Select and Remarkable Epitaphs* (1757), ii. 6; *The Letters of Junius*, ed. J. Cannon (1978), 423.

[6] T. Day, 'Reflections upon the Present State of England', in *Four Tracts* (1785), 101.

Crime and Punishment

Long-standing complaints that the law's workings were socially biased, so that rich and poor received very different treatment from the courts, merged with criticism of its excessive brutality in the treatment of criminal offenders. The severity of England's criminal code, especially the proliferation of capital punishment for relatively minor offences, had come under attack well before 1767, when an English translation popularized the pleas of the Italian jurist Cesare Beccaria (1738–94) for consistent, predictable, and non-retributive penal justice. Thus in 1735 the barrister MP William Hay (1695–1755) deplored what he claimed to be the execution of more persons for theft every six months in London than for offences of all kinds in most other countries over three years. In this view excessive resort to the hangman's noose offset the absence of some of the worst features of Continental penal policy, such as judicial torture. Even Blackstone criticized Parliament's indiscriminate extension of the bloody code, which had resulted in a tripling of capital offences, from around fifty in 1688 to some 160 by George III's accession. Emotional concern and sympathetic compassion for the hundreds of men, women, and children who died on the scaffold every year mingled with distaste for the spectacle of public executions, which were increasingly feared to have a degrading rather than deterrent effect, especially in the unruly, carnivalesque atmosphere of London's Tyburn.[7]

So why did Parliament persist in creating new capital offences, adding another forty or so between 1760 and 1800? One technical reason was the conceptual poverty of English criminal law. In the absence of general definitions of offences, specific enactments were required to criminalize stealing a dog or fish (rather than, say, money or a sheep). But some historians have also seen the proliferation of capital crimes after 1688 as part of a general harnessing of legal process to serve the interests of the powerful and propertied. This view holds that eighteenth-century criminal justice was not just socially biased (in Adam Smith's words, 'a combination of the rich to oppress the poor' by protecting 'the inequality of goods'), but in fact the main ideological and instrumental safeguard of élite power and property. In the absence of an effective police force, or a widely respected national Church, the law allegedly served as social cement, 'constantly recreating the structure of authority which arose from property and in turn protected its interests', while persuading the poor and deprived that the social arrangements which left them in that condition were both inevitable and just.[8]

This ingenious hypothesis starts from a paradox. Although more and more capital offences were created in the eighteenth century, the numbers of executions apparently did not rise in proportion. We lack comprehensive statistics,

---

[7] W. Hay, *Remarks on the Laws relating to the Poor* (1735, 1751), 19; V. Gatrell, *The Hanging Tree: Execution and the English People, 1700–1868* (1994).

[8] D. Hay, 'Property, authority and the criminal law', in D. Hay *et al.*, *Albion's Fatal Tree: Crime and Society in Eighteenth-Century England* (1975).

but there may well have been fewer criminals hanged than in the previous hundred years, and nothing like the increase in absolute numbers which an expanding population and economy would lead us to expect, especially after 1750. Of the persons tried for felonies carrying the death penalty (overwhelmingly offences against property), only a small fraction were actually executed. For example, even of those sentenced to death in the metropolitan county of Surrey over the second half of the eighteenth century, fewer than one-third (1,008 of a total of 3,172) seem to have ended their lives on the scaffold.

There were several recognized avenues of escape from the gallows. 'Benefit of clergy', a medieval relic, gave convicted first offenders an automatic reprieve where many—although not all—crimes were concerned. The King in Council (effectively the monarch and cabinet) also granted pardons on recommendations for mercy by judge or jury, and petitions on behalf of the condemned from employers, landlords, clergy and other notables. So the harsh penalties provided by the criminal code were actually applied on a very selective basis. This process, it is argued, enabled members of the ruling class to reinforce their local status, and reward suitably deferential deportment by their inferiors. Discretionary exercise of the prerogative of mercy supposedly gained added weight from theatrical displays of judicial pomp and ceremony before, during, and after trials, which reinforced the outward majesty of the law, and its ability to intimidate potential malefactors. Finally, although the criminal law's victims were typically plebeian, poor, and propertyless, the occasional trial, conviction, and execution of a socially respectable defendant, like the clergyman-forger Dr William Dodd (1729–77), or the libertine murderer Lord Ferrers (1720–60), vindicated the apparent impartiality and justice of both the legal system and the social order which it protected.

The somewhat patronizing assumption that the labouring poor blindly accepted an ideological message of consent and submission transmitted by the criminal law is difficult to test. Nevertheless it seems unlikely that popular attitudes were totally unaffected by the enormous volume of caricature, criticism, and satire directed against judges, lawyers, and the legal system in general.[9] Nor is it obvious that Georgian society and state teetered on the brink of collapse, saved only by the law's effectiveness as a legitimizing agency. Recent research shows that not just the accused but also the victims of crime, those who brought the vast majority of all criminal charges in the absence of an official state prosecutor, came from the lower ranks of society. At the Old Bailey, London's criminal court, they typically included 'small shopkeepers, artisans, lodging-house keepers, innkeepers'. At the Essex quarter sessions between 1760 and 1800, labourers and husbandmen comprised over one-fifth of those laying prosecutions in cases of serious property crime. So the criminal law was evidently used by the poor as well as the rich (thanks partly to legislation of

[9] J. A. Sharpe, *Crime and the Law in English Satirical Prints, 1600–1832* (1986).

1752 and 1754, which subsidized the costs of successful private prosecutions). Further, most sentencing and pardoning decisions were arguably based on objective criteria, such as the prisoner's reported character, age, and previous record, rather than 'class favouritism and games of influence', even if it seems unlikely that such factors were excluded altogether.[10]

Crime tended to be most prevalent and threatening in and around London. It was often the violent work of gangs and habitual offenders, whose widely reported exploits aroused much anxiety, especially among influential persons likely to support deterrent measures to protect their families and property, including the otherwise seemingly irrational extension of capital punishment. But it is also now clear that significant changes occurred in the trial, sentencing, and punishment of criminals from 1660 onwards. By the late eighteenth century the growing presence of lawyers as counsel for both prosecution and defence had given a new public formality to committal hearings before magistrates, encouraging the refinement of rules of evidence, and shifting the focus of attention in criminal trials from the character of the accused to the evidential strength of the prosecution's case against him (or, much less frequently, her). The physical conditions under which prisoners were held, largely awaiting trial rather than as a mode of punishment, began to show marginal improvement as early as the 1740s; the appalling dirt and disease which the reformer John Howard (1726?–90) exposed in his reports on the *State of the Prisons* from the 1770s onwards were partly due to recent and temporary overcrowding, following the end of transportation to America. Above all, there occurred a major transformation of sentencing options, to supplement and partly replace capital and corporal punishments which were coming to be regarded in at least some quarters as unduly severe, violent, or ineffective deterrents.

Transportation and imprisonment developed as secondary punishments for convicted offenders who might previously have been hanged, whipped, or—most likely—allowed to escape virtually scot-free, after the formulaic literacy test for benefit of clergy was abolished in 1706. Once a government-financed scheme for shipping convicts to the North American colonies had been established in 1718, transportation rapidly became the preferred penalty for property offences. Yet from the 1760s doubts about its deterrent value multiplied. Meanwhile reformers anxious to combat what they saw as the irreligion and moral degeneracy of the lower orders increasingly advocated the discipline of imprisonment with hard labour, solitary confinement, and religious instruction. A sharp drop in the numbers sentenced to transportation was apparent even before the outbreak of war with America in 1776 put a temporary end to that option. A spell in county gaols or houses of correction (reformatory-like institutions where beggars, prostitutes, vagrants, and other petty offenders were set to hard labour) served as the main penal substitute. When transportation

[10] J. Langbein, '*Albion's* Fatal Flaws', *P&P* 98 (1983), 96–120; P. King, 'Decision-makers and decision-making in the English criminal law, 1750–1800', *HJ* 27 (1984), 25–58.

resumed again in 1787 with the dispatch of the First Fleet to Botany Bay, the trend towards incarceration was not reversed. By the end of the century only 30 per cent of males and 17 per cent of females awarded non-capital sentences for offences against property in Surrey were sent to Australia; all but a handful of the remainder received prison terms. Thus popular participation, ritual shaming and terror (as exemplified by the public whipping, pillorying, or hanging of offenders) began to be replaced by forms of correction which occurred out of the public gaze, and which at least some reformers believed should produce repentance and rehabilitation, rather than merely serving to punish and deter.[11]

The Established Church, Dissent, and Disability

A final difficulty with the interpretation outlined above arises from the assumption that criminal justice (so-called) filled a vacuum created by the post-1688 collapse of religion as an instrument of social control. The declining potency of religious ideas and institutions ranks second only to the rising middle class as a hardy perennial of historical explanation. Yet we have already noted (Ch. 11 above) that, despite contemporary lamentation about flourishing immorality and irreligion, the early eighteenth century witnessed neither the unqualified triumph of secularism nor wholesale abandonment of the Anglican Church. Later Hanoverian complaints that religion was 'evidently destroyed' must also be regarded with scepticism, even when backed by a modern historian's characterization of the entire period 1740–1830 as 'an era of disaster' for the Church of England.[12]

That judgement was underpinned by a survey of Easter communicants in a sample of thirty Oxfordshire parishes, whose numbers dropped by a quarter between 1738 and 1802, with most of the decline occurring in the last thirty years of the century. While this finding may point to some contraction of formal Anglican observance, it is not clear how far Easter communion can be used as an index of religious commitment (owing to a lingering belief that the sacrament should be reserved for the old, sick, and well-to-do), nor whether the Oxfordshire experience was typical of the nation at large. Even if it were, some slackening of Anglican religiosity need not necessarily have been fatal to the Church's broad cultural role in marking the communal calendar and individual rites of passage, or its effectiveness in propagating messages of social and political deference.

True, the long-standing structural problems of clerical pluralism and non-residence did not improve and may well have worsened during the second half of the eighteenth century. By 1780 possibly well under half (38 per cent) of

---

[11] This and the previous paragraph draw heavily on J. M. Beattie, *Crime and the Courts in England, 1660–1815* (1986).

[12] J. Brown, *An Estimate of the Manners and Principles of the Times* (1757), 175; A. D. Gilbert, *Religion and Society in Industrial England* (1976), 27.

English parishes were served by a resident beneficed minister, even if pastoral care was often provided by a curate living only a mile or so across the parish boundary. Meanwhile a general improvement in clerical incomes, due to rising agricultural prices and determined efforts to maximize income from church fees and tithes, as well as the greater prevalence of pluralism, helped raise the socio-economic status of the clergy as a whole, even if large inequalities persisted between poorly paid stipendiary curates, at the bottom of the ecclesiastical hierarchy, and the privileged clerical minority who held cathedral livings and other well-endowed benefices. Better material prospects attracted increasingly well-educated and better-born recruits. Whereas a third of the bishops appointed by George I had been peers and gentlemen's sons, nearly half the episcopal promotions in the first thirty years of George III's reign went to representatives of the landed elite; only one bishop can be positively identified as of plebeian stock. The rising economic and social standing of the clergy was also evident in their frequent appointment and vigorous activity as JPs. Of some 9,000 local magistrates in 1761, no fewer than 1,038 were clergymen, whose presence compensated for the growing disinclination of the landed gentry to pull their weight in local government. Clerical JPs ('squarsons') signed more than four out of five quarter sessions convictions in Oxfordshire in 1780.[13]

These developments strengthened personal and social links between the landed ruling class and the Anglican clergy, while simultaneously distancing the latter from the bulk of their congregations, especially where the parson was identified as an enclosing landlord and assiduous tithe collector, appropriating even a tenth of the potato crops grown by poor labourers and other smallholders. A German pastor who attended the Sunday morning service at a parish church outside Oxford in 1782 remarked on the minister's haughty demeanour, as he acknowledged members of his flock 'with a superior nod'.[14] But if the alliance between squire and parson may have fuelled popular anti-clericalism, it could also help reinforce the existing political and social order. From this point of view some degree of popular alienation, if that is what the statistics of falling communicant numbers indicate, may have been a price worth paying in order to cement personal as well as ideological and institutional links between Church and State (or at least the upper ranks of the political nation).

The massive population expansion of the later eighteenth century created more tangible problems for the Established Church, especially as demographic growth was associated with urbanization and internal migration from the south and east of England (where clergy and churches were most numerous) to

[13] N. Ravitch, *Sword and Mitre: Government and Episcopacy in France and England in the Age of Aristocracy* (1966), 118–25; E. J. Evans, 'Some reasons for the growth of English anti-clericalism c.1750–c.1830', *P&P*, 66 (1975). N. Landan, *The Justices of the Peace, 1679–1760* (1984).
[14] C. P. Moritz, *Journeys of a German in England in 1782*, tr. R. Nettel (1965), 127.

the industrializing Midlands and North. Here, it has been argued, the Anglican presence was simply too sparse and under-resourced to meet the spiritual needs of rapidly growing communities, particularly their most vulnerable inhabitants, a rootless, disoriented, and alienated industrial proletariat. Yet the extent to which the traditional, rural, and aristocratic Church of England was overwhelmed by an emerging urban-industrial society must not be exaggerated. Although the population of the cluster of mining and cloth-working settlements formed by Oldham in south-west Lancashire and Saddleworth across the border in Yorkshire mushroomed from around 6,500 to 36,000 persons between 1725 and 1800, the seating capacity of Anglican churches and chapels grew by only a slightly smaller ratio (from 2,817 in 1738 to 8,772 at the end of the century), thanks to the extension of existing structures and the building of at least eight new ones. This construction effort involved both the local manufacturing and landowning elites and their employees; both old and new churches became centres for choral and musical recitals, bell-ringing, and Sunday schools, as well as religious services, while a pub opened next door to the Anglican chapel in the village of Hey to cater for its thirsty congregation. And although the provision of resident beneficed clergy did not keep pace with the expansion of church buildings, 'competent and dedicated stipendiary curates' provided a high level of pastoral care, building upon a strongly felt popular commitment to the Established Church.[15]

Only further research will establish how far the experience of Oldham and Saddleworth may have been typical. But this case history demonstrates that the later eighteenth-century Anglican Church was by no means impotent in the face of demographic and economic change. The continued growth of Wesleyan Methodism, and the broader evangelical movement of which it was the most conspicuous part, provide further reason to doubt that the later Georgian Church of England had become an entirely moribund institution. So too does the revival of the Oxford-based High Church party after 1760, when self-styled 'Orthodox' ministers like Nathaniel Wetherell (1727–1807), master of University College, and his friend George Horne (1730–92), president of Magdalen College and then bishop of Norwich, began to receive official preferment after a fifty-year drought.

The evangelicals' emphasis upon a deeply felt personal faith did undoubtedly represent a reaction against the perceived spiritual and structural inadequacies of mainstream Anglicanism. But whereas laymen and women always figured prominently as Methodist organizers and preachers, Anglican evangelicalism remained under tighter clerical control, guided by godly ministers like Charles Simeon (1759–1836), mentor to successive generations of Cambridge undergraduate 'Simeonites' from 1782 to 1836. The careers of the Revd Henry Venn (1725–97) and his son John (1759–1813) culminated in John's ministry at

[15] M. Smith, *Religion in Industrial Society: Oldham and Saddleworth, 1740–1865* (1994).

Clapham on London's southern outskirts from 1792 to 1813. This influential and wealthy Low Church congregation included the reforming MPs William Wilberforce (1759–1833) and Henry Thornton (1760–1815), the anti-slavery publicist Granville Sharp, and the blue-stocking poet-philanthropist Hannah More (1745–1833); their prominence in campaigns against the slave trade and on behalf of other worthy causes made the 'Clapham Sect' a byword for high-principled moral zeal (see further below, Ch. 14). Lay activism, except in church organizations like the SPCK, was still less encouraged by High Churchmen, who early in the nineteenth century formed the 'Hackney Phalanx', a group of like-minded clergy loosely associated with Joshua Watson (1771–1855), the retired London merchant whose brother John was parish priest at the village of Hackney to the north of London.

Evangelical emphasis on the conversion experience as gateway to an active Christian life lived in accord with Gospel precept did not respect denominational boundaries. Whereas evangelicals of all persuasions comprised only a small and often unpopular minority within the Established Church, the movement had a dramatic impact on Dissent. From the 1760s onwards the long-term decline in Dissenting congregations was reversed, as Baptist and Congregationalist numbers began to rise in response to a continuing surge of evangelical missionary activity. Like Methodism, this 'New Dissent' tended to find its support mainly among urban artisans, the labouring poor, and women, especially in rapidly expanding industrial areas. The better-educated and relatively well-to-do Presbyterians and Quakers remained largely aloof from evangelical enthusiasm and its 'felt', personal religion. Their congregations accordingly continued to dwindle, a tendency accelerated by the Presbyterian drift towards an increasingly intellectualized theology, paralleling similar developments among such advanced Anglican thinkers as Archdeacon Francis Blackburne (1705–87), and Edmund Law (1703–87), an influential master of Peterhouse, Cambridge. The anti-Trinitarian or outright Unitarian outlook of 'Rational Dissent', in which scepticism about the divinity of Jesus Christ joined an optimistic belief in human perfectibility and the power of enlightened human reason, was exemplified in the sermons and writings of two prominent Presbyterian clerical intellectuals and political activists, Drs Richard Price (1723–91) and Joseph Priestley.

The re-emergence of Dissent as a political force after George III's accession reflected new confidence in the security of the Protestant succession, and accumulated impatience with the 'petty apartheid' of limited religious toleration and civil rights imposed (albeit with diminishing rigour) on all non-Anglicans since the Revolution.[16] Yet campaigns for outright repeal of the Test and Corporation Acts were hardly more productive than similar agitation under Walpole, although in 1779 Parliament did free Dissenting ministers and

---

[16] C. Binfield, *So Down to Prayers* (1977), 3–4.

schoolmasters from their obligation to subscribe to the doctrinal articles of the Anglican Church. The King's personal opposition (George took his headship of the Church of England very seriously) and a hostile Anglican majority in both Houses, making much of the interdependence of Established Church and State, of religion and civil government, blocked further movement on this front. Resistance redoubled next year with the shock of the Gordon riots. This massive breakdown of civil order was named after Lord George Gordon (1751–93), the naïve, unstable, but charismatic Scottish founder of the 'Protestant Association', a populist organization dedicated to overturning the 1788 Catholic Relief Act, which had itself repealed a statute of 1700 whereby Roman Catholics were debarred from buying land, or teaching school. These minimal concessions (intended to facilitate recruitment of Catholics to the armed forces) aroused widespread fear and massive anti-papist loathing, which erupted in June 1780 when widespread arson and looting gripped the capital for a week, with minor outbreaks in several provincial centres, arousing understandable fears that the violence might become 'epidemical to the country'. It took 10,000 troops and more than 400 deaths to suppress the London disturbances, which targeted both Catholics and symbols of state authority, including Chief Justice Mansfield's house, the inns of court, Newgate Prison, and the Bank of England. Memories of those traumatic events (marked, according to the historian Edward Gibbon, by 'a dark and diabolical fanaticism' reminiscent of the sectarian mob violence of 1640–1) continued to haunt politicians, policy makers, and the propertied classes for years to come. No further measures to alleviate the disabilities of Dissenters were even proposed to Parliament until 1787.[17]

But it was not only in seeking to better their own lot that Dissenters undertook a significant political role. Many of them also expressed and organized opposition to the American war (see below, Ch. 14), while from the late 1760s onwards Rational Dissenters, in conjunction with their radical Whig allies, supported proposals for institutional, legal, and parliamentary reform which developed alongside and then outstripped the Wilkite agitation. Price and Priestley were both prominent in these campaigns. They also argued for the natural right of every individual to enjoy absolute freedom of religious belief and worship without state interference—a direct denial of the orthodox Anglican view that Established Church, government, and society were intermingled and mutually self-supporting.

Between the mid-1740s and the late 1780s, popular anti-Catholicism, Methodism, and Dissent all showed themselves capable of generating considerable public conflict and disorder, while religious and political dissidents habitually invoked the law's protection against official abuses of power, as well as attacking its subversion by ministerial influence. Radical activists like James

---

[17] C. Haydon, 'The Gordon Riots in the English provinces', *Historical Research*, 63 (1990); E. Gibbon, *Miscellaneous Works* (1814), ii. 240–1.

14

BURDENS AND FRUITS OF EMPIRE
1763–1788

Attitudes to Empire

The peace which concluded the Seven Years War was 'a damned bad one' in the view of a London citizen, recorded by Boswell at Child's coffee house on 11 December 1762. But although the Treaty of Paris saw Guadeloupe, Martinique, and Goree restored to France, while Spain regained Cuba and the Philippines, it nevertheless brought vast territorial gains, especially in India and North America. These massive acquisitions of lands and people inevitably focused attention on England's extra-European interests and presence. The phrase 'British Empire' began to acquire a new significance, denoting the possession of lands and peoples across the seas, in addition to the more familiar assertion of commercial and maritime dominance.[1]

These new connotations of empire did not sit happily with the pervasive Country ideology, which deplored any reason for enhanced executive influence, while celebrating the supposed republican Roman virtues of agrarian independence and public service. Nevertheless, the benefits of colonies or plantations, both as sources of valuable imports and as receptacles for the surplus poor, unemployed, vagrants, and criminals had long been canvassed, especially by mercantilist economic writers. John Bennet's frequently reprinted *National Merchant: or, Discourses on Commerce and Colonies* (1736) celebrated 'our colonies' as 'a charitable benefaction bestowed on this nation by God ... which, if rightly improved, must needs make us a great, happy, and flourishing people'. A decade before the campaign of the poet-philosopher Bishop Berkeley for funds to erect a missionary college in Bermuda was buttressed by more altruistic, even millenarian visions of a new golden age in America's 'happy climes', as 'Westward the course of empire takes its way'. Yet Berkeley had been no more successful in attracting government assistance for this scheme than the eccentric Captain Welbe, a veteran of William Dampier's 1699 voyage to Australia's north-west coast, who twenty years later was still vainly struggling to arouse official interest in 'carrying on a trade to Terra Australis and making very advantageous discoveries there'.[2]

---

[1] *Boswell's London Journal*, ed. Pottle, 74–5. In rural Sussex the peace was thought 'ignominious and inglorious': *The Diary of Thomas Thoner 1754–1765* (1984), 270.

[2] Alexander Turnbull Library, Wellington, New Zealand, qMS-2128. G. Williams and A. Frost (eds.), *Terra Firma to Australia* (1988).

Welbe's proposals were shuffled off to the 'Lords Commissioners of Trade and Plantations' (or Board of Trade), from 1696 the government's advisory body on colonial and commercial matters. The Board also served as main point of contact for pressure groups with special interests in colonial and overseas affairs, including merchant lobbies, missionary societies, and the Dissenting denominations (who maintained close contact with co-religionists across the Atlantic). It participated in negotiations which led to the establishment of Georgia as a chartered colony in 1732, ostensibly to provide a refuge for freed English debtors and persecuted European Protestants, as well as a buffer protecting the English Carolinas from French Louisiana and Spanish Florida. But the limited and reluctant assistance Walpole's government provided to the well-connected philanthropists who backed this project was symptomatic of a generally low level of public interest in colonial and imperial issues before the 1760s.

True, the exotic settings of Dryden's *The Indian Queen* (1664, revived with music by Purcell in 1695), Behn's *Oroonoko* (adapted for the stage 1695, revived 1759), Defoe's *Robinson Crusoe* (1719) and Swift's *Gulliver's Travels* (1726) point to rising fascination with the wider world beyond Europe. So does the popularity of travel books, such as William Dampier's *Voyage to New Holland* (1703, 1709) and *A Cruising Voyage round the World* (1712) by the adventurous Woodes Rogers (d. 1732), whose account of the castaway Alexander Selkirk's rescue from the island of Juan Fernandez helped inspire Defoe's best-seller. Broadened horizons of the imagination paralleled increased population flows, from Scotland and Ireland as well as England and Wales, to the Americas, the West Indies, Africa, India, and South-East Asia, in the first case primarily to settle, otherwise mainly to trade. Absentee West Indian sugar planters, wealthy 'nabobs' returned from India, Virginia tobacco planters' sons attending Oxford or the inns of court, black slaves and personal servants like Samuel Johnson's Francis Barber, ensured that the movement was not entirely one-way. Nor did opposition politicians find difficulty in arousing mercantile and popular support for patriotic aggression against the extra-European colonial and commercial interests of Catholic France and Spain during the later 1730s and 1740s, and again from the mid-1750s. But it took the remarkable victories of Pitt's Seven Years War to bring the British empire beyond Europe close to the forefront of political and public consciousness.[3]

George III, Lord North, and the American Revolution

Long before hostilities formally ended, English politicians were considering how colonial relations should be adjusted to reflect the new imperial realities.

[3] K. Wilson, 'Empire of Virtue: the imperial project and Hanoverian culture *c*.1720–1785', in L. Stone (ed.), *An Imperial State at War* (1994), 128–64; cf. B. Harris, ' "American idol": empire, war, and the middling ranks in mid-eighteenth century Britain', *P&P* 150 (1996).

The national debt had doubled, to some £130m., thanks to spending on the war. One obvious way to reduce that burden was by applying 'user pays' principles to the empire at large. The evident prosperity of just under two and a half million American colonists (whose numbers had increased nearly tenfold since the beginning of the century) made it appear to many both feasible and fair that they should contribute towards the costs of their own defence. Expenditure might also be reduced by restricting westwards territorial expansion, thereby minimizing clashes with the indigenous Amerindians. Another priority was tighter administration of the Navigation Acts and other protective commercial regulations, eliminating illicit American trade with other European states or colonies in order to protect British mercantile and revenue interests. Such measures would address underlying concerns that the colonies had already drifted some distance from Britain in economic, religious, and social terms, and might well seek full independence in the not-too-distant-future, unless handled with appropriate firmness and resolve.[4]

The reception of George Grenville's legalistic efforts to implement a new imperial order hardly calmed such fears. His Sugar Act (1764) and Stamp Act (1765) were revenue-raising measures which explicitly asserted Parliament's right to tax the colonies directly. They provoked not only fierce and ominously concerted colonial resistance, but enormous political controversy, in both England and America. The colonists—or those speaking on their behalf—claimed to be British subjects of George III, owing allegiance directly to the Crown, and not to the British Parliament, where they were unrepresented. Westminster consequently had no more right to legislate for them than their own legislatures in Boston or New York had to make laws for the counties of Middlesex or Yorkshire. Initially the King himself may not have been entirely unsympathetic to this line of reasoning. George did nothing to prevent almost all the offending legislation being repealed, once Grenville was succeeded by an 'Old Corps' Whig ministry under the enormously wealthy but politically lightweight marquess of Rockingham (1730–82). Rockingham and his followers generally favoured a conciliatory approach to the American problem, doubting both the expedience and feasibility of attempts to bind the colonies more closely to the mother country. After a fairly ineffective year in power Rockingham was replaced in mid-1766 by the seriously ailing William Pitt, now ennobled as earl of Chatham, whose support for colonial immunity from British taxes was on the public record. But thereafter the royal attitude hardened, despite some temporary improvement in Anglo-American relations which followed the suspension of colonial boycotts on British goods, and a consequent revival of transatlantic trade.[5]

---

[4] *Gentleman's Magazine* (1764), 104; J. P. Greeme, 'The Seven Years' War and the American Revolution: the causal relationship reconsidered', in P. Marshall and G. Williams (eds.), *The British Atlantic Empire Before the American Revolution* (1980).

[5] P. D. G. Thomas, 'George III and the American Revolution', *History*, 70 (1985), 16–31.

The King's growing intransigence towards his North American subjects in the later 1760s was stiffened by American support for John Wilkes, as another proponent of liberty, and agitation by Dissenters, political radicals, reformers, and republicans, plus a minority of opposition politicians, on behalf of those whom they represented as 'poor Americans' struggling against 'most cruel oppression'.[6] Some in these circles claimed to fear that repressive policies intended ultimately for Britain were being trialled in America, or even that the intended enslavement of the colonists was a popish plot designed to clear the way for a Jacobite *coup d'état* in Britain. Nor did those advocating conciliation rather than repression of the Crown's American subjects have a monopoly on conspiracy theories: High Church Anglican paranoia depicted colonial resistance as part of a sinister transatlantic Presbyterian–republican plot. Certainly Americans' objections to being taxed by a body in which they were unrepresented did help to reinforce the case made by English reformers for measures to ensure that Parliament was henceforth freely elected, independent, and authentically representative. However, the King's hardline stance was supported by most Church of England clergy, and the overwhelming bulk of peers and MPs, including the new prime minister whose appointment in 1770 unexpectedly ended nearly a decade of political instability.

Frederick Lord North (1732–92), who as the heir to a peerage was known by his courtesy title, is irrevocably associated with the outbreak of the American Revolution in 1776, and Britain's subsequent loss of what became from 1778 the United States of America. Yet, given the extent to which the lines of conflict had already been drawn before he came to office, it remains doubtful whether North could have prevented armed hostilities with the thirteen colonies. Nor should the clash be reduced to a mere matter of personalities. In fact Lord North received overwhelming support, from both within and outside Parliament, for the fateful coercive measures which he introduced in response to the Boston Tea Party (1773), when three shiploads of surplus East India Company tea, the sole imported commodity on which a British tax still applied, were dumped in Boston harbour as a calculated gesture of colonial defiance. He and his fellow ministers had no difficulty in representing the defence of Parliament's legislative authority as a matter of constitutional (indeed 'Revolution') principle, or the recalcitrant colonists as an ungrateful faction of self-interested troublemakers, supported only by 'mad enthusiasts and desperate republicans'—and in having that defence accepted by most of the public.

The Strains of War

In response the administration's American opponents depicted themselves as innocent victims of a corrupt and tyrannical government, seeking merely to

[6] *The Diary of Sylas Neville, 1767–1788*, ed. B. Cozens-Hardy (1950), 51 (entry for 4 Nov. 1768); J. Sack, *From Jacobite to Conservative: Reaction and Orthodoxy in Britain, c.1760–1832* (1993), 31–2.

uphold the constitutional liberties of free-born Englishmen. The 1774 Quebec Act, which had realistically recognized French civil law and extended religious toleration to French-Canadian Catholics, was naturally cited as further evidence of the administration's malign intent to subvert both Protestantism and the common law. In fact the extreme stance taken by the Commonwealth of Massachusetts in response to this and other British measures enjoyed nothing like unconditional support in the remaining twelve colonies, while even Boston had its quota of loyalist 'Tories'. But bloody clashes between Massachusetts militiamen and regular British troops at Concord and Lexington in 1775 were sufficient to bring about a general colonial insurrection, from which only Canada and the West Indies remained aloof.

Despite ministerial expectations of rapid victory against presumably ill-equipped and untrained colonials, the formidable difficulties of waging a counter-insurgency campaign across huge tracts of hostile territory on the other side of the Atlantic Ocean soon became painfully apparent. The unexpected surrender of General ('Gentleman Johnny') Burgoyne (1722–92) and his 5,000 men at Saratoga in upper New York province in October 1777 encouraged first France, then Spain, and eventually Holland to enter the war on the American side. Meanwhile Britain remained in diplomatic isolation, unable to persuade other powers such as Austria and Russia to join her struggle against the Bourbon states, whose combined naval strength now easily outnumbered that of the British fleet, which had been allowed to run down after the triumphs of the Seven Years War. At home loyal addresses and subscriptions to support those 'employed in suppressing the American rebellion' were countered by anti-war petitions and sermons.[7] In Parliament North's American policies were fiercely attacked by opposition spokesmen, including the gifted Anglo-Irish orator Edmund Burke (1729–97), Charles James Fox, Rockingham, and the widely unpopular earl of Shelburne (1737–1805). Growing dismay at the government's evident inability to crush the rebels was aggravated by threats of French invasion, unrest in Ireland (see below, pp. 216–18), disruption of maritime trade, and the exploits of John Paul Jones, whose American-French privateering fleet bombarded Edinburgh, captured the fort at Whitehaven, and took numerous prizes in the Channel and Irish Sea. Besides these dangers and humiliations, prolonged warfare inevitably meant higher taxes and a ballooning national debt.

So generalized dissatisfaction supplemented the hostility of the vocal minorities who had consistently opposed the government's American policies since the early 1770s and before. This pervasive mood of discontent gained sharper focus with the launching in 1779 of a grass-roots campaign against political and parliamentary corruption. Led by Christopher Wyvill (1740–1822), a wealthy, liberal-minded clergyman, the cause was taken up enthusiastically

[7] R. J. Fletcher (ed.), *The Pension Book of Gray's Inn, 1669–1800* (1910), 326.

by his fellow Yorkshire landed proprietors, as well as many merchants and professional men. A large public meeting at York formed a county 'Association' of 'gentlemen, clergy and freeholders' to press for economy in government spending by the abolition of sinecures, together with other forms of Crown and ministerial patronage. This demand for what became known as 'economical reform' revived and extended a campaign dating back to the 1760s, which attributed all shortcomings in the political system to the underhand workings of corrupt advisers and 'secret influence' (then usually a code-word for Bute). Once such influence had been eliminated, and Parliament set free to function as it should, other desirable reforms would supposedly become possible, including repeal of the Septennial Act and measures to achieve more equal representation of the people.

But how far should political reform go? The Rockingham Whigs, the most coherent of the various anti-North parliamentary factions, while anxious to jump aboard Wyvill's Association bandwaggon, sought only to reduce the Crown's influence, not to abolish political patronage *per se*. Around London, moreover, the Association movement attracted such alarmingly advanced thinkers as Major John Cartwright, the first public proponent of the vote for all males over the age of 18, and Dr John Jebb (1736–86), one-time academic and would-be university reformer, now a Unitarian advocate of the people's right 'to remodel the constitution'. In April 1780 Cartwright and Jebb, together with the young barrister Capel Lofft (1751–1824) and other radical associates, founded a new Society for Constitutional Information. Unlike the forty or so county and urban associations this body had as its prime objective the advancement of parliamentary reform. These middle-class dissidents and intellectuals, who held that 'the very name of Parliament is a mockery in England', were hardly natural allies of country gentlemen whose main concern was simply to see the land tax fall to a shilling in the pound.[8] So even without the sobering impact of the Gordon riots in the early summer of that year, the diverse aims and character of the reformers help explain their failure to achieve any more substantial outcome than the passage of a famous House of Commons resolution, 'that the influence of the Crown has increased, is increasing, and ought to be diminished'.[9]

Ireland: Patriots and Volunteers

While the North ministry continued to hope in vain for a loyalist counter-revolution to solve its American problem, a second colonial rebellion loomed much nearer home. Anglo-Irish frictions had caused concern since the 1750s, and by the mid-1770s a crisis of some sort seemed imminent. During the Seven

[8] [A Gentleman of the Middle Temple], *The Out-of-Door Parliament* (1780), 82.
[9] J. Almon, *The Parliamentary Register* (1780), xvii. 453; I. R. Christie, *The End of North's Ministry, 1780–1782* (1958), ch. 1.

Years War long-standing resentment of Ireland's constitutional and economic subordination was expressed in the aggressively 'Patriot', anti-English stance adopted by members of the Protestant ascendancy in their Dublin parliament. London's wish to impose more effective political control and tame the aristocratic 'undertakers' who managed the Irish Lower House underlay the appointment in 1767 of the first permanently resident Viceroy or Lord-Lieutenant, and the passage of an Act limiting each Irish parliament to eight years' duration (rather than the reigning monarch's lifetime). But no further progress was made with constitutional reforms, like judicial tenure during good behaviour and a Habeas Corpus Act (to systematize appeals against arbitrary imprisonment, following the century-old English statute to that effect), which Henry Flood (1732–91) and other Patriot spokesmen sought in order to redress the lack of civil rights enjoyed by the King's loyal Protestant subjects in Ireland.

Obvious parallels could be, and were, drawn between the Patriots' ultimate goal of Irish legislative independence and the aims of the recalcitrant American colonists. Continuing sympathy for their cause in both Belfast and Dublin did not readily translate into active support for the Americans. But an accumulation of grievances arising from the war's impact on Ireland's economy turned the volunteer militias raised mainly by local landlords to repel the threat of French invasion into a new and potent nationalist political force. Drawn overwhelmingly from the ranks of the respectable (they had to provide their own—Irish-cloth—uniforms), but not exclusively Protestant in composition, the Volunteers lent weighty out-of-doors support to the parliamentary campaign for the removal of all legislation restricting commerce led by Henry Grattan (1746–1820). Militia parades with posters bearing the ominous slogan 'Free Trade—Or Else' combined with a boycott of British imports helped persuade Lord North, over the objections of domestic manufacturing lobbies, to allow free access of Irish manufactured goods, including glass and woollens, to both Britain and colonial markets, with which Irish merchants could henceforth trade directly.[10]

Yet such substantial if overdue concessions merely whetted Irish appetites for full legislative independence, especially given the possibility, unwisely hinted at by North, of a future reimposition of discriminatory trade measures. Accordingly Grattan and his followers in Dublin co-ordinated with the opposition Whig leadership in London and the local parliamentary reform movement calls for an end both to Poynings' Law and the Declaratory Act (see above, Ch. 7). Their campaign was supported by well-publicized county and Volunteer meetings, like that of representatives from 143 corps of Ulster Volunteers at Dungannon, County Tyrone, in February 1782, which denounced as 'unconstitutional, illegal and a grievance' claims by 'any body of men, other than the King, Lords, and Commons of Ireland, to make laws to

---

[10] J. C. Beckett, *A Short History of Ireland* (1979), 111.

bind this kingdom'.[11] Following the organizational pattern of the English political reform Associations (itself reminiscent of the American constitutional congress, which in turn adapted a model pioneered by English Dissenters in the 1730s), the Volunteers' assemblies set up standing committees to implement their decisions and liaise with counterparts across the country. Nor was pressure applied solely by and on behalf of the Anglican Protestant ascendancy; middle-class Catholics and Ulster Presbyterians were both conspicuously involved, their patriotic fervour doubtless buoyed by recent incremental civil rights gains.

Faced with this formidable alliance, and no obvious alternatives, the reformist Rockingham–Shelburne Whig coalition which took office after the much-bruised North resigned in March 1782 quickly granted Ireland's constitutional demands in full, including legal and legislative independence, security of judicial tenure, and an annual Mutiny Act (to ensure parliamentary control of the military). Patriot suspicions of British good faith raised doubts about the permanency of these concessions, addressed next year by a further Renunciation Act. But Grattan's triumph hardly put an end to the manipulation— and corruption—of Irish politics to serve British interests through the agency of the Lord-Lieutenant. Nor did the further easing of restrictions on Roman Catholic ownership of land in 1782 please hardline Protestants, or satisfy growing pressure for full civil and political rights from 'the potentially dangerous force of resurgent Catholicism', which at least some English ministers were coming to envisage as a possible counterweight to the demands of the Ascendancy patriots.[12]

Pitt and Recovery

Lord North's resignation after twelve years in office inaugurated a brief period of ministerial instability reminiscent of the first decade of George III's reign. The main difficulty, as before, was a shortage of politicians who both commanded sufficient parliamentary following to form a government and were acceptable to the King. With the surrender of General Cornwallis (1738–1805) and his army to George Washington at Yorktown in 1781, it became plain that the rebellious colonies would not be brought to heel by military force. But peace negotiations were protracted, complicated by the involvement of France and other European powers, as well as by differences between George III and his ministers, and indeed among the ministers themselves. After the death of Rockingham in July 1782, it still took more than twelve months to conclude a settlement. This treaty of Versailles saw surprisingly little loss of British territory apart from her former thirteen American colonies, although France regained Tobago and Senegal, while Spain recovered Florida and Minorca.

[11] *EHD, 1714–1783*, 695.
[12] O. MacDonagh, *States of Mind: Two Centuries of Anglo-Irish Conflict* (1983), 130.

Shelburne, who initiated these negotiations, was in turn overthrown in February 1783 by an improbable factional deal struck between the ambitious, charming, and ebullient Fox, a man bred up to politics (in which his interest was said to be exceeded only by his appetite for alcohol, gambling, and women), and his former antagonist Lord North. This cynical, even unnatural coalition deeply disgusted George III. Feeling betrayed by North and regarding the openly anti-monarchist Fox as a politician and person without redeeming features (not least on account of his undesirable friendship with the Prince of Wales), the King determined to bring down their ministry at the first available opportunity.

That came at year's end, when an India Bill drafted by Burke and supported by Fox failed to pass the Upper House, thanks partly to well-publicized royal hostility to the proposal that the entire management of the East India Company's massive territories and patronage should be vested in sixteen appointed commissioners—all known Foxites. George thereupon summarily dismissed Fox and North, inviting the 24-year-old William Pitt (1759–1806) to take their place. Although brought up on the assumption that he would follow his famous father into a brilliant political career, Chatham's extraordinarily able younger son had only two years' parliamentary experience. But at this moment of constitutional crisis and national soul-searching in the aftermath of the American débâcle, young 'Billy' Pitt's main qualifications for office were probably not so much his impressive debating skills as the high seriousness with which he took both himself and his political mission. The connotations of untainted independence and patriotic integrity still attached to his family name were also no handicap. And the King's gamble worked. In the face of successive motions of no-confidence when Parliament met, and Fox's urging that only majority support in the House of Commons (which Pitt lacked) could legitimize a ministry, Pitt refused to resign. Instead he maintained that the King alone had the right to appoint or dismiss his own ministers, and appealed over the head of a discredited, faction-ridden, and conspicuously unreformed Parliament to the nation at large. More than two hundred loyal addresses supporting Pitt and his King from counties and towns all over the country lent weight to this argument, even with some element of government manipulation at work, as it was also and inevitably in the premature general election which George broke convention by calling for March 1784.

The outcome of what was widely depicted as a personal duel between Charles James Fox and George III, as well as a party clash between Whig upholders of the Commons and Pittite supporters of the royal prerogative, could hardly be in doubt. After 1714 governments won all eighteenth-century general elections, but the landslide which reduced Fox's party from about 210 to 132 MPs reflected a genuine rallying to the Crown across the political nation. Buoyed by this triumph, Pitt continued to hold office, without serious challenge, for a further seventeen years. During the rest of the 1780s his main achievement was to preside over an unglamourous but quietly successful process of national economic recovery and modest administrative reform, building upon foundations laid by North and Shelburne. Pitt himself was particularly identified with effecive measures to reduce government spending and the size of the National Debt, to dismantle protective commercial restrictions and lower customs duties, following free-trade principles expounded by Adam Smith's path-breaking *Inquiry into the Nature and Causes of the Wealth of Nations* (1776), and to increase revenue from indirect taxation. While these 'economical' reforms were widely welcomed, and helped restore confidence in government, the much more difficult and divisive issue of parliamentary reform was allowed to founder quietly in a series of failed private members' bills.

India and the East

That the tea tipped into Boston harbour on 16 December 1773 was originally intended both to help the East India Company's tottering finances and to inveigle the Americans into accepting the Westminster parliament's taxing powers underlines the complex and global scale of Britain's post-1760 imperial commitments. Anglo-American relations naturally became the predominant concern from this point onwards, but during the Seven Years War and for a decade afterwards Britain's role and responsibilities in India had attracted at least as much attention. With the loss of the thirteen colonies, Indian affairs returned to prominence. As we have just seen, it was the defeat of Fox's controversial India Bill, with its proposal to entrust all official patronage in the subcontinent to a parliamentary committee of Foxite Whigs, that enabled George III to bring Pitt to power.

 Early eighteenth-century British involvement in India had been largely limited to coastal commerce. Sir Josiah Child's disastrous foray into mainland power politics just after the Glorious Revolution, which effectively bankrupted the old East India Company, provided a long-standing argument against more adventurous policies. But the subsequent decline of the Mogul empire's authority over its feudal vassals and their dependent territories created a power vacuum increasingly open to European intervention. In the 1740s the Company's relatively modest deployment from its trading posts at Bombay, Calcutta, and Madras was challenged by the rapid territorial expansion of its French competitor, *La Compagnie des Indes*. Anglo-French rivalries began to be played out via alliances with indigenous rulers, backed by sepoy armies of native troops with European officers, and occasional actions between naval fleets of both nations. During the 1750s Robert Clive (1725–74), a young East India Company 'writer', or clerk, led some remarkably successful military ventures against the French and their client states. As a result the Company gained control of the Carnatic region in south-east India, together with the much wealthier territories of Bengal, Bihar, and Orissa lying inland from Calcutta along the Ganges Valley, and the French lost their main base at Pondicherry, south of Madras. Clive's exploits brought him not only glory and a peerage, but an immense personal fortune. Other employees quickly sought to follow his dazzling example, conscious that private trading, the traditional means by which East India Company officers accumulated a more or less modest nest-egg for their retirement, was affected by the depressed commercial conditions which had also reduced returns to the Company's shareholders.

So the Seven Years War left the East India Company a colonial power in its own right, with substantial administrative, judicial, and taxing responsibilities. The government's initial response was merely to extract an annual £400,000 levy from 'John Company'. But growing humanitarian disquiet about the methods by which Clive and his fellow nabobs had acquired their riches reinforced pragmatic fears that the Company was creating an administrative, financial, and military burden which the state would sooner or later be called upon to shoulder. Rather than antagonize powerful interests by halting territorial expansion altogether, attempts were made to control and supervise the process. Lord North's Regulating Act (1773) created a Supreme Council in Bengal, whose government-appointed members squabbled incessantly with Warren Hastings (1732–1818), a seasoned administrator appointed by the Company to the newly created office of governor-general. Burke proposed to solve this problem ten years later by simply removing all non-commercial functions from the Company. After the failure of Burke's bill, Pitt's India Act, finally passed in 1785, took a less drastic approach. A ministerial Board of Control in London was appointed to determine overall British policy towards India, but the Company's directors were allowed to continue ruling its annexed territories as well as conducting commercial operations. These expanded considerably in the 1780s, especially with China and South-East Asia, where a trading post was established at Penang on the Malay Peninsula in 1786. Reduced British import duties greatly stimulated demand for China tea, which in turn encouraged the production of Indian cotton, and more ominously opium, as an alternative to the traditional practice of paying for Chinese goods with silver bullion.

India and the East provided Britons not only with consumer goods, careers (the Company's military establishment alone increased from 114 officers in 1763 to 1,069 by 1784), and exotic plunder, but also the opportunity to observe at close quarters an ancient non-Christian civilization. The linguist, poet, and scholar William Jones, who served as a judge in Calcutta for ten years until his death in 1794, committed himself to an ambitious course of study, recently characterized as an intrusive act of European cultural imperialism. Yet his pioneering translations of ancient Indian laws and literature led 'Oriental' Jones to postulate a common source for the Greek, Latin, and Sanskrit languages, thereby challenging naïve Eurocentric notions of Western cultural primacy. Jones also hoped to benefit both East and West by facilitating the use of indigenous law in 'the administration of justice among the natives of Bengal and

Bihar'.[13] His linguistic interests were shared and encouraged by Warren Hastings, before the latter's return to Britain in 1785 to face a parliamentary inquiry and impeachment for his conduct as first governor-general. The trial of Hastings, and by implication not only the Company through whose ranks he had risen, but Britain's entire imperial presence in Asia, initially attracted enormous public attention. This soon slackened as hearings dragged on over nine tedious years, and it became apparent that the charges of corruption and misrule would not stick. Indeed, whatever the rights or wrongs of Hastings's actions, unease about the uglier aspects of British colonialism was increasingly overtaken by national pride in the perceived benevolence and moderation of Britain's presence East of Suez.

The Pacific

The Pacific Ocean's vast immensity remained largely unknown to Europeans for 250 years after its first crossing by Portuguese navigators in the early sixteenth century. Then within the space of a generation after 1760 maritime explorers and scientific observers, mostly British and French, finally made contact with the main Pacific islands and their peoples. This new wave of state-backed oceanic exploration was driven by a mixture of geo-political strategic concerns, commercial ambition, intellectual and scientific curiosity, and competitive national rivalry. Published journals, maps, and illustrations of the voyages and discoveries provided extensive accounts and evocative images of hitherto isolated human societies, whose apparently idyllic existence close to nature seemed at least initially to confirm Rousseau's preference for the 'noble savage' before the civilized but corrupt European.

The best-documented and most extensive expeditions of the whole post-1760 race for the Pacific were those commanded by Captain James Cook (1728–79), a Yorkshire labourer's son who joined the Royal Navy as an able seaman, gaining promotion through the ranks by his outstanding self-taught skills as navigator and surveyor. Cook's first voyage on HMS *Endeavour*, a converted North Country collier similar to those on which he had served his own apprenticeship in the coastal trade between London and Newcastle, left England in 1768 with a crew of seamen and scientists, including the young Joseph Banks (1743–1820), a future president of the Royal Society. After visiting the newly discovered island of Tahiti to conduct astronomical observations only possible in the Southern hemisphere, the *Endeavour* sailed west and south to circumnavigate and map the islands of New Zealand, survey the eastern coast of New Holland (as the continent now known as Australia had been named by Dutch explorers), and finally work north through the Great Barrier Reef to Dutch Batavia and home via the Cape of Good Hope in 1771.

---

[13] E. Said, *Orientalism* (1985), 77–9; *The Works of Sir William Jones, in Six Volumes* (1799), iii. 51.

Cook's two further epic voyages, in 1772–5, and 1776–80, conclusively established the non-existence of both a fabled great southern continent ('Terra Australis') joined to Antarctica, and a navigable north-west passage linking the Atlantic and Pacific. He also made important contributions to European geographical, botanic, and ethnographic knowledge. But Cook's greatest achievement before his violent death at the hands of Hawaiian islanders was to show the feasibility of very long trans-oceanic passages without either massive casualties from scurvy or potentially disastrous navigational errors in determining longitude. Had it not been for his success in these respects, it seems doubtful whether Pitt's administration would eventually have taken up the suggestion first made by Joseph Banks before a parliamentary committee in the late 1770s, to establish a British colony on the shores of Botany Bay, in the region Cook named New South Wales.

Historians have long debated whether that decision was solely motivated by the desperate short-term need to find a dumping ground for convicted criminals sentenced to transportation, following the refusal of the newly independent American colonies to accept them. Although the traditional monocausal explanation has a satisfying simplicity, some decision makers may have been influenced by commercial and strategic considerations, especially the prospect of acquiring new sources of timber and flax for naval spars, sails, and rigging, increasingly required by the expansion of Britain's maritime presence in Asia. Indeed the government very likely sought to kill at least two birds with one stone, achieving a solution to the convict problem while at the same time 'rendering their transportation reciprocally beneficial both to themselves and to the state'.[14]

This is not to postulate a coherent policy of British colonial expansion from 1760 or 1780 within which the settlement of Australia can be located. The abandonment of the Falkland Islands in the South Atlantic ten years after they were first settled by rival British and French expeditions in 1764, the lack of official involvement in the settlement of Sierra Leone as a refuge for repatriated slaves in 1787, and the protracted process leading to the eventual choice of Botany Bay rather suggest an opportunist, case-by-case approach, while the American experience and the theoretical arguments of Adam Smith operated in a powerfully anti-imperialist direction. Even so, the ambitious scale of the Australian venture, in particular the extent to which state resources were committed to the successful voyage of the First Fleet in 1787–8, would have been barely imaginable a mere quarter-century before.

[14] 'Heads of a Plan' (August 1786), in C. M. H. Clark (ed.), *Select Documents in Australian History, 1788–1850* (1950), 34.

15

SENSE AND SENSIBILITY

The British Enlightenment

England was 'the country of philosophers', according to a cosmopolitan French visitor in 1745 (echo Voltaire). Argument and disputation pervaded every level of society, from peers of the realm debating parliamentary business, to common sailors denigrating both French matelots and their own government. Foreign observers often attributed this contentiousness to the national obsession with political and religious liberty, which encouraged all aspects of individualism, including a questioning and rationalist outlook.[1]

By 1780 England was being hailed as 'without doubt the most enlightened country in Europe'.[2] Yet 'the Enlightenment' does not come into the English language until the mid-nineteenth century. Indeed it is only recently that historians have ceased to exclude England from accounts of what was once regarded as a largely, if not wholly, French phenomenon. Yet many characteristic features of the European Enlightenment as manifested in eighteenth-century France were plainly pioneered in England during the seventeenth and early eighteenth centuries, most notably a commitment to using empirically derived scientific knowledge to improve the human condition, as advocated by Francis Bacon and institutionalized by the Royal Society. The focus of historical attention has also widened, from the philosophies of Enlightenment thinkers to the processes by which enlightened attitudes and values were transmitted to a broad audience.

The Enlightenment may be defined as a European-wide intellectual movement, committed to improvement, progress, and reform by means of 'rational use of the human faculties'. Joseph Priestley linked an emphasis upon reason (utilizing the fruits of ordered experience, or designed experiment, rather than authority, precedent, or tradition) as the yardstick against which all existing institutions should be tested, with 'freedom from debasing and vulgar prejudices'.[3] Yet in England, unlike France, this did not usually or necessarily imply freethinking secularism, or the rejection of Christianity. Despite his heterodox Unitarian theology, Priestley was an ordained Presbyterian minister, while

---

[1] J.-B. Le Blanc, *Lettres d'un François*, in R. E. Palmer (ed.), *French Travellers in England, 1600–1900* (1960), 56.

[2] J. Cannon, *Samuel Johnson and the Politics of Hanoverian England* (1994), 192.

[3] J. Priestley, *A Free Discussion of the Doctrines of Materialism, and Philosophical Necessity* (1778), sig. a3v.

Newtonian science provided ideological underpinning for the latitudinarian wing of the Church of England from the later seventeenth to the early nineteenth century. Among laymen, however, enlightened values often went hand-in-hand with anticlericalism, and the rejection of 'priestcraft', whether popish or Anglican, as well as the traditional folk-ways and superstitions of the lower orders.

Unlike their Continental counterparts, and imitators, most English adherents of enlightenment could afford to adopt a relatively relaxed attitude towards the existing régime in Church and State (at least for the first sixty years of the eighteenth century), precisely because they already enjoyed religious toleration, limited monarchy, and substantial personal liberties guaranteed by law. At the same time, optimism about the prospects for human betterment resulting from the application of scientific knowledge to government, agriculture, commerce, manufacturing, and social issues imposed an obligation on the enlightened to assist in realizing those benefits. They sought to do so both by individual effort (in Priestley's case, path-breaking experiments with electricity and the composition of air, and an outpouring of publications on educational, political, religious, and scientific subjects) and through collaboration with like-minded contemporaries. Alongside the pre-eminent Royal Society (of which Priestley was naturally a Fellow), numerous specialist and provincial bodies dedicated wholly or in part to the advancement and practical application of knowledge sprang up during the eighteenth century. They included the London-based Society of Antiquaries (1707–) and the (Royal) Society for the Encouragement of Arts, Manufactures, and Commerce (1754–), together with the quaintly named Spalding Gentlemen's Society (1712–), the Derby Philosophical Society (1784–), the Kentish Society for Promotion of Useful Knowledge (1788–), and many similar voluntary associations based on local landed, mercantile, and professional elites. Priestley himself belonged to the small, informal, and intellectually high-powered Lunar Society of Birmingham (so-called because it met on the nearest Monday to the full moon), where he hobnobbed with the entrepreneurial manufacturer and steam-engine developer Matthew Boulton (1728–1809), the inventor, physician, and poet Erasmus Darwin (1731–1802), the manufacturing chemist James Keir (1735–1820), and the eccentric novelist and educational theorist Thomas Day (1748–89).

Notwithstanding its pre-1688 intellectual origins, the uncomplicated heyday of the Enlightenment in England was the early to middle eighteenth century. From the 1760s onwards republicans, Dissenters, political reformers, American colonists, and Irish Patriots began to harness the values of enlightened rationalism to their own various sectional causes, although the broad consensus they were slowly undermining did not finally shatter until the outbreak of the French Revolution. Even then the optimistic individualism of the Enlightenment continued to exercise considerable if no longer uncontested influence, for example among Benthamite reformers and other exponents of self-help liberalism. An important transitional figure whose advocacy of enlightened values survived into the early decades of the nineteenth century was the long-lived Lincolnshire landowner and amateur botanist Sir Joseph Banks, a personal friend of George III. As president of the Royal Society from 1778 until his death forty-two years later, Banks had the energy, gentlemanly status, gregariousness, and zeal for improvement that perfectly fitted him to play the role of chief government scientist, or scientific adviser, co-ordinating efforts to harness useful knowledge to national and imperial goals.[4]

While the Enlightenment in England largely depended upon intellectual capital generated by Bacon, Locke, and Newton, in Scotland the influence of these luminaries was accompanied by a unique flowering of native talent: 'a galaxy of great and original-minded men ... comparable in brilliance with that of any other such intellectual cluster in a small country in the history of Europe'.[5] *A Treatise of Human Nature* (1739–40) by the philosopher and historian David Hume (1711–76) and Adam Smith's *Wealth of Nations* were only the most outstanding products of a thriving civic culture generated by the interlocking academic, commercial, and professional circles of Edinburgh and Glasgow. Particularly conducive to wide-ranging exploration of the moral and historical dimensions of human society, this lively urban axis contributed crucial foundations to the emerging social sciences of economics, psychology, and sociology by the polymath philosophers Francis Hutcheson (1694–1746) and Thomas Reid (1710–96), the lawyers Lord Kames (1696–1782) and John Millar (1735–1801), and the historians Adam Ferguson (1723–1816) and William Robertson (1721–93). The same environment also generated major achievements in natural science, including the discovery of carbon dioxide and latent heat by Joseph Black (1728–99), and James Hutton's *Theory of the Earth* (1788), a founding work of modern geology.

The Scottish Enlightenment—unlike its English counterpart, a well-recognized historiographical phenomenon—barely got under way before the 1740s, more than a generation after the Act of Union. At one level it looks like a delayed reaction to that event, an assertion of cultural identity and worth in response to traumatic loss of political autonomy. Yet simple nationalist sentiment was neither its idiom nor its overt motivating force. Enlightened Scots sought rather to establish a progressive commercial civilization, on a pattern determined largely by English cultural norms and expectations of politeness and sociability, whereby North Britons might participate as respected partners in a greater British Enlightenment.

[4] J. Gascoigne, *Joseph Banks and the English Enlightenment* (1994).
[5] T. C. Smout, *A History of the Scottish People, 1560–1830* (1972), 451.

Science and Medicine

Once the scientific revolution of the seventeenth century had reconfigured Europe's intellectual map, there followed a long period of intellectual consolidation. Much experimental activity continued, notably on electrical phenomena, and the composition of gases. Scientific instrumentation and observation became more sophisticated: the ex-Hanoverian bandsman and church organist William Herschel (1738–1822) built a series of large reflecting telescopes which led to his discovery of the planet Uranus in 1781, and together with his sister Caroline (1750–1848), who also received a salary from George III for her astronomical work, embarked upon an ambitious attempt to map the universe. But 'natural philosophy' witnessed no major conceptual breakthroughs comparable to the Newtonian synthesis.

Eighteenth-century science was overwhelmingly non-academic, non-professional, and non-specialist. While arithmetic and geometry figured in school and university syllabuses (at Cambridge mathematics effectively dominated the formal curriculum pursued by the minority of students who undertook examinations for the honours degree), general science received little attention outside the Dissenting academies and some private schools, where the emphasis tended to be on practical subjects like navigation, gunnery, and surveying. Hence Benjamin Martin's claim that since 'masters in [natural] philosophy' were 'unheard of in private schools', the 'only way' to learn was from 'books well wrote on that subject'.[6] This was slightly misleading advice, in that public demonstrations and lectures like those given by Martin himself were a major means of spreading scientific culture and information. The content and presentation of these offerings varied considerably. There were the prestigious Boyle lectures (or sermons) delivered in London between 1692 and 1735, which (especially in their relatively expensive published form) served as a channel for disseminating the Newtonian world-view on the harmony of revealed religion, science, and a stable, ordered, society among the educated élite. Much more accessible and indeed enormously popular were coffee-house, 'academy', and local learned society lecture-demonstrations, effectively adult education classes in the new philosophy, offered both in London and the provinces to surprisingly diverse clienteles. Finally, theatrical entrepreneurs exploited fashionable interest in the new science, with displays like the 'Grand Thaumaturgick Exhibition of Philosophical, Mathematical, Sterganographical, Sympathetical, Sciateroconatical, and Magical Operations' staged by the showman known as 'Sieur Herman Boaz' at Birmingham in 1780. In addition to such entertainments, Birmingham was also favoured with no fewer than seven fee-paying lecture courses on aspects of natural philosophy between August 1778 and May 1779; those by the former schoolteacher mathematician

---

[6] B. Martin, *The Young Gentleman and Lady's Philosophy, in a Continued Survey of the Works of nature and Art By Way of Dialogue, i. Containing the Philosophy of the Heavens and the Atmosphere* (1772), 3.

Benjamin Donn (1729–98) promised special attention to 'the most valuable experiments of Dr Priestley' (who provided several itinerant lecturers with detailed instruction on the use of his chemical apparatus for demonstration purposes). While entrance fees obviously restricted the size and social composition of potential audiences, lecturers anxious to maximize their take often admitted women at half the usual charge of between five shillings and a guinea a head.[7]

The varied and growing literature on scientific topics ranged from overviews provided by successive editions of Ephraim Chambers's *Cyclopedia or An Universal Dictionary of the Arts and Sciences* (1728–), and William Smellie's *Encyclopaedia Britannica* (1768–) to original works of the great masters like Isaac Newton's *Opticks*, popularizations of these classics (for example, Elizabeth Carter's *Newton's Philosophy Explain'd for the Use of Ladies*, published in 1739), textbook-like manuals derived from lecture series, and a growing range of publications accessible to a general audience on aspects of natural history—botany, geology, geography, zoology. Access to this diverse body of printed work was assisted by the proliferation of commercial circulating and corporate subscription libraries, as well as the longer-established church and school libraries. Articles on scientific topics in journals like the *Gentleman's Magazine*, and the annual *Ladies' Diary* were another source of scientific information; the latter also printed mathematical puzzles, as did the short-lived *British Museum, or Universal Register of Literature, Politics and Poetry*, whose first issue in 1771 promised 'instruction and entertainment for the fair sex, the gentleman and the mechanic'. So despite a low academic profile, various informal channels both satisfied and stimulated growing public interest in knowledge about the natural world, especially among the urban middle classes. At the same time (as the announcement by 'Sieur Boaz' quoted above indicates), magic and the occult arts of divination and healing retained considerable credibility. Their appeal was not confined to the rural labouring poor; when the mother of the notorious Elizabeth Canning (1734–73), a London maidservant supposedly abducted by gypsies in 1754, sought the aid of 'all the agents and places' she could think of to locate her missing daughter, she consulted an 'astrologer' or 'conjurer' living in the Old Bailey (who sensibly counselled newspaper advertisements and keeping calm until the girl returned, as eventually she did).[8]

Although few clients of such practitioners would have been able or willing to distinguish experimental natural philosophy from the practice of magic, hardly anyone could make a living by working as a scientist without a private patron's support. Direct government funding was scanty, limited to the solution of pressing practical problems, like the reliable determination of longitude at sea,

---

[7] J. Money, *Experience and Identity: Birmingham and the West Midlands, 1760–1800* (1977), ch. 6; J. Golinski, *Science as Public Culture* (1992), 93–105.

[8] J. Treherne, *The Canning Enigma* (1989), 110–11.

for which a cash prize offered by Parliament was eventually awarded to the skilled clockmaker John Harrison (1693–1776), although only after George III's personal intervention. Hence most of what today would be recognized as scientific research was undertaken on an amateur basis, like the 'chemical experiments, of which [Dr Samuel] Johnson was all his life very fond'.[9] Chemistry itself hardly existed as a separate discipline before the middle of the eighteenth century, being practised mostly by physicians, apothecaries, and other medical men, still deriving much of its technical basis from alchemy, and also overlapping in terms of subject-matter with geology and physics. Such characteristically loose disciplinary definition was both cause and effect of the preponderance of part-time dabblers over career professionals, the prospects of the latter only showing a major improvement after the Royal Institution was set up in London as a scientific research centre in 1799.

Although there were many more full-time medical practitioners than full-time scientists, most eighteenth-century medical treatment was probably self-prescribed, reflecting the dominance of the patient-amateur. Indeed medicine and science had much in common. Eighteenth-century medicine was not based upon a new 'scientific' conceptualization of the human body and its disorders, even if the best practitioners increasingly acknowledged the importance of carefully and systematically observing bodily processes, and the effects of different treatment régimes. Because medical practice was wholly unregulated, the small elite of genteel academically trained physicians was far outnumbered by surgeons, apothecaries, and a host of miscellaneous practitioners— folk-healers, wise women, empirics, and quacks, who owed whatever knowledge they had to apprenticeship, or self-tuition, or both.

In terms of formal medical education Oxford and Cambridge lagged far behind the fame of Edinburgh and Glasgow. The teaching of its distinguished professoriate, which linked academic theory to clinical practice, helped Edinburgh gradually outstrip Padua and Leiden as Europe's leading medical school, attracting students from Continental Europe and North America, as well as the British Isles. Cheaper if less thorough training was available from the London teaching hospitals, possibly supplemented by a course of study at a private anatomy school, like that established in London by the immigrant Scottish obstetrician and surgeon William Hunter (1718–83) and his still more eminent brother John (1728–93). Thus after some practical experience gained serving as assistant to his father's Lancashire general practice, the conscientious and devout 27-year-old Richard Kay was sent as pupil to Guy's Hospital in 1743. There he attended lectures, observed operations, and delivered babies 'for being as is designed both surgeon and physician'. But Richard returned home only twelve months later, equipped with 'my new chirurgic instruments' and the pious hope 'may I be well improved'.[10]

[9] *Boswell's Life of Johnson*, ed. R. W. Chapman (1953), 308.
[10] *The Diary of Richard Kay, 1716–51*, Chetham Society, 3rd ser. 16 (1968), 88.

Many contemporaries and later historians would give such aspirations short shrift, asserting that to call for the doctor or be admitted to an eighteenth-century hospital was far riskier than letting nature take its course. Yet such claims ignore a number of authentic medical success stories, including the conquest of smallpox by inoculation and then vaccination, better techniques for difficult deliveries (admittedly often at the expense of the baby) developed by 'male midwife' obstetricians, or 'accoucheurs' as they preferred to be known, and the use of digitalis in the treatment of heart conditions. They also take no account of the prevailing high level of demand for medical services. Of course the customer could be wrong, and the seemingly insatiable contemporary appetite for medical advice and treatment may reflect either rampant consumerism or quiet desperation, rather than well-grounded faith in the efficacy of the available therapies. But even twentieth-century scientific medicine has its own failures and shortcomings.

While it was and is easy to caricature the motives and mock the ignorance of eighteenth-century medical men (and women, notably dentists, herbalists, and midwives), we should not underestimate the intelligence of those who called upon their services. There was, after all, no shortage of competition for patients' fees; indeed, as Roy Porter and others have argued, doctors were in active competition with the sick for the treatment of illness, in what may be characterized as a culture of medical self-help. The sick did not invariably expect a cure, as distinct from advice, relief, and support; moreover, the unregulated and relatively uninstitutionalized context of eighteenth-century medicine gave at least the middling and upper classes far greater bargaining power in their dealings with practitioners of all kinds than most patients can expect today.[11]

Good Works

Hospitals were a major site of eighteenth-century medical improvement. At the long-established St Thomas's in London, the death rate of in-patients declined from 1 : 10.9 in the 1740s to 1 : 14 forty years later. This trend owed much to better bedding, hygiene, sanitation, and ventilation, as long urged by, among others, the Quaker philanthropist John Bellers (1654–1725), the clergyman inventor Stephen Hales (1677–1761), and the army's physician-general Sir John Pringle (1707–82), who coined the word 'antiseptic'. Over the course of the century no fewer than thirty-one new British general hospitals or infirmaries supplemented what had been a mere handful of London-based institutions; from the 1740s various special-purpose hospitals also opened their doors to abandoned children, expectant mothers, and those afflicted with sexually transmitted diseases.

All these were founded, funded, and administered by private individuals, rather than the state. Together with the proliferating charity and Sunday

---

[11] R. Porter, *Disease, Medicine and Society in England, 1550–1860* (1987).

schools (see above, pp. 102–3, 175), London's Asylum for Orphaned Girls (1759), and the Magdalen House (1758), dedicated to rehabilitating ex-prostitutes, they represent the visible outward face of eighteenth-century philanthropy, prompting contemporary claims that their age was distinguished for 'benevolence' and 'humanity', as well as enlightenment. Whereas most earlier almshouses, hospitals, and similar charitable institutions had sprung from the posthumous endowment of a single wealthy benefactor, their eighteenth-century equivalents were generally established and maintained through public donations and subscriptions.

Many characteristic ventures of the age— including joint-stock companies, circulating libraries, Dissenting congregations, and gentlemen's clubs—were similarly organized as voluntary associations of subscribers under an elected committee of management. Pre-eminent among the charitable activists to adopt this model was the retired Russia Company merchant and prolific author Jonas Hanway (1712–86), supposedly the first Englishman to protect himself from the rain with an umbrella. Having served his philanthropic apprenticeship as a reforming member of the Foundling Hospital's governing board, at the outbreak of war with France in 1756 Hanway moved on to set up the Marine Society. This outstandingly successful charity combined patriotism and philanthropy, outfitting poor men and boys with suitable clothing in order to encourage their enlistment in the navy. Hanway was also associated with the Magdalen House, the Troop Society (supporting British soldiers serving overseas), and a special committee of the Marine Society which sought in vain to alleviate the appalling working conditions of boy chimney sweeps by exerting moral pressure on their employers. Despite the ineffectiveness of this last initiative, it serves to demonstrate the operational flexibility of agencies like the Marine Society, as compared to hospitals and other institutional charities, with their expensive single-purpose buildings, and related problems of selecting and maintaining inmates. These advantages were exploited by yet another new philanthropic venture established during the war years, the 'Lying-In Charity for Delivering Poor Married Women in their Own Habitations' (1757), which claimed to provide safer and cheaper obstetrical care than the specialist maternity hospitals. Similar considerations justified the out-patient medical clinics or dispensaries which mushroomed in London and the provinces from the late 1760s onwards, the 'Society for the Discharge and Relief of Persons Imprisoned for Small Debts' (1773), and the Humane Society, established in 1774 to encourage the resuscitation of victims of drowning.

This wide spectrum of benevolent, charitable, and philanthropic activity resists easy categorization. At one end it shaded off into various forms of collective self-help. Thus friendly or mutual benefit societies provided mainly artisan and working poor subscribers with rudimentary medical and funeral insurance, as did the more socially elevated Freemasons, whose lodge brethren worked hard at self-improvement as well as mutual charity. At the other it intersected a growing contemporary preoccupation with 'police', meaning not just law and order, but all aspects of public administration and social welfare. Reform of the poor laws, a perennial of parliamentary and press debate, acquired added urgency for the propertied classes with the doubling of the poor rates from a total £0.7m. in 1748 to £1.5m. by 1775. The demographic and social trends underlying this ominous development were hardly checked by the legislation which the long-serving lawyer MP Thomas Gilbert (1720–98) sponsored in 1782, permitting but not requiring parishes to collaborate, with the aim of reducing costs and promoting greater efficiency in the provision of poor relief. Gilbert also interested himself in the state of prisons and houses of correction, or reformatories, an issue which became an obsession with the well-to-do dissenter John Howard, when as sheriff of Bedfordshire in 1773 he became formally responsible for the dirty and overcrowded county gaol. Howard spent the rest of his life visiting prisons throughout the British Isles and much of Europe, publishing the results of these fact-finding tours as an ongoing report on the progress of prison reform. His attempts to improve conditions for those temporarily deprived of their liberty forms a link to the most ambitious and widely supported humanitarian project of the age, formally inaugurated in 1787 with the establishment of a Committee for the Abolition of the Slave Trade, 'that unhappy and disgraceful branch of commerce ... which contradicts the feelings of humanity ... this stain on our national character'.[12]

The spread of these manifold activities to relieve suffering may have resulted from simple human compassion in the face of unprecedented social strains produced by massive demographic growth, rampant urbanization and economic dislocation. But it has also been interpreted as a form of social control imposed upon the labouring and potentially dangerous classes by the middling and upper sort, in pursuit of their own narrow class interests. In the eyes of their promoters one main function of hospitals, like charity and Sunday schools, was undoubtedly to reform the morals and discipline the manners of in-patients, who came overwhelmingly from the lower orders (the quality were treated at home). Similarly the Marine Society found employment for those without work, who might otherwise have become unproductive beggars, or criminals; lower poor rates and a larger workforce were possibly more valued by some of its propertied supporters than at best marginally better life chances for the deprived individuals whom it 'helped'. Even the anti-slavery campaign has been depicted as a clever diversionary tactic, distracting public attention from the evils of the 'wage slavery' being imposed in the factories of England.

No doubt charity is unavoidably paternalistic and to some extent patronizing, involving as it does more or less subtle direction and manipulation of the afflicted and assisted by their benefactors. Yet genteel Evangelical reformers like Hannah More and the earnest William Wilberforce, both key figures in the

---

[12] J. Newton, *Thoughts on the African Slave Trade* (1788), 1.

mobilization against slavery, did not seek moral improvement among the poor alone; indeed the 'Proclamation Society', founded in 1787 at Wilberforce's instigation to support a reformation of manners campaign against vice and immorality, specifically targeted the shortcomings of those in high places, and the deficiencies of public policy, rather than merely the dissipations of the lower sort. It makes more sense to see the origins of this 'age of benevolence' (as Hannah More characterized it, not altogether approvingly) in a mixture of enabling circumstances and motivations. Rising wealth and middle-class aspirations facilitated charitable endeavours, at a time when by any objective measure social problems, and public consciousness of them, were both expanding fast. The evangelical impulse provided a powerful religious incentive to charitable action. The moral philosophy of the third Lord Shaftesbury (1671–1713), with his theory of 'social affections' as an innate 'natural' force, and Francis Hutcheson's further emphasis on the providential tendency for self-regarding individuals to promote the common good, was a complementary secular formulation. So, more mundanely, was the perception that an expanding economy needed a large and healthy labour force. Small wonder that the prolific man of letters John Campbell (1708–75) should have congratulated his fellow countrymen in 1774 on constituting 'so brave, so generous, so enlightened a nation'.[13]

Humanity and Nature

But as we have just seen in the case of enslaved Africans, even if charity did begin at home, British benevolence was by no means confined to the British Isles. Nor indeed was it limited to human kind. As the seventeenth and eighteenth centuries saw the natural environment ever more closely studied and effectively exploited, so there grew a corresponding appreciation of, and concern for, the world of nature.[14]

On biblical grounds, nature was traditionally regarded as specifically intended for human benefit and exploitation. In the early seventeenth century Francis Bacon had indeed seen one purpose of science as to restore that human dominion over all creation partially lost at the Fall. Civilization meant distinguishing people, made in God's image, from brute beasts without minds or souls. Yet the assumption of absolute human superiority and domination over the animal kingdom was gradually dimished throughout our period. This attitudinal change arose partly from the work of scientists and naturalists, including the great botanist John Ray (1627–1705) in the later seventeenth century, and the less ambitious but more accessible Gilbert White, author of a classic

[13] J. Campbell, *A Political Survey of Britain to show that we have not as yet approached near the Summit of Improvement* (1774), ii. 694; G. Himmelfarb, *The Idea of Poverty: England in the Early Industrial Age* (1985), ch. 1.

[14] The following section draws largely on K. Thomas, *Man and the Natural World: Changing Attitudes in England, 1500–1800* (1983).

Natural History of Selborne, the secluded Hampshire village where he grew up and served as curate from 1751 to 1793. They contributed to a growing realization that fauna and flora might be better approached and understood in terms of their innate qualities, rather than according to traditional, human-centred taxonomies (of beauty, or usefulness, for instance).

The development of closer, less instrumental relationships with animals seems to have been another key influence. While accommodation for sheep and cattle was increasingly segregated from human living space, non-working animals—pets—moved into a more intimate emotional relationship with their human owners. The keeping of pets was becoming a middle-class habit, not merely an aristocratic indulgence, as early as the sixteenth and seventeenth centuries. Cats, regarded as dirty and impure in the Middle Ages, had colonized most London households by the second half of the seventeenth century. Samuel Johnson's love of children, kindness to servants, and fondness for pet animals, especially Hodge (that 'very fine cat'), were thought by Boswell to demonstrate his 'real humanity'. By this time birds, hares, mice, hedgehogs, bats, and even toads were all being accorded the status of pets—kept for company, allowed indoors, given names, and not eaten.

Even insects and pests benefited from a narrowing of the perceived gulf which divided humans from other living things. On the morning of Friday, 2 October 1767 the young republican Sylas Neville 'set at liberty two mice' he had caught the previous night, because he could not bring himself 'to kill the little vermin'. His contemporary Thomas Day, a law student and keen disciple of Rousseau, asserted that he had no more right to kill a spider than a lawyer (and anyway most people preferred spiders to lawyers).[15] The spread of such attitudes generated opposition to various traditional blood sports, notably cock-fighting, dog-fighting, the 'baiting' with dogs of badgers, bears, and bulls, and 'throwing at cocks' (a rural pastime in which clubs and sticks were flung at a tethered chicken). While all these practices continued into the nineteenth century, they were increasingly condemned as barbarous survivals from a less enlightened age. The scenes of disorder and dissipation which often accompanied them were a further cause of objection. However, the field sports or hunting of the gentry as yet attracted little attention from reformers, who concentrated their efforts on the easier (and doubtless more conspicuous) target of plebeian cruelty.

Parallel shifts of attitude transformed rugged mountains and woodland from unattractive and unproductive wilderness to picturesque landscape and romantic vista. In 1775 the 'stupendous cragginess' around Bangor in North Wales appeared far more impressive to a cultivated Irish visitor than the prospect from Richmond Hill outside London, which 'has nothing picturesque to

---

[15] *The Diary of Sylas Neville, 1767–1788*, ed. B. Cozens-Hardy (1950), 25; *DNB*, s.v. Day, Thomas.

be seen from it'.[16] Instead of formally composed gardens laid out in geometrical patterns, the new style of landscape gardening developed by William
Kent (1684–1748) and 'Capability' Brown sought to extend and recreate nature
in a parkland setting. Landscape gardening has been called 'a true spearhead
of romanticism'; another harbinger of the full-blown Romantic movement
was the cult of sensibility, and sentiment, in literature and painting. Novels like
Samuel Richardson's *Pamela* (1740) and *Clarissa* (1747–8) portrayed as never
before the emotional and psychological lives of their much put-upon female
subjects. Sensitive depictions of rural labouring families by the painter
Thomas Gainsborough (1727–88) provided a visual equivalent to the universal
benevolence expressed in Oliver Goldsmith's *Citizen of the World* (1762).
'Gothic' novels of macabre medieval mystery, a genre pioneered by *The Castle
of Otranto* (1764); the cult of the 'noble savage' (invented by Rousseau and
fostered by published journals and sketches of voyagers to the South Seas); fascination with primitive indigenous cultural forms, whether fabricated (like the
epic poetry of Ossian, the supposed British Homer) or merely 'restored', like
the folk ballads published by Bishop Thomas Percy (1729–1811): all these
characteristic cultural forms of the 1760s–1780s might embody implicit or explicit criticism of mainstream Enlightenment values (science, rationality, progress). Yet for that reason they also represent a continued engagement with the
real world; the wholly introverted and self-obsessed Romantic artist remained
in the future.

[16] *Dr Campbell's Diary of a Visit of England in 1775*, ed. J. L. Clifford (1947), 36–8, 83.

PART V

Economic Expansion and Diversification
1750–1815

16

INDUSTRIALIZING ENGLAND

Historiography

In the opening pages of *Headlong Hall* (1816), Thomas Love Peacock's first published novel, the 'perfectibilian' Mr Foster holds forth 'with great energy on the subject of roads and railways, canals and tunnels, manufactures and machinery: "In short", said he, "everything we look on attests the progress of mankind."' His pessimistic opposite Mr Escot does not attempt to deny the existence of these 'improvements'. But he asserts that, far from evidence of human progress, they constitute 'so many links in the great chain of corruption, which will soon fetter the whole human race', thanks to the 'factitious wants and unnatural appetites they engender'. The moral and social benefits, or otherwise, of industrialization have continued to be debated down to the present day.

A vigorous scholarly discussion about the nature, causes, and effects of English economic and social change between the mid-eighteenth and mid-nineteenth centuries is now part of that debate, as the search for the origins of those benefits (or that 'corruption') continues. Whether or not England, let alone Britain, was indeed the world's first industrial nation, a French diplomat is credited with the earliest recorded use of the term 'industrial revolution', claiming in 1799 that his own country had already embarked upon 'la révolution industrielle'.[1] Nearly a century passed before the English equivalent came into general use, aided by the publication in 1884 of a book with that title, based on the adult education lectures of Arnold Toynbee, a young and socially committed Oxford don. Although Toynbee depicted 'the Industrial and Agricultural Revolution at the end of the eighteenth and the beginning of the nineteenth centuries' as 'one of the most important facts of English history', the picture of the Industrial Revolution he presented was plainly a concept or interpretation, drawing upon a particular reading of the evidence. It was also, by his account, a largely retrograde development, at least for the majority of the population. Once traditional 'medieval regulations which had previously controlled the production and distribution of wealth' were swept aside by competitive forces, 'the capitalists used all their power to oppress the labourers and

---

[1] D. S. Landes, 'The Fable of the Dead Horse; or, the industrial revolution revisited', in J. Mokyr (ed.), *The British Industrial Revolution* (1993), 133.

drive their wages down to starvation point'. The agrarian enclosure movement and the factory system, based upon the new technology of steam power, permitted greater efficiencies in production, but only at the cost of heightened class antagonism and depressed living standards for the working poor.[2]

Despite the emergence of economic history as a new academic discipline in the later nineteenth century, Toynbee's pessimism was not seriously challenged until the 1920s. Utilizing what by then had become a substantial accumulation of detailed research on eighteenth- and nineteenth-century English economic activity and institutions, the Cambridge economic historian J. H. Clapham argued that industrialization was a far less rapid and thorough process than the label 'industrial revolution' implied. Clapham also paved the way for more positive views of the social impact of industrial change, suggesting that the upwards trend of wages after 1790 hardly supported the orthodox picture of working-class immiseration. Subsequent debates on what became known as the 'standard of living question' divided economic historians into opposing camps of, crudely, capitalist optimists, and Marxist pessimists. Yet both sides tended to lose sight of the stress Clapham and others had laid on the slow and uneven nature of post-1760 economic change. Instead they concentrated increasingly on a search for the sources of economic growth in eighteenth-century England, not without hope of assisting the development of contemporary third-world economies. The high (or low) point of these efforts was W. W. Rostow's *The Stages of Economic Growth: A Non-Communist Manifesto* (1960), which sought to derive a free-market recipe for economic and social modernization from the British experience of 'take-off into sustained economic growth' during the later eighteenth century.

Rostow's best-seller appeared just as exciting intellectual vistas were opening up for economic history, with the application of increasingly sophisticated quantitative techniques and macroeconomic theory. Adopting the framework of aggregate national income accounting, and utilizing statistical series of wages, prices, trade, and production, assembled by scholarly labourers over the previous century or so, the Cambridge economic historian Phyllis Deane and her collaborator W. A. Cole published in 1961 an ambitious quantitative study of *British Economic Growth, 1688–1959: Trends and Structure*. Their pioneering work appeared to lend qualified support to Rostow's thesis of economic 'take-off' from the 1780s. However, subsequent detailed econometric research, drawing upon more recently compiled demographic, occupational, trade, and other data, and even more highly refined theoretical assumptions, has raised considerable doubts about the reliability of Deane and Cole's original economic growth rate estimates. In a particularly influential book N. F. R. Crafts asserted that 'growth was considerably slower between 1780 and 1821–30 than was believed by Deane and Cole'; real output did not expand at even 2 per cent

2 A. Toynbee, *Lectures on the Industrial Revolution in England* (1884).

a year until after the 1820s, and its acceleration was 'a more gradual process than metaphors such as "take-off"'imply'.[3]

So notions of the industrial revolution as a 'major discontinuity' in English history, a 'dramatic watershed between the old world and the new', came once again under serious challenge in the de-industrializing Thatcherite 1980s. The gradualist conclusions of the new economic history depend upon complex statistical procedures and abstract theoretical reasoning with which few non-economists feel comfortable or familiar. They were nevertheless adopted with enthusiasm by historians inclined to emphasize the conservative, even un-changing character of eighteenth-century England. Thus 'the unchallengeably quantifiable' findings of 'recent conceptual and empirical advances' have been invoked to support the assertion that 'English society before 1832 did not ex-perience an industrial revolution, let alone an Industrial Revolution. . . . England was not *revolutionized*; and it was not revolutionised *by industry*.[4] Of course much depends upon how we define those key terms, industrial and revolution. But it is rash to assume that the quantitative procedures and results of the cliometricians are intrinsically more accurate, objective, solid, or un-biased, especially when expressed as figures in a table or lines on a graph, than a historian's findings based upon non-statistical or qualitative evidence and presented in traditional literary form.

These considerations underlie a good deal of the current scholarly reaction against revisionist attempts to minimize the scale and significance of economic and social change in later eighteenth- and early nineteenth-century England. But quite apart from such methodological issues, we must now look at some of the substantive themes which they address.

Feeding the People

In successive editions of his influential *Essay on the Principle of Population* (first published 1798), the clergyman-mathematician T. R. Malthus effectively inverted traditional fears of national weakness stemming from population shortage. According to Malthus, whereas the numbers of humans, like all living things, tend to increase by an exponential or geometrical ratio ($1 : 2 : 4 : 8 : 16 \ldots$), supplies of food, clothing, and shelter can at best expand by an arithmetical progression ($1 : 2 : 3 : 4 : 5 \ldots$). Therefore demographic growth must, sooner or later, overtake the resources available to sustain it. The in-evitable outcome will be famine and social catastrophe, until the establishment of a new, temporarily manageable equilibrium between the numbers of mouths and the food supply which sustains them.

---

[3] N. F. R. Crafts, *British Economic Growth during the Industrial Revolution* (1985), 2.

[4] J. C. D. Clark, *Revolution and Rebellion: State and Society in England in the Seventeenth and Eighteenth Centuries* (1986), 39.

The adverse circumstances of the 1790s and 1800s might seem to bear out Malthus's grim picture of population numbers pressing ever harder against the means of subsistence. Having risen progressively since mid-century, food prices reached unprecedented peaks in the 1790s, accentuated by the outbreak of war with France and a series of harvest failures in the middle and later years of the decade. Londoners paid 10 pence for a quartern loaf of bread in 1801, the year of the first national population census; while a marked improvement on the prices of the previous two years (13 and 17.5 pence respectively), this was still about 25 per cent above the average price prevailing throughout the ten years before 1795. Nor had wages kept pace with prices; during the first decade of the new century real wages (i.e. money wages adjusted for price inflation) may have dipped to their lowest point since 1700.[5] Overall the war years (1793–1815) saw occasional localized dearth, and extensive food riots in 1795–6 and 1800–1, together with widespread industrial disputation, strikes, and other forms of popular protest (see also above, pp. 163–7).

Yet appearances, and portents, were deceptive: the threatened Malthusian crisis did not eventuate. Despite local shortages, trade interruptions, and harvest failures, the people continued to be fed, by and large. Journalists might write on occasion of 'artificial famine' caused by profiteering, when 'provisions of all sorts' became 'so excessively dear that a family of moderate income can hardly live, and the poor must, literally, starve'.[6] Yet no part of the British Isles experienced anything comparable to the massive famines which continued to sweep across France well into the nineteenth century. Notwithstanding some grain imports from the 1770s onwards, England's food needs continued to be met largely from domestic farm production. In short, although the rate of growth of agricultural productivity may have fallen behind the rate of population increase after 1750, the gap never widened so far as to precipitate political and social catastrophe. The fact that agricultural production levels were already comparatively high at mid-century (when wheat exports peaked) obviously helped cushion the impact of subsequent rapid demographic growth. An increasingly urbanized population working in sedentary occupations may also have required fewer calories than an agricultural peasantry engaged in strenuous manual labour. This last consideration supplements the observations of a visitor to the industrial towns of South Yorkshire in 1781, who believed 'the miserable appearance of many of the poorer sort in these parts' demonstrated that 'men live better by agriculture than manufactory—one tends to preserve health, the other to destroy it'.[7]

By the end of the eighteenth century farms in Belgium and northern France were achieving comparable crop yields to their English counterparts, but only

[5] T. S. Ashton, *Economic Fluctuations in England, 1700–1800* (1959), 181; R. Schofield, 'English population change, 1700–1871' in *EHB* 80–1.

[6] *Gentleman's Magazine*, Mar. 1764, 108.

[7] G. Clark, M. Huberman, and P. H. Lindert. 'A British food puzzle, 1750–1850', *EcHR* 48 (1995), 215–37. *The Diary of Sylas Neville, 1767–1788*, ed. B. Cozens-Hardy (1950), 277.

through employing a significantly larger labour force per hectare, on farms of much smaller area than their English equivalent. Indeed recent estimates put French agricultural labour productivity in 1801 at barely half that of England. This difference underlies the strong growth of urban populations and non-agricultural employment in eighteenth-century England, which would hardly have been possible without an efficient, and improving, farming sector. 'Urban growth and agricultural prosperity were intimately connected, and mutually stimulating', as E. A. Wrigley has remarked, paraphrasing Adam Smith.[8]

Yet no agreement exists as to exactly how much and why English agricultural output grew during the second half of the eighteenth century. This is hardly surprising, given the considerable technical problems involved in estimating both the value and quantity of farm production. Moreover, the extent of regional variation in farming practice makes any conclusions based on national aggregates potentially misleading. For example, a recent study of Norfolk agriculture suggests that grain yields only rose decisively above their medieval peak from the 1740s onwards, thanks to the widespread adoption of nitrogen-fixing clover and turnips as a field crop for cattle, part of what became known as the Norfolk four-course crop rotation. Yet by contrast it has also been claimed that in the South Midlands counties little productivity gain was achieved after the seventeenth century, despite the introduction of similar cropping techniques in appropriate light soil areas. These contradictory findings also embody different conclusions as to the agents of agricultural betterment, who in Norfolk appear to have been large-scale improving landlords, but in the Midlands small yeoman owner-occupiers.[9]

Given the fragmentary nature of the evidence, we cannot be sure how far these apparent disparities reflect real variations in local arable farming technique, or in rural landholding structures. However, the vital importance of livestock husbandry, both as a source of manure for improved crop yields, and of animal power for carting and ploughing, is one subject on which some consensus is emerging. Here again England appears significantly advantaged, with a population of perhaps 700,000 farm horses in 1811, whereas in contemporary France only a million or so horses were available to work an arable area approximately four times as large. Impressed by 'prodigious' numbers of cattle, sheep, and horses, French travellers anticipated recent research findings that agriculture in England was significantly more 'animal-intensive' than in France.[10]

[8] E. A. Wrigley, *Continuity, Chance and Change: The Character of the Industrial Revolution in England* (1988), 14–15.

[9] B. M. Campbell and M. Overton, 'A new perspective on medieval and early modern agriculture: six centuries of Norfolk farming, c. 1250–c. 1850', *P&P* 141 (1993); D. C. Allen, *Enclosure and the Yeoman* (1992).

[10] Wrigley, *Continuity, Chance and Change*, 41–3; F. Crouzet, 'The sources of England's wealth: some French views in the eighteenth century', in id., *Britain Ascendant: Comparative Studies in Franco-British Economic History*, tr. M. Thom (1990).

Infrastructure: Canals and Turnpikes

Of the six symbols of human progress nominated by Peacock's optimistic Mr Foster, the first four—'roads and railways, canals and tunnels'—all relate to transport. What would later come to be known as the railway age had barely dawned when *Headlong Hall* was written, even if a few steam locomotives were already pulling coal trucks along private colliery tracks. Yet the novelist evidently expected his readers to recognize that they were living through an era of significant change in the means and modes of transport and travel.

The most familiar, because geographically widespread, transport development would undoubtedly have been the turnpiked road. The first turnpike gate had been set up in 1665 on a hilly section of the Great North Road in Hertfordshire, after an Act of parliament authorized the collection of tolls from passing traffic to help repair the highway. But it was not until the early eighteenth century that the user-pays principle began to be widely applied to road maintenance, supplementing each parish's traditional responsibility to construct and repair all highways and bridges within its boundaries. Where these included major traffic routes, such as roads leading to and from London, local resources were often swamped, and road surfaces accordingly deteriorated. Turnpikes, administered by bodies of statutory commissioners (usually neighbouring landowners, merchants, and other local men of property) added revenue raised from road users to the mandatory parochial contribution in labour or kind. This formula proved very successful in building up a national network of regularly maintained toll-roads, which initially radiated out from London and the Home Counties, then after mid-century spread across the whole country, with particularly dense clusters linking Birmingham and the industrial Midlands to Lancashire, Yorkshire, and the South-West. More careful construction and systematic maintenance of roads, for which the principles were codified at the very end of our period by the Scots Thomas Telford (1757–1834) and John McAdam (1756–1836), together with improved coach construction and better organization of horse relays, permitted continuous and successive reductions in long-distance travel times. Stage coach services, having averaged less than 5 miles (8 km.) per hour in the 1750s, were achieving average speeds of 6.7 m.p.h. (10.7 km.h.) in the early 1790s, an improvement of over 34 per cent. Those few able to afford the long-distance all-night mail coaches, introduced under contract to the Post Office by the entrepreneur John Palmer (1742–1818), could expect to get from London to Bristol in 1792 at what was the relatively breakneck pace of 8.52 m.p.h. (13.6 km.h.), excluding stops.

Although their origins also date back before the eighteenth century, canals, and railways were both more functionally specialized and hence less frequently met with than turnpikes. After the first English canal was constructed at Exeter in the 1560s, two more centuries passed before the much-publicized opening in 1761 of an artificial and partly underground waterway, built by the self-taught millwright-engineer James Brindley (1716–72), to link the Duke of Bridge-water's colliery at Worsley with domestic and industrial customers in Manchester, some seven miles (11.2 km.) away. Less attention was paid to the opening of the Sankey Brook Canal from Liverpool to St Helens four years earlier because it merely extended an existing stream, not for any lack of aristocratic cachet. Much effort had gone into river improvement, by dredging, straightening, and installation of locks, during the seventeenth and early eighteenth centuries. Besides doubling the length of navigable waterways, this work generated a valuable accumulation of civil engineering expertise, drawn upon by men like Brindley and John Smeaton (1724–92), who in 1768 began to oversee construction of the massive Forth and Clyde canal across Scotland.

Yet canals did not merely exploit and extend existing technology and rivers. These hugely expensive ventures, mostly funded by joint-stock companies, made it possible to overcome the restrictions of nature and topography which had previously advantaged coastal areas and those on navigable waterways. Now the benefits of ready access to water transport (generally far cheaper for bulky, low-value goods than the road wagon or packhorse) could be made available almost anywhere, 'linking places at will by deliberate, rational, economic calculation', and reinforcing regional economic cohesion.[11] On a smaller scale the same was true of the wooden wagonways used originally for transporting coal or ore from inland mines to waiting barges or ships, as with the large Tyneside network upstream of Newcastle. Wagons pulled by horses first ran on iron wheels from the 1730s, on iron rails from the 1760s, and through short tunnels in the 1790s; during the first decade of the nineteenth century stationary steam engines began to haul them up steep gradients. These technical improvements, plus the lower capital costs of building what were increasingly known as railroads or tramways (around £1,660 per mile, as against some £5,000 per mile for canals), encouraged their use to extend, supplement and, in some cases, replace canals, like the 9-mile (14.4 km.) double-track line opened in 1803 which joined Croydon (south of London) to the Thames at Wandsworth.

So the appearance of steam-powered ships and railway locomotives at the very end of our period was no sudden, unheralded event, but the culmination of a continuous stream of incremental transport innovation. By that time some 20,000 miles (32,000 km.) of turnpiked road, 2,125 miles (3,400 km.) of navigable river, 2,000 miles (3,200 km.) of canal, and perhaps 1,500 miles (2,400 km.) of mainly horse-drawn railway enhanced the country's natural endowments of relative compactness, temperate climate, indented coastline, and gentle topography. Together with the growing size and efficiency of coastal shipping, they gave early nineteenth-century England the world's most efficient and reliable transport infrastructure. The comparative ease, inexpensiveness, and speed

[11] G. Turnbull, 'Canals, coal and regional growth in the Industrial Revolution', *EcHR* 40 (1987), 539.

with which goods, ideas, information, and people could be moved from place to place were of enormous economic and social consequence. Above all they facilitated the emergence of something approaching a unified national market and culture, characterized by marked regional economic specialization and significant economies of scale in both agricultural and manufacturing production. Most contemporaries may have been at best only dimly aware of the latter developments. But the transport revolution which gathered pace in the second half of the eighteenth century was highly visible, and no less profound in its demonstration of the potential benefits of technological advance, than in the ambivalent impact upon popular consciousness evidenced by Peacock's novel.

Power

Classical accounts of the industrial revolution emphasized the central role of the steam engine, 'the pivot on which industry swung into the modern age' enabling (according to Mantoux) 'the immense and rapid development of large-scale industry to take place'. But some modern revisionists play down the significance of this new technology, insisting that as late as 1832, 'Britain was still essentially horse-drawn and sail-driven'.[12] Of course much depends on that 'essentially', and whether more significance is attached to elements of continuity than intimations of change. By 1800 perhaps one-fifth of the mechanical energy generated in England came from steam engines, rather than animal, wind, and water power. That relatively modest proportion represents a 100 per cent increase since the building of the first steam (or 'fire') engine in 1695. On the other hand, total capacity (an average of only 23 horsepower per engine, or 34,500 overall) was a mere flea bite compared to the 2 million industrial steam horsepower built up by 1870.[13]

Horsepower, the unit which measures the rate of doing work (in the sense of moving mass through distance), was devised by the Scottish engineer and inventor James Watt (1736–1819), who in 1763–4 developed the separate condenser, which at least trebled the efficiency of Newcomen's steam engines. An eighteenth-century proponent of steam power would naturally seek to compare the output and running costs of his engines with the working capacity of horses. Mine pumps, grinding and mixing mills in potteries, tanneries, and brickyards, spinning and weaving machinery, even building cranes, all continued to be worked by horses (occasionally donkeys and other animals) well into the nineteenth century.[14] Besides relatively modest capital costs, equine labour

[12] T. S. Ashton, *The Industrial Revolution, 1760–1830* (1948), 70; P. Mantoux, *The Industrial Revolution in the Eighteenth Century* (1934), 344–6; J. C. D. Clark, *English Society, 1660–1832* (1985), 65.

[13] G. N. von Tunzelman, *Steam Power and British Industrialization to 1860* (1978).

[14] Two mechanical looms set up at Glasgow in 1793 were powered by a Newfoundland dog: Mantoux, *Industrial Revolution*, 248.

was readily adaptable to different industrial tasks, even if these advantages were offset by restricted output and the ongoing costs of maintaining both animals and their human attendants. A 'machine horse' was some ten times stronger than a man, but munched each year fodder and grass equivalent to the produce of about five acres of farmland.

Wind and water provided the other main sources of mechanical energy. Besides grinding flour, windmills were used for land-drainage and to power a few industrial processes where intermittent operation was no major problem. Waterwheels also ceased to turn when mill streams froze or dried up, while more fundamental difficulties arose from the limited number of optimal sites, and their distance from supplies of raw materials and labour, as well as markets. Nevertheless, water power and its still evolving technology remained vital to British industry until the mid-nineteenth century. In the 1750s John Smeaton conclusively demonstrated the superior efficiency of the radical new 'breast' wheel, driven by water directed to a middle point on the wheel's outer circumference, over its traditional overshot and paddlewheel predecessors. Improved gearing and the use of iron components made it possible to build very large and well-balanced wheels, some capable of generating as much as 200 horsepower, far more than early steam engines could manage. The latter were frequently used merely to provide a head of water, as with one of Watt's early models installed at Matthew Boulton's Soho manufactory, outside Birmingham. At Stockport in 1776 the visiting American Quaker Jabez Fisher was impressed by five water-powered silk mills, one with a wheel 40 feet in diameter 'turned by about as much water as could go out of a pint mug', although the technology of water-powered silk-winding actually showed little advance on Lombe's Derby mill (see above, p. 151).[15] Before 1800 most textile mills were water-powered; even as late as 1830 no fewer than 2,230 British textile factories still used waterwheels, as against some 3,000 steam engines. In other industries—especially metalworking, mining, ceramics, and paper-making—water-power remained dominant well into the nineteenth century. Everywhere human hand and muscle continued to complement and control energy generated by animals, wind, and water.

Yet the persistence of traditional energy sources hardly detracts from the profound significance of the steam engine's ability to transform heat into power. It constituted a wholly new, massively potent, and extremely versatile source of mechanical energy. England was particularly well placed to utilize the new technology, possessing coal supplies of unrivalled abundance (and, thanks to the canal system, increasing accessibility) to fuel steam engines, as well as the precision metalworkers and other skilled artisans needed to construct, maintain, and improve them. The vast potential of steam to transform the conditions and processes of production had been nothing like fully realized

[15] *An American Quaker in the British Isles: The Travel Journals of Jabez Maud Fisher, 1775–1779*, ed. K. Morgan (1992), 235.

by the end of the period which this book covers. Yet the results of its application, in mining, transport, metallurgy, and above all the booming cotton industry, were already more than sufficient to point the way to a very different future.

Industry and Invention

Early eighteenth-century manufacturing industry was far from moribund (see ch. 10 above). So if 'about 1760 a wave of gadgets swept over England' (to cite T. S. Ashton's well-worn account of a school exam answer on the industrial revolution), that burst of inventiveness did not materialize out of a clear blue sky. Yet in the next decade Adam Smith appeared quite unconscious of living in an era of massive mechanization and technical change. His *Wealth of Nations* depicts enhanced industrial productivity as resulting from the organizational principles of division of labour and specialization of function, rather than the application of new or improved technology. Hence Smith saw economic growth in a broader sense as dependent upon abolishing monopolies and other anti-competitive restraints which served the narrow self-interest of merchants and manufacturers.

Perhaps Smith was reluctant to complicate his case against the mercantile system with a digression on the likely benefits of technical 'improvements'. But he was not alone among his contemporaries in attributing less significance to new technology than subsequent historians have done. As late as 1797 an informed commentator could deplore the lack of interest in 'mechanical contrivances and ingenious expedients' shown by British manufacturers, and the alleged consequence that 'the progress of the mechanical arts is much slower than that of commerce'.[16] Indeed the impact of new technology, both real and perceived, was neither instantaneous, nor universal.

The 1760s 'wave of gadgets' was special because, as Fig. 3 indicates, the decade 1760–9 inaugurated a sharp and sustained increase in the number of patents granting exclusive rights to inventors. This is not to say that the sixfold rise in patents between the 1740s and the 1790s implies an equivalent expansion in industrial research and technical change over the same period. Because patenting was an expensive, somewhat esoteric process, by no means all inventions were patented: the spinning mule devised by Samuel Crompton (1753–1827) is the classic case in point. So growing appreciation of the advantages of the patenting system, and the dangers of not using it, account for some—although certainly not all—of the post-1760 rise in enrolled patents. Moreover, patents covered products and processes of varying economic significance, including medicinal nostrums and consumer goods (such as skates, trusses, spectacles, false teeth, musical instruments, gloves, coats, and breeches), as well as

---

[16] R. Koebner, 'Adam Smith and the Industrial Revolution', *EcHR* 11 (1959).

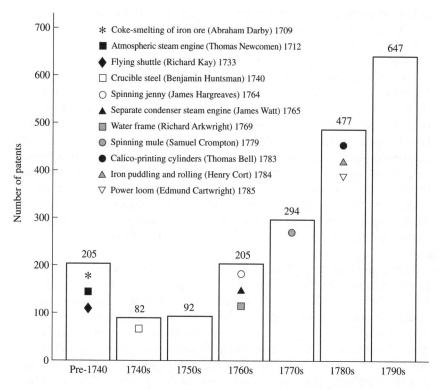

FIG. 3. Patents and Inventions, 1700–99

industrial machinery and techniques. Even within the broad category of capital or producer goods (that is, machines used for productive purposes) patents did not distinguish massive technological breakthroughs from mere incremental improvements. Yet despite these shortcomings, the aggregate patent statistics provide at least a rough-and-ready index of individual and social commitment to inventiveness.

That their post-1760 upturn was no mirage is confirmed by the chronology of the more famous individual 'gadgets' and processes invented during our period. Any selection is inevitably somewhat arbitrary. But it is remarkable how many inventions later seen as significant date from the thirty years after 1760; the sparser record of the preceding decades suggests that this clustering represents something more than the mere culmination of a long-term trend. That five of the seven post-1760 discoveries in Fig. 3 were directly related to textiles, particularly the manufacture of cotton thread (the jenny, water-frame and mule) and cloth (calico-printing from cylinders, and the power-loom), underlines what is readily confirmed from other sources: the existence of a lively industrial culture of experiment and innovation, in this case centred on the rapidly growing cotton-manufacturing region of south-east Lancashire.

Cotton was the great industrial success story of the eighteenth and early nineteenth centuries; in 1795 John Aikin characterized its 'rapid and prodigious increase' as 'absolutely unparalleled in the annals of the trading nations'. The mechanization of spinning reversed a production bottleneck caused by shortages of hand-spun yarn to supply the weavers, whose productivity had risen by half with the general adoption of Kay's semi-automatic fly shuttle. Now the new jennies enabled one worker to spin at least eight, and eventually up to eighty, times the amount of thread previously produced by a single spinning wheel; whereas Indian hand-spinners had taken more than 50,000 hours to process 100 pounds weight (45.5 kg.) of cotton, the cotton mules introduced in the 1790s handled the same amount in around 300 hours. Accordingly raw cotton imports soared and the price of cotton yarn plummeted, while cotton textile exports rapidly outstripped those of woollen cloth, England's traditional export staple.[17]

The original spinning jennies were small enough for home use, and factory-housed power-looms did not seriously challenge the cottage-based hand-loom weavers before 1815. But Arkwright's frame and the associated carding machinery which he developed in the 1770s occupied large, purpose-built, multi-storeyed spinning mills, accommodating several hundred child and female workers, together with male mechanics and overseers. Originally water-powered, some factories soon introduced steam engines; by 1800 steam power processed perhaps a quarter of the cotton yarn produced in Britain. Technologies originally developed for cotton spread to other branches of the textile industry, assisted by specialist machine makers, like William Cannon (1743–1825), yet another émigré Scot who settled in the Lancashire village of Chowbent in the 1780s, employing more than thirty workers to manufacture and install his spindles, jennies, and looms.[18] At first constructed mostly of wood, increasing use was made of cast and wrought iron and other metals (such as the copper cylinders in Bell's calico-printing machinery).

In this context the process developed by Henry Cort (1740–1800) for converting brittle cast pig-iron into malleable bar-iron (used for tools and precision parts) was of comparable importance to Darby's earlier discovery of a workable coal-based smelting technique for iron ore. The new technologies (accompanied by numerous other innovations in forging and metal working) saw a fourfold growth in the output of pig-iron between 1788 and 1806, and a virtual end to expensive imports of high-grade Swedish bar-iron. They also made iron and steel production far more directly dependent on coal and steam

[17] S. D. Chapman, 'The cotton industry and the Industrial Revolution', in L. A. Clarkson (ed.), *The Industrial Revolution: A Compendium* (1990).

[18] F. and K. Wood (eds.), *A Lancashire Gentleman: The Letters and Journals of Richard Hodgkinson, 1763–1847* (1992), 115–16.

power than was the cotton industry, hence encouraging the growth of ever larger and more capital-intensive industrial plants on the coalfields of Staffordshire, Yorkshire, South Wales, and the Scottish Lowlands.

Of course cotton and iron were pace-setters; neither can be regarded as typical of English, let alone British, industry in the late eighteenth and early nineteenth centuries. But neither was technical change, leading to enhanced output, larger production units, and increased use of female and child labour, restricted to cotton and iron alone. Non-ferrous metals, papermaking, chemicals, glass, food-processing, and shipbuilding, among others, experienced significant organizational and technological innovation during our period. The pace of development did vary considerably, even within the most advanced industrial sectors; thus small Lancashire country workshops were still spinning cotton yarn for hand-loom weavers with water-power well into the nineteenth century, while the Bonawe blast furnace on the remote west coast of Scotland continued to smelt iron with charcoal until 1876. Yet despite the persistence of traditional forms and processes, of hand tools and horsepower, the cumulative impact of invention and innovation amply justified the judgement of a visiting Swiss industrialist in 1814, that Britain had 'taken the lead in all kinds of mechanical installations'.

Trade

By now Britain had also acquired global commercial pre-eminence. The same observer noted that Paris was no great trading city: 'London, however, is the capital of an even richer state and ... the centre of the world's commerce.'[19] Of Holland's former commercial and maritime supremacy barely the memory survived the fourth Anglo-Dutch war (1780–4) and the later impact of economic blockade (1805–13). France, with a larger and rising population, an extensive colonial presence, and considerable growth in both agricultural and industrial output, posed a more serious challenge. From 1715 the volume of French foreign trade may actually have expanded faster than that of Britain, albeit from a lower base, to reach something like the same volume by 1789. But thanks largely to the Royal Navy's maritime supremacy, the Revolutionary and Napoleonic Wars (1793–1815) crippled France's overseas commerce, securing economic as well as military hegemony for Great Britain.

That outcome would hardly have been predicted throughout most of the eighteenth century, when English merchants enjoyed much less of a boom time than they had over the previous hundred years. Between 1699/1701 and 1772/4 the volume of English foreign commerce (imports and exports combined) grew some 132 per cent, a far less spectacular increase than during the initial colonial re-exports boom of the later seventeenth century, even if still

[19] W. O. Henderson (ed.), *Industrial Britain under the Regency* (1968), 1, 54.

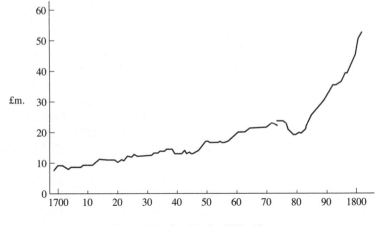

FIG 4. Foreign Trade, 1700–99

comfortably exceeding the rate of population growth over the same period (33 per cent).[20]

And while the post-war recovery phase in the late 1740s saw both exports and imports turn sharply upwards (at an annual rate of 3.9 per cent in 1745–60), the overall yearly rise between 1737 and 1771 was less than half as much (1.7 per cent). Yet shrugging off the disruptions of the American War of Independence, British foreign commerce surged dramatically in the last two decades of the century, registering an average annual growth rate of 4.9 per cent, before slackening somewhat until the end of war with France.

No less striking than the overall expansion of eighteenth-century English overseas trade was its changing direction and composition. The shift from a largely European focus towards a broadly Atlantic economy, already apparent in post-Restoration England, accelerated over the first three-quarters of the eighteenth century. The growing commercial importance of English colonies in North America and the Caribbean, as well as the West African slave trade (which supplied not only English plantations but their French and Spanish competitors), and the oceanic trade with Asia, reflected both an apparently insatiable European appetite for tropical groceries and produce (sugar, tobacco, rice, tea, coffee, and dyestuffs) and heightened colonial demand for English manufactures (mainly textiles and metalwares). By 1774 a quarter of England's total commodity imports came from the West Indies (slave-produced sugar, molasses, and rum, plus raw cotton). But although the English consumed eight times more sugar per head of population than the French, they did not keep it

[20] R. Davies, 'English foreign trade, 1700–1774', *EcHR* 15 (1962), 285; J. M. Price, 'What did merchants do? Reflections on British overseas trade, 1660–1790', *Journal of Economic History*, 49 (1989), 269–70.

all to themselves. Whereas mercantilist tariffs imposed by Continental rivals to protect their manufacturing industries held the level of English exports to Europe virtually static until the 1780s, re-exports of colonial and Asian goods from England, mainly to Europe and Ireland, rose nearly threefold between 1699 and 1774.

Sales of extra-European goods to Britain and on to Europe generated income for their (non-slave) producers. Some of this could be devoted to the purchase of manufactures (which comprised 80 per cent of all English exports at the beginning of the century and 87 per cent of all British exports at its end). Whereas a mere £0.53m. of total English exports (£4.43m.) were shipped across the Atlantic in the late 1690s, on the eve of the American Revolution nearly half (a huge £4.18m.) of Britain's total domestic export sales (now £9.85m.) went to customers in North America, the West Indies, Spanish America, and West Africa, with a further £0.7m. (up from a mere £0.12m.) absorbed by the rising Asian market. Only in the remarkable post-1783 export boom did European markets pick up again, taking perhaps 30 per cent of the addition to British commodity exports between 1784–6 and 1804–6, and up to 47 per cent immediately after 1815. The ratio of exports to total national output (GNP) over the course of the eighteenth century possibly doubled, from 8.4 to 15.7 per cent. As a proportion of total *industrial* output they may have risen from around a quarter to one-third; but of course these estimates are 'in the nature of controlled conjectures rather than definitive evidence'.[21]

Foreign trade and industrialization were closely connected. The fast-growing cotton industry not only depended for raw material on imports from America, but sold overseas between a half (in 1760) and nearly two-thirds (by 1801) of its yarn and cloth output. Although cotton never dominated commodity exports to the extent that woollen cloth had once done (with a 68.7 per cent share at the beginning of the century), its proportion rose to nearly 40 per cent by 1801, by which time the relative share of woollen textiles had plummeted to a mere one-sixth of total exports by value. Perhaps a third of Britain's entire output of woollen cloth was sold overseas; the corresponding figures for cotton and iron were around two-thirds and one-quarter respectively. Export sales were plainly of considerable significance for these last two rapidly expanding sectors. Moreover, most exported woollen cloth came from Yorkshire's relatively young and dynamic West Riding region, rather than the traditional textile centres in East Anglia and the West Country.

Besides importing essential industrial raw materials and supplementary supplies of grain, together with a wide range of exotic consumables, Britain's overseas trade created jobs (especially for unskilled female and child labour) in the major export industries. By extending industrial markets well beyond the limits of Britain's own population, exports also encouraged greater productive efficiency, through economies of scale, the division of labour, and investment in

[21] Crafts, *British Economic Growth*, 9, 131–2.

new technology. Further, profits made in overseas trade were a potential source of capital for industry; merchants from Bristol, Liverpool, Glasgow, and London invested directly in factories, foundries, and mills, as well as extending long-term credit to manufacturers.

Some economic historians play down the significance of overseas trade as a direct source of economic and industrial development. Thus Deane and Cole argued that trade growth was primarily a dependent effect rather than an autonomous cause of domestic expansion, mainly because home demand for foreign goods ultimately provided overseas customers with the means to purchase British manufactures. Furthermore, it is claimed that resources devoted to foreign trade and to manufacturing for the export market might have been better employed in catering for more immediate needs: 'the men and money used to make the excess cotton could have been turned towards making beer, roads, houses, and other domestic things.'[22] Yet eighteenth-century growth in North American population and economic activity, including trading surpluses with the West Indies and Southern Europe, did generate independent demand for British exports. Detailed studies also reveal no positive correlation between British import and export levels. It may additionally be doubted whether the workforce—especially its juvenile and female members—employed in export-oriented industries could readily have found jobs elsewhere, let alone that tropical commodities imported from the New World might have been readily replaced by home-grown substitutes.

Much of the case made against the importance of overseas trade has a somewhat abstract and doctrinaire character, perhaps reflecting the flimsiness of its evidential base. Although customs registers provide the most comprehensive series of contemporary economic statistics, even converting their stereotyped official values into current prices is not a straightforward business, while little can be done to compensate for the unknown volume of illicitly imported tea, tobacco, silks, wine, and spirits. An equally serious omission from the customs registers is the overseas shipping industry. Other sources show that, while the realignment of British trade from Europe to the Atlantic required larger and more expensive vessels, the efficiency of their operation increased quite substantially during the course of the eighteenth century; on the London–Virginia run, for example, the ratio of ships' tonnage to crew members rose from 9 : 1 to 13.9 : 1 between the mid-1720s and the later 1760s.

The slave trade, eulogized in 1772 as 'the foundation of our commerce, the support of our colonies, the life of our navigation and the first cause of our national industry and riches', figures not at all in the customs registers.[23] Yet

---

[22] P. Deane and W. A. Cole, *British Economic Growth, 1688–1959* (1967), 83–9; R. P. Thomas and D. McCloskey, 'Overseas trade and empire, 1700–1860', in *Economic History of Britain since 1700*, ed. Floud and McCloskey (1981).

[23] *A Treatise upon the Trade from Great Britain to Africa* (1772), quoted R. Anstey, *The Atlantic Slave Trade and British Abolition, 1760–1810* (1975), 36–7; P. K. O'Brien and S. L. Engerman,

besides the fluctuating, if frequently lucrative, profits reaped by individual merchants of Bristol, Liverpool, and London who bought and exported black slaves from West Africa before 1807, significant volumes of English cotton cloth exports were either bartered for slaves on the West African coast or sold to clothe slaves in the New World. The cotton industry also depended on slave labour for its raw material, imported first from the Caribbean and then increasingly from North America and Brazil, while the ability of North American non-slave colonies to buy British manufactures depended in part on their sale of surplus agricultural produce to feed slaves in the British West Indies. It is difficult to demonstrate that profits from the slave trade were an essential prerequisite of industrialization, as posited in Eric Williams's 1944 study of *Capitalism and Slavery*. Yet slavery plainly underpinned Britain's participation in the Atlantic economy, not to mention the luxurious lifestyles of many West Indian planters, and some significant architectural achievements, including the splendid Codrington Library at All Souls College, Oxford, and the Gothic fantasy of Fonthill Abbey in Wiltshire. We should recall, with the historian Richard Pares, that the funds came from working half-starved African slaves twelve hours a day in appalling conditions.[24]

Banking and Finance

Adam Smith thought of money as 'the great wheel of circulation, the great instrument of commerce'.[25] Yet barter continued to be widely used for domestic transactions, and not just in the Africa trade, throughout the eighteenth century. Thus during the 1760s Abraham Dent's customers in Kirkby Stephen, Cumberland, paid in kind for their groceries with coal, garden seeds, and shoe repairs. Papermills gladly replenished retail stocks of their finished product in return for bulk collections of rags to be recycled into paper. Towards the end of the century the Lancashire toolmaker Peter Stubs (1756–1806) routinely swapped quantities of his well-regarded wood and metal files for bars of the high-grade Sheffield steel from which they were made, and in his other business capacity exchanged malt, ale, and beer for barley, candles, coal, and the rent of the White Bear, the inn which he leased on Bridge Street, Warrington.[26]

The prevalence of barter, short-term credit, and payment in kind is largely explained by the government's persistent failure to provide sufficient supplies of 'the great instrument of commerce'. After the elaborate recoinage of 1696–8, undertaken on Locke's advice and supervised by Isaac Newton as Warden of

'Exports and the growth of the British economy from the Glorious Revolution to the Peace of Amiens', in B. Solow (ed.), *Slavery and the Rise of the Atlantic System* (1991).

[24] J. I. Inkori, 'Slavery and the Revolution in cotton textile production in England', *Social Science History*, 13 (1989). Cf. R. Pares, *Merchants and Planters* (1960), 40.

[25] *The Wealth of Nations* (1776, 1904), ed. E. Cannan, i. 309.

[26] T. S. Willan, *An Eighteenth-Century Shopkeeper* (1970), 24–5; T. S. Ashton, *An Eighteenth-Century Industrialist* (1939), 38–9, 80, 99.

the Mint, silver coins rapidly disappeared from circulation, because their face value in England was significantly less than what they fetched when melted down for the European bullion market. Gold accordingly became the national circulating medium, supplemented by copper coins for small transactions. The quantity and quality of this coinage left much to be desired. An official inspection in 1787 revealed that perhaps only 8 per cent of circulating copper was of Mint quality; the remainder comprised clipped originals, blanks, counterfeits, and privately minted tokens issued for local circulation by manufacturers and shopkeepers. The acute shortage of both copper and silver currency led to the circulation of both genuine and fake Portuguese moidores, a small gold coin, alongside gold guinea pieces which had frequently lost up to a quarter of their nominal face value and weight by wear and tear combined with filing and other forms of illegal debasement.

Lack of a national paper currency further aggravated these problems. More or less negotiable paper included pawnbroker's, lottery, and navy pay tickets, employer's promissory notes for wages, the occasional personal cheque, and above all bills of exchange ('the principal medium of foreign and inland commerce').[27] The Bank of England issued printed notes, redeemable in cash, which could be used as a means of payment, but these did not circulate widely outside London, and until the 1790s were not available in denominations under £10. The need for smaller notes was met by provincial banks, whose numbers increased from a mere dozen or so at mid-century to perhaps 100 by 1775, some 370 at the end of the century, and well over 600 by 1815. Besides issuing printed notes for local circulation these country banks accepted deposits, discounted bills of exchange, and other securities, remitted funds to London, received specie in return, and advanced loans, to businessmen and industrialists among others. Thus Goldney's of Bristol funded the Darbys of Coalbrookdale, Peter Stubs ran an overdraft with Parr, Lyon and Co. of Warrington, while early in his brilliant career Richard Arkwright, who eventually established his own banking firm, received short-term finance from Wright Brothers of Nottingham.

Utterly unregulated in terms of reserve ratios and lending policies, private note-issuing banks were limited by law to a partnership of no more than six persons, in order to protect the Bank of England's monopoly. Partners in country banks were typically drawn from the ranks of local manufacturers and merchants (who had workers and suppliers of raw materials to pay, and customers requiring credit), lawyers (who frequently had surplus funds available for investment, as well as a shrewd appreciation of local business opportunities), and collectors of land tax and other government revenues (who needed secure means of transferring large sums to London). Yet despite their agency arrangements with London private banks, the limited size and unincorporated status

[27] [T. Cunningham], *The Law of Bills of Exchange, Promissory Notes, Bank-Notes and Insurances* (1770), sig. A2.

of country banking firms meant that they inevitably operated on a narrow capital base. Apart from proprietorial inexperience or recklessness, this feature made them extremely vulnerable during economic crises like those of 1793 and 1798; still worse were the three years of post-war depression in 1814–16, when no fewer than seventy-two private banks closed their doors, and many more temporarily suspended payments to depositors. Such disruptive national slumps in business confidence, characterized by tight money and heightened bankruptcy rates, became an increasingly common phenomenon from the 1770s onwards. They were directly related to the heightened pace of economic activity, largely funded by the expansion of credit in the form of bills of exchange, which linked banks and businesses both across the country and across the world.

The shortcomings of late Georgian banking and finance should not be exaggerated. Indeed the proliferation of country banks after 1750 was part of a second-wave financial revolution, otherwise centred in the City of London. The growth of merchant banks, dealing both in foreign bills of exchange and the burgeoning government debt, the opening in 1773 of a building in Threadneedle Street which became the Stock Exchange (whose broker members gradually added canal, dock, and insurance shares to their mainstays of government and East India Company securities), and a great influx of foreign capital, and capitalists, during the Napoleonic wars, enabled the City finally to supplant Amsterdam as Europe's, indeed the world's, chief financial centre. There seems little doubt that this momentous outcome depended largely upon the commercial and industrial developments outlined above, which in turn would hardly have occurred without a workable and expanding infrastructure of banks, credit, and exchange.

Law, Policy, and the State

Eighteenth- and early nineteenth-century constitutional and legal arrangements both helped and hindered economic development. English law generally supported the rights of private property, but historians routinely assert that it had little direct economic influence during this period. Similarly, the Hanoverian state's main contribution to economic development is often thought to have been the negative one of vacating the field, permitting the eventual triumph of free-market principles. Neither view is entirely persuasive.

To begin with, law in the sense of parliamentary legislation must be distinguished from law as dispensed by the courts. The administration of justice was a legitimate state function even for dedicated champions of *laissez-faire*. But the state's legal apparatus was no mere dependent arm of government. While Parliament legislated at an ever-increasing rate, enacting more than 15,000 statutes (overwhelmingly private Acts) during the sixty-year reign of George III, the courts made law on an even larger scale, in the course of determining cases brought to trial before them. Much statute law did define or redefine property rights in ways favouring both economic development and the well-to-do; thus private enclosure Acts coerced small tenants with token—or no—compensation for forfeited customary rights, anti-embezzlement laws criminalized traditional employee perquisites, and various sixteenth-century statutes against profiteering in foodstuffs were repealed in 1772. But the effectiveness of parliamentary legislation depended both on the draftsman's skill and the attitude of the judges. Even after the 1772 repeal Chief Justice Kenyon continued to sanction proceedings against speculators on the London food market, holding 'these practices so injurious to the poor and middling classes of society as to call forth the immediate punishment of the law'.[28]

Nor did all legislation promote free-market principles, or practice. Besides a mass of laws regulating foreign trade and protecting domestic industries, the Bubble Act (1720) sought to check the formation of limited-liability business companies, while the Stockjobbing Act (1734) outlawed various forms of speculative dealing in securities. Despite limited success in achieving their avowed ends, neither measure had any positive economic effect. The 'profoundly obtuse and procedurally labyrinthine' law of partnerships, under which most businesses were obliged to operate until the mid-nineteenth century, tended to perpetuate inefficient family firms, while restrictions on share transactions depressed investment, and—in so far as that were possible—the already abysmal reputation of stockbrokers. Judicial decisions (like those of Chief Justice Mansfield, assisted by special merchant juries) might help alleviate such problems, especially in the field of commercial law. But there were limits to the distance even activist judges could go in the face of combined common-law and statutory chaos; the notoriously defective bankruptcy laws, for example, remained basically unreformed throughout our period. The difficulty of pursuing claims for small debts through Westminster Hall was solved not by restructuring the central courts, but by establishing ad hoc provincial 'courts of requests', with part-time amateur commissioners rather than professional lawyers as judges. Yet attorneys and barristers also played a key role in mobilizing investments and devising new arrangements for the holding and transfer of property. In short, the relationship between law, legal institutions, and the economy in eighteenth-century England was anything but straightforward, and merits further investigation.

Considerable recent scholarly attention has focused on the fiscal, protectionist, and welfare roles of the Hanoverian state. Both the burden and the yield of taxation rose sharply over the course of the eighteenth century, most notably in times of war, since at least four-fifths of government revenues were earmarked for foreign and military expenditure. Between 1693–7 and 1812–15 the tax level rose more than fivefold in real terms, or from 6.7 to 18.2 per cent of national income. This massive fiscal burden, by far the highest in Europe,

---

[28] J. Oldham (ed.), *The Mansfield Manuscripts and the Growth of English Law in the Eighteenth Century* (1992), 932–3.

doubtless weakened domestic demand, even if much of the money returned to the home market to purchase food and equipment for British armies and navies. War also boosted specific industries, notably coal, textiles, and metallurgy, and employment in general, at least partially offsetting the inevitable commercial disruptions. But in both peace and war the whole external orientation of the economy, with its emphasis on exploiting a protected British-Atlantic free-trade area, and gaining additional markets at the expense of France, Spain, Portugal, and Holland, ultimately depended upon maintaining a formidable military and naval capability: 'Hanoverian governments knew some big things, namely that security, trade, Empire, and military power really mattered.'[29]

Free trade was not among those big things. While the Eden Treaty (1786) between England and France did see some bilateral tariff cuts, the level of protection for English manufactures and farming rose again with the outbreak of war in 1793. The inexorable rise in taxation between the Glorious Revolution and 1815 was largely effected by indirect levies, including customs duties on a wide range of imported manufactured goods. These tariffs were not initially motivated by systematic mercantilist goals. But despite their original fiscal purpose they considerably assisted the competitive position of domestic producers. Thus the flowering of the English linen industry between 1740 and 1790 has been attributed to high duties imposed after 1688 on imported Continental linen goods, reinforced by subsequent bounties which subsidized both English linen exports and domestic production of flax and yarn. The latter measures were introduced in response to pressure from industry lobbies, on the assumption that import substitution could help reduce unemployment, and hence the burden of the poor rates—always a major issue for Hanoverian policy makers.

As a secular, comprehensive, compulsorily funded and locally administered social welfare scheme, England's national system of poor relief was unique, in the British Isles as well as Europe. By contemporary standards the scale of aid provided was also generous; during the 1780s English expenditure on poor relief per head of population may have been over seven times higher than comparable assistance in France. Despite persistent complaints from those taxed to support their less fortunate neighbours, as a social welfare provision the poor law had considerable macro-economic benefits, including enhanced labour mobility (despite the harsh absurdities of the law of settlement) and lower workforce resistance to waged employment than might otherwise have been the case. For all their dread of the workhouse, a minimal but guaranteed level of food and shelter in sickness, unemployment, and old age may well have reduced the incentives for workers to cling to rural smallholdings (hence assisting the process of agricultural consolidation), or to rear large families of children as a form of social insurance.

[29] P. K. O'Brien, *Power with Profit: The State and the Economy, 1688–1815* (1991), 33.

To conclude: our present state of knowledge makes it difficult to lay down hard-and-fast conclusions about the overall economic impact of eighteenth-century English law and lawyers. However, in the light of recent research the economic role of government and the state appears clearer and more positive than was once thought. British governments eschewed the ambitious efforts of their European counterparts to foster industrial and infra-structure developments. But England's massive external naval and imperial commitments played a roughly equivalent role to these mercantilist projects. Meanwhile agriculture and manufactures were fostered by a dense barrier of protective tariffs, which had barely begun to be dismantled before the end of our period. Not until 1814 did the repeal of the Elizabethan Statute of Artificers underline the state's evident willingness to abrogate its remaining responsibilities for regulating wages, working conditions, and the supply of food.

Nor was government non-intervention always economically advantageous. Even where state-sponsored action plainly proved counter-productive (as with the overvaluing of silver in the 1690s), subsequent governmental inaction did not necessarily improve matters. Lack of commitment to a comprehensive law-reform agenda, despite the legal system's long-standing inability to provide cheap and speedy resolution of property disputes, provides a further example of state abstention perpetuating significant diseconomies in transaction costs, to say nothing of an unpopular and expensive professional cartel. Failure to establish a national system of weights and measures until 1826 (especially as between England and Scotland), or to curb child labour, crime, occupational disease and injury, overcrowding, pollution, and related public-health problems in and around fast-growing industrial towns, provide additional instances of counter-productive official inertia in the medium to longer term, however limited or unquantifiable their immediate effects on output.

Organization of Work and Workers

The proliferation of large, urban, steam-powered 'manufactories'—those 'dark satanic mills' of the poet William Blake (1757–1827)—has long been regarded as the defining characteristic of English industrialization. But what is, or was, a factory? Originally denoting a merchants' trading post, during the eighteenth century the word came to be applied to textile 'mills', initially human-, horse-, or water-powered, which concentrated both workforce and production under one roof, not necessarily in a town or 'cottonopolis'. Factories came in various shapes and sizes, but the large, multi-storey establishments which employed hundreds of workers, like Arkwright's original cotton-spinning plants at Nottingham, Belper, Cromford, Derby, Chorley, and Manchester, or the huge New Lanark works in Scotland, were very much the exception before 1815. In the early days of mechanized spinning most cotton mills were housed in cottages, shanties, or sub-let floors of a larger building, with perhaps a carding engine, some small mules, or a few jennies, worked by anything from a handful to twenty or thirty employees. Size and power-source were less significant than organization and managerial structure. Centralized control of the entire production process was what essentially distinguished small-scale factories from larger enterprises in which workshop space was leased to numerous independent artisan subcontractors, as at Boulton's Soho complex outside Birmingham.

Transition to the factory from the decentralized domestic or putting-out system was slow, uneven, and far from universal. Some industries never experienced the domestic phase: concentration of production, specialized machinery, and workforce at a single site was always characteristic of the manufacture of chemicals, iron, and non-ferrous metals, as also mining and shipbuilding. Nor was the factory age anything like fully established by 1815, even within the textile industry, where woollens and worsteds lagged well behind cotton or silk. Indeed the mechanization of spinning more than a generation before power-looms came into general use created an Indian summer boom-time for hand-loom weaver outworkers. In other industries most manufacturing (for example, of pottery, cutlery, small metal wares, boots, shoes, and leather goods) long continued to be carried out by small workshops, each producing its own few distinctive product lines, or by 'sweated' outworkers, like the men, women, and children who hand-made chain-links and nails in the industrial villages of the Staffordshire Black Country.

Yet factories could offer employers more than merely technological benefits. Besides efficiency gains from the use of capital-intensive powered machinery, and savings of time and trouble (transaction costs) in physically conveying work over considerable distances at each successive stage of production, the factory facilitated close supervision of the labour force. A Mr Atkinson of Huddersfield explained in 1806 that it was 'principally to prevent embezzlement' of materials that he preferred to bring together all the weavers working for him.[30] Better quality control and more effective scheduling of production were also possible in the factory environment.

From the employee's viewpoint, factory work held considerably fewer attractions. Conventional belief that the strong 'leisure preference' of English workers necessitated a low wages regime, since they would only labour under threat of imminent starvation, was increasingly challenged after 1750 by those who agreed with David Hume and Adam Smith that rising real wages could stimulate heightened industriousness among the lower orders. Yet the relatively high wages paid to factory workers came at a considerable price. When Malachy Postlethwayt (1707?–57) praised the 'ingenuity and dexterity' of English craftsmen in 1751, he specifically linked these attributes to freedom to work as and how they pleased. But the outworker artisan's and agricultural labourer's irregular work patterns, 'alternate bouts of intense labour and of idleness', task-

---

[30] H. Heaton, *The Yorkshire Woollen and Worsted Industries* (1920), 352.

rather than time-oriented, were incompatible with the insistent demands of concentrated, mechanized production.[31] Instead of being able to keep 'St Monday' as a holiday, and work at an increasingly frenetic pace as the end of the week approached, the ceaseless rhythm of the machine demanded long, constant, and monotonous attendance. Nor was recruitment encouraged by the architectural and disciplinary associations of large factories with bridewells or houses of correction, and workhouses, whose inmates were typically put to work on cloth and yarn production. The substantial contingents of orphan and pauper children routinely supplied—in effect sold—by southern parishes to northern factories, underlined the point. Difficulty in attracting and keeping free labour (the giant Manchester spinning firm of McConnel and Kennedy typically experienced a complete turnover of workforce every year), was exacerbated by attempts to inculcate a new work-discipline, aided by fines for drunkenness, fighting, lateness, shouting, loud talk, whistling, 'calling foul names, all mean and vulgar language, and every kind of indecency'. Widespread concern with the notorious 'immorality' of factory life suggests that these efforts had little immediate success. Finally, although working conditions in cottage industry could be squalid, factories were often dusty, hot, ill-ventilated, noisy, and very dangerous places. Industrial health and safety remained a matter for individual employers, and only an exceptional minority placed guards on moving machinery, or sought to enforce safe work practices. Management and workforce alike generally adopted a fatalistic attitude to occupational hazards; a visitor touring the extensive Tyneside glass works in 1772 was told—and noted without comment—'that the excessive heat generally kills the workmen employed in glass making in 7 or 8 years'.[32]

So it is not just their remote locations in upland valleys which explains why many early factories were worked mainly by impoverished Irish, Scots, and Welsh immigrants, together with parish apprentices and women. Child and female labour had long been used in both outwork and workshop manufacturing, especially of cloth, as well as on the land and in mining. But the nature and extent of work opportunities for women and children varied widely across the country. Lack of occupational statistics makes it difficult to know how they were affected by economic growth and industrialization from the mid-eighteenth century onwards. The consolidation of large arable farms in southern England, and changes in farming practice such as the substitution of scythes for sickles, saw family agricultural employment fall, even if women day-labourers still found some seasonal work, and played a major year-round role on farms in the pastoral north and west. But overall a substantial release of female labour from agriculture seems to have occurred after 1750, and it is unclear how far manufacturing industry took up the slack.

[31] E. P. Thompson, 'Time, work-discipline, and industrial capitalism', in *Customs in Common* (1991), 373.

[32] Neville, *Diary*, 158.

Certainly the mechanization of textile production brought women and children into the factories as a relatively docile and low-wage labour force. Children under 18 years of age made up more than half the cotton factory workforce in 1816, and some textile machinery was specifically designed for operation by small boys and girls. While mechanization largely eliminated demand for home-spun yarn produced by women on a wheel or distaff, many of the hand-loom weavers who gained a temporary increase in work from the increased supply and cheapness of thread were women. Yet most industries offered less scope than textiles for child or female employment, and some, like the primary production of iron and steel and the better-paid jobs in textiles, were effectively monopolized by men. The resistance of male artisans to female labour as a serious threat to prevailing wage levels complemented respectable opinion that 'the superintendence of domestic economy is the natural and proper province of the female'.[33] Moreover, the inhabitants of non-industrial towns and villages, and workers in contracting industries, were often unable or unwilling to pursue opportunities in the booming industrial areas. Many young women found domestic service in London or their immediate neighbourhood a more accessible and attractive option than emigration to a distant factory town. Meanwhile, judging by public concern from the 1780s onwards about the moral and social evil of children 'nurtured in idleness', young people of both sexes were frequently unable to find employment of any kind, a problem enhanced by their prominence in an increasingly youthful as well as expanding population.[34]

Labour and Capital

Since women's and children's earnings could contribute significantly to family incomes, the extent of their participation in paid employment is crucial to weighing up the gains and losses of industrialization. Not surprisingly, contemporary disagreements on this major issue have been echoed by commentators down to the present day. In his challenge to Victorian eulogies of material improvement and progress, Toynbee declared that the new regime of unrestrained *laissez-faire* ushered in by the final collapse of medieval collectivism had devastating consequences. Not only did feral 'capitalists' combine to oppress the 'labourers' with savage wage cuts; even where money wages actually rose, the degraded working conditions of the factory system, the impact of price inflation, and severe recurrent economic crises brought 'misery' and 'bitter distress' to 'large sections of the working people'.[35] Like the more optimistic counter-claims of subsequent scholars, this broadly pessimistic account of

[33] *Principles of Law and Government with an Inquiry into the Justice and Policy of the Present War* (1781), 165.
[34] H. Cunningham, *Children of the Poor: Representations of Childhood since the Seventeenth Century* (1991), 23.
[35] *The Industrial Revolution*, ch. 8.

the socio-economic impact of competition, capitalism, and industrialization (or industrial capitalism), relates to a period extending beyond the chronological limits of this book. But before examining as much of their basis as falls within our time frame, we should review Toynbee's assertion, elaborated by subsequent writers, that the cluster of events which he termed the industrial revolution also saw a sharp polarization of capital and labour.

Some prima-facie evidence of heightened class consciousness in the later eighteenth and early nineteenth centuries may be provided by the appearance of the terms 'working class' (as distinct from previous variations on the 'low' or 'lowliest' classes) and 'capitalist', first recorded in 1789 and 1792 respectively.[36] The demographic pressures, rampant inflation, soaring taxes, harvest failures, trade crises, ideological turmoil, millenarian fervour, radical political activism, and repressive state reaction, which characterized the era of the French Revolution and Napoleonic Wars (see below, Chs. 17–18), also did little to advance the cause of social harmony. To these aggravations must be added the discriminatory Combination Acts of 1799 and 1800 (which criminalized trade union activity in defence of working conditions, without affecting employers' associations), together with a succession of serious food riots, strikes, and other industrial action, culminating in the violent machine-breaking of the 'Luddite' framework-knitters and their allies in 1811–12. Even so, it does not follow that English society as a whole emerged from the French wars more seriously polarized along class lines than had been the case a quarter of a century before.

Expressions of class hostility, and hatred, are not difficult to cite from the 1790s and 1800s. But similar verbal manifestations of enmity and fear between rich and poor occured in many, perhaps most, previous decades of early modern English history: there was nothing novel or unprecedented in the reported anticipation by female food-rioters in 1795 of 'the downfall of all the clergy and of every rich person'.[37] The high level of popular disturbance during the French wars is adequately explained by the combined impact of poor harvests, high taxes, and bruising trade recessions, without any need to invoke the spectre of class warfare. Industrial conflict was endemic throughout the eighteenth century, especially in London and the textile trades of the West Country, Yorkshire, and Lancashire. Tailors, hatters, coal-miners, dockyard workers, and sailors were also prone to collective mobilization, including work-stoppages, protest demonstrations, lobbying local authorities and Parliament, and destructive attacks on job-threatening new machinery. From the early 1740s onwards, Dr Dobson tells us, 'strikes or "turn-outs" became commonplace in London and the provinces'.[38] Many trades had more or less informal mutual provident associations, box or subscription clubs, and friendly societies, which,

[36] P. Corfield, 'Class by name and number in eighteenth-century Britain', *History*, 72 (1987), 56.
[37] J. Bohstedt, 'Women in English riots, 1760–1810', *P&P* 120 (1988), 103.
[38] C. R. Dobson, *Masters and Journeymen: A Prehistory of Industrial Relations, 1717–1800* (1980), 21.

besides providing workers with sickness and other benefits, served as a base for industrial action. By the 1750s the London society of journeymen tailors included some forty affiliated clubs based on inns and taverns known as 'houses of call', each sending delegates to a central House of Representatives, whose policies were implemented by a five-member executive, the Grand Committee for the Management of the Town. This formidable organization continued to operate throughout our period, in defiance not only of the general Combination Acts, but also of industry-specific anti-union legislation obtained by the master tailors in 1721 and 1768.

Yet confrontations between masters and men, although not infrequent, were limited by locality and industry, rather than involving general, or national, strikes. On the workers' side these conflicts did not necessarily or usually invoke the rhetoric of class interest, but often appealed to an idealized vision of harmonious employer–employee relations advancing the well-being of the entire trade. The 1803 rulebook of the union of journeymen papermakers expressed this ideal in verse:

> May masters with their men unite
> Each other ne'er oppress
> And their assistance freely give
> When men are in distress.[39]

Such aspirations may not have been very realistic, and were by no means universal. Yet according to E. P. Thompson, they expressed the distinctive cultural consensus of the working poor, who whether striking against wage cuts, or rioting against high food prices, sought to assert a traditional communal 'moral economy' against the market economy of emergent capitalism. They stood for just prices and fair shares, enforced if necessary by paternal magistrates, against the amoral, market-dominated 'political economy' of Adam Smith and his economic rationalist disciples. Thompson's critics dismiss the moral economy concept as a romanticized historiographical construct, not a contemporary reality. Invocations of traditional popular rights or usages are explained away as bargaining counters deployed in the struggle for economic advantage by men and women already immersed in a monetized market economy. Yet such scepticism fails to explain the peculiarly controlled, orderly, almost ritualistic form of many popular protests, as when crowds sold off commandeered grain or cheese at customary prices, then returned the proceeds to the original owners, rather than simply appropriating the foodstuffs. It also overlooks the possibility that communitarian rhetoric had a self-validating quality, especially when local governors placated insurgent plebeians by agreeing to fix wages or enforce ancient fair-marketing and apprenticeship regulations.

A more damaging objection is that the skilled urban industrial workers whose actions provide the main evidence for Thompson's moral-economy

---

[39] J. Rule, *The Experience of Labour in Eighteenth-Century Industry* (1981), 210.

thesis constituted only a small minority of the total working population. According to the earliest reliable census data, as late as 1831 adult males employed in agriculture—among whom industrial and political activism was largely unknown before 1815—still made up around a third of the workforce, as against just over one male in ten employed in manufacturing (both factory and outwork).[40] Working-class solidarity was also hindered by the intricate hierarchy of crafts and trades, each with its own culture and traditions, and the considerable disparities in income and status separating skilled and relatively highly paid masters, or self-employed artisans, from working journeymen and unskilled hands or labourers.

Similar diversity characterized the other side of the industrial and social divide. From the middle of the eighteenth century the term 'manufacturer' gradually shed its original ambiguous reference to either workman or master, contracting to the modern meaning of one who employs labour to manufacture goods. But many manufacturers, or industrialists, came from relatively modest backgrounds, even if the contemporary myth of the wholly self-made man, exemplified by the 'cotton lord' who rose from operative to proprietor by dint of sheer hard work, must be heavily discounted. Fewer than 10 per cent of a sample of 226 individuals who founded industrial firms employing at least one hundred workers during the century after 1750 appear to have been the sons of wage-earning manual workers. However, the proportion who could be described as having risen from humble origins would expand significantly with a broader sample which included the proprietors of smaller spinning mills and similar enterprises, or by adding in the sons of yeomen farmers, shopkeepers, and skilled craftsmen. Opportunities for the proverbial ascent from rags to riches varied between industries. The capital-intensive nature of iron-making, the large London breweries, and spinning with the Arkwright water frame (at least until Arkwright's patent expired) meant that successful ventures in these lines of business generally required much larger resources than, say, ceramics, light engineering, or the Birmingham and Sheffield metal trades, where individual enterprise and skills were the critical factor. Even so, Samuel Whitbread I (1720–96), founder of a great London brewing dynasty, was a self-made yeoman's son, while it took three generations for successive heads of the Darby family to rise from small ironmasters to proprietors of the largest metallurgical plant in the kingdom. The ranks of the aristocracy and landed gentry supplied hardly any active industrialists (as distinct from sleeping partners); businesswomen, usually widows, were even rarer, although a Miss Rachel Leach of Keighley, in the West Riding of Yorkshire, built and operated a cotton mill from the 1780s to the early 1800s.

The middling-to-humble social origins of most industrialists, and especially the smaller 'yeomen capitalists', such as Yorkshire's artisan clothiers, did not

---

[40] Wrigley, *Continuity, Chance, and Change*, 84–7; those producing goods and services for local markets in retail trades and handicrafts amounted to another third.

necessarily guarantee more humane treatment of their workforce. Indeed the reverse might be true, as conservative and radical critics alike were quick to point out, blaming the oppressions of the factory system on the vulgar avarice of new-rich mill owners. Yet at the end of our period most industrial workers were still found in relatively small concerns, where master and worker could interact on a face-to-face basis. Even in Manchester, where 44 per cent of the cotton-spinning labour force in 1815 worked for firms with over 500 employees, only 8 per cent of all concerns were so huge, the remainder constituting 'a thick undergrowth of very small-scale enterprises'.[41]

Contemporaries do not seem generally to have interpreted the partial deregulation of the economy and the labour market between the 1780s and 1815, with the repeal of long-standing apprenticeship, fair-marketing, and wage-fixing legislation, as a victory for capitalism or the industrial bourgeoisie. Besides lacking the requisite vocabulary, they could observe that manufacturers and industrialists exhibited little more solidarity than their employees. In 1800 the cotton-weavers' successful campaign for compulsory arbitration to settle pay and other disputes received support from at least some masters, while smaller employers also joined abortive attempts to revive the old apprenticeship system in 1813–14. Earlier, in 1802, Parliament had passed an 'Act for the preservation of the health and morals of apprentices and others, employed in cotton and other mills, and cotton and other factories'. The limited effectiveness of the initial Factory Act's attempt to enforce a maximum twelve-hour working day and some rudimentary educational provision for parish apprentices should not diminish its significance as the first attempt to regulate employment conditions with the welfare of the workforce in mind. Yet the parliamentary sponsor of this unprecedented challenge to *laissez-faire* and the autonomy of private property was none other than Sir Robert Peel (1750–1830), proprietor of the largest calico-printing business in England.

Standards of Living

There seems little reason to suppose that the bulk of the population was more fiercely united in class-conscious antagonism to the middling and upper sort by the end of the Napoleonic wars than they had been in the 1750s. But were their material conditions of life significantly different? How did the early stages of industrialization affect the living standards of ordinary people? Unfortunately this question has no simple answer, despite (and only partly because of) over fifty years of intense scholarly debate.

The argument really began in the 1920s, with Clapham's suggestion that rising real wages (that is, money wages adjusted to take account of price inflation)

---

[41] F. Crouzet, *The First Industrialists* (1985); R. Lloyd-Jones and M. J. Lewis, *Manchester and the Age of the Factory: the Business Structure of 'Cottonopolis' in the Industrial Revolution* (1988), 33.

during the first half of the nineteenth century contradicted Toynbee's gloomy picture of severely deteriorating living standards among the working poor.[42] During the 1950s and 1960s this case was championed and extended by several writers, most notably R. M. Hartwell, and severely criticized by Eric Hobsbawm, in a scholarly exchange embittered by Cold War divisions. Increasingly sophisticated efforts to refine the measurement of real wages have continued with both regional and national studies, despite the difficulties involved in moving from statistical series of piece rates, prices, and daily or weekly money wages (put together by averaging numerous individual instances) to general conclusions about living standards across the country as a whole. Wages and earnings were not identical, even in the case of individuals (much less families), thanks to the uneven and variable impact of self-, under-, and unemployment; money wages often constituted only part of an individual or family income, because of job-related perquisites and payments in kind (the miner's free coal, the agricultural labourer's subsidized cottage, or less advantageously the employee's payment by ticket redeemable for groceries at a factory 'truck' shop); consumption patterns varied with changing income levels and relative costs of food and other commodities; prices fluctuated not only over time but also regionally, while money wages differed according to locality and season as well as occupation. Moreover, despite new wages and prices data, and attempts to factor in women's and children's earnings, huge gaps remain in our knowledge, particularly on housing costs, while much potentially valuable archival evidence on these matters remains unexplored.

Similar difficulties, and more, are posed by possible quantitative alternatives to the real wages yardstick, such as estimates of GNP or per capita income, and trends in consumer goods imports. For example, the impact of rising national productivity on living standards for the mass of the population would obviously depend on how evenly the benefits of productivity gains were distributed, a complex question in itself. In any case, money isn't, and wasn't, everything. Calculations of financial gain or loss ignore many fundamental aspects of physical, psychological, and social well-being. How do we measure the costs, and benefits, of movement from an attractive rural village to an overcrowded and polluted industrial town, let alone from artisan self-employment to factory wage labour? (Some ingenious calculations suggest that in the early nineteenth century a wages premium of between 10 and 24 per cent was necessary to attract labour to the industrial towns; but whether this was a fair price, even in the limited sense that those accepting it had adequate knowledge of the health and welfare implications of their choice, is another question.)[43] An alternative strategy is to track biological yardsticks, such as life expectancy, infant mortality,

---

[42] J. H. Clapham, *An Economic History of Modern Britain: The Early Railway Age, 1820–1850* (1926), 125–31, 466–7, and ch. 14.

[43] J. G. Williamson, *Coping with City Growth during the British Industrial Revolution* (1990), 255–6.

and physical height, on the assumption that these mirrored changes over time in living conditions, particularly nutrition and public health. Demographic studies have now been supplemented by analyses of the recorded height of soldiers, Marine Society boys, indentured servants, and transported convicts, both male and female. This work relies on a well-established correlation between adult height and nutritional intake during childhood and adolescence, and the more dubious assumption that such groups can provide a representative cross-section of England's working poor.

Unfortunately, but unsurprisingly, these investigations have yielded contradictory results. Adult male real wages may either have stagnated before and actually declined during the war years, or alternatively risen substantially between 1781 and 1821. Industrial workers in the North and Midlands evidently experienced significant wage gains before 1815, but London real wages seem to have fallen between 1770 and 1800. However, wives' and children's earnings cushioned the wartime squeeze on family finances, even if adult male wage rates were usually at least a half to one-third higher than those paid to women.[44] The productivity and consumption data are also inconsistent and inconclusive, although average per capita food intake may actually have decreased between the later eighteenth and mid-nineteenth centuries, as an increasingly urbanized and industrialized workforce ingested fewer (and less nutritious) calories than agricultural workers required. Demographic findings nevertheless indicate a gradual improvement in both overall life expectancy and infant mortality rates from the mid-eighteenth to the early nineteenth century. Finally, the height studies also point in different directions. The earliest and most comprehensive survey reports a sustained rise in the heights, and hence presumed childhood nutritional status, of male military and naval recruits born from the 1760s to the 1820s. But the statistical bases of this finding have been challenged, while studies of smaller samples of convicts transported to Australia yield diametrically opposite results, showing a marked decline in the heights of both males and females— most pronounced in the case of women—from both rural and urban backgrounds born during the Napoleonic wars.[45]

It may be possible to reconcile some of these discrepancies; for example, over-representation of Londoners among the convicts sampled could help

[44] N. F. R. Crafts, 'Real wages, inequality and economic growth in England, 1750–1850', in P. Scholiers (ed.), *Real Wages in 19th and 20th Century Europe* (1989); S. Horrell and J. Humphries, 'Old questions, new data, and alternative perspectives: families' living standards in the Industrial Revolution', *Journal of Economic History*, 52 (1992).

[45] R. Floud, K. Wachter, and A. S. Gregory, *Height, Health and History: Nutritional Status in the United Kingdom* (1990). J. Komlos, 'The secular trend in the biological standard of living in the United Kingdom, 1740–1860', *EcHR* 46 (1993); S. Nicholas and R. H. Steckel, 'Heights and living standards of English workers during the early years of industrialization, 1770–1815', *Journal of Economic History*, 51 (1991); S. Nicholas and D. Oxley, 'The living standards of women during the Industrial Revolution, 1795–1820', *EcHR* 46 (1993); R. V. Jackson, 'The heights of rural-born English women convicts transported to New South Wales', *EcHR* 49 (1996).

account for their apparently less favoured nutritional status, as compared with soldiers and sailors. However, an aggregate standard of living index for the period 1750–1815 could only be obtained by smoothing out substantial gender, occupational, and regional variations, and in the process blurring real differences between the experiences of north and south, industry and agriculture, men and women. Even if this task were feasible, its completion would still leave two major puzzles. First, did changes in living standards, however defined, and in whatever direction, occur because of, or despite, industrialization (bearing in mind the unprecedented demographic pressures of the later eighteenth century, the prolonged run of bad harvests which coincided with the strains of war during the 1790s and 1800s, and the still relatively limited scale of the industrial as compared with the agricultural labour force)? Even more problematic is the question of how those most directly affected by the impact of economic change among the mass of the population perceived their situation. We know that enclosures were generally unpopular among the rural poor, but little direct testimony survives about the attitudes of labouring men and women towards mechanized factory work, or urban-industrial squalor. Internal migration trends (discussed further below) suggest that many people voted with their feet, for reasons adequately implied by aristocratic condemnation of 'great manufacturing towns', where labour shortages meant 'the workman demands excessive wages, is insolent, abandoned, and drunk half the week'.[46] Yet we should not suppose that contemporaries were any more single-minded in their attitudes towards the emergent industrial society than we are about its modern manifestations.

Regional and National Dimensions

Economic change and industrial growth were not evenly distributed across England, let alone Britain, during the two-thirds of a century before 1815. Dynamic development occurred in distinct, cohesive, and specialized economic regions, notably southern Lancashire and parts of the adjoining counties of Derbyshire and Cheshire (cotton), the West Riding of Yorkshire (wool), Shropshire (iron), the Staffordshire Potteries (ceramics), Birmingham and Warwickshire (metalworking), Tyneside (coal, iron, salt, glass), and Cornwall (copper- and tin-mining and smelting). With its large population base and advanced manufacturing and service sectors—docks, warehouses, shipbuilding, engineering, financial, government, and legal institutions, printing, publishing, silk-weaving, entertainment and luxury trades—London constituted an economic region in itself. Although not the scene of dramatic economic change, the capital had already reached a relatively sophisticated stage of industrial development, 'where spinning, weaving, baking, brewing, and candle-making

---

[46] *The Torrington Diaries Containing the Tours through England and Wales of the Hon. John Byng*, ed. C. B. Andrews (1936), iii. 115.

were no longer done by housewives'.[47] De-industrialization also exhibited a regional character. Besides the decline of East Anglian and West Country textile manufacturing, the later eighteenth century saw the final disappearance of the iron industry from the Kentish Weald, and the eclipse of Whitehaven and the Cumberland coalfields; towards its end Shropshire iron-making and Cornwall non-ferrous mining were both fading fast.

Many, if not most, industrial enterprises depended on one or more of the following: running water as a power source and/or means of processing; a workforce with occasional or part-time agricultural commitments; ready access to coal and other minerals. So the regions and their industries tended to retain to varying degrees a rural character, despite the growing cheapness and efficiency of steam-power, which enabled mills to cluster together away from waterside sites. They also incorporated urban centres, providing financial, legal, retail, transport, and other services. Some handicraft manufacturing was a feature of most long-established provincial capitals, but the eighteenth century also saw the rapid expansion of towns mainly preoccupied with various industries. In 1776 Adam Smith referred to 'the manufactures of Leeds, Halifax, Sheffield, Birmingham, and Wolverhampton', while a German visitor the previous year reported Birmingham 'a very large and thickly populated town, where almost everyone is busy hammering, punching, pounding, rubbing and chiseling'.[48] Around each of these urban centres clustered smaller towns and industrial villages, whose artisan outworkers often specialized in particular lines, like the shoe buckles described as the 'staple manufacture' of Walsall in the Black Country, the saddler's ironmongery of nearby Bloxwich, and Willenhall's tobacco boxes.[49]

Although industry and towns were far from synonymous, industrial and urban growth were closely interrelated. Town-dwellers both consumed and produced manufactured goods, while the expanding market which they created for foodstuffs and other agricultural produce enhanced the farming sector's ability to purchase the fruits of industry. Concentration of specialized commercial and industrial services, not least skilled labour, in and around towns was a significant advantage for urban businessmen, who also benefited from easy access to an increasingly dense road and water transport infrastructure, as necessary for obtaining supplies of fuel and raw materials as for distributing finished goods.

So it is not surprising that both the number and size of urban centres, and the proportion of the population living in them, continued to grow strongly throughout the later eighteenth and early nineteenth centuries. According to

[47] M. George, *London Life in the Eighteenth Century* (1930), 169.

[48] *Wealth of Nations*, i. 431; *Lichtenberg's Visits to England*, ed. M. Mare and W. H. Quarrell (1938), 98–9.

[49] W. Pitt, *General View of the Agriculture of the County of Stafford* (1794), quoted *EHD, 1783–1832*, 521–2.

one estimate the urban component of England's population rose from a quarter to a third between 1776 and 1811; another suggests a rise from 23 per cent to 31 per cent of the population living in towns of more than 2,500 inhabitants between 1750 and 1801. The number of such towns in England and Wales together increased from 104 in 1750 to 188 at the century's end. By that time England was among the world's most urbanized countries, and the rate of urban growth had still not peaked. With one million inhabitants London—the largest city in Europe, and close to the biggest in the world—continued to head the urban league table. But in relative terms the capital's predominance had somewhat declined, since its share of national population remained steady at around 9 per cent, whereas the biggest provincial centres (with populations of between 20,000 and 100,000) more than doubled their share of the total urban population over the previous half-century. This same demographic shift saw Manchester and Liverpool displace Bristol and Norwich as the country's second- and third-largest towns, with Birmingham, Leeds, and Sheffield following close behind: an observer noted disapprovingly in 1792 that 'Birmingham, Manchester, and Sheffield, swarm with inhabitants'.[50]

The remarkable growth of the Northern and Midlands industrial centres during the second half of the eighteenth century resulted largely from migration, not natural increase. Underlying this major population movement was another significant regional phenomenon, the reversal of the traditional north–south wages differential. Within one generation, from the 1760s to the 1790s, the level of money wages paid to craftsmen in Manchester, and to Lancashire agricultural labourers, rose from a little lower to substantially higher than what their counterparts in southern England received. Thus in the late 1760s Buckinghamshire farm workers were paid on average eight shillings a week, 20 per cent above the Lancashire rate; but by the mid-1790s a Lancashire day-labourer's wage was more than ten shillings, or over a third higher than in Buckinghamshire, where money wages actually fell during those same thirty years. This dramatic turnabout, which transformed the previously low-wage Midlands and North into the nation's pace-setting pay zone, was clearly a twin consequence of industry's insatiable demand for labour and the difficulties facing regions where population increase was not accompanied by industrialization.[51]

Although we have concentrated on developments within England, a regional, rather than indiscriminately national, approach would take account of the emergence of Glasgow and the Clyde Valley as Britain's second-largest cotton-spinning and weaving area, the site of New Lanark mill (where Robert Owen developed his critique of competitive capitalism), together with major coal-mining, iron, shipbuilding, and engineering industries. Coal and iron in Wales,

[50] *Torrington Diaries*, iii. 32.
[51] E. H. Hunt, 'Wages', in *Atlas of Industrializing Britain, 1780–1814*, ed. J. Langton and R. J. Morris (1986).

both north and south, and linen in Ulster, should also be added to the list. Nor should human contributions from across the borders be overlooked, such as those made by Irish canal-building navvies and Scots engineers to the construction of England's transport and mechanical infrastructure. To this extent it is not absurd to speak of British rather than merely English industrialization.

Revolution or Evolution?

The term 'industrial revolution' implies a fundamental and rapid transformation of England's economy and society. But how long can a revolution last before losing its revolutionary character? While constitutional and political revolutions typically take the form of short sharp shocks to, or reversals of, the status quo, economic and social change is by its nature likely to involve more complex processes, continuing for decades, if not centuries. Yet a broad distinction between political and other revolutions aggravates the problem of periodization, since an *industrial* revolution can hardly be expected to possess a clearly marked starting point or finishing post. Exactly when the English transition from an agricultural to a commercial-industrial basis of economic and social life began or ended is impossible to say. No doubt the process commenced before 1750 and continued long after 1815. But have we sufficient evidence for a quickening tempo of change over the intervening sixty-five years to justify regarding this period as at least the decisive initial phase of the world's first industrial revolution?

Much recent quantitative research has tended to emphasize the relatively limited extent and nature of socio-economic transformation before the end of the Napoleonic wars. Although it is possible to trace a continuous thread of technological innovation in manufacturing and agriculture back to the later seventeenth century and before (see above, Ch. 10), the immediate impact of these changes on national productivity, as measured by economic growth rates, seems relatively slight. Thus estimated gross domestic product increased at something less than 1 per cent per annum between 1700 and 1780, rising to 1.4 per cent from 1780 to 1800, and then to an annual rate of 1.9 per cent over the next thirty years. Industrial (i.e. non-agricultural) growth turned in a slightly more impressive performance, averaging perhaps 2 per cent or a little over in the 1780s and 1790s, then possibly reaching as much as 2.7 per cent over the first decade of the new century.[52] Although showing a generally upwards trend since *c.*1700, and perceptible acceleration towards the end of the eighteenth century, these figures are well below the growth rates achieved by modern industrializing societies, and substantially less than those for mid-nineteenth-century Britain.

[52] *EHB* 47; R. V. Jackson, 'Rates of industrial growth during the industrial revolution', *EcHR* 45 (1992), 19.

Yet aggregate output statistics depend upon exceedingly fragile and frag-mentary evidence, while illuminating only part of the total picture. Far from constituting reliable and comprehensive series, the limited nature of the output data means that modern estimates for some key industries show truly alarming discrepancies; for example, the production of coal during the first half of the eighteenth century is variously estimated to have grown at a compound annual rate of 0.64 per cent, or alternatively at nearly twice that pace (1.13 per cent). Aggregate figures also blur crucial differences between the experience of dif-ferent regions and industries, over what was still in some respects a highly localized economy (if not a federation of local economies). They also tend to encourage a mistaken assumption that 'the industrial revolution and growth are virtually interchangeable concepts'.[53] Yet qualitative or structural change, such as investment in new technology, was not necessarily and immediately fol-lowed by quantitative expansion of output. Some early steam-powered cotton mills were expensive disasters for their owners. Other industries which under-went considerable restructuring in the later eighteenth and early nineteenth centuries (such as woollen textiles and paper manufacturing) experienced lower growth rates than sectors relatively uninfluenced by mechanization or organizational change (like coal-mining, where the widespread adoption by the mid-eighteenth century of Newcomen engines for pumping water had no effect on hand-hewing techniques at the coal-face).

This last example reminds us that technological change itself was a long-drawn-out process, with origins dating back, if not to the dawn of time, cer-tainly well before the eighteenth century, despite the accelerating tempo of invention and innovation apparent from the 1760s onwards. Apart from schol-arly conservatism and convenience, what sustains the concept of an English industrial revolution in the face of revisionist and quantifying doubt is the evident bunching of associated demographic, economic, and social change throughout the later eighteenth and early nineteenth centuries. Significant de-velopments (outlined above) in agriculture, transport, banking and finance, the management and organization of work, the composition and remuneration of the labour force, economic theory, and urban growth complemented the re-markable dynamism of cotton and iron, while extending their influence well beyond the industrial North and Midlands.

Contemporary awareness of living through a period of great change was widespread:

> All things are changed, the world's turned upside down
> And every servant wears a cotton gown.

according to the two 'aged females' who deplore the rising generation in a poem written by Susanna Blamire (1747–94) around the year 1776. In the early 1790s

---

[53] J. Hoppit, 'Counting the Industrial Revolution', *EcHR*, 43 (1990), 180, 187.

another author referred to 'times which are passed, before manufactures and commerce enriched us'; a parliamentary Select Committee of 1806 assumed that the 'rapid and prodigious increase in the manufactures and commerce of this country is universally known'. In a work published next year the former radical Robert Southey (1774–1843) asserted that 'no kingdom ever experienced so great a change in so short a course of years ... as England has done during the present reign'; among the changes Southey identified were 'the invention of the steam engine' and 'the manufacturing system carried to its utmost point'.[54] Even the novelist Jane Austen, whose portrayals of genteel family life in rural southern England are seemingly far removed from the bustling worlds of commerce and industry, wrote 'a lampoon of modernization' in her final, unfinished novel *Sanditon*. Composed during the last months of her life (January–March 1817), *Sanditon* satirizes consumerism, fashion, patent medicines, and speculative property-developers, like the energetic Mr Parker, whose efforts to promote the small Sussex village of Sanditon as a 'young & rising bathing-place' mirror the new middle-class fad for seaside holidays, a taste which in due course would come to be shared by the working masses, at Blackpool and elsewhere.[55]

[54] *New Oxford Book of Eighteenth-Century Verse*, 647; T. Ruggles, *The Barrister* (1794), i. 15; *EHD, 1783–1815*, 505; R. Southey, *Letters from England* (1807), 200.
[55] O. MacDonagh, *Jane Austen: Real and Imagined Worlds* (1991), ch. 7.

PART VI

Reform, Revolution, Reaction
1789–1815

17

RADICALS, REFORMERS, AND THE FRENCH REVOLUTION

Radical and Reformist Traditions

In 1781 the clergyman economist Dean Josiah Tucker (1712–99) attacked English supporters of the American rebels, claiming that among other 'gross errors and absurdities', they must logically uphold the principle that 'not even women nor children ought to be excluded from the right of voting'. Yet seven years later a London audience characterized as 'numerous and polite' endorsed the proposition that 'the extraordinary abilities of the ladies in the present age demand academical honours from the universities', together with the rights both to vote and stand for Parliament. Few who heard or participated in this public debate would have regarded themselves as radicals or reformers. The former term was not yet in common use, and it seems likely that 'rational entertainment', not the promotion of constitutional or social change, was the main purpose of the evening. Nevertheless, this was by no means the first time that one of the numerous public debating societies and venues which flourished in London and some larger provincial towns during the later eighteenth century had discussed the political rights and status of women. Thus even before the French Revolution challenged the legitimacy of England's whole social and political system, so fundamental a matter as the theoretical male monopoly of public life had come under extra-parliamentary questioning and scrutiny.[1]

No detailed account of the substance of this debate survives; virtually the only evidence for it and similar events takes the form of brief newspaper advertisements and reports. But even if the proceedings were not entirely straight-faced, any serious advocacy of civic equality for women would have invoked the natural-rights arguments increasingly deployed from *c*.1760 onwards to justify extension of the parliamentary franchise and associated political reforms. Originally voiced by Leveller spokesmen in the mid-seventeenth century, and further elaborated by Locke, this intellectual strategy depended on the premiss that all humans were originally endowed by God with mental and moral capacities equal in kind, if not in degree. Thanks to that natural equality, any restriction on the people's rights to determine the laws under which they lived through their choice of government could be regarded as a human denial

---

[1] R. L. Schuyler (ed.), *Josiah Tucker: A Selection from his Economic and Political Writings* (1931), 424, 425; *London Debating Societies, 1776–1799*, ed. D. T. Andrew, London Record Society, 30 (1994), 223, 97, 111, 135, 146, 181.

of the original Divine purpose. The subversive potential of insistence upon universal natural rights divorced from the possession of property meant that during the half-century or so after 1688 Locke's ideas were eclipsed by a 'Country' opposition ideology, which sought to safeguard the ancient constitution, traditional liberties, and civic virtues of free-born Englishmen against the corrupting influences of commerce and an overpowerful 'Court', or executive. But from the early 1760s the influence of Locke, or at least of natural-rights arguments building upon aspects of his thought, revived with a vengeance.[2]

The emergence of 'ultra-Lockian radicalism' among Wilkites, supporters of the insurgent American colonists, and the County Association movement for parliamentary reform in 1779–80 (see above, pp. 195–8, 214, 215–16) did not wholly replace earlier appeals to law and history. Thus Dr Jebb's call in 1780 for adult male suffrage, annual Parliaments, elections by secret ballot, and salaried members of Parliament invoked the dictates of reason and 'the natural feelings of mankind', while also asserting that these very measures had been 'substantially' enjoyed in the times of King Alfred. Next year Wyvill's Yorkshire Association similarly juxtaposed 'the natural rights of men and the ancient privileges of Englishmen' to buttress their less ambitious reform agenda. However, some 'friends of liberty' now began to elevate natural over historical rights, contrasting 'the evil principle of the feudal system, with his dark auxiliaries, ignorance and false philosophy and the good principle of increasing commerce, with her liberal allies, true learning and sound reasoning'. In this progressive scenario, inherited constitutional forms carried less weight than 'the true theory and genuine principles of freedom', understanding of which had supposedly unfolded with economic expansion and 'the great transactions of the last century' (that is, the civil war and Glorious Revolution).[3]

Religious millenarianism, an expectation of some imminent more or less apocalyptic change ushering in the last days of the world, reinforced a secular sense of expanding political enlightenment. Among those so influenced were leading Rational Dissenters like the ministers Priestley and Price, together with the well-to-do manufacturers, merchants, and professional men who formed their congregations in London, the West Country, the Midlands, and the industrializing North. Rational Dissent played a key role in the various overlapping reform initiatives which from the 1770s onwards sought to remodel not only Parliament, but the courts and the legal system, the prisons and hospitals, the administration of government, the poor law, and the universities. Agitation for the repeal of discriminatory legislation against Protestant Dissent continued in the 1780s even after the Association movement for parliamentary

---

[2] J. C. D. Clark, *The Language of Liberty, 1660–1832* (1994), 143; H. T. Dickinson, *The Politics of the People in Eighteenth-Century England* (1995), 184–5; J. Cannon, *Parliamentary Reform, 1640–1832* (1973), 96.

[3] S. Maccoby (ed.), *The English Radical Tradition* (1966), 36–9, 40; 'Speech . . . 28 May 1782', in *The Works of Sir William Jones* (1799), vi. 719–20.

reform had temporarily run out of steam. Indeed Rational Dissenters increasingly professed a willingness to extend to Roman Catholics the same absolute liberty of religious belief and practice which they were demanding for themselves.

Yet three successive attempts between 1787 and 1790 to repeal the Test and Corporation Acts were voted down in the House of Commons, on the last occasion by an increased margin, before the bill even reached the Lords. Reform of any kind was obviously still far from commanding majority support, either within or outside Parliament. Significant differences also separated opportunist politician-aristocrats like Fox (who hardly commanded a united Whig opposition) from middle-class extra-parliamentary radical activists such as Jebb, high-minded evangelical MPs like Wilberforce, or a committed single-issue campaigner like Major John Cartwright. So it is hardly surprising that the would-be reformers failed to present a coherent and united front on various central issues, such as the extent to which religious belief should be treated as a purely private matter, or whether the franchise might safely be extended to the poor and propertyless. Although much of what they advocated did eventually come to pass (if well after our period, and with some conspicuous exceptions, such as annual Parliaments and disestablishment of the Church of England), we should not take their ultimate triumph for granted, nor write off their opponents as wholly self-interested and intellectually negligible.

It is also important to recognize that for many contemporaries parliamentary and ecclesiastical reform seemed less feasible or urgent than amelioration of the costs and efficiency of government (economical reform), improvements in both the substance and administration of the law, and what might be broadly characterized as reformation of the nation's morals and manners. These various objectives were pursued both by committed individuals like Thomas Clarkson (1760–1846), the campaigner against slavery, or the Whig lawyer-politician Samuel Romilly (1757–1818), whose long-term parliamentary agitation for criminal law reform came to fruition only after his death, and numerous more or less well-organized lobbies and pressure groups. Such bodies might either concentrate on influencing the political and social elite (like Wilberforce's Proclamation Society), or (as with the anti-slavery London Abolition Society and its provincial offshoots) seek to mobilize an irresistible force of public opinion behind their cause, through newspaper advertisements, pamphlets, public meetings, and parliamentary petitions. The variety of aims and methods which characterized the later eighteenth and early nineteenth century reform impulse was matched by a great diversity of outcomes. Thus much economical reform, and the abolition of the slave trade, were both achieved long before the first parliamentary Reform Act of 1832. Another relatively early reform measure was Charles Fox's Libel Act of 1792, which provided that in criminal trials juries might determine not only whether particular words had actually been published by the defendant, but also whether their intent and effect were indeed libellous, instead of reserving this crucial question of law and fact for a judge to decide.

One major stumbling-block in the path of would-be reformers was George III's known hostility to any change in existing constitutional or, especially, ecclesiastical arrangements. For a few months from October 1788 the King's incapacitating mental illness (now thought to have resulted from the hereditary disease porphyria) and the proposed regency of his disaffected and dissolute elder son and heir, Fox's drinking companion, seemed to offer a way around that obstacle. True, in demanding that his young ally be granted full and immediate royal powers, Fox found himself maintaining a view of the relative authority of Crown and Parliament entirely at odds with his previous constitutional stance, and more akin to that of his arch-rival Pitt. For his part the prime minister, in resisting a change which would have guaranteed his own dismissal from office, argued a Whiggish case for parliamentary supremacy, which would have seen the Prince of Wales appointed regent for only a year's term and with limited powers, while the royal assent required for the necessary legislation was provided by a body of parliamentary commissioners. However, in February 1789 the widely acclaimed news of a royal recovery curtailed the bizarre political acrobatics of the Regency crisis, and with them Foxite hopes of superseding Pitt. After focusing on the opening stages in the trial of Warren Hastings, political attention turned largely to matters overseas, including confrontations between English and Spanish ships in Nootka Sound off Vancouver Island, a nationalist uprising in the Austrian Netherlands, and the developing crisis of the French monarchy.

'Bliss was it in that Dawn to be Alive'

'Very great rebellion in France' was how the Norfolk clergyman James Woodforde (1740–1803) recorded the fall of the Bastille in his diary for July 1789. His learned Whig fellow-cleric Dr Samuel Parr (1747–1825) reportedly celebrated the news by dancing around a Tree of Liberty, while an elated Fox rhapsodized: 'How much the greatest event it is that ever happened in the world! & how much the best!'[4] These 'friends of civil and religious liberty' assumed that France had at last moved to reject arbitrary power in Church and State, thereby following England's auspicious example set to the nations of Europe a hundred years before. The Dissenting ministers, lawyers, and merchants who had met in London a year before to commemorate the centenary of the Glorious Revolution with dinner and a sermon found their number remarkably augmented on 5 November 1789. The veteran activist Dr Richard Price, 'disdaining national partialities', moved a congratulatory address from the Revolution Society to the National Assembly in Paris. He hoped that their

---

[4] *The Diary of a Country Parson: The Rev. James Woodforde, 1758–1802*, ed. J. Beresford (1924–31), iii. 124. W. Derry, *Dr Parr* (1966), 128; L. G. Mitchell, *Charles James Fox* (1992), 111.

'glorious example' might encourage others to 'assert the *unalienable* rights of mankind, and thereby to introduce a general reformation in the governments of Europe', which would 'make the world free and happy'. The sermon or 'Discourse on the Love of our Country' delivered by Price at this same occasion had an equally optimistic, quasi-millenarian conclusion. It also attacked 'defects' and 'absurdities' of 'our established codes of faith and worship', while criticizing recent loyal addresses to the King on his recovery 'from the severe illness with which God has been pleased to afflict him' as excessively adulatory ('civil governors are properly the servants of the people'). Price's condemnation of continued discrimination against Dissenters, and political 'inequality of representation' gave added point to his stirring peroration, which urged all 'friends of freedom' to take heart from 'the light you have struck out, after setting America free, reflected to France', while warning the 'oppressors of the world' to 'consent to the correction of abuses, before they and you are destroyed together'.[5]

Many who shared none of Price's prejudices, or principles, nevertheless welcomed the Revolution simply because it seemed likely to distract and weaken England's hereditary enemy. But the more idealistic and generous thrilled to the dawning of a new and better age: 'From hence we are to date a long series of years, in which France and the whole human race are to enter into possession of their liberties', wrote the novelist and philosopher William Godwin (1756–1836) in the *New Annual Register* for 1789. The artisan book-engraver and poet William Blake proclaimed his revolutionary sympathies by wearing the 'bonnet rouge', the red cap of liberty, on the streets of London.[6] Another poet, William Wordsworth (1770–1850), was still a Cambridge undergraduate when he first visited France in 1790. Later he recalled his elevated state of mind in a famous phrase:

> Bliss was it in that dawn to be alive
> But to be young was very heaven!

Wordsworth and his young friends believed that they were witnessing the birth of a new age:

> When Reason seemed the most to assert her rights . . .
> Not favoured spots alone, but the whole Earth,
> The beauty wore of promise—that which sets . . .
> The budding rose above the rose full blown.
> What temper at the prospect did not wake
> To happiness unthought of?
>
> . . . .

---

[5] *An Abstract of the History of the Proceedings of the Revolution Society in London* (1789); A. Cobban (ed.), *The Debate on the French Revolution, 1789–1800* (1963), 59–64.

[6] Cf. P. Ackroyd, *Blake* (1995), 155–6; J. A. Epstein, *Radical Expression: Political Language, Ritual and Symbol in England, 1790–1850* (1994), ch. 3.

Not in Utopia—subterranean fields,—
Or some secreted island, Heaven knows where!
But in the very world, which is the world
Of all of us,—the place where, in the end,
We find our happiness, or not at all!
                        (*The Prelude* (1805–6), vi. 108–44)

Burke and Paine

Many shared in these sentiments, or at least believed that 'dissolution of the despotism in France, effected at first without bloodshed or apparent struggle, would be a fortunate event for mankind'.[7] Nor was it until the massacres following Louis XVI's overthrow in August 1792 that the promise of the new French dawn began to sour, and not even then for Blake, Wordsworth, and many like-minded sympathizers. However, the individual who became the Revolution's most famous English antagonist had expressed misgivings about the course of events across the Channel almost from the fall of the Bastille in July 1789. In a dramatic speech to the House of Commons some six months later, Edmund Burke broke publicly with his former Whig allies by denouncing the principles and proceedings of the French revolutionaries. He also warned that England now faced the threat of being led to 'an imitation of the excesses of an irrational, unprincipled, proscribing, confiscating, plundering, ferocious, bloody, and tyrannical democracy', by 'wicked persons' (notably Dr Price, whose 'Discourse' of November 1789 Burke had read on its publication in January 1790).[8] Both the substance of these sentiments and their highly charged language foreshadowed the appearance in November 1790 of the most famous political pamphlet in the English language, Burke's *Reflections on the Revolution in France and on the Proceedings of Certain Societies in London relative to that Event.*

The fundamental point of this former passionate defender of the American Revolution was that its French sequel must not be welcomed as a belated re-enactment of Britain's Glorious Revolution. Whereas that had been an essentially moderate, conservative event, 'made to preserve our *ancient* indisputable laws and liberties', France was now plunged by her 'men of theory' into a novel and dangerous experiment. This 'most astonishing thing that has hitherto happened in the world' threatened 'a general earthquake' to the established institutions of Church and State. Its destructive tendencies recalled not 1688–9, but the disastrous civil wars of the mid-seventeenth century. By the same token, the republican sentiments recently addressed to the Revolution Society by Dr Price resembled the regicide pulpit rhetoric of 1648.

---

[7] P. C. Scarlett, *A Memoir of the Right Honourable James, First Lord Abinger* (1877), 36.
[8] E. Burke, *Works*, ed. F. Wills (1906), iii. 277.

Burke nevertheless maintained that Price (this 'political divine' or 'professor of metaphysic'), and those of his lay followers who shared a similarly doctrinaire approach to constitutional change, were entirely unrepresentative of the English people:

Because half a dozen grasshoppers under a fern make the field ring with their importunate chink, whilst hundreds of great cattle, reposed beneath the shadow of the British oak, chew the cud and are silent, pray do not imagine, that those who make the noise are the only inhabitants of the field; that of course, they are many in number; or that, after all, they are other than the little shrivelled, meagre, hopping, though loud and troublesome insects of the hour.

On the contrary, Burke claimed, 'thanks to our sullen resistance to innovation', the abstract principles of the Enlightenment philosophers had as yet made little progress in England, where 'we are generally men of untaught feelings', with little trust in 'naked reason': 'We have real hearts of flesh and blood beating in our bosoms. We fear God; we look up with awe to kings; with affection to parliaments; with duty to magistrates; with reverence to priests; and with respect to nobility.'[9]

This passionate counterrevolutionary appeal to experience, law, nature, religion, and tradition, over abstraction, idealism, reason, and theory sold perhaps 19,000 copies in its first six months of publication. The ensuing paper war generated over a hundred published rebuttals and twice as many pamphlets broadly supporting Burke's position. The first hostile response, a *Vindication of the Rights of Man* by the young Anglo-Irish radical author Mary Wollstonecraft (later to become William Godwin's wife), claimed that Burke was callously defending the rights of property at the expense of the poor, while his pessimistic arguments from history and prescription amounted to no more than the proposition that 'time sanctifies crimes'. But the most formidable and successful rejoinder came in March 1791, when the seasoned Anglo-American controversialist Thomas Paine (1737–1809) brought out Part I of his *Rights of Man*, a work which may have sold no fewer than 50,000 copies during its first three months in print, and perhaps as many as 200,000 over the next three years.[10]

Burke, the veteran Anglo-Irish politician, and Paine, son of a Norfolk maker of stays (or corsets), actually had more in common than their former friendship and American sympathies. Both were self-made men of letters, although Burke received a gentleman's education and aristocratic Whig patronage, whereas young Tom was taken away from school at the age of 12 to be apprenticed to his father's trade. After unsuccessfully trying various occupations, Paine emigrated to America in 1774. There the popularity of his pro-independence

[9] E. Burke, *Reflections on the Revolution in France*, ed. C. C. O'Brien (1968), 92, 94–5, 118–19, 181–3.
[10] M. Philp (ed.), *The French Revolution and British Popular Politics* (1991), 5; J. Ehrman, *The Younger Pitt: The Reluctant Transition* (1983), 77.

pamphlet *Common Sense* earned him fame and office, including a diplomatic mission to France, where he made an impression on advanced political circles, as he had done in America. Brought up a Quaker, Paine's own religious stance was Deist and anticlerical; his republicanism reflected both a robust suspicion of hereditary privilege and optimistic faith in the rational capacities of ordinary folk. The plain, conversational style of his writing contrasts sharply with Burke's theatrical rhetoric (characterized by Paine himself as 'the spouting rant of high-toned exclamation').[11]

The brevity, clarity, and determined reasonableness of Paine's *Rights of Man* go far towards explaining its runaway initial success. Paine kept his case simple, in essence asserting that Burke's account of the revolution in France was blatant propaganda which totally ignored the plight of the French people under the *ancien régime*. By concentrating instead on the purported sufferings of Louis XVI and his queen at the hands of the Paris mob, Burke 'pities the plumage, but forgets the dying bird'. Custom, precedent, and prescription, which for Burke embodied the wisdom of the ages, Paine denigrated as 'badges of ancient oppression', asserting that no previous generation could bind its successors, nor detract from their natural and civil rights ('government is for the living, not for the dead'). All regimes originating other than by the free consent of the sovereign people must be the product of force, or fraud. Hereditary monarchies, like Britain's, with their attendant corruptions—specified and condemned in detail—were doomed to replacement by democratic republics, as the rapid ascent of reason overcame ignorance and superstition in all spheres.[12]

Jacobins and Loyalists

Burke had sought to arouse the educated and propertied elite, by showing how recent developments in France imperilled what George III neatly characterized as 'the cause of the gentlemen'.[13] Yet the cautious initial reception of the *Reflections* by Pitt and his ministerial colleagues, not to mention Fox and the Whig grandees, reflected widespread scepticism towards Burke's alarmist stance among his intended audience, at least until the Revolution took a decidedly more radical and bloodthirsty turn in 1792. Paine, who 'possessed the peculiar art of addressing the people in a plain, forcible, and interesting manner', may have aimed at a more plebeian readership. But many of the middling and upper sort found his critique well informed and persuasive, especially so long as the actual course of events across the Channel scarcely seemed to bear out Burke's grimmer predictions. Moreover, Paine's scathing attack on the shortcomings of Britain's existing political institutions in the light of recent French constitutional reforms echoed long-standing dissatisfactions with

---

[11] T. Paine *Rights of Man, Common Sense, and other Political Writings*, ed. M. Philp (1995), 100.

[12] Ibid. 91–2, 95, 102, 117. Cf. R. Dishman (ed.), *Burke and Paine on Revolution and the Rights of Man* (1971).

[13] *The Correspondence of Edmund Burke*, ed. T. Copeland (1958–78), vi. 237–9.

domestic political abuses and anomalies. So it is hardly surprising that the *Rights of Man* was 'read and approved by many whose sentiments were in general by no means favourable to republicanism'.[14]

The wide circulation of Paine's views outside the ranks of the propertied political nation, assisted by special cheap editions of his *Rights of Man* printed and distributed by radical clubs, and the continuing pamphlet warfare between Burke's opponents and supporters, coincided with a revival and extension of earlier reform campaigns. The Society for Constitutional Information stepped up its propaganda activities and welcomed a trickle of new, more radically inclined members, even as some veteran reformers like Christopher Wyvill were worrying that Paine had 'formed a party for the republic among the lower classes of the people, by holding out to them the prospect of plundering the rich'.[15] The publication in February 1792 of the second part of *Rights of Man* only heightened such concerns. Here Paine proposed that the material hardships of the labouring poor should be relieved by the creation of an embryonic welfare state, providing maternity allowances, child endowment, and old age pensions. This development would be entirely feasible once political reform had eliminated the exorbitant taxes which currently maintained an unnecessary monarchy, avaricious aristocrats, parasitic placemen, and an inflated military establishment. Henceforth public debate on the French Revolution and its implications embodied a new and distinct element of class tension, as well as more traditional political and religious divisions.

Besides holding celebratory dinners, publicizing reform activities and principles in newspaper advertisements, and circulating pro-reform literature, the Society for Constitutional Information followed what was now standard procedure for political and social reform movements, by developing an extensive correspondence network. As well as linking similar-minded organizations in London, provincial England, Ireland, and Scotland, it established contacts with individual French republican leaders, and the political clubs in Paris and some provincial centres. Like their predecessors at the time of the American war, the English constitutional associations and societies were initially drawn from the ranks of the socially respectable—lawyers, doctors, Dissenting clergy, merchants, industrialists, and the occasional country gentleman. But the winter of 1791/2 witnessed a momentous new departure in extra-parliamentary politics, with the emergence of the Sheffield Society for Constitutional Information and the London Corresponding Society, since the membership of these radical reform clubs consisted mainly of artisans, journeymen, mechanics, small shopkeepers, and tradesmen.

According to Thomas Hardy (1752–1832), the Scottish-born master bootmaker and devout Dissenter who founded the more famous London

[14] *The New Annual Register, or General Repository of History, Politics, and Literature, for the Year 1793* (1794), 4.

[15] C. Wyvill, *Political Papers* (1804), v. 51, quoted J. Keane, *Tom Paine* (1995), 329.

Corresponding Society, his own political interests, dating back to the 1780s, were reawakened when he perused some pro-reform literature originally circulated by the Society for Constitutional Information. In October 1791 Hardy first met with a few friends at the Bell Inn off the Strand to discuss setting up a society dedicated to advancing the cause of political reform. Membership of the London Corresponding Society, formally constituted the following January, cost one penny a week (comparable to a journeyman's club or trade union), in sharp contrast to the annual subscription of one guinea charged by the Society for Constitutional Information. And whereas that body admitted no more than 133 new members in the three years from April 1791, by late 1792 the London Corresponding Society was claiming over 800 members, each committed to promoting universal manhood suffrage and parliamentary reform 'by all justifiable means'. Following the example of the Sheffield body founded a few months before, and also reminiscent of the practice of London trade unions, members were organized into twenty-nine regional cells or divisions spread across the metropolis. Besides maintaining an elaborate structure of elected office-holders and delegates meeting weekly in General Committee, these local divisions also functioned as adult education classes, with regular 'readings, conversations and discussions'.[16]

The advent of the London Corresponding Society and similar self-styled 'various, numerous and respectable societies' inevitably aroused fears that those whom Burke had memorably termed 'a swinish multitude' were mobilizing against their betters, for all their formal disavowal of 'tumult and violence'. The wide circulation of radical newspapers like the weekly *Sheffield Register* and the *Manchester Herald*, and of pamphlets issued by reform-minded booksellers, journalists, and printers, like Daniel Eaton (d. 1814) and Thomas Spence (1750–1814), inevitably increased these anxieties. In May 1792 a royal proclamation against 'divers wicked and seditious writings . . . tending to excite tumult and disorder', speedily endorsed by both Houses of Parliament, seemed to constitute grudging official admission that Burke's warnings were not entirely exaggerated.

Besides giving free publicity to Part II of the *Rights of Man*, the government's move further split the parliamentary Whig party (whose radical wing had just launched a pro-reform Society of Friends of the People, to Fox's considerable dismay). A still more important effect of the proclamation lay in strengthening the resolve of those who shared Burke's alarm, and accordingly feared that

> . . . if French schemes we imitate
> And pull down Nobles, Church and State
> Believe me, my Countrymen, we're undone![17]

[16] *The Autobiography of Francis Place, 1771–1854*, ed. M. Thale (1972), 129–31.
[17] Cobban, *The Debate on the French Revolution* (1960), 273; 'Ode for his Majesty's Birthday, 1791', in L. H. Halloran, *Poems on Various Occasions* (1791), 56.

According to a near-contemporary account, three distinct political groupings now began to emerge: 'the Tories, or devoted advocates for the royal policy; the Whigs, or constitutional assertors of the rights of the people; and the republicans'. Of these, 'the first were perhaps the most numerous, the latter the most active party'.[18] The conservatism of what was already a far from silent majority owed much in the first instance to long-standing antagonism between Churchmen and Dissenters. Indeed the occasion for establishing provincial reform societies during the early 1790s was frequently the emergence of local 'Church and King' clubs, like that founded by Manchester Anglicans and Tories in March 1790 to celebrate Parliament's failure to repeal the Test and Corporation Acts. In July of the following year their Birmingham counterparts, with the connivance of local magistrates, staged a violent demonstration and riot against those 'Friends of Freedom' who had gathered for a well-publicized banquet to celebrate the second anniversary of the fall of the Bastille. Before attacking the homes of nearly thirty prominent local Dissenters and radicals, including Joseph Priestley, who escaped with his life but lost his laboratory and library, the Church and King mob destroyed Birmingham's two Presbyterian chapels. This last violent action was evidently provoked by Priestley's claim that his writings were 'laying a train of gunpowder, grain by grain, under the old building of error and superstition, which a single spark may hereafter inflame'.[19]

The Birmingham riots of mid-1791, together with less violent disturbances at Manchester and elsewhere, suggested that proponents of the rights of man might have overestimated the extent of their support among the population at large. Of course these outbreaks were not wholly spontaneous manifestations of popular sentiment; as with earlier Sacheverell, anti-Jewish, anti-Methodist, and Wilkite riots, a considerable element of incitement, legitimation, and orchestration by parsons and other authority figures was involved. Nor did the central authorities, for their part, allow Paine and the activists of the reform societies to operate entirely unchecked. The government's initial countermeasures were covert and low-key, including attempts to restrict the circulation of *Rights of Man* by intimidating printers and booksellers, commissioning a scurrilous biography of Paine, and promulgating anti-Painite material in the nine subsidized pro-administration London newspapers. But the proclamation of May 1792, which was devised by Pitt in consultation with the duke of Portland (1738–1809), nominal leader of the parliamentary Whigs, signalled an openly tougher stance (albeit one still 'more precautionary than alarmist').[20] Criminal prosecutions were launched against Paine, his printer, and various booksellers accused of selling radical literature; innkeepers were

[18] *New Annual Register . . . 1793*, 3.

[19] A. Goodwin, *Friends of Liberty* (1979), 145; *An Authentic Account of the Riots at Birmingham* (n.d.), pp. vi, 1–12.

[20] T. C. W. Blanning, *The Origins of the French Revolutionary Wars* (1986), 144.

warned against allowing seditious meetings on licensed premises, and spies sent out to infiltrate the reform societies. Meanwhile public assemblies of local notables held across the country to consider the proclamation forwarded to London nearly 400 addresses of support for government and constitution.

Satisfied with the immediate impact of these measures (not least on the severely divided Whigs), the ministry shrugged off protests about their chilling effect on free speech. At the same time, there was as yet little indication of impending change in Britain's official policy of aloof neutrality towards events in France, despite mounting appeals for intervention from aristocratic French *émigrés*, and growing concern about the course of events in Paris, notably the suspension of the monarchy and imprisonment of the royal family, followed by the widely reported September massacres. While these last atrocities appalled and dismayed even many supporters of the Revolution, Pitt and his colleagues saw as yet no compelling reason why Britain should join the Austrians and Prussians in attempting to reverse its progress by military means. Then a series of unexpected defeats suffered by the counter-revolutionary forces at the hands of the new republic's citizen armies was capped early in November by their crushing defeat at the battle of Jemappes, which left the Austrian Netherlands (Belgium) open to French occupation. The prospect of the entire Low Countries (including the United Provinces, with whom Britain had been formally linked in a defensive alliance since 1788) falling under French control provided the decisive strategic argument to abandon neutrality. Besides the direct threat such a development would pose to British naval supremacy in the Channel and North Sea, the government had also become seriously concerned about the state of internal security. A poor harvest with consequent rising grain prices and food shortages, industrial disputes and bread riots in north-east England, reported stockpiling of arms, the quickening tempo of fraternal addresses and visits between English radicals and French revolutionaries, widespread political and social unrest in Ireland and Scotland, and the enthusiasm which greeted France's military successes: all these portents aroused fears of popular insurrection, fomented by revolutionary agents and their republican British sympathizers. Seeking to counter and if possible overawe pro-French sentiment with a convincing display of national patriotic zeal, the administration encouraged and was itself encouraged by a massive rallying in support of Crown, Church, and Constitution.

On 19 November 1792 the National Convention in Paris endorsed a Fraternal Edict, promising French military aid to export the revolutionary principles of the rights of man to oppressed peoples throughout Europe. Later that month John Reeves (1752?–1829), a middle-aged law officer, legal historian, and former Oxford don with strong ministerial connections, announced the founding of the first 'Association for the Preservation of Liberty and Property against Republicans and Levellers'. Government-funded advertisements appearing in the London and country newspapers under Reeves's name invited 'friends to the established law and to peaceable society' to follow suit in their own neighbourhoods, in order to check 'the progress of such nefarious designs as are meditated by the wicked and senseless reformers of the present time'. The response was overwhelming, doubtless swelled by reaction to the trial and execution of Louis XVI, who went to the guillotine on 21 January 1793. Reeves himself later claimed that no fewer than two thousand loyalist associations had sprung up by February 1793; even if the true figure were half that, and the number of active supporters less than the million suggested by a pro-government journalist, the scale of the loyalist response was absolutely without precedent. Moreover, although the gentry and well-to-do dominated the loyal associations, many much humbler folk joined in their activities. These included mass meetings, collections of signatures for addresses of loyalty to Crown and Parliament, ceremonial burnings in effigy of Tom Paine (complete with stays), and the dissemination of anti-French, pro-constitutional propaganda, directed at both middling and lower orders.[21] Moves early in December to call out the militia and secure the Tower of London, combined with continued rumours of plotting and subversion, doubtless bolstered this overwhelming rejection of the French approach to constitutional change. Its success in turn helped sustain the confidence of Pitt and his colleagues in their resolve to make no concessions to republican, regicidal France.

[21] R. R. Dozier, *For King, Constitution, and Country* (1983).

18

THE LAST FRENCH WARS, 1793–1815

Mobilization and Repression

Despite the powerful loyalist reaction against French revolutionaries and their English sympathizers, France's actual declaration of war on 1 February 1793 evoked widespread misgivings. The cultivated Sussex clergyman Thomas Twining (1735–1804), an anti-democrat who professed disgust at Gallic atrocities (that 'ferocious and butcherly mob'), nevertheless questioned the necessity of hostilities and feared their outcome, correctly predicting that 'war will unite the French nation'.[1] In this respect Twining endorsed the views of Fox, who steadfastly maintained that for all their faults the French people were defending liberty against monarchical despotism, and hence should be treated as allies, not enemies. The underlying implication, that Robespierre posed less of a threat than George III, led inevitably to the disintegration of the Foxite Whigs, although it was not until mid-1794 that Portland formally brought his depleted parliamentary following into coalition with Pitt. But the feasibility, morality, and prudence of war with France continued to be questioned, both inside and outside Parliament, throughout the following two decades, except for two brief periods (1797–8 and 1803–5) when the country was directly threatened by invasion.

Military clashes between Britain and France were no novelty, and this latest round in a long struggle between two 'natural' enemies appeared to open along traditional lines. Three years before, when the Revolution broke out, Britain had had some 40,000 men under arms, about a quarter of the French monarchy's land forces. Since then the peaceful resolution of two potentially serious diplomatic incidents (the Nootka Sound confrontation with Spain in 1790, and a brief crisis over Russia's seizure of the Black Sea port of Ochakov the following year) had encouraged Pitt to slash troop numbers back still further, to around 17,000 men. The army's relative numerical weakness, exacerbated by problems of administration, command, morale, and training, was however offset to some extent by Britain's clear naval pre-eminence. With some 195 ships of the line, more than double the size of the French fleet, Pitt, even more than his father before him, essentially planned to fight a blue-water extra-European war, anticipating only a brief struggle before France capitulated. Military engagements on the Continent were expected to be only small-scale, with hastily hired German mercenaries supplementing native English, Irish, and

---

[1] R. Twining (ed.), *Recreations and Studies of a Country Clergyman of the Eighteenth Century* (1882), 154, 169, 172.

Scots troops. The bulk of military manpower would be provided by European allies, in return for cash payments and diplomatic inducements. Meanwhile Britain's maritime strength not only guaranteed command of the seas, and hence security for the nation's vital commerce, but also held out the promise of significant colonial gains; indeed Pitt's friend William Wilberforce suspected that annexation of the French West Indies was the prime minister's real war goal.[2] However, as events were to show, the prolonged struggle against revolutionary France could not be won outside Europe, nor without a substantial commitment of British men and material.

Some French sugar colonies (Guadeloupe, Martinique, St Lucia, Tobago) were indeed captured by British expeditions during the opening years of the war, but at very high cost, thanks to the ravages of yellow fever, which forced the abandonment of Gaudeloupe towards the end of 1794. By then it was abundantly clear that, contrary to optimistic official expectations, the war in Europe would not be easily and quickly won. Far from forcing France's capitulation and restoration of the Bourbon monarchy, the imperfectly co-ordinated military efforts of Britain, and her subsidized First Coalition partners (Austria, Prussia, Spain, Sardinia, Tuscany, and Naples) had effectively fulfilled the Revd Thomas Twining's prophecy. The revolutionary response to foreign invasion of *la patrie* was mass mobilization, and the application of conscription to Europe's most populous country created the 'nation in arms', a new and awesomely potent military phenomenon.

French citizen armies totalling around half a million men (and rising to some 750,000 by the spring of 1794) repelled allied incursions and consolidated their hold on the Low Countries (with predictably serious strategic consequences in terms of control of the Channel and North Sea, and British vulnerability to invasion). Meanwhile at home the great loyalist upsurge was long past. Some friends of peace, supporters of reform, and republican radicals had been frightened or persuaded into silence. Others continued to agitate in pamphlets, sermons, and newspaper columns, at fastdays, dinners, and public meetings. However, they were now very conscious of representing 'the side which is, for the moment, the least popular', as the secretary to the Society of Friends of the People put it at the end of 1793; he likened the current dominance of 'Tory, or High Church and King opinions' to the royalist reaction in the last years of Charles II.[3] More or less indirect, communal, and private pressures, as when Derbyshire villagers refused to drink with a reputed Jacobin, or the 'bigots and timeservers of Cambridge' expelled the Unitarian reformer William Frend (1757–1841) from his college fellowship, reinforced occasional intimidatory outbreaks of mob violence, and various forms of legal and official coercion.[4]

[2] *EHD, 1783–1832,* 886.

[3] D. Stuart, *Peace and Reform against War and Corruption* (1794), 1–2.

[4] *An Account of the Proceedings in the University of Cambridge against William Frend* (1793), p. ii.

Prosecutions and convictions for sedition rose sharply in 1793. The first of a series of widely reported political trials saw the Edinburgh advocate Thomas Muir (1765–98) and the Dundee Unitarian minister Thomas Fyshe Palmer (1747–1802) sentenced to transportation by a blatantly partisan Edinburgh court for their roles in a national convention of Scots reformers the previous December. A subsequent British Convention met in Edinburgh during the autumn of 1793, attracting delegates from England and the radical nationalist Society of United Irishmen, before it was dispersed by the authorities. Secret operations co-ordinated by the government's spymaster William Wickham (1761–1840) penetrated networks linking reform societies across the three kingdoms with French agents. Their own published propaganda adopted French revolutionary language and symbolism, including the title 'Citizen', while proposing a 'General Convention' to be summoned in the event of any government move 'inimical to the liberties of the people'.[5] The administration responded in May 1794 by arresting Thomas Hardy and other leading lights of what the rising young back-bench MP George Canning (1770–1827) dubbed the 'treasonous societies'.[6] At the same time Parliament agreed to suspend the Habeas Corpus Act, which not only enabled political suspects to be held indefinitely without trial, but intensified the political and cultural isolation of dissidents, liberals, radicals, and reformers.

Dearth and Famine, Discontent and Mutiny

Food rioting, the characteristic popular mode of protest, reached its eighteenth-century peak in the years 1794–6. Two successive harvest failures pushed the price of a quarter of wheat, the staple food grain of the poor throughout most of England, to 75 and then over 78 shillings in 1795–6 (from an average of 43 shillings per quarter in 1792). Although money wages also increased, they generally lagged far behind soaring prices. It has been calculated that after purchasing a minimum wheat-based subsistence diet a Sussex agricultural labourer's family with two children would have had no cash surplus whatever for other food, fuel, clothing, or rent during nine of the twelve months from September 1794. Both humanitarian and prudential motives underlay the decision of the Berkshire JPs, meeting at Speenhamland in May 1795, to subsidize wages from the poor rates whenever they fell short of an agreed minimum scale. This example was widely followed, although—or perhaps because—it forced workers into dependence on parish welfare, rather than compelling employers to pay a living wage. The radical London tailor Francis Place (1771–1854) believed that the purchasing power of his fellow tradesmen's earnings in 1795 was nearly one-third lower than it had been in the 1770s. Modern

---

[5] *At a General Meeting of the London Corresponding Society Held at the Globe Tavern Strand; on Monday the 20th Day of January 1794, Citizen John Martin in the Chair* (1794), 7.

[6] *The Letter-Journal of George Canning, 1793–1795*, ed. P. Jupp (1991), 100.

research suggests that real wage rates for skilled workers in London may have fallen by nearly 15 per cent over the last decade of the eighteenth century.[7] The inflationary effects of bad harvests in 1794–5 were exacerbated by heavy military spending, and the impact of associated government borrowings and taxes.

As early as June 1794 a worried conservative expressed doubts in the privacy of his diary 'about fighting for the wrong of France ... when our country is desolate, our poor oppressed', especially since 'discontent will increase with taxes'.[8] Widespread economic distress, and the lack of military success against France, helped build support for the London Corresponding Society, and similar bodies in Norwich and Sheffield. A further fillip to the radical cause was provided by successive jury acquittals of Thomas Hardy and the young John Thelwall (1764–1834), together with a veteran clergyman radical, John Horne Tooke (1736–1812) of the Society for Constitutional Information, the only three of the 'Twelve Apostles' originally charged with high treason ever actually brought to trial. Reports of 'much discontent in England' and numerous desertions from the Royal Navy were circulating in Dutch newspapers by May 1795.[9] Famine, or at least severe food shortages, and food rioting were now widespread, occasionally involving militia soldiers unable to feed themselves on their meagre daily pay of one shilling. Next month the first of several mass open-air protest meetings held at St George's Fields (where troops had bloodily dispersed Wilkes's supporters nearly thirty years before) attracted at the very least 10,000, and possibly as many as 100,000 people; estimates of attendance at subsequent gatherings in October and November vary even more widely. However, in conjunction with events at the state opening of Parliament that autumn, when an 'immense number of people ... hissed and groaned' the royal procession, and a window in the King's coach was broken, either by a stone or a bullet, these events provided ample pretext for further repressive measures.[10] Pitt's 'Two Acts' radically extended the scope of the crime of treason, made incitement to hatred or contempt of king or constitution a crime punishable by transportation, and subjected all public meetings to the control of local magistrates.

Despite vigorous petitioning against this legislation and some ingenious attempts to evade it ('Citizen' Thelwall, for example, evaded a provision which may have been directed specifically against his popular pro-reform public lectures by rewriting them as a course on 'Classical History, and especially the Laws and Revolutions of Rome'), the Treasonable Practices and Seditious Meetings Acts did help curtail the membership and activities of the radical

---

[7] J. Rule, *Albion's People: English Society, 1714–1815* (1992), 184; L. D. Schwarz, 'The standard of living in the long run: London, 1700–1860', *EcHR* 38 (1985), 31.

[8] *The Torrington Diaries*, ed. C. B. Andrews (1938), iv. 42–3.

[9] Historical Manuscripts Commission, *Report on the Manuscripts of J. B. Fortescue* (1899), iii. 74

[10] *The Autobiography of Francis Place, 1771–1854*, ed. M. Thale (1972), 145–6.

societies.[11] Ever more embattled and harassed, those still committed to working for peace and reform frequently found themselves diverted into unproductive personal and tactical squabbles. Given the difficulty of proceeding as before, they tended either to take up ever-more extreme positions, including the revolutionary-republican option of armed insurrection, or alternatively to withdraw entirely from further political activism. Not all succumbed to these pressures; for example, after his acquittal the sociable parson Horne Tooke played an important role in sustaining the reformist cause, while also working to improve relations between committed democrats and more moderate Foxite parliamentarians. But intimidation and reprisals created a very bleak environment for radicals who did not enjoy Tooke's gentlemanly status and economic independence.

Besides the formidable battery of legal and official measures now arrayed against the administration's critics, a rapid improvement in food supplies by the summer of 1796 lessened one major stimulus to anti-government agitation. It also seems unlikely that the volume of printed propaganda for peace and reform ever matched the enormous output of conservative, loyalist, and patriotic ballads, caricatures, cartoons, newspapers, pamphlets, plays, poems, and tracts. Like the crusading counter-revolutionary pamphlets of the prolific John Bowles (1751–1819), some of this material was government-subsidized, but nevertheless represented the author's own intensely held personal convictions. The evangelical Hannah More certainly required no official urging to counsel the poor against the wiles of democratic agitators in her widely distributed *Village Politics* (1793). Even the libertine Scots poet and democrat Robbie Burns (1759–96) wrote a chauvinistic verse challenge to 'haughty Gaul' and all those who would 'set the mob above the throne' in 1795, although his last couplet suggests a certain lingering political ambiguity:

> And while we sing *God Save the King*
> We'll ne'er forget the People!
> ('The Dumfries Volunteers', 1795)

Invasion fears and threats provided the strongest stimulus to pro-government loyalism, or quietism. The tides of diplomacy and war had both turned against Britain by 1796, after the withdrawal of Prussia and Spain from the First Coalition in 1795, following successful French campaigns in the Low Countries, Spain, and the Rhineland. But while Pitt was prepared to explore the possibility of a negotiated peace with the apparently more moderate Directory which came to power in November 1795, Spain's re-entry to the war as France's ally, followed by the young Napoleon's dazzling victories in 1796–7, hardly encouraged the French to seek terms. Although Britain's maritime strength had permitted the seizure of numerous French and Dutch colonial possessions in the West Indies, Africa, and Asia, these gains made little or no impression on the worsening strategic situation in Europe. Indeed, it was unusually prolonged

---

[11] E. P. Thompson, 'Hunting the Jacobin fox', *P&P* 142 (1994), 95.

bad weather, not the Royal Navy, which prevented a 15,000-strong French expeditionary force from getting ashore at Bantry Bay on Ireland's remote southwest coast in December 1796. Two months later the news that a much smaller French contingent had actually landed at Fishguard in Wales generated widespread panic and threatened a disastrous run on the banks, forcing the government to suspend cash (i.e. non-paper) payments by the Bank of England, notwithstanding the almost immediate surrender of this motley band. Only a hard-fought naval action off Cape St Vincent that same month prevented a much larger Spanish flotilla from uniting with their French allies and thus achieving tactical superiority in numbers, which was the necessary condition for a more successful invasion attempt. The fragility of the nation's maritime shield was further underlined by the eruption in April and May 1797 of a string of naval mutinies, beginning with the Channel fleet based at Portsmouth (Spithead), then spreading, in more serious form, to the North Sea fleet, and ships based at the Nore (in the Thames estuary). The Nore mutineers managed to defy their officers and the government for a month before the revolt collapsed, whereupon thirty-six sailors were summarily court-martialled and hanged from the yardarm. While initially sparked by lower-deck discontent over grossly inadequate pay (sailors' wages had not been raised since the mid-seventeenth century) and miserable shipboard conditions, the form and rhetoric of these events betrayed strong democratic and Painite influences, conveyed via the London Corresponding Society and (through the growing Irish presence among the Royal Navy's largely conscript crews) the clandestine and revolutionary Society of United Irishmen.

Ireland: Rebellion and Union

In Ireland, as in England and Scotland, the French Revolution had given many would-be reformers an uplifting sense of participation 'in a great European drive against tyranny and anachronistic privilege'.[12] Confidence that the obvious righteousness of their cause guaranteed its speedy triumph, mixed with frustration at the continued dominance of Irish government by English interests even after the winning of legislative independence in 1782 (above, pp. 217–18) impelled a mixed group of liberal Dissenters and Catholics to found the Society of United Irishmen at Belfast in October 1790. The following month a Dublin branch emerged, professing its desire 'to make an United Society of the Irish nation; to make all Irishmen citizens—all citizens Irishmen'. The rhetoric of these nationalistically Anglophobe and self-consciously enlightened merchants and professional men was in fact directed at two goals: Catholic emancipation and political reform. Many members of Pitt's administration were favourably predisposed to the first of these demands, particularly since the war with France had created an urgent need to recruit more Irish

---

[12] R. B. McDowell, *Ireland in the Age of Imperialism and Revolution, 1760–1801* (1979), 363.

soldiers, making concessions to the Catholic majority appear prudent as well as just. However, their London-based perspective discounted or ignored the fears and interests of the local Anglo-Irish Protestant ascendancy, now facing an ominous upsurge of Catholic militancy. The conventional pressure-group tactics of the relatively respectable Catholic Committee—whose organizing secretary, the barrister Wolfe Tone (1763–98), also served, however, as the United Irishmen's leading ideologue—were repudiated by the Defenders, an armed, anti-Protestant, lower-class secret society, which, having expanded well beyond its Ulster birthplace, was urging violent solutions to traditional Catholic grievances.

In these circumstances it was not just the Viceroy's administration in Dublin Castle but most Anglo-Irish politicians and their constituents who viewed with alarm the United Irishmen's linkage of an advanced political reform agenda with the granting of full civil rights to Catholics. Revival of the armed Volunteer movement (in uniforms barely distinguishable from those of the French *garde nationale*), and revelations of extensive contacts between Irish liberals and revolutionary Paris naturally added to these concerns. After the declaration of war with France attempts to suppress the United Irishmen were inevitable (the movement was formally outlawed in 1794). So was the failure to enact even token political reform, and the grudging nature of the concessions finally extended to Catholics, which enabled them to vote for, but not sit in, the Dublin Parliament. Disappointed hopes, crowned by the premature recall early in 1795 of Earl Fitzwilliam (1748–1833), Rockingham's heir and now a Portland Whig, whose somewhat naïve attempts as Viceroy to implement total Catholic emancipation had been blocked in London, brought new and sharply radical courses.

The United Irishmen went underground, maintaining close contact with the French government, which undertook to assist an anti-British rising in Ireland in return for Irish help to invade England. While Wolfe Tone prepared the way in Paris, at home sectarian conflict flared. Animosity between Catholic and Protestant artisans and farmers was especially fierce in Ulster's County Armagh, where economic pressures linked to the burgeoning linen trade had for some time sharpened denominational tensions. However the 'Armagh outrages' of 1795–6 brought sectarian rioting and gang warfare to a new level of institutionalized violence, as an ultra-Protestant Orange Order confronted a Catholic-dominated fusion of Defenders and United Irishmen, the latter now actively recruiting among the peasantry. The end of 1796 saw the first of four French attempts to establish a beachhead in Ireland. Despite the aborted landing at Bantry Bay and the decisive defeat (by the recently disaffected North Sea fleet) of another attempted invasion force under Dutch command at the battle of Camperdown in October 1797, the conclusion of the Peace of Campo Formio between Austria and France that same month left England dangerously isolated, and vulnerable. Meanwhile denominational polarization and internal security across St George's Channel had deteriorated to such an extent that the Viceroy in Dublin characterized the whole kingdom as in a state of 'warfare', while simultaneously admitting his government's reliance upon a policy of 'terror' matching that of 'the rebellious'.[13]

In March 1798 a government swoop on United Irishmen meeting in Dublin severely disrupted the movement's leadership and lines of communication. Hence the uncoordinated mass rising-cum-sectarian civil war which sputtered into life two months later south of Dublin, not waiting for the arrival of a French army. The two French forces which did eventually materialize—both little more than raiding parties—came only after 'probably the most concentrated episode of violence in Irish history' had reached its bloody climax, with the army's storming of the rebel camp at Vinegar Hill, County Wexford, on 21 June.[14] By then Pitt had already determined on a formal legislative union as the only means of resolving what had clearly become a major threat to Britain's own security. The growing financial burden which recurrent Irish budget deficits placed on the British taxpayer, and the evident inability of existing government structures to cope with the country's glaring economic, political, and religious problems were further powerful incentives. Abolition of Dublin's corrupt and recalcitrant Parliament would remove a significant sounding-board for Irish nationalism, as well as the possibility of an Irish legislature formulating its own foreign policy in opposition to that of England. Direct representation at Westminster (with 100 Irish seats in the Commons and 32 in the Lords), together with further concessions to the Catholics, might even offer the country a positive way forward, as part of a truly United Kingdom.

Unfortunately the Act of Union which eventually passed in mid-1800 was 'an act of ambiguity, not to say self-contradiction'.[15] The machinery of English colonial rule via Dublin Castle remained, while Ireland's MPs at Westminster represented the Ascendancy minority, not the dispossessed Catholic majority (who continued to be ineligible for public office or return to Parliament until 1829). In any case, mere legislative union could hardly ameliorate long-standing cultural, economic, and religious divisions, let alone erase the potent ideal of a free Ireland taking her rightful place among the nations of the earth. The year 1800 also saw 'the Liberator', Daniel O'Connell (1775–1847) launch his public political career, which would be devoted to the twin goals of Catholic emancipation and repeal of the Act of Union.

A Peace to be Glad of

The 40-year old William Pitt had just commenced his eighteenth year as prime minister when the Act of Union came into force on New Year's Day 1801. No hawk, especially by contrast to the passionate counter-revolutionary Burke,

---

[13] HMC, *Fortescue*, iii. 388–9.   [14] R. Foster, *Modern Ireland, 1600–1972* (1988), 280.
[15] O. MacDonagh, *States of Mind* (1983), 52–5.

from the outset Pitt and his war minister Henry Dundas (1742–1811) were nevertheless determined to resist an expansionist France and its threat to the European balance of power, on which Britain's own security ultimately depended. His enormous energies and talents were accordingly flung into the all-demanding task of wartime administration, at a personal cost reflected in recurrent bouts of ill health, mercurial mood swings, and consumption of port wine in quantities which alarmed even his far from abstemious colleagues.

The strain, on both Pitt and the country, would obviously have been less if the war could have been succesfully concluded. Yet despite nearly eight years of hostilities, military victory seemed as elusive as ever. Instead a stalemate had emerged, with neither France nor Britain able to deal the other a decisive blow, despite their respective dominance on land and at sea. While revolutionary fervour no longer gripped France, partial restoration of internal stability had actually strengthened the country's fighting capacity. Bonaparte's decision not to mount a major invasion of England or Ireland, but rather to strike with maximum force against British interests in the eastern Mediterranean and India, had been indirectly responsible for the failure of the Irish rising in 1798. But after the destruction of his naval force anchored off the Nile estuary in the battle of Aboukir Bay by the dashing Admiral Horatio Nelson (1758–1805), whose victory gained him a peerage and instant national hero status, Napoleon succeeded in escaping from Egypt. His seizure of dictatorial power in November 1799 appeared bound to strengthen France's diplomatic and military potential, especially when the anti-French Second Coalition (of Britain, Russia, Austria, Turkey, Portugal, and Naples) constructed by Pitt and his foreign secretary Lord Grenville (1759–1834) earlier that same year seemed to unravel even faster than its predecessor.

The unsatisfactory situation abroad added weight to mounting pressures for peace, both within and outside Parliament. There had been intermittent negotiations with France since 1796, varying in intensity and seriousness with the changing strategic balance. But the economic burdens of war, including escalating direct taxes, notably the massively unpopular income tax first introduced in 1799, and widespread disruption to industry and trade, were accentuated in 1799–1800 by the decade's second major harvest failure and food crisis. In February 1800 the Revd James Woodforde worried that the price of wheat at Norwich market had reached an unprecedented 120 shillings a quarter, with consequent 'very great grumbling amongst the poor'. Twelve months later a Lancashire businessman feared that 'the high price of provisions' had broken 'every link that bound subjects to government'.[16] By mid-1801 thirty persons were being held on suspicion of involvement in treasonable activities. Government informants from Lancashire and Yorkshire reported sinister gatherings at night, associated with yet another subversive organization, the United

---

[16] *Diary of a Country Parson* (see Ch. 17 n. 4), v. 241 (25 Feb. 1800); A. Booth, 'Popular loyalism and public violence in the north-west of England, 1790–1800', *Social History*, 8 (1983), 312.

Britons (probably an offshoot of the United Englishmen, which had incorporated ultra-radical members of the London Corresponding Society, as well as Irish migrant workers in northern England). Such reports, although often exaggerated and alarmist, nevertheless confirmed that attempts to stifle popular political activism following the Irish rising, and the disclosure of further plots involving Irish and English conspirators early in 1799, had met with only limited success. (These sweeping measures included the outlawing of the London Corresponding Society and all bodies with similar aims and organizational structures; provisions for the detention of suspected insurrectionists without trial; and the formal if somewhat redundant outlawing of trade unions and collective industrial action, under the Combination Acts of 1799 and 1800.)

While such pressures alone might not have persuaded Pitt to press for peace, the matter was unexpectedly resolved by George III's adamant and continued refusal to permit any relaxation of the penal laws against Catholics, Irish or otherwise. Faced with this 'consecrated obstruction' to a key element of his Irish policy, and unwilling to risk the personal and constitutional consequences of proceeding regardless of the King's position, the exhausted and overwrought Pitt resigned from office in February 1801. He did not move into opposition against his successor Henry Addington (1757–1844), the competent if somewhat uncharismatic son of the Pitt family physician. Fully supported by public opinion, and the King (after his recovery from another bout of insanity), Addington's ministry made peace with France its first priority. Despite yet another invasion scare in the summer of that year, an Anglo-French accord was announced in October. The joy which greeted this news was only a little muted when the terms of the final treaty signed at Amiens in May 1802 became widely known. But whereas Britain had agreed to give up almost all her overseas conquests, France retained effective control over a larger area of Western Europe—the Netherlands, Germany, Switzerland, and northern Italy—than any of Napoleon's royal predecessors had enjoyed.

Worldwide War

This imbalance in itself hardly made a resumption of hostilities inevitable. But persistent bickering over implementation of the peace settlement and various other mutual irritants deepened reciprocal mistrust between Addington's ministry and Napoleon's regime. The immediate causes of renewed fighting were British fears that Napoleon would reoccupy Egypt instead of allowing the Ottoman Turks to resume control after a British garrison had departed, and Britain's associated refusal to abandon the island of Malta, which she had occupied as a naval base since 1800. This geographical context reflected the growing importance of what came to be known as the Eastern Question, resulting from a long-term decline of Ottoman power in the eastern Mediterranean, and the corresponding expansion of Russian influence. It stood in marked contrast to the more traditional concern over control of the Netherlands, which had touched off the previous Anglo-French conflict. That war had also to some extent the character of an ideological contest, with considerable domestic sympathy for the enemy, or at least for the revolutionary French ideals of liberty, equality, and fraternity. By 1803, however, hardly anyone could or did maintain that Napoleon's boundless ambition for power, amply demonstrated both within and outside France, was motivated by such principles. Indeed the fact that the aggressive expansionism of 'Boney's' France had come to focus primarily on Britain now galvanized a massive patriotic reaction, of a scale and intensity which surpassed even the loyalist rallying a decade before.

Having once recognized the effectiveness of French total mobilization in the early 1790s, British policy makers determined to make maximum use of their own much smaller population. A parish-by-parish survey of men and resources under the Defence of the Realm Act of 1798 preceded the first national population census, authorized by Parliament and conducted by John Rickman (1771–1840) in 1801. Rickman sought to establish the precise numbers available for military service, and possibly also to demonstrate that recent demographic growth had reduced France's traditional numerical advantage. But the British 'armed nation' which confronted Napoleon in 1803–4 was not wholly the creation or creature of the state. Besides the regular army and the county militia (that government-subsidized home defence force revived by Pitt's father in 1757 and further expanded in 1796 and 1802, to which each parish contributed its compulsory levy of men), there were numerous privately funded and locally recruited volunteer corps. The largely middle-class ranks of the Volunteers had swelled to some 116,000 men during the invasion scare of 1797–8. The more ominous threat posed by Napoleon's intensive preparations to launch an invasion armada from Boulogne in 1803–4 saw a still larger and more socially inclusive response. No fewer than 380,000 Volunteers rallied to the colours in England and Scotland, with a further 70,000 in Ireland, amounting in all to more than double the number of regular army troops, both at home and abroad. In July 1803 a young liberal Dissenter reported from his native Essex that 'Everything is military, and the common salutation now, to what [Volunteer] corps do you belong?... There is no longer a difference of political opinions, but we are united hand and heart to drive back invaders'.[17]

Patriotic journalists boasted that Britain now actually had more men under arms than France. Indeed a national league table produced for the future prime minister Lord Liverpool (1770–1828) put military participation per 'male active population' in Britain at around 1 : 5, whereas the French ratio was a mere 1 : 14. Direct civilian involvement in national defence included the systematic enrolment of agricultural workers as 'pioneers', guides, and drivers of carts and wagons. Women's committees busied themselves in providing clothing for

---

17 P. J. Corfield and C. Evans (eds.), *Youth and Revolution in the 1790s: Letters of William Pattisson, Thomas Amyot and Henry Crabb Robinson* (1996), 39.

the troops, and raising contributions to patriotic subscription funds. Military displays and parades, such as the 1803 royal review of volunteers in Hyde Park, attracted enormous crowds of onlookers. Indeed the early stages of the struggle against Napoleon's France saw a level of mobilization closely resembling the era of total warfare with which modern industrial societies have become only too familiar, rather than typically more limited eighteenth-century conflicts, fought out mainly between professional armies with minimal civilian involvement.

But if war against Napoleonic France enjoyed much wider domestic support than the previous Anglo-French conflict, the strategic situation abroad had not changed. Despite his efforts to bolster French naval strength, Napoleon was still prevented by British maritime supremacy from gaining temporary control of the Channel for long enough to allow an invasion force to cross and land safely. And after a series of minor naval setbacks, Nelson's decisive defeat of a combined Franco-Spanish fleet at the battle of Trafalgar off southern Spain (1805) effectively ended the invasion threat. Yet however crucial for national defence, and the continuance of overseas trade, British maritime supremacy could not in itself defeat the French. And because victory on land in Europe was hardly to be expected from British arms alone, despite the considerable expansion and reorganization of the British army under the direction of Frederick, duke of York (1763–1827) as its Commander-in-Chief from 1795, concerted action with European allies seemed essential. The construction of such an alliance, in the form of the Third Coalition (between Austria, Russia, and Britain) was a major preoccupation of William Pitt's second ministry, formed after the uninspiring Addington had succumbed to the sniping of parliamentary critics in 1804. However, Pitt only just managed to outlast the collapse of the Austrian component of the coalition, the result of Napoleon's brilliant victories at Ulm and Austerlitz. His death early in 1806, followed soon after by that of his ancient adversary Fox, ushered in a phase of factionalized ministerial instability, which ended only with the formation of Liverpool's ministry in 1812.

The first of these short-lived administrations, the 'Ministry of All the Talents' (so-called because headed by Pitt's former colleague Lord Grenville, although composed largely of Foxites), impatient with the expensive but apparently fruitless policy of coalition, adopted an essentially defensive, isolationist posture towards the ongoing war. As Napoleon meanwhile extended and tightened his control over the heartland of Europe, he also adopted a new strategy against Britain, appropriate to crushing what he had once contemptuously dismissed as a 'nation of shopkeepers'. His 'continental system' relied on the fact that French allies and satellite states ruled by members of his family included most of the major European markets for British manufactured and colonial goods, as well as the Baltic sources from which Britain acquired naval stores (notably pine for masts and tar for caulking). But the attempted exclusion of British goods from European markets, although damaging in the short term, proved a less effective form of economic warfare than the retaliatory blockade imposed from 1807 by Orders in Council and enforced by the British navy on French-controlled ports and neutral shipping. Moreover Britain's trade also continued and expanded beyond Europe, especially to Asia and South America, while the failure of an improbably long-distance expedition mounted out of Cape Town (seized from Holland in 1806) against Spanish Buenos Aires was offset by numerous colonial gains, including the former French Caribbean sugar islands of Martinique and Guadeloupe, the strategically placed island of Mauritius in the Indian Ocean, and Java (also annexed from the Dutch satellite regime).

But it was two military campaigns in south-western and eastern Europe which finally tilted the strategic balance against Napoleonic France. The first of these was the result of a nationalist uprising and guerrilla war in Spain against the French army of occupation which installed Napoleon's brother Joseph as puppet ruler in 1808. In response to Spanish appeals an British expeditionary force of 15,000 troops commanded by Sir Arthur Wellesley (1769–1852) was sent to Portugal to assist their struggle. This substantial commitment of men and money paid several dividends, not only demonstrating British military effectiveness and French vulnerability, but also creating a constant drain on Napoleon's thinly stretched resources. Having failed to dislodge Wellesley from the Iberian Peninsula, the French found themselves increasingly pushed on the defensive by the combination of British troops, Portuguese auxiliaries, and local guerrillas, effectively supported from the sea by the British navy. Britain, however, played no direct part in the second campaign which followed the breakdown of Tsar Alexander's alliance with France, when Napoleon's over-ambitious assault on Russia was succeeded by an ignominious and costly retreat from Moscow in the dreadful winter of 1812/13.

Victory and Misery

As the threat of French invasion subsided, so had any semblance of national unity on the home front, except perhaps for general approval of the anti-French risings in Portugal and Spain. The realm of high politics was destabilized by the Whigs' internal divisions, as well as by constant infighting among Pitt's former colleagues and followers. These squabbles reached their extraordinary climax when two of the most capable cabinet ministers in Portland's administration, the foreign secretary George Canning and Robert Stewart, Viscount Castlereagh (1769–1822), secretary for war, resigned their offices and fought a pistol duel over personal and policy rivalries in September 1809. Other disruptive factors included uncertainties associated with the King's deteriorating mental and physical health (which led finally to the appointment of the Prince of Wales as Regent in 1811, although his father was to live on, blind and insane, for nine more years), and the revival of the movement for constitutional reform. Alongside veteran campaigners like John Cartwright, Capel Lofft, and Francis Place, new leaders emerged. The most notable were Sir Francis Burdett (1770–1844), a radical baronet MP who achieved national notoriety and attracted huge crowds of supporters when he was committed to the Tower in 1810 for attacking parliamentary restrictions on free speech, and the former conservative journalist William Cobbett (1762–1835), whose outspoken *Political Register* was one of thirteen London newspapers to denounce Burdett's arrest. These comparatively respectable reformers and their middle-class supporters increasingly distanced themselves from the parliamentary Whigs, while also shunning the disreputable metropolitan fringe of ultra-radical activists and ex-Jacobins, such as Thomas Spence, a former schoolteacher turned bookseller, journalist, and republican-revolutionary theorist.

Blunders, reverses, and scandals, military and otherwise, stimulated both burgeoning war-weariness and the radical cause. Prefaced by the impeachment of the veteran Scottish political operator Henry Dundas in 1805 on a charge of misappropriating Admiralty funds, these included the misnamed 'delicate investigation' of 1806 into the sordid personal life of Princess Caroline, the Prince of Wales's estranged wife; the Convention of Cintra, whereby a 'confused and incapable' general (not Wellesley, shortly to be ennobled as Viscount Wellington) permitted a defeated French army to be evacuated from Portugal with arms, equipment, and booty intact in 1808; next year's disastrous Walcheren expedition against the major French naval base off Antwerp, resulting in the loss of 4,000 troops for no apparent military gain; and an unfolding saga of commissions and promotions obtained by bribes paid to Mary Anne Clarke (1776–1852), an actress and ex-mistress of the duke of York, which eventually forced his resignation from the position of army Commander-in-Chief. Widely publicized in the press, these incidents and revelations were also the subject of caricatures and engravings, chalked slogans, debates, handbills, meetings, and petitions; the Clarke affair even figured marginally in the long-running 'O[ld] P[rice]' demonstrations against increased ticket prices at the rebuilt Covent Garden theatre in September 1809.[18] They reinforced claims that only radical and thorough reform could eliminate what was in fact a pervasive system of corruption, political, governmental, financial, and administrative. Piecemeal initiatives like John Curwen's private member's bill of 1809 against the sale of parliamentary seats were scorned as simply too little, too late.

The reform cause drew support from Dissenters, industrial artisans and employers in the North and Midlands, urban merchants and shopkeepers, and members of the professions. However, it made very little headway among the landed interest which dominated both Houses of Parliament. Thus in 1810 the Commons voted down a very mild pro-reform motion by 234 votes to 115;

---

[18] M. Baer, *Theatre and Disorder in Late Georgian London* (1992), 164–5.

although this was the largest minority for reform since the rejection of Pitt's proposals in 1785, a mere 88 MPs supported a further attempt in 1812. One main reason for this drop in support was the fears of imminent social disorder aroused by machine-breaking riots which began in 1811, spreading from the Nottingham framework knitters and lacemakers to other textile trades in Lancashire and the West Riding of Yorkshire. These 'Luddite' disturbances were so termed after the mythical General (and even Lady) Ludd, under whose name dire threats were directed at employers attempting either to cut wages or introduce labour-saving machinery. While they represented in the first instance a response to extremely harsh economic and industrial conditions, there is sufficient evidence of regional co-ordination, secret meetings, quasi-military formations, and stockpiling of weapons in and around major industrial centres to suggest that small groups of workers were actively preparing for armed insurrection by 1812.

That no successful uprising actually occurred was due mainly to the efficient ferocity with which the ministry headed by Spencer Perceval (1762–1812) deployed both military and legal means of repression (seventeen Luddites were hanged at the York assizes in January 1813). The bumper grain harvest of that year brought food prices down from a peak not seen since the famine years at the beginning of the century. A commercial upturn, thanks to easing of the Anglo-French trade blockades following repeal of the British Orders in Council, also helped. Unfortunately it came too late to prevent the outbreak of war with the United States, a conflict sparked by combined resentment at British interference with American merchant ships and crews attempting to trade with France, and American schemes for the acquisition of both Canada and Florida. But while the Luddites were temporarily suppressed, the overall economic outlook seemed anything but promising, with the prospect that wartime inflation and high taxes would soon give way to post-war recession and mass unemployment.

Wellington's decisive victory at Vitoria in June 1813 ended France's occupation of Spain. Four months later the combined forces of the Fourth (British, Austrian, Russian, Prussian, and Swedish) Coalition destroyed French power in Germany by overwhelming Napoleon's weakened army at the battle of Leipzig. While military action continued on France's southern and eastern borders, the main focus now shifted to complex and prolonged diplomatic negotiations conducted on Britain's behalf by Castlereagh, first between the coalition partners and then with the Bourbon monarchy restored after Napoleon's abdication in April 1814.

But before the peace treaty of Vienna was ready for signing, Napoleon staged a dramatic comeback. His hundred days of power ended appropriately enough in a series of grim encounters with the allied armies on the fields of Belgium. The outcome remained far from certain until the final hard-fought battle at Waterloo on 18 June 1815. A narrow but decisive victory by 74,000 troops (of whom only a half were British) under Wellington's command, with the arrival late in the day of the Prussians under Marshal Blucher, brought to a close Britain's last and longest struggle against France. As Wellington commented in his dispatch from the field next day, 'such a desperate action could not be fought without great loss'.[19] Casualties (dead, wounded, and missing) on both sides reached around 50,000 men, and 10,000 horses, or approximately the level of total British losses over the six years of the Peninsular campaign. During the whole twenty-two years from 1793, while the national debt had tripled, somewhere between 200,000 and 250,000 British sailors and soldiers died from causes directly attributable to the war.

Allowing for a much smaller total population, that human loss was comparable to what the country would suffer during the First World War a century later, even if those casualties were due largely to enemy action rather than disease, and crammed into a much shorter timeframe.[20] For these and other reasons the French wars lacked the Great War's direct and devastating impact on the home front. Yet the struggle with revolutionary and Napoleonic France was not unlike the First World War, in that it generated powerful, if episodic, surges of patriotic unity, and also strains which both exacerbated existing tensions and created new ones. Traumatic post-war economic depression, massive unemployment, and widespread social distress, continuing campaigns for legal and political reform, conflicts over economic policy between landed and manufacturing interests (focused on Liverpool's immensely divisive Corn Law of 1815, which sought to maintain agricultural profit margins by restricting foreign grain imports), the Catholic emancipation issue, and the Irish Question, soon overshadowed the victory celebrations.

[19] *EHD, 1783–1832*, 935.
[20] R. Muir, *Britain and the Defeat of Napoleon, 1807–1815* (1996), 363, 377.

19

RETROSPECT AND CONCLUSION

Change and Continuity, 1660–1815

The proverbial long-lived time-traveller who visited England after Charles II's restoration in 1660, then returned again to hear the news of Waterloo, would have found much that appeared unchanged. In 1815 England still retained a hereditary monarchy, ruling with a bi-cameral Parliament and an avowedly undemocratic, gender-biased, property-based political nation; agriculture was the largest economic sector in terms of both employment and production, aristocratic landowners dominated high politics, and most people lived in rural villages rather than towns; poverty was massive, social inequality pervasive; the Church of England retained a privileged status, with its bishops holding seats in the Lords and its clergy supported by compulsory universal payment of tithes and other church dues. Yet on closer inspection many of these apparent continuities turn out to be formal rather than substantive, while others were offset by real and significant change, in kind as well as degree.

The first and most obvious discontinuity was demographic. Twice as many persons, and a much higher proportion of young people among them, occupied England's fields and streets in 1815 than had been there 155 years before. Whereas population growth then was stagnant or negative, in the early years of the nineteenth century the compound rate of annual population increase was running at well over 1 per cent, and still rising. Between 1660 and 1815 England's inhabitants had more than doubled in number, from just over 5 to 10.5m., a pace of growth seemingly unmatched on the Continent (if exceeded in Ireland). Moreover, while three-quarters of the population still lived in rural villages, or towns of fewer than 10,000 inhabitants (the proportion drops to around two-thirds if those in large provincial towns of 2,500 and up are included), only about 40 per cent of the adult male labour force worked the land, a far smaller proportion than anywhere else in Europe. The remainder, and many women and children as well, found or at least sought various forms of non-agricultural employment, especially in manufacturing (despite spasmodic disruptions to commerce and industry associated with the French wars).

Population growth, booming urban centres, and expanding non-agricultural employment affected both landscape and townscape. The average size of farms had increased—in northern England, from around 65 to some 100–150 acres— and it has been calculated that by 1800 peasant families occupied under 10 per cent of all farmland.[1] The enclosure of common pastures and open fields, already well under way during the seventeenth century, had continued, using private Acts of Parliament to overcome local resistance, which was often both fierce and violent. Perhaps 13 per cent of England's total surface area was enclosed between 1700 and 1799, with significantly higher proportions in the heavier soils of East Anglia and the Midlands counties. The 6.8m. acres enclosed by parliamentary process between 1750 and 1820 may have amounted to as much as 30 per cent of the country's agricultural land; the economic and social impact upon small farmers dispossessed of ancient common rights was often traumatic, and bitterly resented. Of course both the amalgamation and consolidation of farms, and the legal privatization and subsequent physical enclosure of commons and fields, were hardly novel developments, any more than the spread of manufacturing in the countryside. But the multi-storey, purpose-built mills now found in river valleys on both sides of the Pennines and elsewhere were quite new, as also the occasional iron bridges crossing those rivers, and the still expanding network of canals and turnpiked roads, which 'afford communication between some of the greatest manufacturing towns in the kingdom'.[2]

Brick, slate, stone, and tile had largely replaced timber and thatch as the building materials of choice, especially in towns. The physical vastness of London, now a city of a million inhabitants, overwhelmed foreign visitors, who were well advised to buy one of several available directories, guidebooks, or street-maps to help them find their way around. At least the capital's main thoroughfares had now been substantially upgraded, or as contemporaries would say 'improved', by ratepayer-funded boards of commissioners. These bodies supervised the installation of stone pavements, separated by gutters from the horse-drawn traffic in the streets, which were illuminated by oil-lights from dusk to dawn; the first gas-lighting had been introduced in 1807. Further help for strangers and inhabitants alike came with the numbering of houses (rather than their identification by name and appearance), particularly in the newer squares, terraces, and crescents created by fashionable architects like John Nash (1752–1835) not only in London, but in elegant provincial resorts such as Bath, Brighton, Buxton, Cheltenham, and Tunbridge Wells. Additional architectural evidence of change included the purpose-built Dissenting chapels and meeting houses, and the rows of cheap and often nasty workers' cottages and tenements, hastily erected to accommodate the labour force attracted to major industrial centres in the Midlands and North of England. Although slightly safer places since the disappearance of bubonic plague after the epidemic of

---

[1] P. K. O'Brien, 'Path dependency, or why Britain became an industrialized and urbanized country before France', *EcHR* 49 (1996), 237.

[2] J. Neeson, *Commoners: Common Right, Enclosure and Social Change in England, 1700–1820* (1993); R. Warner, *A Tour through the Northern Counties of England, and the Borders of Scotland* (1802), i. 23.

the mid-1660s, the promotion by Edward Jenner (1749–1823) of vaccination against smallpox, and some marginal improvements in urban sanitation, cities and towns of any size were ever more heavily polluted by a pall of smoke from coal fires, with industrial areas particularly badly affected. Extensive exploitation of the massive coal deposits which constituted industrializing England's major natural resource came at a considerable environmental price.

A full catalogue of outward signs of change between the mid-seventeenth and early nineteenth centuries would list clothing and hairstyles (particularly the discarding of wigs and swords by men other than lawyers and soldiers, and some simplification of dress for both sexes), gesture and bodily deportment, food and table-manners (including the multiplication of cutlery after the mid-seventeenth century), titles and modes of address, sexuality, sport and recreation, among many other aspects of everyday life. But while it certainly should not be assumed that any of these areas was unaffected by larger shifts in economic conditions, ideas, or social and political institutions, we must now focus on two fundamental and systemic discontinuities. As the title of this book suggests, the most remarkable and consequential development during the century and a half with which we have been concerned was a great enlargement of state power, both domestic and, especially, external. In geopolitical terms England had moved from a subsidiary to a central, indeed pre-eminent position *vis-à-vis* Continental Europe. London was the capital city not just of England but a formally constituted United Kingdom, as well as the metropolis of a world empire on which the sun barely set. Astonishingly enough, the loss of the thirteen North American colonies in 1783 had been followed almost immediately by further massive acquisitions. By 1815 Britain had clearly succeeded Spain as the world's leading imperial power, holding territories of some 2 million square miles in extent inhabited by some 25 million people (see Appendix II). For the first time a majority of the Crown's subjects were non-white, non-Christian, and ruled from London; in 1793 the first British embassy to China had been received by the Emperor Qianlong.

This global projection of commercial, diplomatic, and maritime strength would hardly have occurred without what has been termed the 'fiscal-military state' (see above, Ch. 5). That compound of 'large armies and navies, industrious administrators, high taxes, and huge debts',[3] did not fully emerge until after the Glorious Revolution, although it is important to recognize that some of its key elements (including the development of a range of new consumption taxes, an expanded supervisory role for Treasury, and a decentralized bureaucracy of customs and excise collectors) date back to the 1660s, and before. Nevertheless, those institutional devices which so greatly expanded the scope of public finance—the Bank of England, the National Debt, and the regular annual sessions of Parliament which guaranteed payments to government

---

[3] J. Brewer, *The Sinews of Power: War, Money and the English State, 1688–1783* (1989), 250.

creditors from assigned revenue sources—were all post-1688 developments, as likewise the clustering of bankers, brokers, dealers, investors, and jobbers in public and private securities which constituted the City's embryonic financial centre. On the military side, a standing army and the Royal Navy both pre-date 1660, but a world of difference separated the military resources available to Charles II from those deployed by the later Hanoverian state. The establishment of 6,000 soldiers grudgingly accepted by Parliament in 1660 had become by the end of the Seven Years War in 1763 a peacetime standing army of some 45,000 men (although all but 17,000 or so were stationed abroad), still formally serving the King, but paid and disciplined by Parliament's authority. During the Napoleonic wars the payroll swelled to some 250,000 regular troops, over twice the size of the military force which lost the War of American Independence, and not counting the large subsidized allied contingents. The 156 warships of all kinds manned by nearly 20,000 seamen which Charles II inherited from Cromwell represented a fleet three times larger than his father's: yet 150 years later the Royal Navy included well over 1,000 vessels, and 214 ships of the line, manned by a complement of more than 142,000 sailors.[4]

The second major discontinuity between 1660 and 1815 was the emergence of a workable constitutional settlement and political system in the aftermath of the Glorious Revolution. It seems most improbable that the state's interlocking military, administrative, and financial capabilities could have expanded as far or as fast as they did without a resolution, one way or another, of Charles II's dangerously unstable political inheritance. Had his younger brother managed to repel Dutch William's challenge, England might still have developed a significantly more powerful state apparatus, along lines pioneered by absolutist monarchs in France and Spain. As it was, the adjusted balance of power between Crown and Parliament after 1688 largely removed any threat of a monarch using enhanced financial or military resources to pursue policies unacceptable to the landed and mercantile elites represented in Parliament. For despite the appearance of continuity which the victors of 1689 were so anxious to maintain, and the quite serious differences between William III and his parliaments, the terms of their relationship had clearly shifted, and by no means in the monarch's favour.

This is not to say that kings and queens were henceforth mere ceremonial figures or rubber stamps. But well before 1815 political conflict and decision-making had come to centre on Parliament and cabinet, not the royal court. A ruler's personal views could still carry considerable weight, and might well prove decisive, at least in the short run, as with the adamant opposition of both George III and his son to Catholic Emancipation. But while monarchs quite often made themselves troublesome to politicians, they could no longer expect

---

[4] Ibid. 29–31; L. Colley, *Britons: Forging the Nation, 1707–1837* (1992), 286–7; M. Duffy (ed.), *The Military Revolution and the State, 1500–1800* (1980), 82–3.

to conduct their own foreign policy (as Charles II and even William III had done), nor even to determine the composition of the ministries which governed in their names (especially after George III's reluctant acceptance of his *bête noire* Fox as foreign secretary in 1806). The resources of Crown influence and patronage (considerably diminished by several decades of Pittite 'economical' reform from the mid-1780s) were now largely commanded by ministers, and essentially employed to maintain control of parliamentary business. From George I's reign onwards ministers normally met as an executive which had come to be known as cabinet council, or cabinet, 'the spring and heart of government', without the sovereign's presence.[5] The old privy council, out of which this body had evolved, and over which the monarch usually presided, retained only formal pre-eminence, although it did act decisively at Queen Anne's death to secure the Hanoverian succession. The conventions of collective cabinet solidarity and responsibility to Parliament under prime-ministerial leadership took much longer to solidify. But the process was well advanced under Pitt's long tenure of office, even before George III's incapacity, the personal inadequacies of the Regent, and the exigencies of war bestowed virtually executive autonomy on the ministry. Meanwhile, despite the enormous political influence of individual peers and their families, both in cabinet and through dependants and relatives in the Commons, the numerically larger and procedurally more sophisticated Lower House was generally coming to be recognized as enjoying 'ultimate superiority, not only over the Crown, but also over the House of Lords'.[6]

So the apparent continuity of political institutions during the period covered by this book is very misleading. While the names remain the same, the nature and relations of Crown, Lords, and Commons changed very markedly. At the same time wholly new institutions and offices (cabinet, political parties, the prime ministership) came into being. The nature of political issues and the manner in which they were expressed and contested were also transformed in the last third of our period, as extra-parliamentary public opinion was regularly mobilized by the power of the press and through numerous associations, clubs, lobbies, special-purpose organizations, and pressure groups. These bodies and their members engaged in systematic national collective action, by means of newspaper advertisements, correspondence, delegations, demonstrations, public meetings, petitions, and publications, all directed at concrete political goals, usually through parliamentary legislation. Far and away the most momentous and successful of these campaigns was conducted over thirty-five years by the Abolition Society, culminating with the passage in 1807 of an Act of Parliament banning the slave trade. Further popular pressure (including a petition bearing no fewer than three-quarters of a million signatures)

---

[5] D. Lemmings, 'Lord Chancellor Cowper and the Whigs, 1714–16', *Parliamentary History*, 9 (1990), 168, 174.

[6] R. Pares, *King George III and the Politicians* (1953), 43.

was mobilized in 1814 to ensure that the terms of the peace treaty did not permit France to continue trafficking in slaves. While the organizational antecedents of the abolitionist movement can be traced back through the Wilkite, anti-Walpole, pro-Sacheverell, and Exclusionist agitations to the mass petitions, newsbooks, and pamphleteering of the 1640s and 1650s, all these earlier mobilizations were by comparison relatively disorganized, ephemeral, unruly, and ineffective.

The Peculiarities of the English

Some things, of course, did not change. Belief in the innate and distinctive superiority of everything English (or, increasingly, British) continued to generate an 'enveloping haze of patriotic self-congratulation'(E. P. Thompson). That miasma spread and thickened throughout the eighteenth century, fanned partly by the admiration of foreign commentators like Voltaire and Montesquieu for England's post-1688 constitution and social institutions, but still more by successive military and naval exploits, and the growth of an imperial presence overseas. Popular nationalist sentiment found encouragement and expression in patriotic songs and ballads ('Rule Britannia' and 'God Save the King' were both first publicly performed in the early 1740s, during the War of the Austrian Succession), in cartoons and satirical prints, in plays and theatrical spectacles representing past and present triumphs of British arms. So the assertion of the eccentric poet Christopher Smart that 'English cats are the best in Europe', was hardly more indicative of mental unbalance than his aspiration that English might become 'the language of the West', a goal facilitated by Dr Johnson's path-breaking dictionary of the English language (compiled over ten years from 1746 to 1755). The publication from 1747 of the *Biographica Britannica*, a national biographical dictionary, the founding of the British Museum (opened in 1759), a striking revival of interest in Shakespeare as national dramatist from the 1760s onwards, establishment of the Royal Academy to foster the visual arts in 1768, and the commemoration in 1784 of the death a quarter-century earlier of Handel, the great German-born but long-term resident English composer, all reflected a drive to contest French artistic and cultural pre-eminence. Parochial complacency was to some extent counterbalanced by the cosmopolitanism of the cultural elite, and tempered by the fierce criticism which an increasingly vocal band of radicals and reformers directed at most national institutions after 1760. However, the massive loyalist reaction to French revolutionary excesses, and still more the threat of Napoleonic invasion, inevitably tended to swamp such minority doubts and reservations.

Yet perhaps contemporaries, native-born and foreigners alike, were mistaken in their insistence upon the distinctive and exceptional character of England and the English. Historians have recently begun to question whether the political, social, and economic structures of eighteenth- and early nineteenth-century England, or Britain, were indeed essentially different from those of leading contemporary European states. Thus post-1688 England, or Britain, has been characterized as an aristocratic Christian polity, a 'confessional state' founded on the marriage or mutual interdependence of Crown and altar, hereditary monarchy and Established Church of England. After all, Britain, like Russia, was geographically on the periphery of Europe, to some extent protected from invasion, yet still capable of involvement in European power politics. Like Russia also, Britain's state church was headed by the sovereign and confined to the dominions of the British Crown. Once it is accepted that *ancien régime* absolutism did not conform to a single type, other apparent similarities may be discerned between the old order in England and its counterparts on the Continent. For example, administrative and military consolidation and expansion after 1688 has been seen as an enhancement of central government power which represents 'another element of convergence with the Continental situation'.[7] Again, the privileged status of English (increasingly British) landed aristocrats, the ease with which they interacted with their European counterparts, and the tenacity with which their influence and wealth was defended, and indeed extended, from the 1780s onwards, may appear to exemplify a pre-revolutionary aristocratic resurgence throughout Western Europe. Lastly, it is clear that population growth, commercial expansion, upgrading of transport infrastructure, and selective industrial innovation were by no means unknown outside the British Isles. With revisionist economic historians busily cutting the industrial revolution down to size (and sometimes to nothing), the perceived economic and social gulf separating offshore England from Continental Europe seems much diminished, if not entirely obliterated.[8]

From a sufficient distance—say the perspective of an extra-terrestrial visitor—features common to all, or most, eighteenth-century European societies (such as an agrarian economic base, the Christian religion, nuclear families, private property, and a patriarchal gender order) may well appear to outweigh their individual differences. Yet closer vantage points permit finer discrimination, enabling other distinguishing characteristics, which did differentiate English institutions from those of Continental Europe, to come into focus. For example, the privileged status of the established Anglican Church, and its close working relationship with the state, are undeniable, as is also the cultural and ideological centrality of Christianity throughout the eighteenth century. Nevertheless, the Church of England hardly enjoyed the cultural and political dominance exercised by its counterparts throughout most of Europe, especially in those states where repressive Counter-Reformation agencies still threatened non-Roman Catholics with fines, imprisonment, and even death.

[7] J. Black, 'Britain and the Continent, 1688–1815: convergence or divergence?', *British Journal of Eighteenth-Century Studies*, 15 (1992).
[8] J. A. Davis, 'Industrialization in Britain and Europe before 1850: new perspectives and old problems', in P. Mathias and J. A. Davis (eds.), *The First Industrial Revolutions* (1989).

Accordingly, while the formal restriction of full civic rights to Anglicans was fiercely resented by many Dissenters, their sense of grievance fell somewhat short of the bitter anticlericalism and widespread hostility towards the Church expressed, for example, in pre-Revolutionary France. Again, the effectiveness of the Hanoverian church in promoting political cohesion and social deference is difficult to establish, and certainly cannot be inferred from England's avoidance of revolution in the 1790s. Despite claims for the near-universality of Christian belief in eighteenth-century England, our knowledge of religious attitudes among the bulk of the population is actually very limited. Nevertheless, evidence of diminishing congregations during the second half of the century (a clergyman who made the rounds of Sunday afternoon services in the City of London in 1781 reported that even on a fine day 'it was melancholy to observe how few attended') suggests that the Anglican Church by then enjoyed a far from universal reach.[9] In this respect, England may actually not have differed very much from parts of Continental, Catholic Europe, where similar signs of pre-1789 'dechristianization' have been noticed; but to the extent that was so, it becomes more difficult to regard the Church of England as a secure bulwark against innovation in a typical traditional society.

That other mainstay of the old order, the 'landed, rentier, privileged, hereditary' English aristocracy, also had much in common with the nobilities of Europe.[10] There was certainly a common obsession with honour and its defence in the duel, together with an ostentatiously leisured lifestyle in which the gaming table and field sports (various forms of hunting) featured prominently. The economic, political, and social power of the great landowning families may well have been expanding during the last twenty or thirty years of our period. George III and Pitt reversed the somewhat parsimonious attitude towards the creation of peerages which had prevailed since the opening of the Hanoverian era, so that the numbers of peers rose by 55 per cent (from 189 to 292) in the thirty years after 1780. A landlord's bonanza in the form of vastly inflated rent-rolls was created by the sharp rise in food prices during the later eighteenth century and Napoleonic wars. This agricultural boom in turn encouraged the extension and amalgamation of landed estates, and the merging of titled English families with their Irish, Scots, and Welsh counterparts, to create at least the beginnings of a consolidated British upper class (to a lesser extent in Scotland than elsewhere). Meanwhile the considerable political influence exercised by the peerage through direct control of nominations to over two hundred borough seats in the House of Commons, and the return of their sons as MPs, continued to grow, as did their influence and representation in the upper reaches of the professions (especially the Church and the army).[11]

[9] *Letters of Theophilus Lindsey*, ed. H. McLachlan (1920), 30.
[10] M. L. Bush, *The English Aristocracy* (1984), 215.
[11] D. Cannadine, *Aspects of Aristocracy* (1994), ch. 1; J. V. Beckett, *The Aristocracy in England, 1660–1914* (1986), ch. 1, app.; J. Cannon, *Aristocratic Century* (1984), ch. 4.

But the enlargement of aristocratic power and influence in late eighteenth- and early nineteenth-century Britain contrasts sharply with the difficult times encountered by most Continental European nobilities during the era of the French Revolution. One immediate reason for that divergent experience was the broadly united front with which the British propertied classes met a common threat posed by the egalitarian slogans of actual and would-be revolutionaries, both at home and abroad. Yet in seeking to explain why England experienced no Painite revolution to overthrow the political and social hegemony of the landed élite, it is also necessary to take account of the unique long-term structural characteristics of the English aristocracy. A very small, tightly defined, and by Continental standards underprivileged (because tax-paying) core of titular peers shaded off into a broad lesser nobility/gentry, which in turn blended with a large, amorphous, and virtually self-defining body of gentlemen. How far the landowning élite was open to constant replenishment from upwardly mobile industrialists, businessmen, and professional persons, as well as smaller gentry families, is still a hotly debated issue, one which turns largely on how 'élite' and 'constant' are defined and measured. But in our present state of knowledge it cannot be concluded that the openness of England's social hierarchy was merely a long-lived myth, based upon unjustified generalization from a tiny handful of spectacularly successful self-made individuals like Sir James Brydges (1673–1744), the fabulously wealthy ex-paymaster of the forces who became first duke of Chandos in 1719. And while the actual permeability or level of movement in and out of both the foothills and loftiest peaks of the landed hierarchy remains a matter of scholarly controversy, there can be no doubt that contemporaries generally believed and behaved as though the English aristocracy was anything but a closed and isolated caste.

Moreover, the élite's dealings with their social inferiors, the plebeian and middling sorts of people, while by definition inegalitarian, and in many respects exploitative, were not entirely one-sided. Deference and paternalism functioned as reciprocal incorporative mechanisms, reinforcing what a Kentish clergyman characterized in 1733 as the 'dependence and mutual check which all orders of men amongst us have upon one another'.[12] In other words, at one and the same time they defined, legitimated, and restricted the authority of superior over inferior, as was most notably apparent in the distinctive and time-honoured ritual of the parliamentary election, but also in the relatively novel settings of the cricket match and the Masonic lodge. So without succumbing to Whiggish exceptionalism, or viewing interactions between Hanoverian rulers and ruled through nostalgically rose-tinted glasses, it is possible to conclude that the English aristocracy may well have been somewhat more flexible and accommodating in both composition and social relations than its Continental European counterparts. If so—and such differences are difficult enough to

---

[12] J. Bate, *An Assize Sermon Preach'd at Maidstone in Kent* (1734), 14.

specify, let alone measure —that variance might help to explain not only its extraordinary longevity, but the pervasive preoccupation with marks of social class and status which still lingers in England today.

The sense of difference, if perhaps no longer assured superiority, apparent in current British attitudes towards Europe probably owes less than it once did to an appeal to history. For most of our period, however, widespread consciousness of the English nation's distinctive course of historical development filled the function of a nationalist ideology. History was utilized not only to form the basis of Burke's conservative political philosophy, but also by the reformers and radicals whom he attacked (as when the London Corresponding Society's republished political pamphlets of the early 1680s in order to rally support against official repression a century later).[13] The magnitude of the break with the past represented by the French Revolution tended subsequently to overshadow its seventeenth-century English precursor. But the excesses of revolutionary France also reinforced long-standing suspicion of enthusiasm (dating back indeed to the 1640s and 1650s), and a predilection (rationalized in David Hume's philosophical scepticism) for the concrete, individual, and practical over the abstract, general, and theoretical. Even the emerging social philosophy of Benthamite utilitarianism reflected this pragmatic cast of mind, with its concern to judge institutions by the measurable real-world benefits which they conferred on the population at large, rather than in terms of their origins, development, or ostensible purpose. While the restoration of the monarchy in 1660, the Revolution of 1688–9, Union with Scotland in 1707, and with Ireland in 1801, the loss of one empire and the expansion of another after 1783 were all major national turning points, only the Glorious Revolution was dignified by any form of official rhetoric or documentary justification, other than brief preambles to parliamentary statutes. It is also worth noting that none of these momentous events, with the possible exception of the Anglo-Scottish Union, were long-anticipated outcomes of careful strategic planning, rather than opportunistic responses to rapidly developing situations.

Good fortune—luck, in short—played a considerable part in Albion's ascent to geopolitical pre-eminence. That was hardly a smooth, uninterrupted, one-way process: after the humiliating—if perhaps in the long term advantageous—loss of her American colonies in 1783, the Austrian Emperor Joseph II maintained that Britain had sunk to the status of a second-rate power, another Sweden or Denmark.[14] Although endorsed by some contemporaries, this judgement underestimated the country's underlying comparative advantages, as well as the strains imposed upon the resources of France and her allies by the attempt to reverse the outome of the Seven Years War. The national endowment of temperate climate, fertile soil, ample mineral resources (especially coal) and a relatively small population continued to be sheltered

---

[13] e.g. J. Hawles, *The Englishman's Right* (1680, 1793).

[14] H. M. Scott, *British Foreign Policy in the Age of the American Revolution* (1989), 389.

from large-scale invasion by the sea, which at the same time facilitated peaceful interchange of goods, ideas, and people with Europe and the world. Having spared England (although not Ireland and Scotland) the worst horrors of the wars of religion which devastated much of Continental Europe during the sixteenth and seventeenth centuries, this fortunate insularity helped ensure that the commercial, dynastic, and at last revolutionary wars of the later seventeenth and eighteenth centuries actually occurred elsewhere. The partial exception— a prolonged and largely ineffective threat of foreign-backed Jacobite invasion— served on the whole to strengthen national cohesion at minimal economic and military cost. These favourable circumstances were managed, on the whole, by competent, sometimes outstanding political leaders. They permitted what were, by comparison with other contemporary European societies and states, high levels of political pluralism and ideological tolerance, a distinctive blend of individual freedom and communal solidarities, and an impressive record of economic innovation and expansion. They also facilitated the continued development of systems of law and government which have turned out to be Britain's most significant, and certainly most durable, export. Indeed, for all its inequalities and injustices, England between 1660 and 1815 might well be classed as not merely a lucky, but a remarkably successful society.

APPENDIX I: MONARCHS AND FIRST MINISTERS, 1660–1815

Prime or first ministers were not formally appointed as such. The Stuarts often did without a recognized first minister, while those politicians who did fill the role held various different offices, including Lord Chancellor, Secretary of State, and Lord Treasurer. From Walpole onwards the acknowledged head of government, who usually presided in cabinet, normally took the post of First Lord of the Treasury. The term 'Prime Minister' (or 'Premier') only lost its derogatory sense during Pitt the Younger's long tenure of office. In the following list the name by which each minister was generally known is capitalized, and followed in parentheses by the office he held.

RULERS	MINISTERS
(i) Stuarts	
Charles II (1660–1685)	1658–67: Edward Hyde, Earl of CLARENDON (Chancellor) [1667–73: The CABAL] 1673–9: Thomas Osborne, Earl of DANBY (Treasurer)
James II (1685–1688)	1683–8: Robert Spencer, 2nd Earl of SUNDERLAND (Secretary of State)
William III (1689–1701) and Mary (1689–1694)	[1696–1700: Whig JUNTO]
Anne (1701–1714)	1702–10: Sidney, Lord GODOLPHIN (Treasurer) [1708–10: Whig JUNTO] 1710–14: Robert Harley, Earl of OXFORD (Chancellor → Treasurer)
(ii) Hanoverians	
George I (1714–1727)	1717–21: Charles Spencer, 3rd Earl of SUNDERLAND (Secretary of State → 1st Lord of Treasury) 1717–21: James, 1st Earl of STANHOPE (1st Lord of Treasury → Secretary of State) 1721–42: Sir Robert WALPOLE (1st Lord of Treasury)
George II (1727–1760)	1727–42: Sir Robert WALPOLE (1st Lord of Treasury) 1742–4: John, Lord CARTERET (Secretary of State) 1744–54: Henry PELHAM (1st Lord of Treasury): BROAD-BOTTOM MINISTRY 1754–6: Thomas Pelham-Holles, Duke of NEWCASTLE (1st Lord of Treasury) 1756–7, 1757–61: William PITT (Secretary of State), with (i) Duke of DEVONSHIRE and (ii) Duke of NEWCASTLE (as 1st Lord of Treasury)

RULERS	MINISTERS
George III (1760–1820)	1760–2: John Stuart, Earl of BUTE (1st Lord of Treasury)
	1763–5: George GRENVILLE (1st Lord of Treasury)
	1765–6: Charles Watson-Wentworth, Marquess of ROCK-INGHAM (1st Lord of Treasury)
	1766: August Fitzroy, Duke of GRAFTON (1st Lord of Treasury)
	1766–9: William PITT, Earl of CHATHAM (Lord Privy Seal)
	1770–82: Lord NORTH (1st Lord of Treasury)
	1782: Marquess of ROCKINGHAM (1st Lord of Treasury)
	1782–3: William Petty, Earl of SHELBURNE (1st Lord of Treasury)
	1783: William Bentinck, Duke of PORTLAND (1st Lord of Treasury)
	1783–1801: William PITT (Prime Minister)
	1801–4: Henry ADDINGTON (Prime Minister)
	1804–6: William PITT (Prime Minister)
	1806–7: William Wyndham, Lord GRENVILLE (Prime Minister)
	1807–9: Duke of PORTLAND (Prime Minister)
	1809–12: Spencer PERCEVAL (Prime Minister)
Prince of Wales (later George IV) Regent, 1811–20	1812–27: Robert Jenkins, Lord LIVERPOOL (Prime Minister)

APPENDIX II: British Colonies and Overseas Possessions, 1660–1815

(i) *Held 1660*

Anguilla
Antigua and Barbuda
Bahamas
Barbados
Belize
Bermuda
Jamaica
Montserrat
St Christopher, Nevis
St Vincent and the Grenadines
Surinam

Connecticut
Maryland
Massachusetts
Rhode Island
Virginia

Newfoundland

(ii) *Held 1763*

Those listed above, *less* Surinam, *plus*:

Delaware
Georgia
New Hampshire
New Jersey
New York
North Carolina
Pennsylvania
South Carolina
Florida

Canada, Upper and Lower
New Brunswick
Nova Scotia
Prince Edward Island
Rupert's Land

Cayman Islands
Dominica
Gambia
Gibraltar

Grenada
India (Bombay, Bengal, Bihar, Carnatic, Orissa)
Minorca
St Helena
Senegal

(iii) *Held 1815*

Those listed under (ii) above, *less* Connecticut, Delaware, Georgia, Maryland, Massachusetts, New Hampshire, New Jersey, New York, North Carolina, Pennsylvania, South Carolina, Rhode Island, Virginia (the Thirteen Colonies), Florida, and Minorca;

plus:

British Columbia and Vancouver Island
Essequibo, Demerara, Berbice; Trinidad, Tobago; St Lucia

Heligoland; Malta; Corfu; Ionian Islands

Sierra Leone; Cape Colony; Gambia; Ascension Island; Pitcairn Island; Falkland Islands

Mauritus; Seychelles; India (including Bengal, Bhutan, Carnatic, Cochin, Madras, Mysore, Orissa; Pondicherry, Surat, Travancore, Ceylon); Java; Penang

New South Wales; Van Dieman's Land, Lord Howe Island; Norfolk Island

CHRONOLOGY

1660 Long Parliament recalled; Convention Parliament votes to restore monarchy; Charles II returns; Navigation Act.

1661 Venner's Rising; 'Cavalier' Parliament meets; Corporation Act.

1662 Charles II m. Catherine of Braganza. Act of Uniformity; Act of Settlement. Royal Society incorporated.

1663 Yorkshire rising; Royal Africa Company founded; Samuel Butler publishes *Hudibras*.

1664 Triennial Act; Conventicle Act.

1665 Second Anglo-Dutch War (to 1667); Great Plague (London and provinces).

1666 Great Fire of London. Dryden publishes *Annus Mirabilis*.

1667 Dutch burn English fleet in the Medway; Clarendon dismissed; Milton publishes *Paradise Lost*.

1668 Triple Alliance (against France); Bombay to East India Company.

1670 (Secret) treaty of Dover; Hudson's Bay Company established; Dryden appointed Poet Laureate.

1672 Stop of the Exchequer; Declaration of Indulgence (2nd); Third Dutch War (to 1674), in alliance with France.

1673 Test Act; James, duke of York, resigns as Admiral, m. Mary of Modena; Wren begins rebuilding St Paul's Cathedral; Danby Lord Treasurer; Shaftesbury dismissed.

1675 *Shirley* v. *Fagg* upholds House of Lords' jurisdiction; Parliament prorogued until 1677.

1676 Bishop Compton conducts religious census; further treaty between Charles II and Louis XIV.

1677 William of Orange m. Mary, daughter of duke of York; Anthony Marvell publishes (anonymously) *Account of the Growth of Popery and Arbitrary Government*; Shaftesbury imprisoned.

1678 Bunyan publishes *The Pilgrim's Progress* (Pt. I); 'Popish Plot' revealed.

1679 Danby falls; Exclusion Crisis (to 1681); Habeas Corpus Act.

1680 Lords reject Exclusion Bill.

1681 Oxford Parliament dissolved; Shaftesbury acquitted of treason; Whig JPs purged.

1682 Borough charters called in; Shaftesbury flees to Holland.

1683 Rye House Plot revealed; Russell and Sidney executed

1685 Charles II d.; succession of James II. Parliament summoned (May), prorogued; Monmouth's rising; Bloody Assizes. Louis XIV revokes Edict of Nantes; 2nd parliamentary session prorogued (Nov.).

1686   *Godden* v. *Hales* upholds dispensing prerogative; Ecclesiastical Commission established.

1687   First Declaration of Indulgence; Father Petre made privy councillor; expulsion of fellows of Magdalen College, Oxford; Halifax publishes *Letter to a Dissenter*.

1688   Second Declaration of Indulgence; birth of Prince James Edward; acquittal of Seven Bishops; William lands Torbay; James escapes to France.

1689   Convention offers Declaration (later Bill) of Rights, and joint sovereignty to William and Mary. James in Ireland with French army; Nine Years War with France begins (to 1697). Toleration Act.

1690   Archbishop Sancroft deprived; William defeats James at River Boyne.

1691   Defeat of Irish Jacobites at Aughrim; treaty of Limerick ends Irish war.

1692   Anglo-Dutch naval victory off La Hogue; Glencoe massacre. First Boyle lecture delivered.

1694   Triennial Act; Bank of England incorporated; Queen Mary d.

1695   Licensing Act lapses; Purcell adapts *The Indian Queen*.

1696   Trial of Treason Act; Last Determinations Act; Board of Trade and Plantations established; Newton supervises recoinage.

1697   Treaty of Ryswick ends war with France; Louis XIV recognizes William III as king of England.

1698   Blasphemy Act; Society for Promoting Christian Knowledge (SPCK) founded. Savery invents first 'fire' (steam) engine.

1700   Spanish succession crisis.

1701   Act of Settlement; revival of convocation. James II d., Prince James Edward (Old Pretender) recognized by France as James III and VIII.

1702   William III d., succession of Queen Anne. England joins War of Spanish Succession (to 1713). Publication of Clarendon's *History of the Rebellion*; first daily newspaper (*Daily Courant*).

1703   Methuen treaty with Portugal.

1704   Marlborough victorious at Blenheim; Queen Anne's Bounty established.

1705   First (pirated) edition of Mandeville's *Fable of the Bees*.

1706   Marlborough's victory at Ramillies; G. Farquhar, *The Recruiting Officer*.

1707   Treaty of Union between Scotland and England.

1708   Last royal veto of legislation; Prince George d., Whigs monopolize ministry.

1709   Peace talks begin; first issue of the *Tatler*; Abraham Darby smelts iron with coke.

1710   Impeachment of Henry Sacheverell; Whig ministry falls; Qualifications Act; general election.

1711   South Sea Company formed; Newcomen develops steam pump; first issue of the *Spectator*.

1712	Last assize trial and conviction for witchcraft; Handel settles in England.
1713	Peace of Utrecht (end of War of Spanish Succession).
1714	Schism Act; Tories split between Oxford and Bolingbroke. Queen Anne, d., George, Elector of Hanover succeeds.
1715	Riot Act; Earl of Mar declares for Pretender; Jacobite risings.
1716	Septennial Act; Anglo-French alliance.
1717	Walpole resigns; inauguration of Union of the English Freemasons Grand Lodge; Convocation suspended.
1718	Innoculation for smallpox introduced by Lady Mary Wortley Montagu; Lombe's silk mill.
1719	Spanish pro-Jacobite invasion of Scotland defeated; repeal of Occasional Conformity and Schism Acts.
1720	South Sea Bubble; Walpole returns to office; Declaratory Act reaffirms Irish legislative and judicial subordination.
1721	Walpole First Lord of Treasury.
1722	Atterbury plot revealed; Defoe publishes *Moll Flanders*.
1723	Patent for Wood's halfpence; Christopher Wren d.
1724	Defoe's *Tour* and Swift's *Drapier's Letters* published.
1725	Impeachment of Lord Chancellor Macclesfield.
1726	The *Craftsman* launched; Swift publishes *Gulliver's Travels*.
1727	George I d., George II succeeds.
1728	John Gay's *Beggar's Opera* first performed.
1729	Wesley begins Holy Club meetings at Oxford; statutory registration of attorneys and solicitors.
1730	Resignation of Townshend.
1732	Colony of Georgia founded; Protestant Dissenting Deputies established.
1733	Excise crisis; John Kay patents his 'flying shuttle'.
1734	Walpole wins general election with reduced majority.
1736	Failed attempt to repeal Test and Corporation Acts; witchcraft decriminalized.
1737	Frederick, Prince of Wales, expelled from court, moves to Leicester House; Queen Caroline. d. Licensing Act.
1738	John Wesley's conversion experience.
1739	War of Jenkins (Jenkin's) Ear (against Spain); Admiral Vernon captures Puerto Bello; Coram's Foundling Hospital incorporated.
1740	War of the Austrian Succession (to 1748); Thomas Arne composes *Rule Britannia*; Samuel Richardson publishes *Pamela*.
1741	General election; famine in Ireland; military failures in Spanish America and West Indies; first performance of Handel's *Messiah* (Dublin).
1742	Walpole resigns (Feb.), succeeded by Carteret.

1743   George II leads British–Austrian–Hanoverian force against French at Dettingen.

1744   Broadbottom ministry, following Carteret's dismissal.

1745   Charles Edward Stuart lands, takes Edinburgh, invades England; Arne's setting of *God Save the King* played at Drury Lane Theatre.

1746   Defeat of Jacobites at Culloden; William Pitt joins ministry.

1747   General election; *Biographica Britannica* published.

1748   Peace of Aix-la-Chapelle (ends War of the Austrian Succession).

1749   Bugging Act; Henry Fielding publishes *The History of Tom Jones*; British settlement of Halifax, Nova Scotia.

1751   Frederick, Prince of Wales, d., New Style (Gregorian) calendar instituted; Clive captures Arcot.

1752   Murder Act.

1753   Jewish Naturalization Act; Hardwicke's Marriage Act; Sir Hans Sloane's library acquired for British Museum.

1754   Henry Pelham d., succeeded by Newcastle; general election.

1755   Samuel Johnson's *Dictionary* published.

1756   Britain (in alliance with Prussia) declares war on France (Seven Years War, to 1763); loss of Minorca, resignation of Newcastle, Pitt–Devonshire ministry.

1757   Byng shot; Pitt–Newcastle ministry; Militia Act.

1758   Blackstone first Vinerian Professor of English Law; Bridgewater's Canal begun.

1759   British capture Gaudeloupe, Goree, Quebec; naval victories: off Lagos, and at Quiberon Bay.

1760   George II d., George III succeeds; Montreal captured; Lord Ferrers hanged.

1761   Pitt resigns; war with Spain; capture of Pondicherry.

1762   Newcastle resigns, replaced by Bute; peace terms debated.

1763   Peace of Paris ends Seven Years War. Bute resigns, replaced by Grenville; *North Briton*, no. 45, published, Wilkes arrested; Catharine Macaulay publishes vol. i of *History of England*.

1764   Wilkes expelled from Parliament; Watt invents separate condenser; Hargreaves invents spinning jenny; Sugar Act. Horace Walpole publishes *The Castle of Otranto*.

1765   Stamp Act; Grenville dismissed, replaced by Rockingham; American trade boycotts.

1766   Rockingham dismissed, replaced by Chatham; Stamp Act repealed; Declaratory Act; widespread food riots.

1767   Townshend duties; New York Assembly suspended; American boycotts reimposed; food riots.

1768   St George's Fields Massacre; Chatham resigns, replaced by Grafton; Royal Academy of Arts established.

1769   Society of Supporters of the Bill of Rights founded; repeal of Townshend duties, except on tea; Wedgwood opens Etruria pottery.

1770   Grafton resigns, replaced by North; Boston Massacre; Falklands Islands crisis.

1771   Cook returns from Pacific; food riots; Arkwright's first spinning mill opens at Cromford.

1772   Food riots; Lord Mansfield's judgment in Somersett's case.

1773   Food riots; Boston Tea Party; Warren Hastings Governor-General of India.

1774   Coercive Acts; Quebec Act; general election. Priestley isolates oxygen ('dephlogisticated air'); Theophilus Lindsey establishes Essex Chapel.

1775   Battles of Lexington-Concord and Bunker Hill; proclamation of American rebellion.

1776   American Declaration of Independence; Smith publishes *The Wealth of Nations*; Gibbon publishes *Decline and Fall*, vol. i; Paine publishes *Common Sense*.

1777   Burgoyne surrenders at Saratoga; William Dodd hanged; Howard's *State of the Prisons* published.

1778   France joins war against Britain; Catholic Relief Act.

1779   Spain joins war against Britain; completion of iron bridge at Coalbrookdale; machine-breaking riots; Crompton invents spinning mule; Yorkshire Association established.

1780   Holland joins war against Britain; Gordon riots; Society for Constitutional Information founded; Sunday schools begin.

1781   Cornwallis surrenders at Yorktown; Herschel discovers Uranus.

1782   North resigns, replaced by Rockingham, who d., replaced by Shelburne; Irish Declaratory Act repealed.

1783   Shelburne resigns, replaced by Fox–North coalition; peace of Versailles (ends War of American Independence); India Bill; dismissal of Fox–North ministry, replaced by Pitt.

1784   General election endorses Pitt, who begins fiscal and administrative reform; India Act.

1785   Pitt's parliamentary reform proposals defeated. Boulton–Watt rotary steam engine applied to spinning; first issue of *Daily Universal Register* (renamed *The Times*, 1788).

1786   Eden commercial treaty with France; Sinking Fund established.

1787   Impeachment of Warren Hastings; Association for Abolition of Slave Trade founded; First Fleet leaves for Botany Bay.

1788   Charles Edward Stuart d.; George III temporarily insane: Regency crisis.

1789   Outbreak of French Revolution; Nootka Sound crisis.

1790   Burke publishes *Reflections on the French Revolution.*

1791   Paine publishes *Rights of Man*, pt. 1; anti-Dissenter riots; Ochakov crisis.
       Boswell publishes *Life of Samuel Johnson.*

1792   Formation of London Corresponding Society; proclamation against sedi-
       tious publications; loyalist associations; Libel Act; Mary Wollstonecraft pub-
       lishes *Vindication of the Rights of Women.*

1793   War with France; first anti-French Coalition (with Austria, Prussia, Holland,
       Spain); British Convention meets Edinburgh.

1794   Treason trials; Portland Whigs join Pitt; Howe's naval victory in Channel;
       France invades Holland.

1795   Food riots, anti-war demonstrations; Speenhamland decision authorizes
       wage supplementation; Spain declares war on Britain.

1796   Peace talks fail; French attempt landing at Bantry Bay; Jenner tests vaccina-
       tion against smallpox.

1797   Bank crisis; Jervis and Nelson defeat Spanish fleet off Cape St Vincent; naval
       mutinies.

1798   Irish rebellion; Malthus publishes *Essay on the Principle of Population*;
       French fleet destroyed at battle of Aboukir Bay; Newspaper Publication Act.

1799   Income tax first levied; Second Coalition (with Russia, Austria, Turkey,
       Portugal, Naples); Combination Act; Seditious and Treasonable Societies
       Act.

1800   Act of Union with Ireland; second Combination Act; Malta captured; estab-
       lishment of Royal Institution; Census Act.

1801   Pitt resigns, succeeded by Addington; Danish fleet destroyed by Nelson at
       battle of Copenhagen.

1802   Peace of Amiens ends French Revolutionary War. William Cobbett founds
       Political Register; First Factory Act.

1803   Britain declares war on France (Napoleonic War, to 1815).

1804   Addington resigns, succeeded by Pitt; invasion force assembles at Boulogne.

1805   Third Coalition (with Austria and Russia); Nelson d., after defeating Franco-
       Spanish fleet at Trafalgar; impeachment of Dundas.

1806   Pitt d., succeeded by Grenville ('All the Talents') ministry; Continental System
       embargoes British exports to Europe.

1807   Britain blockades France and her allies; Portland succeeds 'Talents' ministry;
       general election; Russia declares war on Britain; abolition of slave trade.

1808   British expeditionary force to Portugal.

1809   Failed expedition to Walcheren; investigation of sale of army commissions;
       Portland resigns, succeeded by Perceval; Curwen's Act against electoral
       bribery.

1810   Burdett riots; capture of Mauritius; George III incapacitated.

1811   Prince of Wales made Regent; Luddite riots begin; Hansard issues verbatim reports of parliamentary debates.

1812   Economic crisis; Luddism spreads; assassination of Spencer Perceval, succeeded by Liverpool. Wellington defeats French in Spain; Anglo-American war (to 1814).

1813   Following victory at Vitoria, Wellington invades France. Fourth Coalition; repeal of 1563 Statute of Artificers.

1814   Napoleon abdicates, exiled to Elba; George Stephenson builds steam locomotive.

1815   Battle of Waterloo, Napoleon finally defeated; peace of Vienna (ends Napoleonic war); Corn Law.

FURTHER READING

The following suggestions concentrate on printed books, but some significant articles are also included, as well as items already cited in footnotes. Publication dates are usually of the most recent edition.

Bibliography

The standard Oxford *Bibliography of British History: Stuart Period, 1603–1714*, ed. G. Davies and M. F. Keeler (1970); *The Eighteenth Century, 1714–1789*, ed. S. Pargellis and P. J. Medley (1951); *1789–1851*, ed. L. M. Brown and I. R. Christie (1977), remains useful; a comprehensive forthcoming revision will incorporate successive volumes of the Royal Historical Society's *Annual Bibliography of British and Irish History* (1975–). Annotated bibliographies include the American Historical Association's two-volume *Guide to Historical Literature*, ed. M. B. Norton (3rd edn., 1995); the more specialized *Restoration England, 1660–1689*, ed. W. L. Sachse (1971), and *Late Georgian and Regency England, 1760–1837*, ed. R. A. Smith (1984); see also G. R. Elton, *Modern Historians on British History, 1485–1985* (1970), and J. S. Morrill, *Seventeenth-Century Britain, 1603–1714* (1980). Two valuable subject listings are *British Economic and Social History: A Bibliographical Guide*, ed. R. C. Richardson and W. H. Chaloner (1996), and the *New Cambridge Bibliography of English Literature* (1969–74). The *Annual Bulletin of Historical Literature* gives a conspectus of each year's publications, while the *EcHR* and *EHR* carry twelve-monthly surveys of periodical publications.

Reference

For information on events, institutions, people, and places: *The History Today Companion to British History* (1995); *S. H. Steinberg's Dictionary of British History* (1970); the *Dictionary of British History*, ed. J. P. Kenyon (1981); the *Cambridge Historical Encyclopedia of Great Britain and Ireland*, ed. C. Haigh (1985); *A Dictionary of Eighteenth-Century World History*, ed. J. Black and R. Porter (1994); *Atlas of Industrializing Britain, 1780–1914*, ed. J. Langton and R. J. Morris (1986); and *British Historical Facts, 1688–1760*, ed. C. Cook and J. Stevenson (1988).

Primary Source Collections

The standard bulky compilations of *English Historical Documents: VIII (1660–1714)*, ed. A. Browning (1966); *X (1714–1783)*, ed. D. B. Horn and M. Ransome (1969); and *XI (1783–1832)*, ed. A. Aspinall and E. A. Smith (1959), cover a wide range; *The Stuart Constitution*, ed. J. P. Kenyon (1966; 2nd edn. 1986), and its companion volume *The Eighteenth-Century Constitution, 1688–1815*, ed. E. N. Williams (1960) have a narrower focus. Unfortunately there is no sequel to the excellent selection provided by *Seventeenth-Century England: A Changing Culture, i. Primary Sources*, ed. A. Hughes (1980). *Eighteenth-Century Women: An Anthology*, ed. B. Hill (1984), provides a gendered perspective. Illustrated commentaries on *The English Satirical Print, 1600–1832* (1986) include *The Common People and Politics, 1750s–1790s*, ed. J. Brewer, *Religion in the Popular Prints, 1600–1832*, ed. J. Miller, and *Crime and the Law in English Satirical Prints, 1600– 1832*, ed. J. A. Sharpe. The creative and imaginative literature of the period could take several enjoyable lifetimes to explore; useful departure points include *The New Oxford Book of Eighteenth-Century Verse*, ed. R. Lonsdale (1984), and the encylopaedic *Norton Anthology of English Literature*, ed. M. H. Abrams (1986).

Overviews and Surveys

Absolute beginners might turn to the brisk middle chapters of *The Oxford Illustrated History of Britain* (1984), ed. K. O. Morgan, and the first 150 pages of R. K. Webb's classic *Modern England: From the Eighteenth Century to the Present*, (1968, 1990). Livelier yet is R. Porter's *English Society in the Eighteenth Century* (1990), best supplemented with relevant chapters from A. Briggs's masterly *Social History of England* (1987). Broader and deeper, more up-to-date, if more conventional coverage of all but the last thirty years of our period is provided by G. Holmes, in *The Making of a Great Power: Late Stuart and Early Georgian Britain, 1660–1722* (1993) and *The Age of Oligarchy: Pre-Industrial Britain, 1722–1783* (1993), the latter co-authored with D. Szechi.

Few single volumes attempt to span even what J. B. Owen termed *The Eighteenth Century, 1714–1815* (1974). The older multi-volume series concentrate on high politics at the expense of social, economic, and cultural history, although not uniformly—cf. J. R. Jones, *Country and Court: England, 1658–1714* (1978) and I. R. Christie, *Wars and Revolutions: Britain, 1760–1815* (1982), with W. A. Speck, *Stability and Strife: England, 1714–1760* (1979). A once notable exception, still well worth reading, is C. Hill, *The Century of Revolution, 1603–1714* (1961, 1980). In *A Polite and Commercial People: England, 1727–1783* (1989) P. Langford adopts a no less wide-ranging approach. G. N. Clark *The Later Stuarts, 1660–1714* (1955) has worn better than B. Williams, *The Whig Supremacy, 1714–1760* (1962) or S. Watson, *The Reign of George III, 1760–1815* (1960). A classic modern text, A. Briggs, *The Age of Improvement* (1959, 1966, 1979) covers the last thirty-five years of our period; B. Coward, *The Stuart Age: England, 1603–1714* (1994) has the most recent and comprehensive account of its first half-century or so; I. Gilmour, *Riot, Risings and Revolution: Governance and Violence in Eighteenth-Century England* (1992) is the lively personal interpretation of a perceptive and well-informed non-academic historian.

Able economic and social surveys include D. C. Coleman, *The Economy of England, 1450–1750* (1977); C. Wilson, *England's Apprenticeship, 1603–1760* (1984); J. A. Sharpe, *Early Modern England: A Social History* (1987); M. J. Daunton, *Progress and Poverty: An Economic and Social History of Britain, 1700–1850* (1995); M. R. Berg, *The Age of Manufactures, 1700–1820* (1985, 1994); *The Economic History of Britain since 1700, i. 1700–1860*, ed. R. Floud and D. McLoskey (1981, 1994); J. Rule, *Albion's People: English Society, 1714–1815* (1992) and id., *The Vital Century: England's Developing Economy, 1714–1815* (1992). *The Cambridge Social History of Britain, 1750–1950*, ed. F. M. L. Thompson (1990), a three-volume multi-author work, should not be neglected despite its later modern emphasis. A. Laurence, *Women in England, 1500–1760: A Social History* (1994) is better integrated than A. F. Fletcher's ambitious *Gender, Sex and Subordination in England, 1500–1800* (1995).

On foreign policy and relations, D. McKay and H. M. Scott, *The Rise of the Great Powers, 1648–1815* (1983) has a comprehensive and non-Anglocentric account of

Britain's diplomatic and military interaction with Europe; see also J. Black, *A System of Ambition: British Foreign Policy, 1660–1793* (1991)

Chapter 1

E. A. Wrigley and R. S. Schofield, *The Population History of England, 1548–1871: A Reconstruction* (1989), is helpfully contextualized and glossed by R. A. Houston in *The Population History of Britain and Ireland, 1500–1750* (1992). G. N. Clark, *Science and Social Welfare in the Age of Newton* (1937) discusses the political arithmeticians. R. Davis, *English Overseas Trade, 1500–1700* (1973) and J. Thirsk, *Economic Policy and Projects: The Development of a Consumer Society in Early Modern England* (1978) are also useful. On social structure, see K. Wrightson, 'Estates, degrees, and sorts: changing perceptions of society in Tudor and Stuart England', in P. Corfield (ed.), *Language, History and Class* (1991), and id., *English Society, 1580–1680* (1982). Later Stuart government and politics are discussed by J. Miller, *Bourbon and Stuart: Kings and Kingship in France and England in the Seventeenth Century* (1987); A. Fletcher, *Reform in the Provinces: The Government of Stuart England* (1986); and T. Harris, *Politics under the Later Stuarts: Party Conflict in a Divided Society, 1660–1715* (1993). For the complex religious background, try S. Doran and C. Durston, *Princes, Pastors and People: The Church and Religion in England, 1529–1689* (1991). On culture and ideas, R. H. Tawney's classic *Religion and the Rise of Capitalism* (1926, 1938) is extended by the last chapter of D. Underdown, *Fire from Heaven: Life in an English Town in the Seventeenth Century* (1992); B. Reay (ed.), *Popular Culture in Seventeenth-Century England* (1985) should be read in conjunction with R. Hutton, *The Rise and Fall of Merry England* (1994). See also M. Hunter, *Science and Society in Restoration England* (1981) and H. Kearney, *Science and Change* (1971). England's foreign relations are variously treated by H. Kearney, *The British Isles* (1989), chs. 7–8; S. G. Ellis and S. Barber (eds.), *Conquest and Union: Fashioning a British State, 1485–1725* (1995); P. Jenkins, *The Making of a Ruling Class: The Glamorgan Gentry, 1640–1790* (1983); and J. R. Jones, *Britain and Europe in the Seventeenth Century* (1966).

Chapter 2

There are comprehensive accounts of Charles II's return in R. Hutton, *The Restoration* (1985) and G. Davies, *The Restoration of Charles II, 1658–1660* (1955).

   J. Miller, *An English Absolutism? The Later Stuart Monarchy, 1660–88* (1993); T. Harris, *Politics under the Later Stuarts* (1993); P. Seaward, *The Restoration, 1660–1688* (1991) and R. M. Bliss, *Restoration England: Politics and Government, 1660–1688* (1985) provide excellent introductory overviews; for a fuller narrative, see D. Ogg, *Charles II* (1963), and *England in the Reigns of James II and William III* (1955). L. K. Glassey (ed.), *The Reigns of Charles II and James VII & II* (1997) is a wide-ranging collection of essays on themes relevant both to this and the previous chapter. On religion's political dimensions, there are J. Miller, *Popery and Politics in England, 1660–1688* (1973); T. Harris, P. Seaward, and M. Goldie (eds.), *The Politics of Religion in Restoration England* (1990); R. L. Greaves, *Deliver us from Evil: The Radical Underground in Britain, 1660–1663* (1986), and its sequels (1990 and 1992); S. C. Pincus, *Protestantism and Patriotism: Ideologies and the Making of English Foreign Policy, 1650–1668* (1996) and J. Scott's two-volume political biography of *Algernon Sidney* (1988 and

1991), which dominates a symposium on Restoration politics in *Albion*, 25 (1993), 565–651.

For James II's reign and the causes of the Glorious Revolution, see J. P. Kenyon, *Robert Spencer Earl of Sunderland* (1957); J. R. Western, *Monarchy and Revolution: The English State in the 1680s* (1972), and works cited under Ch. 3 below.

Chapter 3

W. A. Speck, *Reluctant Revolutionaries* (1989) remains the best general introduction to 1688–9. The recent tercentenary spawned numerous volumes of collected essays, including E. Cruickshanks (ed.), *By Force or By Default?* (1989); O. P. Grell, J. I. Israel, and N. R. N. Tyacke, *From Persecution to Toleration: The Glorious Revolution and Religion in England* (1991); J. I. Israel (ed.), *The Anglo-Dutch Moment* (1991); R. Beddard (ed.), *The Revolutions of 1688* (1991); L. G. Schwoerer (ed.), *The Revolution of 1688–1689: Changing Perspectives* (1992); J. R. Jones (ed.), *Liberty Secured? Britain before and after 1688* (1992); and D. Hoak and M. Feingold (eds.), *The World of William and Mary: Anglo-Dutch Perspectives on the Revolution of 1688–89* (1996). G. M. Trevelyan, *The English Revolution, 1688–1689* (1938) judiciously encapsulates the Whig interpretation, of which L. Pinkham, *William III and the Respectable Revolution* (1954) was an attempted revisionist debunking. Two articles with a long perspective are A. McInnes, 'When was the English Revolution?', *History*, 67 (1982), and H. T. Dickinson, 'The Debate on the "Glorious Revolution" ', *History*, 61 (1976), 28–45.

Chapter 4

The work of G. Holmes is fundamental; besides his *British Politics in the Reign of Anne* (1987), see *The Trial of Dr Sacheverell* (1973) and *Politics, Religion and Society in England, 1679–1742* (1986), Holmes also edited *Britain after the Glorious Revolution, 1689–1720* (1977); other valuable collections of essays are C. Jones (ed.), *Britain in the First Age of Party, 1660–1750* (1987), and J. Cannon (ed.), *The Whig Ascendancy* (1981). H. Horwitz, *Parliament, Policy and Politics in the Reign of William III* (1977) complements Holmes. The ideological context is illuminated by G. V. Bennett, *The Tory Crisis in Church and State, 1688–1730* (1975); J. P. Kenyon, *Revolution Principles* (1977); and J. C. D. Clark, *English Society, 1688–1832* (1986), chs. 2–3. On the threat (or promise) of Jacobitism, see E. Gregg, *Jacobitism* (1988); E. Cruickshanks and J. Black (eds.), *The Jacobite Challenge* (1988) and P. Monod, *Jacobitism and the English People, 1688–1788* (1989). J. H. Plumb, *The Growth of Political Stability, 1675–1725* (1967), ch. 5, is a masterly introduction to many of these topics, while K. Feiling, *History of the Tory Party, 1641–1714* (1924) still repays study.

Chapter 5

The key themes of J. Brewer, *The Sinews of Power: War, Money and the English State, 1688–1783* (1989), are summarized in his 'The eighteenth-century British state: contexts and issues', in L. Stone (ed.), *An Imperial State at War: Britain from 1689 to 1815* (1994), whose other contributors explore various aspects of the 'fiscal-military state'. Brewer built upon P. G. M. Dickson's massive *The Financial Revolution in England: A Study of the Development of Public Credit, 1688–1756* (1967), but apparently without the benefit of D. W. Jones, *War and Economy in the Age of William III and Marlborough* (1988).

H. Roseveare provides compact guidance to *The Financial Revolution, 1660–1760* (1991) and *The Treasury, 1660–1870* (1973). On the state's civil and military servants there is G. Holmes, *Augustan England: Professions, State and Society* (1982), chs. 8–9; J. Childs, *The British Army of William III, 1689–1702* (1987); J. Ehrman, *The Navy in the War of William III, 1689–1697* (1953); and J. D. Davies, *Gentlemen and Tarpaulins* (1991).

D. Hayton and D. Szechi present a joint essay on post-revolutionary Ireland and Scotland in Jones, *Britain in the First Age of Party* (see above, under Ch. 4). See B. Levack, *The Formation of the British State: England, Scotland, and the Union, 1603–1707* (1987) for the origins of Anglo-Scottish Union. The reconquest of Ireland and its consequences are detailed by J. G. Simms, *The Williamite Confiscation in Ireland, 1690–1703* (1956) and R. F. Foster, *Modern Ireland, 1600–1972* (1988), ch. 7.

Chapter 6

L. Davison, T. Hitchcock, T. Keirn, and R. B. Shoemaker (eds.), *Stilling the Grumbling Hive: The Response to Social and Economic Problems in England, 1689–1750* (1992), and J. Barry and C. W. Brooks (eds.), *The Middling Sort of People: Culture, Society and Politics in England, 1550–1800* (1994) are volumes of collected essays highly relevant to the themes of this chapter.

R. Davis, *A Commercial Revolution* (1967) condenses his own pioneering work, some of which is reprinted in (ed.), *The Growth of English Overseas Trade in the 17th and 18th Centuries* (1969). C. Wilson's *Mercantilism* (1958) is both succint and expansive; see also his *England's Apprenticeship*, chs. 8, 13. J. A. Chartres, *Internal Trade in England, 1500–1700* (1977), supplementing T. S. Willan, *River Navigation in England, 1600–1750* (1936), is itself revised by D. Gerhould, 'The growth of the London carrying trade, 1681–1838', *EcoHR*, 41 (1988).

Traders feature prominently in P. Earle, *The Making of the English Middle Class: Business, Society and Family Life in London, 1660–1730* (1989), and R. Grassby, *The Business Commmunity of Seventeenth-Century England* (1995). On the professions, see Holmes, *Augustan England* (see above, under Ch. 5), and W. Prest (ed.), *The Professions in Early Modern England* (1987). P. J. Corfield, *The Impact of English Towns, 1700–1800* (1982), examines the socio-economic influence of the expanding urban sector, while P. Borsay's *The English Urban Renaissance: Culture and Society in the Provincial Town, 1660–1770* (1989) looks at how towns themselves changed. E. A. Wrigley, 'London's importance in changing English society and economy, 1650–1750', *P&P* 37 (1967), remains fundamental, as does M. D. George, *London Life in the Eighteenth Century* (1930). M. Ingram, 'Reformation of manners in early modern England', in P. Griffiths, A. Fox, and S. Hindle (eds.), *The Experience of Authority in Early Modern England* (1996) takes a long view of moral reformation, while J. O. Appleby elucidates *Economic Thought and Ideology in Seventeenth Century England* (1978).

Chapter 7

Daniel Defoe's *A Tour Thro' the whole Island of Great Britain* (1724–7) was reprinted in 1927 with an introduction by G. D. H. Cole; there are several modern paperbound editions. On Defoe, see P. Earle, *The World of Defoe* (1976); his legendary literary output is downsized by P. N. Furbank and W. R. Owens, *The Canonization of Daniel Defoe* (1988).

S.J. Connolly, 'Varieties of Britishness: Ireland, Scotland and Wales in the Hanoverian State' in A. Grant and K. J. Stringer (eds.), *Uniting the Kingdom* (1995) provides a splendid overview. Modern introductions to Welsh society and culture include J. Davies, *A History of Wales* (1993); G. E. Jones, *Modern Wales* (1994) and G. H. Jenkins, *The Foundations of Modern Wales* (1987). On Lhuyd, cf. S. Piggott, 'Antiquarian thought in the sixteenth and seventeenth centuries', in L. Fox (ed.), *English Historical Scholarship in the Sixteenth and Seventeenth Centuries* (1956). T. C. Smout, *A History of the Scottish People, 1560–1830* (1970) is an unsurpassed general history. See also B. Lenman, *An Economic History of Modern Scotland* (1977); id., 'A client Society: Scotland between the '15 and the '45', in J. Black (ed.), *Britain in the Age of Walpole* (1984); J. D. Mackie, *A History of Scotland*, ed. B. Lenman and G. Parker (1978); R. Houston and I. Whyte (eds.), *Scottish Society, 1500–1800* (1990).

Besides the standard multi-author *A New History of Ireland*, iv. *Eighteenth-Century Ireland, 1691–1800*, eds. T. W. Moody and W. E. Vaughan (1986), useful surveys include J. C. Beckett, *The Making of Modern Ireland, 1603–1923* (1966); D. Dickson, *New Foundations: Ireland, 1660–1800* (1987) and S. J. Connolly, *Religion, Law and Power: The Making of Protestant Ireland, 1660–1760* (1992).

Chapter 8

On the first two Hanoverian monarchs, see G. C. Gibbs, 'English attitudes towards Hanover and the Hanoverian succession in the first half of the eighteenth century', in A. M. Birke and K. Kluxen (eds.), *England and Hanover* (1986); R. Hatton, *George I Elector and King* (1978), and J. B. Owen, 'George II reconsidered', in A. Whiteman, J. Bromley, and P. Dickson (eds.), *Statesmen, Scholars, and Merchants* (1973).

For the political impact of the Hanoverian succession, L. Colley, *In Defiance of Oligarchy: The Tory Party, 1714–1760* (1982); G. S. de Krey, *A Fractured Society: The Politics of London in the First Age of Party, 1688–1715* (1985), and N. Rogers, *Whigs and Cities: Popular Politics in the Age of Walpole and Pitt* (1989). Besides J. H. Plumb's standard but unfinished two-volume biography of *Sir Robert Walpole* (1956, 1960), there is H. T. Dickinson's succinct *Walpole and the Whig Supremacy* (1973), and B. W. Hill's *Sir Robert Walpole* (1989). On Walpole's political opponents, see A. S. Foord, *His Majesty's Opposition, 1714–1830* (1964), chs. 4–5; I. Kramnick, *Bolingbroke and his Circle* (1968); P. Langford, *The Excise Crisis* (1975); H. T. Dickinson, *Liberty and Property: Political Ideology in Eighteenth-Century Britain* (1977), ch. 5; and K. Wilson, *The Sense of the People: Politics, Culture and Imperialism in England, 1715–1785* (1995), chs. 2–3.

Chapter 9

The editorial introduction to J. Walsh, C. Haydon, and S. Taylor (eds.), *The Church of England, c.1689–c.1833* (1993) is comprehensive, judicious, and up-to-date, if less chatty than E. G. Rupp's survey of *Religion in England, 1688–1791* (1986). J. Spurr, *The Restoration Church of England, 1646–1689* (1991), provides more than chronological background to the influential work of N. Sykes, especially *Church and State in England in the Eighteenth Century* (1934). F. C. Mather, 'Georgian churchmanship reconsidered: some variations in Anglican church worship, 1714–1830', *Journal of Ecclesiastical History*, 36 (1985); W. R. Ward (ed.), *Parson and Parish in Eighteenth-Century Surrey* Surrey Record Society, 34 (1994); and M. G. Jones, *The Charity School Movement*

(1938), explore grass-roots Anglican religious life. J. A. I. Champion, *The Pillars of Priestcraft Shaken: The Church of England and its Enemies, 1660–1730* (1992), traces clerical responses to various intellectual challenges. M. Watts, *The Dissenters: From the Reformation to the French Revolution* (1978) is a reliable survey; see also J. E. Bradley, *Religion, Revolution and English Radicalism* (1990), and D. L. Wykes, 'Religious dissent and the penal laws: an explanation of business success?', *History*, 75 (1990).

On Methodism, H. D. Rack, *Reasonable Enthusiast: John Wesley and the Rise of Methodism* (1989), may be balanced by R. E. Davies and E. G. Rupp, *A History of the Methodist Church in Great Britain* (1965); there are also important articles by J. Walsh, including 'Methodism and the mob', in G. J. Cuming and D. Black (eds.), *Popular Belief and Practice* (1972), 229–36. The same author has discussed 'The Origins of the Evangelical Revival', in G. V. Bennett and J. D. Walsh (eds.), *Essays in Modern English Church History* (1966).

The relationship between Church, chapel, sect, society, and state is discussed by J. C. D. Clark in 'England's Ancien Regime as a confessional state', *Albion*, 21 (1989), and P. Corfield, 'Georgian England: one state, many faiths', *History Today*, 45 (Apr. 1995).

Chapter 10

M. Overton, *Agricultural Revolution in England: The Transformation of the Agrarian Community, 1500–1850* (1996); J. V. Beckett, *The Agricultural Revolution* (1990); and J. Thirsk, *England's Agricultural Regions and Agrarian History, 1500–1750* (1987), offer helpful guidance across a well-worked field, less intimidating than the bulky *Agrarian History of England and Wales, v. 1640–1750*, ed. J. Thirsk (1985).

Berg, *The Age of Manufactures, 1700–1820* (see above, under Overviews and Surveys) discusses domestic and workshop production, especially in the metal trades.

Early modern consumerism has become a scholarly industry; its products include N. McKendrick, 'The consumer revolution of eighteenth-century England', in N. McKendrick, J. Brewer, and J. Plumb, *The Birth of a Consumer Society: The Commercialisation of Eighteenth-Century England* (1982); L. Weatherill, *Consumer Behaviour and Material Culture in Britain, 1660–1760* (1988); C. Shammas, *The Pre-Industrial Consumer in England and America* (1990); H. and L. H. Mui, *Shops and Shopkeeping in Eighteenth-Century England* (1989); B. Fine and E. Leopold, 'Consumerism and the Industrial Revolution', *Social History*, 15 (1990), 151–79; B. Lemire, *Fashion's Favourite: The Cotton Trade and the Consumer in Britain, 1660–1800* (1991); and J. Brewer and R. Porter (eds.), *Consumption and the World of Goods* (1993).

The economic role of government is also attracting attention: e.g. J. Innes, 'The domestic face of the military-fiscal state: government and society in eighteenth-century Britain', in Stone, *An Imperial State at War* (see above, under Ch. 5), and P. K. O'Brien, 'Central governnment and the economy, 1688–1815', in *EHB*.

Chapter 11

See demographic sources already mentioned (under Ch. 1 above); important methodological issues are addressed by P. Razell, *Essays in English Population History* (1993).

J. Rule *Albion's People* (see above, under Overviews and Surveys) is a sympathetic introduction; broader implications of wage labour are postulated by C. Tilly, 'Demographic origins of the European proletariat', in D. Levine, *Proletarianization and*

Family History (1984), 27–9. J. Styles, 'Embezzlement, industry and the law in England, 1500–1800', in M. Berg, P. Hudson and M. Sonenscher (eds.), *Manufacture in Town and Country before the Factory* (1983), examines attacks on customary work practices, also a preoccupation of D. Hay and N. Rogers, *Eighteenth-Century English Society: Shuttles and Swords* (1997).

The social heights are surveyed by J. V. Beckett, *The Aristocracy in England, 1660–1914* (1986); M. Bush, *The English Aristocracy* (1984); J. Cannon, *Aristocratic Century* (1984); and L. and J. C. F. Stone, *An Open Elite* (1984); but see also D. and E. Spring, 'Social mobility and the English landed elite', *Canadian Journal of History*, 21 (1986). Children have attracted much scholarly attention, especially since the appearance of L. Stone's path-breaking *The Family: Sex and Marriage in England, 1500–1800* (1977); general studies include H. Cunningham, *Children of the Poor: Representations of Childhood since the Seventeenth Century* (1991), and I. Ben Amos, *Adolescence and Youth in Early Modern England* (1994). Women's achievements and struggles are variously treated by S. H. Myers, *The Bluestocking Circle* (1990); J. Todd, *The Sign of Angellica: Women, Writing and Fiction, 1660–1800* (1989); S. Staves, *Married Women's Separate Property in England, 1660–1825* (1990); B. Hill, *Women, Work and Sexual Politics in Eighteenth-Century England* (1989); and E. Spring, *Law, Land and Family: Aristocratic Inheritance in England, 1300–1800* (1990).

N. Hans, *New Trends in Education in the Eighteenth Century* (1966); V. E. Neuberg, *Popular Education in Eighteenth-Century England* (1971), and T. W. Laqueur, *Religion and Respectability* (1976) highlight the diversity of educational provision; its effectiveness is scrutinized in R. S. Schofield, 'Dimensions of illiteracy, 1750–1850', *Explorations in Economic History*, 10 (1993), 437–56; R. A. Houston, *Scottish Literacy and the Scottish Identity* (1985), chs. 2–3; and M. Sanderson, *Education, Economic Change and Society in England, 1780–1870* (1983). Higher education is well served by *The History of the University of Oxford*, v. *The Eighteenth Century*, ed. L. S. Sutherland and L. G. Mitchell (1986), and J. Gascoigne, *Cambridge in the Age of the Enlightenment* (1989). J. Gillis, *For Better, For Worse: British Marriages, 1600 to the Present* (1985), chs. 1–4, explores the social meanings of marriage; L. Stone's *Road to Divorce: England, 1530–1987* (1990) chronicles its making and ending. Accessible accounts of ethnic minorities include D. Katz, *The Jews in the History of England, 1485–1850* (1994); R. D. Gwynn, *Huguenot Heritage* (1985); P. Fryer, *Staying Power* (1984), and N. Myers, *Reconstructing the Black Past: Blacks in Britain, c.1780–1830* (1996).

Chapter 12

J. Owen recounts *The Rise of the Pelhams* (1957). R. Poole, ' "Give us our eleven days!": calendar reform in eighteenth-century England', *P&P* 149 (1995) and Katz, *Jews in England* (see above, under Ch. 11), ch. 6, examine Pelhamite legislative initiatives; the impact of the post-war crime wave is discussed by J. M. Beattie, *Crime and the Courts in England, 1660–1815* (1986), while J. Innes, 'Parliament and the shaping of eighteenth-century social policy', *Transactions of the Royal Historical Society*, 5th ser. 40 (1990) contextualizes this activity.

S. Ayling, *The Elder Pitt* (1976), is a full life-and-times; M. Peters, *Pitt and Popularity* (1980), explores the patriot minister's relationship with his London supporters; R. Middleton, *The Bells of Victory* (1985), discounts Pitt's role in winning the Seven Years War, contrary to J. Black in *Pitt the Elder* (1992).

J. C. Clark, *The Dynamics of Change: The Crisis of the 1750s and English Party Systems* (1982) analyses high politics, whereas J. Brewer's *Party Ideology and Popular Politics at the Accession of George III* (1976) examines the interplay between parliamentary politics and public opinion; on a broader canvas so does F. O'Gorman, *Voters, Patrons, and Parties: The Unreformed Electoral System in Hanoverian England, 1734–1832* (1989). For the press and politics, see J. Black, *The English Press in the Eighteenth Century* (1987), and G. Cranfield, *The Development of the Provincial Newspaper, 1700–1760* (1962). P. D. Thomas, *John Wilkes: A Friend to Liberty* (1996) reinterprets both the man and his politics.

Chapter 13

There is no modern biography of Blackstone, nor a general history of eighteenth-century law; but see D. Lieberman, *The Province of Legislation Determined: Legal Theory in Eighteenth-Century Britain* (1989), especially chs. 1–2. The shrinkage of legal business is mapped by C. W. Brooks, 'Interpersonal conflict and social tension: civil litigation in England, 1640–1830', in A. L. Beier *et al.* (eds.), *The First Modern Society: Essays in English History in Honour of Lawrence Stone* (1989). J. Brewer outlines 'The Wilkites and the law, 1763–1774: a study of radical notions of governance', in J. Brewer and J. Styles (eds.), *An Ungovernable People: the English and their Law in the Seventeenth and Eighteenth Centuries* (1980); the work of a politically conservative but reforming judge is documented in J. Oldham (ed.), *The Mansfield Manuscripts and the Growth of English Law in the Eighteenth Century* (1992).

Crime and criminal justice are better served, from D. Hay *et al.*, *Albion's Fatal Tree* (1975), through J. Beattie's magisterial *Crime and the Courts, 1660–1815* (1986) and M. de Lacy's revisionist *Prison Reform in Lancashire, 1700–1850* (1986), to the powerful study of *The Hanging Tree: Execution and the English People, 1770–1868* by V. Gatrell (1994).

W. Gibson, *Church, State and Society, 1760–1850* (1994), and D. Hempton, 'Religion in British society, 1740–1790', in J. Black (ed.), *British Politics and Society from Walpole to Pitt, 1742–1789* (1990) are useful modern surveys. P. Virgin, *The Church in a State of Negligence: Ecclesiastical Structure and Problems of Church Reform, 1700–1840* (1989); E. J. Evans, 'Some reasons for the growth of English Anti-Clericalism, c.1750–c.1830', *P&P* 66 (1975) and A. D. Gilbert, *Religion and Society in Industrial England* (1976) provide a range of perspectives on Anglican pastoral effectiveness. The evangelical impulse is traced by W. R. Ward, *The Protestant Evangelical Awakening* (1992); D. W. Bebbington, *Evangelicalism in Modern Britain* (1989); and P. B. Nockles, *The Oxford Movement in Context: Anglican High Churchmanship, 1760–1857* (1994). For the interplay between religion and politics, see J. Gascoigne, 'Anglican latitudinarianism, Rational Dissent, and political radicalism in the later eighteenth century', in K. Haakonssen (ed.), *Enlightenment and religion* (1996); J. E. Bradley, *Religion, Revolution and English Radicalism: Nonconformity in Eighteenth-Century Politics and Society* (1990); G. Rudé, 'The Gordon Riots', in *Paris and London in the Eighteenth Century* (1971); and I. McCalman, 'Mad Lord George and Madame La Motte: riot and sexuality in the genesis of Burke's *Reflections on the Revolution in France*', *Journal of British Studies*, 35 (1996).

Chapter 14

Wilson, *The Sense of the People*; L. Colley, *Britons: Forging the Nation, 1707–1837* (1992); C. A. Bayley, *Imperial Meridian: The British Empire and the World, 1780–1830* (1989); and J. M. Price, 'Who cared about the colonies? The impact of the Thirteen Colonies on British society and politics, *c*.1714–1775', in B. Bailyn and P. D. Morgan (eds.), *Strangers within the Realm* (1991) are stimulating introductions to the themes of this chapter. T. O. Lloyd, *The British Empire, 1558–1983* (1989) is a helpful general survey.

In *Revolution in America: Britain and the Colonies, 1763–1776* (1992), P. D. Thomas draws on his multi-volume study of British policy towards America. For its divisive domestic impact, see J. Derry, *British Politics and the American Revolution* (1976), and Bradley, *Religion, Revolution and English Radicalism* (see above under Ch. 13). I. Christie recounts the course of the war in *Crisis of Empire* (1976) and has also discussed *Wilkes, Wyvill and Reform: The Parliamentary Reform Movement in British Politics, 1760–1785* (1962).

The Irish crisis is best approached via R. B. McDowell, *Ireland in the Age of Imperialism and Revolution, 1760–1801* (1979).

J. Ehrman, *The Younger Pitt: The Years of Acclaim* (1969) is the first volume of the authoritative biography; on the political background to Pitt's accession to office, see J. Cannon, *The Fox-North Coalition: Crisis of the Constitution, 1782–4* (1969). The underlying constitutional issues are discussed by B. Kemp, *King and Commons, 1660–1832* (1957) and R. Pares, *George III and the Politicians* (1953). For the British and India, the work of P. J. Marshall is indispensable, including '*A Free though Conquering People': Britain and Asia in the Eighteenth Century* (1981); and ' "Cornwallis Triumphant": war in India and the British public in the late eighteenth century', in L. Freedman, P. Hayes, and R. J. O'Neill (eds.), *War, Strategy and International Politics* (1992).

Attitudes towards the wider world are traced in P. J. Marshall and G. Williams, *The Great Map of Mankind. British Perceptions of the World in the Age of Enlightenment* (1982); and B. Smith, *European Vision and the South Pacific, 1768–1850* (1965). J. C. Beaglehole, *The Life of Captain James Cook* (1974), is the standard biography. For New Holland, see J. Hardy and A. Frost (eds.), *Studies from Terra Australis to Australia* (1989), ch. 8; J. Kociumbas, *The Oxford History of Australia, ii. 1770–1860 Possessions* (1992) and A. Frost, *Botany Bay Mirages: Illusions of Australia's Convict Beginnings* (1994).

Chapter 15

R. Porter, 'The Enlightenment in England', in R. Porter and M. Teich (eds.), *The Enlightenment in National Context* (1981), is an excellent overview, while in *Joseph Banks and the English Enlightenment* (1994) J. Gascoigne provides an exemplary case study. A. C. Chitnis on *The Scottish Enlightenment: A Social History* (1976) is complemented by N. Phillipson's chapter in the Porter and Teich volume cited above. The audience for science is discussed by G. S. Rousseau, 'Science books and their readers in the eighteenth century', in I. Rivers (ed.), *Books and their Readers in Eighteenth-Century England* (1982), and J. Money, *Experience and Identity: Birmingham and the West Midlands, 1760–1800* (1977), ch. 6. D. Sobel's *Longitude* (1995) is an engaging account of the eventual winner of Parliament's longitude prize. On medicine, see R. Porter, *Disease, Medicine and Society in England, 1550–1860* (1987); D. Porter and R. Porter, *Patient's Progress* (1989) and J. C. Riley, *The Eighteenth-Century Campaign to Avoid Disease* (1987).

D. Owen, *English Philanthropy, 1660–1960* (1964), is a general survey; D. T. Andrew, *Philanthropy and Police: London Charity in the Eighteenth Century* (1989), more tightly focused, draws out some broader implications, as does J. Innes, 'Politics and morals: the reformation of manners movement in later eighteenth-century England', in E. Helmuth (ed.), *The Transformation of Political Culture: England and Germany in the late Eighteenth Century* (1990).

K. Thomas, *Man and the Natural World: Changing Attitudes in England, 1500–1800* (1983), deploys a wealth of ideas and learning; R. W. Malcolmson, *Popular Recreations in English Society, 1700–1850* (1973), ch. 7, discusses campaigns against popular cruel sports. Proto-romantic sensibilities in landscape gardening, painting, and literature are discussed by E. Hyams, *Capability Brown and Humphrey Repton* (1971); J. Burke, *English Art, 1714–1800* (1976); and M. Butler, *Romantics, Rebels and Reactionaries* (1981).

Chapter 16

Helpful introductory surveys include P. Hudson, *The Industrial Revolution* (1992) and P. K. O'Brien and R. Quinault (eds.), *The Industrial Revolution and British Society* (1993). Although specifically intended for students of economic history, *EHB* is generally accessible to other readers. The debate on the very existence of an 'industrial revolution' is outlined by D. Cannadine, 'The present and past in the English Industrial Revolution, 1880–1980', *P&P* 103 (1984); see also M. Berg and P. Hudson, 'Rehabilitating the Industrial Revolution', *EcHR* 45 (1992).

On agricultural productivity and change, Overton, *Agricultural Revolution in England* (see above, under Ch. 10) is invaluable; see also R. Allen, 'Agriculture during the Industrial Revolution', in *EHB*.

For transport, see R. Szostak, *The Role of Transportation in the Industrial Revolution* (1991); D. H. Aldcroft and M. J. Freeman (eds.), *Transport in the Industrial Revolution* (1983); W. Albert, *The Turnpike Road System in England, 1663–1840* (1972); B. Austen, 'The impact of the mail coach on public coach services in England and Wales, 1784–1840', *Journal of Transport History*, 3rd ser. 2 (1981); P. J. G. Ransom, *The Archaeology of the Transport Revolution, 1750–1850* (1984).

Industrial power sources are surveyed by A. E. Musson, 'Industrial motive power in the United Kingdom, 1800–70', *EcHR* 29 (1976); J. W. Kanefsky, 'Motive power in the British industry and the accuracy of the 1870 Factory Return', *EcHR* 32 (1979); R. L. Hills, *Power from Steam: A History of the Stationary Steam Engine* (1989) and G. N. von Tunzelman, *Steam Power and British Industrialization to 1860* (1978). C. MacLeod, *Inventing the Industrial Revolution* (1988), is concerned with much more than machines; see also J. Mokyr, 'Technological change, 1700–1830', in *EHB*. On the rise of 'King Cotton', there is S. D. Chapman, 'The cotton industry and the Industrial Revolution', in L. A. Clarkson (ed.), *The Industrial Revolution: A Compendium* (1990); and M. M. Edwards, *The Growth of the British Cotton Trade, 1780–1815* (1967).

Aspects of British commercial expansion are treated by F. Crouzet, *Britain Ascendant: Comparative Studies in Franco-British Economic History* (1990); P. Deane and W. A. Cole, *British Economic Growth, 1688–1958* (1967); R. P. Thomas and D. N. McCloskey, 'Overseas trade and empire, 1700–1860', in R. Floud and D. McCloskey (eds.), *Economic History of Britain from 1700* (1981), 89; P. K. O'Brien and S. L. Engerman, 'Exports and the growth of the British economy from the Glorious

Revolution to the Peace of Amiens', in B. Solow (ed.), *Slavery and the Rise of the Atlantic System* (1991); C. J. French, 'Productivity in the Atlantic shipping industry', *Journal of Interdisciplinary History*, 17 (1987); B. L. Solow, 'Capitalism and slavery in the exceedingly long run', in B. L. Solow and S. L. Engerman (eds.), *British Capitalism and Caribbean Slavery* (1989).

On the financial sector, see L. S. Pressnell, *Country Banking in the Industrial Revolution* (1956); R. Cameron, *Banking in the Early Stages of Industrialization* (1967); J. Styles, ' "Our traitorous money makers": the Yorkshire coiners and the law, 1760–83', in Brewer and Styles (eds.), *An Ungovernable People* (see above, under Ch. 13); J. Hoppitt, *Risk and Failure in English Business, 1700–1800* (1987); L. Neal, 'The finance of business during the industrial revolution', in *EHB*, and id., *The Rise of Financial Capitalism: International Capital Markets in the Age of Reason* (1990).

The complex interactions between law, government, and the economy are discussed in the Introduction to G. R. Rubin and D. Sugarman (eds.), *Law, Economy and Society, 1750–1914: Essays in the History of English Law* (1984); H. Horwitz, 'Liberty, law, and property, 1689–1776', in Jones (ed.), *Liberty Secured?* (see above, under Ch. 3); R. M. Hartwell, *The Industrial Revolution and Economic Growth* (1971), 244–61; N. B. Harte, 'The rise of protection and the English linen trade, 1690–1790', in N. B. Harte and K. G. Ponting (eds.), *Textile History and Economic History* (1973). On the poor laws, see P. M. Solar, 'Poor relief and English economic development before the industrial revolution', *EcHR* 48 (1995) and M. D. George, *England in Transition* (1953).

F. Crouzet, *The First Industrialists* (1985), and S. Pollard, *The Genesis of Modern Management* (1965), examine the identities and roles of entrepreneurs and managers, while J. Rule, *The Experience of Labour in Eighteenth-Century Industry* (1981), takes the workers' perspective, as do A. Randall, *Before the Luddites* (1991), and P. Linebaugh, *The London Hanged: Crime and Civil Society in the Eighteenth Century* (1991). On women in the workforce, see D. Valenze, *The First Industrial Woman* (1995); J. Rendall, *Women in an Industrializing Society: England, 1750–1880* (1990); and D. Bythell's essay in O'Brien and Quinault (eds.), *Industrial Revolution and British Society*.

J. Stevenson's essay, 'Social aspects of the industrial revolution', in O'Brien and Quinault, *Industrial Revolution and British Society*, provides a good overview; Perkin, *Origins of Modern English Society* and Thompson, *Making of the English Working Class*, both see industrialization as intensifying class divisions; on class as an analytical concept, cf. N. McCord, 'Adding a touch of class', *History*, 70 (1985). Early trade unionism is surveyed by R. W. Malcolmson, 'Workers' combinations in eighteenth-century England', in M. and J. Jacob (eds.), *The Origins of Anglo-American Radicalism* (1984) and C. R. Dobson, *Masters and Journeymen: A Prehistory of Industrial Relations, 1717–1800* (1980); still earlier by G. Unwin, *Industrial Organization in the Sixteenth and Seventeenth Centuries* (1904).

E. P. Thompson, *Customs in Common* (1991), chs. 4–5, expounds and defends the 'moral economy' thesis; see also A. Randall, 'The industrial moral economy of the Gloucestershire weavers in the eighteenth century', in J. Rule (ed.), *British Trade Unionism, 1750–1850* (1988). For the standard of living debate, see Rule, *Albion's People* (above, under Overviews and Surveys), ch. 7; A. Taylor (ed.), *The Standard of Living Controversy in Britain in the Industrial Revolution* (1975); and S. Horrell and J. Humphries, 'Old questions, new data, and alternative perspectives: families' living standards in the industrial revolution', *Journal of Economic History*, 52 (1992). For the newish sub-field of historical auxology, or the study of human stature, see R. Floud, K. Wachter, and A. S. Gregory, *Height, Health and History: Nutritional Status in the United Kingdom* (1990); J. Komlos, 'The Secular Trend in the Biological Standard of Living in the United Kingdom, 1740–1860', *EcHR* 46 (1993); S. Nicholas and R. H. Steckel, 'Heights and living standards of English workers during the early years of industrialization, 1770–1815', *Journal of Economic History*, 51 (1991); S. Nicholas and D. Oxley, 'The living standards of women during the Industrial Revolution, 1795–1820', *EcHR* 46 (1993).

On regional economic development, see P. Hudson, *Regions and Industries* (1989); S. Pollard, *Peaceful Conquest: The Industrialization of Europe, 1760–1970* (1981), ch. 1; C. H. Lee, *The British Economy since 1700* (1986), ch. 14; Corfield, *Impact of English Towns* (see above, under Ch. 6); J. G. Williamson, *Coping with City Growth during the British Industrial Revolution* (1990), ch. 2.

Chapter 17

H. T. Dickinson, *Liberty and Property* (1977), offers an overview of eighteenth-century political thought; see also J. G. A. Pocock, *Virtue, Commerce and History* (1985), ch. 11, and I. Kramnick, *Republicanism and Bourgeois Radicalism: Political Ideology in Late Eighteenth-Century England and America* (1990). J. Seed discusses 'Rational Dissent and political opposition in England, 1770–1790', in his contribution to K. Haakonssen (ed.), *Rational Dissent and the Enlightenment* (1996). On the impact of the French Revolution, see M. Philp (ed.), *The French Revolution and British Popular Politics* (1991); H. T. Dickinson (ed.), *Britain and the French Revolution* (1989) and his *British Radicalism and the French Revolution, 1789–1815* (1985); A. Cobban (ed.), *The Debate on the French Revolution, 1789–1800* (1963); and P. A. Brown, *The French Revolution in English History* (1918). See also J. Keane, *Tom Paine* (1995); J. Ehrman, *The Younger Pitt: The Reluctant Transition* (1983); L. G. Mitchell, *Charles James Fox* (1992); and C. C. O'Brien, *The Great Melody: A Thematic Biography and Commented Anthology of Edmund Burke* (1993).

T. C. W. Blanning, *The Origins of the French Revolutionary Wars* (1986) anatomizes the international context; a more expansive treatment is J. Black, *British Foreign Policy in an Age of Revolutions, 1783–1793* (1994). On the loyalist movement, see R. R. Dozier, *For King, Constitution, and Country* (1983), and H. T. Dickinson, 'Popular Loyalism in Britain in the 1790s', in E. Hellmuth (ed.), *The Transformation of Political Culture* (1990).

Chapter 18

C. Emsley, *British Society and the French Wars* (1979), and J. Cookson, *The Friends of Peace* (1982) chronicle reactions to the outbreak of war. For the ministry's perspective there are vols. ii–iii of J. Ehrman's standard biography of *The Younger Pitt* (1983) and (1996); also P. Jupp, *Lord Grenville, 1759–1834* (1985). M. I. Thomis and P. Holt, *Threats of Revolution in Britain, 1789–1848* (1977); C. Emsley, 'Repression, "Terror" and the Rule of Law in England during the decade of the French Revolution', *EHR* 100 (1985) and E. Sparrow, 'The Alien Office, 1792–1806', *HJ* 33 (1990) cover the internal security issue.

A. Charlesworth, 'Labour protest, 1780–1850', in *Atlas of Industrializing Britain, 1780–1914*, surveys a broad picture; a complementary overview is provided by R. Wells,

'The development of the English rural proletariat and social protest, 1700–1850', in M. Reed and R. Wells (eds.), *Class, Conflict, and Protest in the English Countryside, 1700–1880* (1990). On the economic causes of discontent, see B. R. Mitchell and P. Deane, *Abstract of British Historical Statistics* (1962), 487, and R. Wells, *Wretched Faces: Famine in Wartime England, 1793–1801* (1988). I. R. Christie, *Stress and Stability in Late Eighteenth Century England: Reflections on the British Avoidance of Revolution* (1984), is concise but wide ranging; an alternative perspective is offered by R. Wells, *Insurrection: The British Experience, 1795–1803* (1986). Diverse political responses are discussed by I. McCalman, *Radical Underworld: Prophets, Revolutionaries, and Pornographers in London, 1795–1840* (1988); A. Hone, *For the Cause of Truth: Radicalism in London, 1796–1821* (1982); and E. Vincent, ' "The Real Grounds of the Present War": John Bowles and the French Revolutionary Wars, 1792–1802', *History*, 78 (1993).

Irish events may be followed in M. Elliott, *Partners in Revolution: The United Irishmen and France* (1982); G. C. Bolton, *The Passing of the Irish Act of Union* (1966); and A. J. Ward, *The Irish Constitutional Tradition: Responsible Government and Modern Ireland, 1782–1992* (1994), ch. 1.

International strategy and its domestic ramifications are traced in P. Mackesy, *The Strategy of Overthrow* (1974), and *War without Victory* (1984), while M. Duffy, *Soldiers, Sugar, and Seapower: The British Expeditions to the West Indies and the War against the French Revolution* (1987), and R. Muir, *Britain and the Defeat of Napoleon, 1807–1815* (1996) deal respectively with the West Indian and Peninsular campaigns. J. Cookson, *The Armed Nation* (1997) is an important recent study, which somewhat qualifies L. Colley, *Britons: Forging the Nation, 1707–1837* (1992), ch. 7, and R. Glover, *Britain at Bay: Defence against Napoleon, 1803–14* (1973). A. D. Harvey, *Britain in the Early Nineteenth Century* (1978) is a general history, usefully supplemented by J. W. Derry, *Politics in the Age of Fox, Pitt and Liverpool* (1990).

Chapter 19

J. C. D. Clark, in *Revolution and Rebellion: State and Society in England in the Seventeenth and Eighteenth Centuries* (1986) and *English Society, 1688–1832* (1985), is the main modern proponent of 'no change', against what he regards as Whig–Marxist orthodoxy, which depicts 1688 as a genuine break in historical continuity: cf. J. Innes's critique (with Clark's response) in *P&P* 115 and 117 (1987), and a symposium on '1688 and all that', *British Journal of Eighteenth-Century Studies*, 15 (1992), 131–49. Other long-range perspectives are provided by C. Hill, 'The place of the English Revolution in English History', in id., *A Nation of Change and Novelty* (1990); P. Corrigan and D. Sayer, *The Great Arch* (1985); and C. Tilly, *The Formation of National States in Western Europe* (1975).

On the construction of national identity, see Colley, *Britons* (see above, under Ch. 18); G. Newman, *The Rise of English Nationalism: A Cultural History, 1740–1830* (1987); W. Weber, 'The 1784 Handel commemoration as political ritual', *JBS* 28 (1989); G. Russell, *The Theatres of War: Performance, Politics, and Society, 1793–1815* (1995); and pt. IV of A. Grant and K. G. Stringer (eds.), *Uniting the Kingdom? The Making of British History* (1995).

J. Black, *Convergence or Divergence? Britain and the Continent* (1994) is a stimulating survey. Issues of social openness or otherwise are canvassed by D. and E. Spring, 'The English landed elite, 1540–1879: a review', *Albion*, 17 (1985); F. M. L. Thompson,

INDEX

Aboukir Bay, battle of 300
absolutism 17, 45, 64
academics 26, 103, 169
Acadia 190
actresses 180
Acts of Parliament:
  Act of Artificers, repeal of (1814) 260
  Act of Indemnity and Oblivion (1660) 37
  Act of Settlement (1701) 63, 74, 89, 120
  Act of Uniformity (1662) 22
  Act of Union (1707) 226, 299
  Aliens Act (1705) 89
  Bill of Rights (1689) 62–5, 68, 72, 83, 198
  Bishops Exclusion Act (1642) 38
  Blasphemy Act (1698) 139
  Bubble Act (1720) 258
  Bugging Act (1749) 166
  Catholic Relief Act (1788) 209
  Combination Acts (1799, 1800) 264, 265,
    301
  Conventicles Act (1670) 42
  Corporation Act (1661) 127, 135, 208, 281
  Declaratory Act (1720) 116, 117
  Defence of the Realm Act (1798) 302
  Factory Act (1802) 267
  Gin Act (1751) 189
  Habeas Corpus Act (1679) 200, 217, 294
  Hardwicke's Marriage Act (1753) 136, 183,
    189
  India Act (1785) 221
  Jew Bill (1753) 189
  Last Determinations Act (1696) 125
  Libel Act (1792) 281
  Licensing Act (1662) 66, 70, 193, 196
  Murder Act (1752) 189
  Navigation Acts (1651, 1660) 11, 32, 93, 95,
    158, 213
  Occasional Conformity Act (1711) 79
  Qualifications Act (1710) 125
  Quebec Act (1774) 215
  Reform Act (1832) 81
  Regulating Act (1773) 221
  Riot Act (1715) 121
  Schism Act (1714) 80
  Seditious Meetings Act (1795) 295
  Septennial Act (1716) 122, 126, 216
  Stamp Act (1765) 213
  Stockjobbing Act (1734) 258
  Sugar Act (1764) 213

  Test Act (1673) 43, 50–1, 127, 135, 208, 281
  Test and Corporation Acts, repeal of 127,
    208, 281
  Toleration Act (1689) 66, 68, 76
  Toleration Act (1712) 115
  Treasonable Practices Act (1795) 295
  Trial of Treason Act (1696) 63
  Triennial Acts (1641 and 1664) 38
  Triennial Act (1694) 63, 70, 74
actuarial calculations 105
Addington, Henry 301, 303
Addison, Joseph 81, 85, 98
Admiralty 87, 88, 305
  see also navy
advertisements 145, 155, 172, 178, 279
affective individualism 179, 184
Africa 10, 16, 32, 33, 94, 157, 186, 191, 255
agricultural revolution 148, 151
agriculture 5, 10, 166
  depression of 147
  productivity of 10, 148–50, 163, 241–3
  urbanization and 150, 242–3
Aikin, John 250
alchemy 27, 229
Alcock, Thomas 153
alcohol 28, 84
  beer 38, 103, 152, 175, 266
  cider 172
  gin 155
  rum 95, 252
  wine 38, 129
ale houses 153
Alexander I, Tsar 304
Alfred, King 280
almshouses 231
America, North 11, 91, 95, 157, 186
  English colonies in 16, 32, 67, 141–2, 152,
    186, 212–19
American Revolution 164, 212–19, 279–80
Americas 32, 94, 129, 157
Amsterdam 257
Anabaptists, *see* Baptists
ancient constitution, the 60, 128, 280
Anglican, *see* Church of England
Anglo-Scots antagonism 89, 115
animals, attitudes to 233–4
Anne, princess, later queen of England 53, 55,
  63, 69, 312
  reign of 75–80

annuities 85, 105
Antarctica 223
anticlericalism 25, 139–40, 206, 225, 264, 286
anti-semitism 185, 189
anti-trinitarianism 66, 139–40
Antwerp 305
apothecaries 13, 98, 229
apprenticeship 15, 19, 98, 158, 174, 265, 267
architects and architecture 13, 24, 179
Argyll, Archibald Campbell, earl of 49, 80
Arianism 139
Arians 66
aristocracy 12, 38, 49, 102, 168–72, 266
   composition and social relations of 315–16
   English and European 314
Aristotle 26
arithmetic 227
Arkwright, Richard 249, 250, 256, 266
arms, right to bear 68
arms, stockpiling of 290
army 35–6, 50, 123, 171, 230
   German mercenaries in 293
   lifeguards, the 36, 48, 78, 87
   New Model 21, 36
   officers 50, 51, 55
   recruiting 87–8
   Scots in 116
   size of 82, 87, 292, 311
   standing 37, 44, 49, 62–3, 74, 88, 124
   Volunteers 302
   William III's 55
   see also militia, navy
artisans 52, 97, 98, 168, 180, 194
artists 171
Ashton, T. S. 248
Asia 7, 16, 32, 94, 157, 186
Asiento 123
Association movement 215–16, 280, 312
Associations for the Preservation of Liberty
   and Property 290–1
Astell, Mary, *Reflections upon Marriage* 180
astrologers 145, 228
astronomers 188, 227
atheism 20, 27, 35, 139–40, 143
Atterbury, Francis 76
Aubrey, John 26, 173
Aughrim, battle of 73
Augusta of Saxe-Gotha, widow of Frederick
   Louis, prince of Wales, queen mother
   192
Austen, Jane, *Sanditon* 275
Austerlitz, battle of 303
Australia 186, 205, 211, 222–3
Austria 73, 146, 191, 215, 290, 293, 298, 303
Austrian Netherlands (Belgium) 242, 282,
   290
Austrian succession, war of the 129–31, 188

baby farmers 174
Bacon, Francis 224, 226, 233
Bailey, Nathan 169
bakers 15, 164
balance of payments 103
balance of power, European 300
balance of trade 7, 103
Baltic, the 303
Bangor 137, 234
bankers 74, 99
banking and finance 82–6, 145, 255–7
Bank of Amsterdam 84
Bank of England 74, 78, 92, 105, 123, 209,
   310
   founding of 85–6
   notes, issued by 256
   suspends cash payments 297
bankruptcy laws 258
Banks, John 14
Banks, Joseph 222–3, 226
banks, provincial 256–7
Bantam 32
Baptists 21, 22, 24, 45, 134, 208
Barbados 32, 67
Barber, Francis 212
Barbon, Nicholas 100, 103
barter, continued use of 255
Basingstoke 101
Bastille, fall of the 282, 284
Batavia 222
Bath 101, 171, 309
Beachy Head, battle of 73
Beccaria, Cesare 202
Bedfordshire 178
beggars 184, 204, 232
Behn, Aphra*** 18, 53
   Oroonoko 212
Belfast 118, 216, 297
Bellers, John 230
Bell, Deborah 181
Bell, Thomas 249
Belper 260
benefit of clergy 203, 204
Bennet, John, *The National Merchant* 211
Bennet, Henry, later earl of Arlington 42
Bentham, Jeremy 200, 226
Berkeley, George 119, 140, 211
Berkshire 294
Bermuda 211
Berridge, John 143
bills of exchange 256, 257
Biographica Britannica 313
Birmingham 244, 266, 270, 271, 272
   Church and King riots at 289
   Lunar Society of 225
   science lectures at 227
   Soho manufactory near 247, 261

Blackburne, Francis 208
Blackburne, Lancelot 137
Black Country, the 261, 271
Black, Joseph 226
Blackpool 275
blacksmiths 10
Blackstone, William 136
  Commentaries on the Laws of England
    199–200
Blake, William 260, 283, 284
Blamire, Susanna 274
Blenheim, battle of 77
Blenheim Palace 171
blood sports 234
'bloody assizes' 49
Bloxwich 271
Blucher, Marshal 307
Blue Stocking Circle 180–1, 182
blue-water strategy 76, 292–3
Board of Trade 104, 212
Bolingbroke, Henry St John, Viscount 80, 93,
    121, 128
Bonaparte, Joseph 304
Bonaparte, Napoleon 296, 300–4, 306–7
book-keeping 176
books and book trade:
  booksellers 144, 288, 305
  Dutch imports 115
  guidebooks 31, 110, 309
  see also print media
Booth, George 34
boots and shoes, manufacture of 261
Bordeaux 30
boroughs, parliamentary 126, 194
Boscawen, Edward 181
Boscawen, Frances 180
Boston 214, 215, 220
Boswell, James 185, 211, 234
botany 228, 233
Boulogne 302
Boulton, Matthew 172, 225, 247, 261
Bowles, John 296
Boyle lectures 140, 227
Boyle, Robert 26, 27, 104
Boyne, battle of the 73
Bradford 166
bread 103, 164, 242
  see also riots
Brecknock 112
Breda, declaration of 21, 35, 37
bridewells 262
Bridgewater, Francis Egerton, duke of 245
Bridport 135
Brighton 309
Brindley, James 245
Bristol 102, 112, 121, 244, 272
  foreign trade of 11, 94, 95, 186

Goldney's bank 256
  merchants of 95, 118, 129, 150, 254, 255
Britain:
  and empire 211–12, 213–23, 310
  and Europe 81–2, 91, 313–18
  as confessional state 146, 314–15
  free trade area 109
British Museum 313
British Museum, or Universal Register 228
Broadbottom ministry 130, 187–90
Brome, Alexander 22
Brown, Lancelot ('Capability') 171, 235
Brownists 21, 24
Brydges, James, duke of Chandos 316
Buckingham, George Villiers, 1st duke 125
Buckingham, George Villiers, 2nd duke 42
Buckinghamshire 196, 272
Buenos Aires 304
building craftsmen 8
building materials 150, 309
Buller, Francis 181
bullion 7, 94, 104, 256
Bunyan, John 28
Burdett, Francis 305
Burgh, James 209
Burgoyne, John 215
Burke, Edmund 215, 221, 288, 299, 317
  Reflections on the Revolution in France
    284–6
Burnet, Gilbert 19, 68
  History of His Own Time 59 n.
Burney, Fanny 179
Burns, Robert, 'The Dumfries Volunteers'
    296
Bute, John Stuart, Lord 191, 192–3, 196, 216
Butler, Joseph 140
Butler, Samuel, *Hudibras* 22
Buxton 171, 309
Byng, John 190, 191

Cabal 42–3
cabinet 123, 311–12
Calamy, Edmund 135
calendar, Gregorian 3, 188
calorific intake 163–4
Calvinism 24, 72, 141
Cambridge University 30, 135, 177, 207, 283,
    293
  Latitudinarians at 138
  mathematics at 227
  medical education at 229
  Peterhouse 208
  theological heterodoxy at 139–40
Campbell, Archibald, earl of Islay, later duke
    of Argyll 116
Campbell, John 233
Campbell, Thomas 184, 234–5

Camperdown, battle of 298
Campo Formio, peace of 298
Canada 94, 190, 191, 215, 306
canals 244–6
Canning, Elizabeth 228
Canning, George 294, 304
Cannon, William 250
Cape Breton Island 190
Cape of Good Hope 222
Cape St Vincent, battle of 297
Cape Town 304
Capel, Arthur, earl of Essex 48
capitalism 166, 263–4, 267
Caribbean 32, 76, 130, 190
Carlisle 114
Carolinas, North and South 32, 212
Caroline of Ansbach, queen of England 127, 128, 129
Caroline of Brunswick, princess 305
Carteret, John 130
Carter, Elizabeth, *Newton's Philosophy Explain'd for the Use of Ladies* 228
Cartwright, Edmund 249, 281, 305
Cartwright, John 209, 216
Cary, John 95, 150
Casaubon, Meric 27
Castle Rising 122
Castlemaine, Barbara, countess of 27
Castlereagh, Robert Stewart, viscount 304, 306
cathedrals 20, 134
Catherine of Braganza, queen of England 32
Catholics, Roman 20, 21, 28, 43, 48, 50, 66, 68, 79, 136–7, 184
emancipation of 209, 308, 311
Cavalier Parliament 22, 37–49
Cavendish, Georgiana, duchess of Devonshire 182
censorship 37, 66, 70, 110, 128, 139
census 6, 24, 105, 302
ceramics 152, 154, 172, 245, 247, 261, 266
cereals, export of 148, 163, 242
Chamberlayne, Edward, *Anglia Notitia* 4, 6, 10, 16, 28
Chambers, Ephraim, *Cyclopedia* 228
Channel Isles 16
Channel 30, 215
charities 174, 230–3
charity schools 102, 112, 138, 143, 175, 230
Charles I, 3, 21, 37, 38, 70
Charles II 29, 34–49, 311, 312
religious attitudes of 21–2, 41
and trade 11
Charles Edward Stuart, the 'Young Pretender' 130, 187
charters, borough 48, 54
Cheltenham 309

chemicals 251, 261
chemistry 229
Cheshire 34, 270
Chesterfield, earl of, *Letters to his Son* 182
see also Stanhope, Philip Chester 112
Cheviot hills 4
Child, Josiah 104, 220
children 9, 172–4
employment: agricultural 147; in cotton mills 250; in factories 262–3; in navy 231
chimney sweeps 174, 231
China, 153, 221, 310
Chippendale, Thomas 172
chocolate 38, 84, 153
Chorley 260
Chowbent 250
Churchill, John, duke of Marlborough 55, 59, 68, 75, 77
Churchill, Sarah, duchess of Marlborough 55, 75, 78, 182
Church of England 3, 20–3, 51, 64, 75–80, 134–46, 205–10, 225, 314–15
and Tories 45, 76–80, 289
Arminians 21
Book of Common Prayer 22
bishops of 17, 20, 22, 23, 38, 40, 76, 206; in House of Lords 41, 46, 126; non-jurors 72; Whig 76, 137
Convocation 76, 138
Hackney Phalanx 208
High Church 76–7, 127, 135, 207
latitudinarians 76–7, 138–40
Low Church 76, 135
see also clergy
churchwardens 18, 182
Cintra, Convention of 305
cities, see towns
City, see London
civil engineering 245
civil list 127, 128
civil service 13, 18, 37, 43, 84, 86–7, 99, 125
civil wars, English 6, 11, 22, 35, 59, 284
Clapham, J. H. 240, 267
Clapham Sect 207–8
Clarendon, Edward Hyde, earl of 22, 37, 39–40, 41, 173
History of the Rebellion 41, 70
Clarke, Mary Anne 305
Clarkson, Thomas 281
clergy 16, 22–3, 25, 26, 76–8, 102, 205–6
incitement of violence by 144, 289
as profession 13, 98–9, 171
resistance to James II 51, 53–5
Clifford, Thomas, Lord 42
Clive, Robert 220–1
clocks 3, 229

clothing 153, 155, 164, 172, 310
    second-hand 154
clubs 70, 102, 193, 264–5, 287, 312
    gaming 177
    London 113
    political 47, 55, 121, 289, 301
Coalbrookdale 151, 256
coal 10, 97, 112, 157, 244, 245, 250, 268, 317
    coalfields 247, 251
    sea-coals 101
Cobbett, William, *Political Register* 305
cocoa 153
coffee-houses 70, 102, 113, 153, 178, 193, 227
coffee 38, 84, 153, 252
coin 103, 158, 255–6
Coleman, Edward, secretary to James, duke of
    York 44
Coleraine, Gabriel Hanger, Lord 172
College of Arms 14, 169
Collins, Anthony 139
colonies 6, 16, 31–3, 95, 211–23
    emigration to 116, 161, 186
    as market 152, 252–4
commerce, corrupting influence of 280
commercial revolution 93–6
Commissioners of Accounts, parliamentary
    83
commissions of the peace 48, 54, 121
    see also justices of the peace
Committee for the Abolition of the Slave
    Trade 232
common lands 5, 164
    see also enclosure
Commonwealth, the 19, 22, 37, 48, 138
Compton, Henry 51, 54
Concord 215
Congregationalists 21, 22, 24, 45, 134, 208
Consols, 3 per cent 188
consumerism 11, 152–6, 197, 221, 275
contraception 6, 7, 162
Convention Parliament (1660) 32
Convention Parliament (1689) 72
convicts 94, 223, 269
Cook, James 222–3
copyhold tenants 38, 149
Coram, Thomas 174
Cornwall 10, 270–1
Cornwallis, Charles, Earl Cornwallis 217
coronation oaths 64
corruption, political 124–8, 198, 215–16, 305
Cort, Henry 249, 250
cottagers 13, 165
cotton industry 32, 154, 249–51, 252
    dependence on slave labour 255
    McConnel and Kennedy, Manchester 262
    mills 261
    size of firms 267

steam engines and 248
Counter-Reformation 31, 52
country houses 168, 170
Court and Country 43, 45, 71–2, 88, 128, 211,
    280
Court, the royal 18, 27, 86, 127
    and politics 132, 311
Crafts, N. F. R., *British Economic Growth dur-
    ing the Industrial Revolution* 240
Craftsman 128
craftsmen 10, 155, 166, 247
Crawley ironworks 152
cricket 316
crime and criminals 87, 102, 203, 211, 232
criminal law 102, 168, 189, 202–5
crockery 11, 154
Cromford 260
Crompton, Samuel 249, 248
Cromwell, Oliver 18, 19, 21, 34, 37, 311
Cromwell, Richard 34
Crown:
    and Parliament, 16–17, 42, 62–5, 69, 131–3,
        311–12
    patronage of 126, 216, 312
    prerogatives of 17, 50, 62, 62, 64
Croydon 245
Cullen, L. M. 118
Culliford, Edward 104
Culloden, battle of 156, 187
Cumberland 97, 178, 255, 271
Cumberland, William Augustus, duke of 187
Curwen, John 305
customary rights 148–9, 164, 258
customs 94, 156, 220
    collectors 310
    duties 129
    revenues 11, 38, 49, 83, 86
    registers 254
cutlery 11, 150, 155, 261, 310

d'Adda, Ferdinand 51–2
Daily Courant 70
Dampier, William 211,
    Voyage to New Holland 212
Danby, Thomas, earl of 54, 68, 73, 125
Danube, the 87
Darby, Abraham 151, 249, 250, 256
Darby family 266
Darwin, Erasmus 225
Davenant, Charles 84, 101, 104
Day, Thomas 225, 234
Deane, Phyllis, and Cole, W. A. 240, 254
debating societies 279
Declaration of Indulgence 43, 51
Declaration of Independence 63
Declaration of Rights 60, 62–4, 68
Declaration of the Rights of Man 63

Defoe, Daniel 110–14, 152, 155, 165, 179
    Robinson Crusoe 110, 212
    Tour 110–14
    The True-born Englishman 110
deindustrialization 271
Deism 139, 140, 285
Delmayne, Thomas, *The Patricians* 171
demonstrations, popular 47–8, 53–4, 78,
    121–2, 130, 142, 164, 168, 184, 191, 193,
    197–8, 217, 289, 290–1, 295, 305, 312–13
    see also food riots
Denbighshire 112
Denmark 317
Dent, Abraham 255
dentists 230
Derby 130, 260
Derby Philosophical Society 225
Derbyshire 270, 293
deregulation 260, 267
Derwent river 151
Dettingen, battle of 130
Devon 10, 55
Devonshire, William Cavendish, duke of 196
Diggers 12, 21
diplomacy 30, 191, 303, 306
disease 7
    epidemic 161
    gout 79, 190
    influenza 161
    plague 7, 18, 40, 161, 309
    porphyria 282
    scurvy 223
    smallpox 7, 161, 162, 180, 230; inoculation
        162, 180, 230; vaccination 310
    typhus 7, 161
    yellow fever 293
dispensaries 231
Dissenters 22–5, 42, 43, 66, 76–8, 134–8,
    208–10
    disabilities of 123, 135–6, 280–2
    as political force 51, 53, 208–10, 214
Dissenting academies 110, 175, 227
Dissenting chapels and meeting houses 134,
    309
divine-right monarchy, doctrine of 60, 64,
    132–3
Dobson, C. R. 264
dockyards 86, 88, 152, 264
Dodd, William 203
Doddridge, Philip 143
domestic servants 165, 174, 263
Doncaster 101
Donn, Benjamin 228
Dorset 5, 10, 59, 111
Dover 29, 36
Downing, George 84
Dryden, John 53

Absolom and Achitophel 39, 48
'Annus Mirabilis' 33, 41
The Indian Queen 212
duelling 15, 171, 315
Dundas, Henry 300, 305
Durant, Robert 23
Durham 178
'Dutch finance' 74, 85, 124
Dutch Wars
    first (1652–4) 31
    second (1665–7) 33, 40
    third (1673–4) 43
    fourth (1780–4) 251
    see also Netherlands

Eachard, John 25
East Anglia 5, 10, 149, 253, 271
Eastern Question 301
East Hoathly 175
East India Company 7, 94, 153, 154, 186, 188,
    220–1
    and French 192
East Indies 94
Eaton, Daniel 288
Ecclesiastical Commission 54
economical reform 216, 281, 312
economic growth 167, 240–1, 273–4
economics 7, 95, 103–5, 226
Eden Treaty 259
Edgehill 35
Edict of Nantes, revocation of 52
education 13, 134, 174–8, 181, 227
Egypt 300, 301
elections 18, 51, 62, 65, 70–1, 194–6, 280, 316
    general 78, 80, 121, 122. 125–7, 129, 187,
        218
Elizabeth I 20, 47, 75, 93
emigration 161–2, 186
employment 10, 102, 147, 308
    see also children, women
enclosure 10, 148–50, 166, 240, 270, 309
Encyclopaedia Britannica 228
Endeavour 222
engineers and engineering 99, 245, 266, 273
English language 30, 175, 313
English Revolution 317
    see also civil wars
Enlightenment 224–6, 280, 285
enthusiasm 25, 26, 28, 140, 142, 317
equity of redemption 149
Erastianism 76, 137
Essex 30, 302
estate stewards 99, 149
Eton College 175
Eugene, prince of Austria 77
Europe and England 28–33, 91, 313–18
evangelicalism 207–8, 233

Evelyn, John 36, 53
Exchequer 86, 87
excise 38, 83, 84, 86, 129, 156
Exclusion Crisis 19, 44–5, 61
Exeter 11, 59, 101, 152, 244

factories 151–2, 240, 250–1, 260–3, 267
Falkland Islands 223
Familists 21
farms and farming, 147–50, 164, 242–3, 308
Farquhar, George, *The Recruiting Officer* 87
fathers and daughters 13, 72, 183
Faversham 99
Ferguson, Adam 226
Ferrers, Laurence Shirley, Earl Ferrers 203
feudalism 38, 166, 280
Fielding, Henry 178
    The History of Tom Jones 167
Fielding, Sarah 179
Fiennes, Celia 100, 114
Fifteen, the 80, 121
Fifth Monarchists 12, 21, 37
Filmer, Sir Robert, *Patriarcha* 60–1
financial revolution 83–6, 257
financiers 78, 99, 104, 171, 185
Finch, Daniel, earl of Nottingham 73
Finland 161
'fiscal-military state' 91–2, 157, 310
Fisher, Jabez 247
fishermen 29, 99, 165, 168
Fitzwilliam, William Wentworth, Earl 298
Flanders 29, 87, 92, 94, 187
Flood, Henry 216
Florida 212, 217, 306
flying shuttle 151, 250
folklore 113, 145, 235
Fonthill Abbey 255
food, shortage of 10, 113, 163–4, 242, 295
food prices 154, 163, 242, 290
food riots 18, 164, 264, 294, 295
foreigners 29, 63, 78, 184, 188
foreign policy 40, 63, 70, 91, 127, 129–30, 215, 282, 290, 292–3, 301–2, 303
    Crown and 11, 17, 31–2, 42–3, 187–8, 311–12
foreign trade 10–11, 32–3, 84, 93–8, 104, 251–5
    expansion of 32, 49, 93, 252, 304
    London and 94, 101
    re-exports 11, 95, 251, 253
    triangular trades 94
    see also trading companies
Forth and Clyde canal 245
Forty-five, the 130, 163, 187
forty-shilling freeholders 126, 172
Fox, Charles James 182, 215, 219, 220, 281, 282, 286, 288, 292, 303, 312

Fox, Henry, Baron Holland 173, 190
Fox, Lady Caroline 190
Fox, Sir Stephen 84
France 4, 17, 30, 40, 41, 43, 49, 59, 146, 170, 188, 218, 242
    colonies of 96, 190–2, 220–1, 293
    commerce of 95, 251
    English attitudes to 29, 31–2, 43, 104, 282–6
    Estates-General 17
    immigrants from 52, 100
    population of 99, 161
    war with 64, 69, 72–7, 82–3, 91, 130, 190–2, 215, 292–307
French-Canadians 215
French language 30, 176
French Revolution 279, 282–91, 296, 317
    war of the 292–301
Frederick, duke of York 303
Frederick, prince of Wales 129, 189
Frederick the Great 191
Freemasonry 231, 316
Freethinkers 139
Frend, William 293
friendly societies 231, 264
Frittenden 24

Gaelic language 30, 178
Gainsborough, Thomas 235
gambling 102, 171
game laws 168
Gay, John 110
    The Beggar's Opera 128
gender 13–14
    see also fathers and daughters; husbands and wives; women
general warrants 196–7
Gentleman's Magazine 180, 228
gentlemen 12–15, 169, 386
gentry, landed 12–16, 23, 38, 49, 98, 102, 170–1, 266, 316
geology 226, 228, 229
geometry 227
George I 79, 80, 120–1, 127, 190, 312
George II 120, 123, 130–3, 187–8, 190–2
    accession of 127–8
    mistress of, *see* Schulenberg, von der, Melusine
George III 195–6, 218–19, 229, 292, 312, 315
    accession and character of 192–3
    and American colonists 212–14
    on Burke 286
    defends Church of England 209, 301, 311
    friend of Sir Joseph Banks 226
    insanity of 282, 304–5
    opposes reform 282
George, prince of Denmark 75

George, prince of Wales, regent, later George
    IV 282, 304, 311, 312
Georgia 141–2, 212
German language 31
Germany 95, 100, 120, 301
Gibbon, Edward 177, 209
Gibraltar 89, 91
Gibson, Edmund 137, 142
Gideon, Samson 185
Gilbert, Thomas 232
Glanvill, Joseph 27
glass 11, 118, 150, 151, 251
Glencoe massacre 67
Glorious Revolution 59–68, 77, 81, 85, 133,
    282
Gloucester 10, 152, 175
Gloucester, William Henry, duke of 75
Gloucestershire 172
Godden v. *Hales* 50
Godfrey, Sir Edmund Berry 44
'God Save the King' 313
Godolphin, Sidney 71, 77, 78
Godwin, William 283, 285
Goldsmith, Oliver 200
    Citizen of the World 235
Gooch, Thomas 143
Gordon, Lord George 209
Gordon riots 167, 184, 209, 216
Gordon, Thomas 144
Grand Alliance 73, 76
Grand Tour 29, 31, 178
Grattan, Henry 216
Graunt, John 8
Great Chain of Being 12
Great Marlow 111
Great North Road 244
Greek language 30, 175, 221
Grenville, George 196, 213
Grenville, Hester 190
Grenville, William, Lord 300, 303
Grew, Nehemiah 150, 154
groceries 153–6, 252, 153
grocers 15, 97
Grosley, Jean-Paul 168
Grotius, Hugo 115
Guadeloupe 191, 196, 293, 304
Guest, Ralph 96
Gulf of Mexico 190
gypsies 228

Hague, The 14
Hales, Stephen 230
Halifax 15, 271
Halifax, George Savile, marquis of 28, 41, 47,
    53
Halley, Edmund 5
Hall, Thomas 23

Hamilton, David 70
Hampshire 234
Hampton Court 40
Handel, George Frederick 313
Hanover 75, 120, 123, 135, 188, 190, 192
Hanway, Jonas 174, 231
*Hardships of the English Laws in Relation to
    Wives* 181
Hardwicke, Philip Yorke, earl of 183, 188, 190
Hardy, Thomas 287, 294, 295
Harewood House 171
Hargreaves, James 249
Harley, Robert, later earl of Oxford 78–80,
    104, 110, 122
Harrington, James 20, 40
Harris, Howel 142
Harrison, John 229
Harrogate 101, 171
Hartwell, R. M. 268
harvest failure 78, 103, 161, 164, 167, 242,
    264, 270, 290, 294, 295, 300
Hastings, Selina, countess of Huntingdon 142
Hastings, Warren 221–2, 282
Hawkins, John 199
Hay, William 202
hearth tax 40, 86
Heathcote, Gilbert 96
height 12, 268–70
Hell-fire Club 196
Henrietta-Maria, queen of England 21
Herring, Thomas 140
Herschel, Caroline and William 227
Hertford 27
Hertfordshire 145, 170, 172, 244
Hey 207
highland zone 5
Highmore, Joseph 171
history, appeals to 47, 70, 109, 209, 280, 284,
    293, 317
Hoadly, Benjamin 137–8
Hobbes, Thomas 20, 25, 61
    Leviathan 60
Hobsbawm, E. 268
Hogarth, William 195
Holkham Hall 171
Home counties, the 101
honour 15, 315
Hooke, Robert 25
Horne, George 207
horses 243, 246–7
hospitals 88, 174, 200, 230–2
House of Commons 17, 34, 50–1, 62–5, 74,
    114, 189–90, 196–8, 218–20, 281, 284, 312
    alignments in 71–2, 129
    audit commission 41
    disputes with House of Lords 41
    franchise 65, 125–6, 194, 216, 279–80

management of 43, 125–7
members of 59, 78, 79, 114, 121, 123,
    125–7, 172, 198, 280
rejects reform 305–6
see also elections; Parliament
House of Lords 13, 17, 23, 38, 41, 46, 78, 114,
    135, 169, 170, 182, 197, 312
bishops in 41, 46, 126
see also Parliament; peers,
houses of correction 102, 204, 232, 262
Howard, John 232
    State of the Prisons 204
Huddersfield 261
Hudson's Bay 91
Hudson's Bay Company 94
Humane Society 231
humanitarianism 168, 232
Hume, David 261, 317
    A Treatise of Human Nature 226
Hunter, John and William 229
hunting 168, 234
Huntsman, Benjamin 249
husbandmen 13, 15, 166
husbands and wives 13, 47, 179–84
    see also marriage
Hutcheson, Francis 226, 233
Hutton, James, *Theory of the Earth* 226
Hutton, R. 39
Hyde, Anne, duchess of York 41, 43
hygiene 162, 230

illegitimacy 6, 27, 162
immigrants 29, 52, 137, 162, 184–6
income tax 300
India 32, 188, 190, 219, 220–2, 250, 300
    see also East India Company
individualism 12, 179–80, 224
industrialists, 266–7
industrialization, gains and losses 239, 263
industry, manufacturing 10–11, 24, 104, 114,
    150–2, 248–51
cottage or domestic 152, 166
disputes in 167, 242, 264–5, 290, 301, 306
    see also manufacturers
infant mortality 100, 172–3, 174, 269
insurance 94, 97, 145, 231
insurrection 37, 45, 80, 290, 301, 306
intelligence, counter insurgency 19, 37, 294
    see also spies
inventions 110, 248–51
Ireland 4, 17, 29–30, 67, 90, 97, 100, 116–19,
    148, 216–18, 287, 297–9, 302
Bantry Bay 297, 298
Cork 30, 118
County Armagh 298
Dublin 39, 90, 117, 118, 216, 297, 299;
    Dublin Castle 299; Dublin Society 119

Dungannon 216
King's County 119
Queen's County 109
Ulster 30, 117, 119, 217, 272, 298
Vinegar Hill 299
irreligion 25, 27, 143, 204, 205–6
Irish 45, 100, 137, 162, 184–5, 301
Irish Sea 30, 215
iron 10, 151, 249, 250–1, 261, 266
Islam 139
Isle of Man 16
Italian language 30, 176
Italy 4, 31, 81, 94, 301

'Jack Presbyter' 48
Jacobite risings 136
Jacobites 67, 76, 128, 129, 214
    Irish 90
    Scots 115, 187
    smugglers 153
    strength of 79–80, 121–2, 187
    Welsh 112
Jamaica 31, 32, 67, 185
James I and VI 29, 75
James, duke of Monmouth 46–7, 49, 59, 110
James, duke of York, later James II and VII
    33, 41, 43, 45–7, 49–55, 59–60, 61, 64, 66,
    69, 72, 75, 81, 95, 121, 134, 311
James Stuart, prince of Wales, the 'Old
    Pretender' 53, 59, 69, 75, 76, 79–80, 112,
    122, 127, 128
Java 32, 304
Jebb, John 216, 280, 281
Jeffreys, George 49, 52, 112
Jemappes, battle of 290
Jenkin's Ear, war of 130
Jenner, Edward 310
Jesuits 28, 44, 51
Jews 66, 185, 189
John Bull 168
Johnson, Samuel 182, 185, 212, 229, 234
    Dictionary 313
joint-stock companies 231, 245
Jones, John Paul 215
Jones, Thomas 113
Jones, William 199, 221–2
Joseph II, emperor of Austria 317
Josselin, Ralph 35
journalists 103, 110, 171, 175, 184, 242, 288,
    302, 305
Juan Fernandez Island 212
Judaism 139
judges 17, 50, 63, 257
    tenure of 37–8, 63, 65, 74, 145
Junius 201
Junto, Whig 74, 78, 122
juries 15, 18, 48, 65, 145, 200, 281

justices of the peace 22, 37, 51, 87, 102, 157,
    164, 167, 204, 206,
    powers of 18, 19, 87, 265, 294, 295

Kalm, Per 172
Kames, Henry Home, Lord 226
Kay, John 151, 249, 250
Kay, Richard 229
Keighley 266
Keir, James 225
Kent 10, 15, 24
Kent, William 235
Kentish Society for Promotion of Useful
    Knowledge 225
Kentish Weald 271
Kenyon, Lloyd 258
Kielmansegge, Count Frederick 185
Killiecrankie 67
Kineton 14
King, Gregory 5, 8, 13, 97, 104, 165
King's Evil, touching for 75, 124
King's Lynn 122
Kirkby Stephen 255
knights 13, 15, 169

labourers 13, 15, 148, 164–5, 174, 272, 294
Ladies' Diary 228
La Hogue, battle of 73
laissez-faire 260, 263
Lake District 111
Lambert, John 35
Lancashire 163, 165, 178, 207, 229, 244, 270,
    300, 306,
    cotton industry in 250, 264, 270, 272, 306
Lancaster 97
landholding 134, 147–50, 243, 308–9
land tax 74, 77, 84, 98, 124, 127, 149, 150, 216
    collectors of 256
landscape 4–6, 234–5
landscape gardening 99, 171, 235
Lassells, Richard, *The Voyage of Italy* 31
Latin language 30, 175, 180, 201, 221
Lauderdale, John Maitland, duke of 42 n.10,
    451
law 16, 28, 65, 135, 158, 168, 199–205, 257–8,
    260
    common 16, 65, 199
    Roman 115
    rule of 16, 93
    Scots, 116
lawcourts 16, 63, 70, 71, 86
    Chancery 201
    church 23, 136, 138, 201
    Council in the Marches of Wales 38
    Court of Chivalry 169
    Court of Common Pleas 196
    courts of requests 201, 258
    Court of Wards 38
    Court of King's Bench 50, 181
    local 19
    quarter sessions 203
    Star Chamber 38
law-French 201
Law, Edmund 208
Law, William 140, 175
law reform 201, 260, 280
lawyers 13, 14, 26, 65, 98, 145, 171, 234, 256,
    282
    advocates 294
    articled clerks 174
    attorneys 201, 258
    barristers 99, 199, 258
    in criminal trials 204
    hostility towards 200–1, 234
    solicitors 201
Leach, Rachel 266
Le Blanc, J. B. 224
Leeds 166, 271, 272
Leeward Islands 67
legislation, private 189
    see also Acts of Parliament
Leicester 71
Leipzig, battle of 306
Lennox, Charlotte 179, 181
Levant Company 94
Levellers 12, 61, 197, 279
Leveson-Gower family 149
Lexington 215
Lhuyd, Edward 113
liberties 18, 65–6
'Liberty and Property' 109
libraries 102, 228, 231
Lichtenberg, Georg Christoph 183, 271
life expectancy 173, 268, 269
Lilburne, John 197
Lincolnshire 23
Lincolnshire Wash 163
linen 114, 118, 153, 259
Lisle, Alice 49
literacy 26, 110, 144, 175, 178, 194, 204
litigation 99, 201
Liverpool 94, 111, 184, 186, 245, 254, 255, 272
Liverpool, Robert Jenkinson, earl of 302, 303,
    308
living standards 9, 163–9, 242–3, 267–70
lobbies 103, 135, 281, 312
local government 18, 37, 49, 70, 71, 157, 182
    see also justices of the peace
Locke, John 60–3, 104, 175, 180, 226, 279, 280
    Some Thoughts Concerning Education 173
    Two Treatises of Government 61
    The Reasonableness of Christianity 139
Lofft, Capel 216, 305
Lombe, Thomas 151, 247

London 11, 30, 34, 47, 59, 99–103, 111, 121, 167, 255, 272, 309
    aldermen and councillors of 59, 188
    Asylum for Orphaned Girls 230
    Catholics in 137
    Child's coffee-house 211
    City, the 84, 92, 100, 128, 171, 196, 257, 311
       see also Bank of England
    Coram Hospital 174
    Covent Garden 55
    Covent Garden theatre 305
    economy of 152, 185, 255, 270, 295, 311
    fire of 33, 40–1
    Fleet Prison 183
    Fleet Street 183
    Foundling Hospital 231
    Guildhall 99
    Guy's Hospital 229
    Hackney 208
    Hyde Park 303
    inns of court 176–7, 209, 212
    Kennington Common and Moorfields 141
    King's Bench Prison 139, 197
    Leicester House 129, 189, 191, 192
    Lord Mayor of 77
    Magdalen House 230
    minorities in 52, 184–6
    Newgate Prison 209
    Old Bailey 203, 228
    Richmond Hill 234
    riots in 78, 129, 184, 209
    St George's Fields 295
    St James's Palace 123, 129
    St Paul's Cathedral 77, 100
    St Paul's churchyard 144
    St Thomas's Hospital 230
    Strand 36, 100, 288
    Thames River 55, 110, 245
    Threadneedle Street 257
    Tower of 35, 48, 53, 100, 122, 133, 196, 291, 305
    Tyburn 100, 202
    Westminster 100, 126, 183, 197
    Westminster Hall 78
    Westminster School 175
    Whitehall Palace 38, 59–60
London Corresponding Society 287, 295, 297, 301, 317
London Evening Post 191
Long Parliament 4, 12, 19, 21, 34, 38, 47
longitude, determination of 223, 228–9
Louisburg 190
Louis XIV 39, 42–4, 67, 74, 77, 191
    support for Jacobites 73, 81–2
    threatens Protestantism 52, 54, 72, 75
Louis XVI 284, 286, 291
Louisiana 190, 212

Lovelace, John, Lord 47 n.
loyalism 290–1, 292, 293, 296, 302
lowland zone 5
Lowther, James 126
Luddites 264, 306
Ludlow, Edmund 62
Lunar Society 225

McAdam, John 244
Macaulay, Catharine 181
Macaulay, Thomas Babington, Lord, *History of England* 66, 120
Macclesfield, George Parker, 2nd earl of 188
Macclesfield, Thomas Parker, 1st earl of 128
MacDonalds, massacred at Glencoe 67
Magalotti, Lorenzo 15, 41
magic 26–7, 145, 227–8
Malplaquet, battle of 77
Malta 301
Malthus, Thomas Robert 7
    Essay on the Principle of Population 241–2
Manchester 184, 245, 260, 267, 272, 289
Manchester, George Montagu, duke of 186
Manchester Herald 288
Mandeville, Bernard 144
    Fable of the Bees 105
manners, polite 179
    societies for the reformation of 102
Mansfield, James Murray, Lord 181, 186, 201, 209, 258
Mantoux, P. 246
manufacturers 13, 95, 97, 110, 266
Mar, Erskine, John, earl of 80
Marine Society 231, 232, 269
marriage 6, 7, 14, 15, 162, 176, 179–84, 195, 201
Martin, Benjamin 181, 227
Martinique 196, 293, 304
Marvell, Andrew, *Account of the Growth of Popery and Arbitrary Government* 44
Mary of Modena, queen of England 43, 53, 59
Mary Stuart, princess of Orange, later queen of England 47, 52, 53, 64, 72, 102
Maryland 32, 153
Massachusetts 215
Massacre of St George's Fields 197, 295
Massie, Joseph 165, 169
mathematics 8, 26, 176
Mauritius 304
medicine 115, 136, 150, 177, 229–30
Mediterranean 76, 94
Medway, the 41, 191
men of letters 13, 171, 285
mercantilism 95–6, 104, 158, 259
Merchant Adventurers, Company of 93
merchants 11, 13, 26, 84, 96–8, 102, 110, 113, 171, 282
    immigrant 29, 52, 185–6

metalworking 5, 10, 247, 251, 261. 266, 271
Methodism 141–3, 207–9
Methuen, Paul 77
Middlesex 102, 197–8, 199
middling sort 13, 24, 96–9, 110, 135, 154, 165, 169–72
midwifery, midwives 18, 165, 183, 230
migration, internal 100–101, 163, 206–7, 273
militia 34, 70, 216, 291, 295, 302
Millar, John, 226
millenarianism 23, 33, 192, 280, 283
Miller, James, *The Man of Taste* 180
Milton, John 139
miners 164, 165, 264
mines and mining 110, 111, 247, 248, 261, 264, 274
Ministry of All the Talents 303
Minorca 89, 91, 190, 217
minorities, ethnic 29, 32, 184–6
moidores 256
monarch, powers of 36, 131–3, 311–12
 see also Crown
Monck, General George, duke of Albermarle 34–5, 37
Monitor 191
Monmouth, James, duke of 46–7, 49, 59, 110
Montagu, Charles, earl of Halifax 77, 81, 85
Montagu, Elizabeth 180
Montagu, Lady Mary Wortley 120, 180
Montcalm, Louis Joseph 192
Montesquieu 313
moral economy, the 265–7
Moravian Brethren 141–2
More, Hannah 208, 232, 233
 Village Politics 296
More, Henry 27
Moritz, Carl 169, 206
mortality 6, 100, 162, 163, 172–3, 268–9
Moscow 304
Moss, Robert 140
Muggletonians 21
Muir, Thomas 294
Mun, Thomas 7, 103
musicians 99, 180
Myddle 96

nabobs 212
Namier, L. B. 192, 193
 The Structure of Politics at the Accession of George III 71
Naples 293
Napoleonic wars 267, 296–307
Naseby 36
Nash, John 309
National Debt 85, 123, 157, 188, 213, 215, 220, 270, 310
nationalism, *see* patriotism

natural philosophy, *see* science
natural religion 138, 139, 140
natural rights 61, 279–80, 283, 286
Nature 182, 222, 233–5
naval stores 95, 223, 303
navigation 222–3, 228–9
navvies, Irish 273
navy 31, 43, 86–9, 130, 157, 171, 190, 222, 231, 251, 311
 desertions from 295
 disbandment of 36
 enforces blockade 304
 impressment for 88, 168
 mutinies in 297
 officers 13, 43, 88–9
 size of 88–9, 99, 292, 311
 treasurer of the 122
 in war of American Independence 215
Navy Board 87, 89
Neal, Daniel 135
Nelson, Horatio 300, 303
Netherlands, the 4, 35, 47, 52, 54, 61, 73, 215, 290, 301–2
 and agricultural innovation 10, 148
 commercial rivalry with 11, 32, 42, 95
 decline of 91, 251
 immigrants from 29, 100, 105
 universities in 30, 195, 229
 see also Dutch Wars
Nettlebed 169
Neville, Sylas 234
New Amsterdam 33
New Annual Register 283
Newcastle, Thomas Pelham-Holles, duke of 121, 126, 176, 188, 191, 196
Newcastle-on-Tyne 152, 245
Newcastle–Pitt coalition 191
Newcomen engines 151, 274
Newcomen, Thomas 151, 246, 249
new draperies 11, 94
New England 32, 67
Newfoundland 32, 91, 94
Newmarket 48
New Orleans 190
newspapers 48, 70, 84, 128, 153, 193–4, 289, 312
 advertisements in 228, 281, 287, 312
Newton, Isaac, 26, 27, 104, 139, 226, 227, 255
 Opticks 228
New York 33
New Zealand 222
Nicolson, William 119
Nine Years War 64, 74, 82–5
noble savage 222, 235
non-jurors 72, 77, 79, 137, 140
non-resistance, doctrine of 39, 51, 60, 64, 77

Nootka Sound 282, 292
Nore, the 297
Norfolk 111, 122, 130, 149, 243, 282
Northampton 143
Northamptonshire 170, 175
North Briton 196–7
North, Dudley 96–7, 103, 104
Northern risings 37
North, Frederick, Lord North 212–18
North, Roger 52
North Sea 30
Northumberland 80, 101, 170, 178
north-west passage 223
Norwich 11, 29, 99, 101, 152, 185, 207, 272, 295, 300
Nottingham 78, 135, 256, 260, 306
Nova Scotia 91, 190
novelists and novels 167, 178, 180, 182, 235

Oates, Titus 44
oaths 64, 72
occasional conformity 24, 77, 79
Ochakov crisis 292
O'Connell, Daniel 299
October Club 78
Ohio 190
O P demonstrations 305
Oldham 207
Old Corps 187–92
  see also Whigs
Orange, principality of 52
Oriental languages 31, 221–2
Ossian 236
Ottoman Turks 301
Oudenarde, battle of 77
outports 94, 101
Owen, Robert 272
Oxford 26, 47, 80, 100, 121
Oxford Parliament 47–8
Oxford University 30, 47, 51, 104, 135, 141, 169, 195, 199, 212
  All Souls College 255
  Balliol College 177
  Magdalen College 55, 177, 207
  University College 207
Oxfordshire 169, 195, 205

Pacific Ocean 222–3
Padua University 229
Paine, Thomas 285–6, 291
  Common Sense 286
  Rights of Man 285–9
Palmer, John 244
Palmer, Thomas Fyshe 294
papermaking 111, 150, 151, 247, 251, 255
parent–child relations 173–4
Pares, R. 255

Paris 80, 99, 197, 282, 286, 287, 290
Parliament 19–20, 37–49, 51, 69–80, 125–7, 192–8. 215–16, 218–20
  Dissenters in 135
  colonies, taxation of 213
  and Crown 16–17, 36, 62–5, 131–3, 187–91, 310–13
  legislative functions 157, 257
  opening of (1795) 295
  petitioning of 172, 281, 312–13
  reform of 198, 214, 215–18, 220, 280–1, 286–8, 305–6, 317
Parr, Samuel 282
parties, political 45, 70–1, 125, 189, 193, 312
  see also Tories; Whigs
patents 248–9
Paterson, William 85
patriotism 4, 109–10, 187–98, 212, 216–19, 231, 290–1, 296, 302–3, 307, 313
patronage 39, 70, 86, 125–7, 216
pedlars 96, 113, 155
Peel, Robert 267
peers 13, 15, 26, 48, 59, 72, 121, 126, 169–72, 316–17
  Irish and Scots 114, 169
  at universities 177
Pelham, Henry 187–9
Penang 221
Pengelly, Thomas 143
Peninsular campaign 304, 308
Pepys, Samuel 12, 22, 27, 40, 41, 88, 179
Perceval, Spencer 306
Percy, Thomas 235
Petre, Edward 51
Petty, William 8
Petworth 101
physicians 13, 60, 70, 98, 105, 229–30
physics 26, 229
Picardy 119
picturesque, cult of the 234
Pitt, Thomas 188
Pitt, William, the elder, earl of Chatham 188, 190–3, 213, 302
Pitt, William, the younger 218–20, 282, 286–92, 295–301, 303, 312, 315
Place, Francis 294, 305
placemen 63, 74, 86, 124, 129
Playford, Thomas 124 n.
plots 23, 37, 44–5, 48, 80, 122, 214, 300–1
Plumb, J. H., *The Growth of Political Stability in England, 1675–1725* 133–4
Plymouth 3, 152
political arithmetic 8, 104–5
poor 13–14, 65, 84, 102, 164–8, 185, 202–5, 211, 259, 308, 316
  law 232–3, 280
  overseers of the 18, 135, 157, 182

poor (*cont.*)
  rates 151, 232, 294
  relief 24, 158, 167, 185, 259
pope-burnings 47, 121
Pope, Alexander 124
  Essay on Man 197
popish plot, the 44–5, 50
popular culture 3, 23, 113, 144–5
  see also magic
population 6–7, 11, 99–100, 113, 118, 147, 161–3, 166, 308
Porter, R. 230
Portland, William Bentinck, duke of 289, 292
Portsmouth 152, 175, 297
Portugal 32, 77, 94, 96, 185, 304
Post Office 86, 128, 244
Postlethwayt, Malachy 261
Poyning's Law, repeal of 216
preachers 23, 25, 27, 47, 64, 77–8, 98, 140–2
prerogative, royal 17, 19, 31, 39, 41, 43, 45, 47, 50, 62–5, 133 n.
Presbyterians 21–2, 25, 36, 37, 45, 134–6, 208, 228
Preston, battle of 80
Price, Richard 208, 209, 280, 282, 284
  Discourse on the Love of Our Country 283
Priestley, Joseph 176, 208, 209, 224–5, 228, 280, 289
prime minister 127, 196, 299, 312
Pringle, John 230
print media 47, 48, 70, 155, 178, 193–4, 281, 296, 305
  see also newspapers; novels
prisons 102, 139, 183, 201, 204–5, 209, 232, 280
privateering 88, 95, 103
privy council 17, 37, 104, 113, 312
Proclamation Society 233, 281
proclamations, royal 102, 288, 289
professions 13, 70, 98–9, 102, 155, 170, 171, 176
  Irish and Scots in 116, 185
proletarianization 166
propertied classes, solidarity of 206–7, 316
prostitutes 102, 165, 183, 204, 231
protection, economic 152, 158, 258–60
Protectorate 29, 34, 37, 81
Protestant Association 209
Protestant Dissenting Deputies, the 135
protest, popular 18, 47, 121, 195, 295, 265
  see also demonstrations, riots
proto-industrialization 151
Prussia 130, 191, 290, 293, 296, 307
public finance 42, 82–6, 156–8, 188, 213, 220, 258–60, 300, 310–11
public opinion 3, 40, 47, 48, 103, 128–30, 184, 187, 190–4, 197–8, 211–12, 215–16, 219, 281–2, 312–13

Pulteney, William 128, 129, 130
Purcell, Henry 212
Puritans 20, 24, 35

Quakers 12, 21–2, 24, 35, 45, 134–5, 178, 208, 230, 247, 286
Quebec 192
Queen Anne's Bounty 76, 137
Queensberry, Catherine Douglas, duchess of 182
Quo Warranto, writs of 48

Raikes, Robert 175
railways 244–5
Ramillies, battle of 77
Ranters 21
Rational Dissent 208, 209, 280–1
Ray, John 233
Reading 59 n.
real wages 8–9, 154, 164, 242, 267, 269
reason 224, 283, 286
recoinage 92, 104, 255
Reeves, John 290–1
reformation of manners 102, 233
reform, parliamentary 198, 214, 215–18, 220, 280–1, 286–8, 305–6, 317
Regency crisis 282
regions 4–5, 111, 163, 246, 270–3
Reid, Thomas 226
religious societies 141
Repton, Humphrey 171
republicans 34, 26, 49, 214, 284, 286
restoration of Stuart monarchy 34–8
'Revolution Principles' 122, 214
Revolution Society 282
Reynham 149
Reynolds, Edward 23
Reynolds, Joshua 171
Rhineland 54, 296
Richardson, Samuel 178, 179
  Clarissa and *Pamela* 235
Richelieu, Cardinal 40
Rickman, John 302
riots 78, 121, 129, 144, 168, 242, 306
  see also food riots, demonstrations
roads 96, 244–6
Robertson, William 226
'Robinocracy' 124
  see also Walpole, Robert
Rockingham, Charles Watson-Wentworth, marquess of 213, 215, 217, 298
Rockingham-Shelburne coalition 217
Rockingham Whigs 216
Rogers, Woodes, *A Cruising Voyage Round the World* 212
Romaine, William 143
romanticism 235

Rome 100, 211
Romilly, Samuel 281
Romney, George 171
Rostow, W. W., *The Stages of Economic Growth* 240
Rotherhithe 100
Rousseau, Jean-Jacques 222, 234, 235
  Émile and *Julie* 182
Rowlands, Henry 113
Royal Academy 313
Royal Africa Company 40
Royal Charles 36, 41
Royal Institution 229
Royal Military College, Woolwich 175
Royal Mint 158
Royal Navy, *see* navy
Royal Society 25–6, 222, 224, 225, 226
royalists 35, 38, 40, 60
'Rule Britannia' 313
Rump, *see* Long Parliament
Russell, Edward, earl of Orford 54
Russell, William, Lord 48
Russia 146, 215, 292, 301, 303, 304
Russia Company 231
Ryder, Dudley 179
Rye House plot 48

Sabbath 19, 24, 102
Sacheverell, Henry 77–8, 122
Saddleworth 207
Saffron Walden 30
sailors 29, 88, 99, 165–6, 168, 186, 189, 264, 297, 311
St George's Channel 30
St Germain 73, 79
St Helens 245
St Kitts 91
St Lawrence River 190
St Lucia 293
'St Monday' 262
Salisbury 59
Salvador, Joseph 185
Samuel, Richard, 'Nine Living Muses of Great Britain' 181
Sancho, Ignatius 186
Sancroft, William 51, 72, 138
Sankey Brook Canal 245
Sanskrit language 221
Saratoga 215
Sardinia 293
Saussure, César de 109
Savery, Thomas 151
Scarborough 5
Schofield, R. S. 162, 163
schools 30, 71, 80, 174–6, 232
school teachers 13, 98, 99, 183, 208, 305
  see also tutors

Schulenberg, Melusine von der 117
science 24, 25, 27, 225, 227–30
Scotland 3, 4, 16, 17, 29, 30, 34, 67, 80, 89–90, 100, 111, 113–16, 117, 119, 184, 287, 302
  Argyll's rebellion 83
  Bonawe furnace 251
  Covenanters' rising 45
  Dumfries 296
  Dundee 294
  Edinburgh 89, 130, 215, 226, 294; University 229
  Glasgow 30, 94, 226, 254, 272; University 177, 229
  Gretna Green 184
  Highlands 101
  Lowlands 30, 251
  New Lanark 260, 272
  parliament 17, 29, 89, 113
  political patronage in 125
  Volunteers in 302
Scots 115, 193, 196
Secker, Thomas 136
secret service funds 125
secularism 145–6, 224
  see also atheism
Sedgemoor, battle of 49, 59
Selkirk, Alexander 212
Senegal 217
servants 29, 94, 113, 165, 179, 269
  see also labourers
Seven Bishops, trial of 53
Seven Years War 190–2, 196, 211, 212, 216–17
  aftermath of 164
Severn river 163
sexuality 183–4
sexual morality 24, 27, 38–9, 171, 181, 182
Seymour, Algernon, duke of Somerset 173
Shaftesbury, Anthony Ashley Cooper, 1st earl 37, 43, 44, 48, 61
Shaftesbury, Anthony Ashley Cooper, 3rd earl 233
Shakespeare, William 120, 313
Sharp, Granville 186, 208
Sheffield 255, 266, 271, 272, 287, 295
Sheffield Register 288
Shelburne, William Petty, earl of 215, 217
shipbuilding 101, 164, 251, 261
ships and shipping 32, 88–9, 95, 97, 245, 254, 292, 311
Shirley v. *Fagg* 41
shopkeepers 96, 97, 102, 155, 175
shops and shopping 155
Shrewsbury 87, 101
Shropshire 87, 96, 151, 270, 271
Sidney, Algernon 48, 54
Sidney, Henry, earl of Romney 54
Sierra Leone 223

Simeon, Charles 207
slaves 94, 123, 186, 212, 223
slave trade 33, 40, 94, 252, 254–5
  abolition of 176, 208, 232, 281, 312–13
Smart, Christopher 313
Smeaton, John 245, 247
Smellie, William, *Encyclopaedia Britannica*
  228
Smith, Adam 202, 223, 243, 255, 261, 265, 271
  on mercantile system 95, 104
  at Oxford 177
  The Wealth of Nations 220, 226, 248
Smollett, Tobias, *The Briton* 196
smuggling 94, 153
social sciences 226
social structure 12–16, 96–9, 169–72, 315–17
  class relations 165, 263–5
Society for Constitutional Information 216,
  288, 295
Society for Constitutional Information,
  Sheffield 287
Society for Promoting Christian Knowledge
  (SPCK) 112, 138, 175, 208
Society for the Relief of Persons Imprisoned
  for Small Debts 231
Society for the Propagation of the Gospel in
  Foreign Parts 138
Society of Antiquaries 225
Society of Friends of the People 293
Society of Gentlemen Practisers 201
Society of Supporters of the Bill of Rights
  198
Society of United Englishmen 301
Society of United Irishmen 294, 297–9
Socinianism 66, 139
Soho, nr. Birmingham 247, 261
soldiers 29, 30, 87–8, 157, 165, 186, 189, 231,
  269, 292–3, 311
Somerset 10, 49
Somerset, Charles Seymour, duke of 52
Somersett, James 186
Somers, John, Lord 71, 77
Sophia, electress of Hanover 75, 79
Southampton, Thomas Wriothesley, earl of
  100
Southey, Robert 275
South Sea Bubble 123
South Sea Company 123, 129
Southwark 126, 197
South Yorkshire 152
Spain 17, 28, 31, 32, 82, 87, 94, 129, 130, 170,
  185, 215, 217, 293, 296
  colonies of 91, 96, 123
Spalding Gentlemen's Society 225
Spanish language 30
Spanish succession, war of the 74–7, 79
Spectator 98, 116, 180, 294

Spence, Thomas 288, 305
Spencer, Charles, earl of Sunderland 124
spices 7, 84, 94
spies, government 19, 37, 290, 294, 300
spinning 5, 10, 248–50
Spithead 297
sports 71, 102, 168, 234
Sprat, Thomas 29
Staffordshire 137, 149, 152, 163, 251, 261,
  270
standard of living 7, 163–4, 167, 240, 267–70
Stanhope, Philip, earl of Chesterfield 126
state 16–20, 81–92, 134, 157, 310–11
State Lottery 87
states system, European 82
stature, *see* height
status and degree 13–14
  see also social structure
steam power 151, 240, 244–8, 250
Steele, Richard 98
steel 250
  see also iron
Sterne, Laurence 179
Stillingfleet, Benjamin 181
stockbrokers 74, 99, 257, 258
Stock Exchange 257
Stockport 247
Stone, J. 170
Stone, L. 170, 173, 179
Stop of the Exchequer 85
Stout, William 97, 123
street-signs 178
strict settlement, the 149, 181–2
strikes, *see* industry, disputes in
Stubs, Peter 255, 256
Suffolk 168
sugar 11, 32, 94, 95, 153, 212, 252
suicide 145
Sunday schools 175, 178, 207, 230
Sunderland, Robert Spencer, earl of 51, 55,
  71, 125
surgeons 98, 189, 229
Surrey 203, 205
suspending power 43, 50, 62
Sussex 10, 137, 175, 294
Sweden 42, 317
Swift, Jonathan 110, 124
  Drapier's Letters 117
  Gulliver's Travels 212
Switzerland 62, 301
swords 15, 310

table manners 179, 310
'Tack', the 77
Tahiti 222
tailors 10, 164, 264
Tatler 98

Taunton 49
taverns 193
taxation 16, 17, 62, 64, 69, 74, 83–5, 103, 105, 156, 300
  indirect 38, 127, 156–7, 310
  level of 258–9, 264
  non-parliamentary 19, 39, 65
tea 38, 84, 153, 155, 214, 220, 252
Telford, Thomas 244
Tenison, Thomas 139
Terra Australis 223
textiles 7, 9, 10–11, 15, 84, 94, 104, 111, 118, 152, 155, 166, 250–1, 253, 270–3
  see also cotton, woollen cloth
Thelwall, John 295
Thirsk, J. 152
Thompson, E. P. 165, 265, 313
Thornton, Henry 208
Tillotson, John 138, 140
Tindal, Matthew 139, 143
tobacco 11, 32, 94, 95, 97, 129, 153, 155, 252
Tobago 217, 293
Toland, John, *Christianity not Mysterious* 139
Tone, Wolfe 298
Tooke, John Horne 295, 296
Tooley, Michael 87
Torbay 55
Tories 23, 45, 70–2, 74, 76–80, 88, 121, 123, 125, 129, 130, 134, 189–92
  American 215
Townshend, Charles, viscount Townshend 127, 149
towns 3, 10, 22, 49, 99–103, 150, 178, 270–2, 309–10
  population of 11, 101, 271, 308
Toynbee, A. *Industrial Revolution in England* 239–40, 263, 268
trade 10–11, 24, 93–105, 152–8, 223, 251–5
  see also foreign trade
trade unions 264–5, 288, 301
trading companies 84, 94, 105
Trafalgar, battle of 303
transportation 19, 204, 223, 244–6, 295, 309
'Treason Club' 55
Treasury 84–6, 125, 310
treaties:
  of Aix-la-Chapelle 188, 189
  of Amiens 301
  of Dover 42–3
  of Limerick 90
  of Paris 196, 211
  of Ryswick 74
  of Utrecht 79, 91, 123, 129
  of Versailles 217
  of Vienna 306

  see also Eden Treaty
Trevelyan, G. M. 65, 66, 111 n. 4
Triple Alliance 42
Troop Society 231
truck 268
Tucker, Josiah 279
Tunbridge Wells 101, 171, 309
Turkey 180
Turner, Thomas 175, 192
turnips 10, 149, 243
turnpike commissioners 135, 157
turnpikes 244–6
Tuscany 293
tutors, private 176, 183
Twining, Thomas 292, 293
Tyneside 101, 245, 262, 270

Ulm, battle of 303
unemployment 9, 164, 211, 263
Union, of England and Scotland 29, 89, 113–16, 156, 187
Union, of Britain and Ireland 298–9, 301
Unitarians 66, 130, 139, 216, 224, 293, 294
United Britons 301
United Kingdom 299
universities 30, 51, 126, 134, 176–8, 280
  see also Cambridge University, Oxford University
utilitarianism 200, 317

vaccination 230, 310
vagrants 165, 204, 211
Vale of Evesham 111
Vane, Henry 40
Vatican 52
'Venetian Oligarchy' 122
Venner, Thomas 37
Venn, Henry and John 207
Versailles 75
Vesey, Elizabeth 180
Vicar of Bray 121
Virginia 32
Vitoria, battle of 306
Voltaire 224, 313
voluntary associations 231
  see also clubs

wages 8–9, 164–5, 166, 265, 267–8, 272, 297
Walcheren expedition 305
Wales 4, 16, 29, 30, 111–13, 142, 161
  Fishguard 297
  Neath 30, 112
  South Wales 112, 251
  Swansea 30, 112
Wallis, John 104

Walpole, Horace 187, 188, 189, 190, 194
  The Castle of Otranto 235
Walpole, Robert, later earl of Orford 77,
  122–30, 133, 134, 158
Walsall 271
Wandsworth 245
Wapping 100
wardship 38
War of 1812 306
warfare:
  impact on government 74, 81–92, 302–3
  socio-economic consequences 95, 103, 109,
  189, 258–9, 295, 307
warming-pan 53
Warrington 255
Warrington Academy 175
Warwickshire 14, 35, 270
Washington, George 217
Waterloo, battle of 306
water power 10, 151, 247
Watson, John and Joshua 208
Watt, James 246–7, 249
weavers 10, 29, 166, 184, 250, 251, 261, 263,
  267
weaving 5, 151–2, 246, 249–50, 270, 272
Webster, Edward 86
Wedgwood, Josiah 172
Week St Mary, Cornwall 10
weights and measures 260
Welbe, John 211
Wellesley, Arthur, duke of Wellington 304,
  305, 306
Welsh language 30, 111
Wesley, Charles 141
Wesley, John 141–3, 145
Wesley, Susannah 173
West Country 118, 253, 264, 271
West India merchants 127
West Indies 7, 11, 31, 49, 95, 186, 215, 252,
  293
  see also Caribbean
West Midlands, 10, 152
Westmorland 178
Westphalia 119
Wetherell, Nathaniel 207
Weymouth 5
Wharton, Thomas, Lord 71, 77
Whigs 45–8, 51, 62, 63, 65, 66, 69–80, 121–31,
  187–90, 192–4, 216, 281, 286, 289, 305
  Foxite 220, 286, 288, 292, 303, 304
  view of history 65, 66–8, 132, 316
Whiston, William, *Primitive Christianity
  Revived* 139
Whitbread, Samuel 266
White, Gilbert, *Natural History of Selborne*
  233–4
Whitehaven 94, 97, 215, 271

Whitfield, George 141, 142
Wickham, William 294
wigs 172, 310
Wilberforce, William 208, 281, 293
Wilkes, John 195–8, 214
  Essay on Woman 197
  The North Briton 196–7
Wilkites 196, 200, 209, 280
Willenhall 271
William III 47, 52–5, 59–60, 71, 72–5, 311,
  312
  anti-French designs 82
  authoritarianism of 73
  religious tolerance of 68
  threatened abdication 74
Williams, E. *Capitalism and Slavery* 255
Wilson, Richard 171
Wiltshire 10, 255
windmills 150, 247
witchcraft, 27, 145
Woburn Abbey 171
Wolfe, General James 192
Wollstonecraft, Mary, *Vindication of the
  Rights of Man* 285
  Vindication of the Rights of Woman 182
Wolverhampton 271
women 13–14, 61, 149, 156, 162, 169, 178,
  181–4, 194, 279
  education of 175, 176, 181, 228, 279
  employment of 10, 147, 150, 151, 165, 166,
  250, 251, 262–3
  food riots and 18, 164, 264
  and Methodism 141, 181, 207
  occupations of 97, 175, 180, 181, 183, 230,
  266
  wages of 9, 164–5
  and war effort 302, 303
Woman not inferior to Man (1739) 180
Woodforde, James 282, 300
wool 9, 10, 93, 147, 148
woollen cloth 10, 96, 152, 154, 166, 253, 261,
  270–1, 274
  Irish 118, 217
  Scotch 114
Woolston, Thomas, *Six Discourses on
  Miracles* 139
Woolwich 175
Worcestershire 23
Wordsworth, William 283–4
  The Prelude 283–4
work-discipline 261–2
workhouses 102, 259, 262
working class 264
Worsley 245
Wren, Christopher 100, 104
Wrigley, E. A. 162, 163, 243
Wyvill, Christopher 215, 216, 280, 287

xenophobia 28, 32, 74–5, 89, 109–10, 115,
    186, 189

yeomen 13, 15, 97, 166, 243
York 101, 171
York Chronicle 193
York Courant 193
York, Frederick, duke of 305

Yorkshire 5, 10, 43, 152, 163, 178, 207, 244,
    251, 264, 266, 300
    West Riding of 10, 111, 166, 253, 270,
    306
Yorkshire Association, the 216, 280
Yorktown 217

zoology 228